TOWARD
A LITERATE
SOCIETY

Committee on Reading, National Academy of Education

John H. Fischer, Chairman
  Teachers College, Columbia University

John B. Carroll
  University of North Carolina at Chapel Hill

Jeanne S. Chall
  Harvard University

Kenneth B. Clark
  City College of the City University
    of New York

James S. Coleman
  University of Chicago

John I. Goodlad
  University of California at Los Angeles
    and Institute for Development of
    Educational Activities, Inc.

Harry Levin
  Cornell University

Mark R. Shedd
  Harvard University

CONTRIBUTORS

John R. Bormuth
Oliver S. Brown
Richard H. de Lone
Barbara R. Fowles
William Furlong
Samuel Y. Gibbon, Jr.
Eleanor J. Gibson
Norris G. Haring
Guilbert C. Hentschke
Vivian M. Horner

Nathan Maccoby
David G. Markle
Nancy Hamilton Markle
Edward L. Palmer
Helen M. Popp
Lauren B. Resnick
Betty H. Robinson
T. A. Ryan
Natalie Saxe
Rose-Marie Weber

TOWARD
A LITERATE
SOCIETY

*The Report of the Committee on Reading
of the National Academy of Education.*
= Committee on Reading.

**WITH A SERIES OF PAPERS
COMMISSIONED BY THE COMMITTEE**

John B. Carroll
UNIVERSITY OF NORTH CAROLINA
AT CHAPEL HILL

and

Jeanne S. Chall
HARVARD UNIVERSITY

Editors

McGRAW-HILL BOOK COMPANY

*New York   St. Louis   San Francisco   Düsseldorf
London   Mexico   Sydney   Toronto*

Library of Congress Cataloging in Publication Data

National Academy of Education.   Committee on Reading.
    Toward a literate society.

    Includes index.
    1.   Reading.   2.   Illiteracy—United States.
I.   Carroll, John Bissell, 1916–   II.   Chall,
Jeanne Sternlicht, 1921–   III.   Title.
LB1050.N298   1975   428'.4'071073   75-4860
ISBN 0-07-010130-2

123456789 BPBP 798765

The editors for this book were Thomas Quinn, Phyllis McCord, and
Cheryl Love, the designer was Christine Aulicino, and the production
supervisor was Milton Heiberg. It was set in Caledonia with display
lines in News Gothic and Craw Clarendon by Cherry Hill Composition.

Printed and bound by the Book Press.

CONTENTS

FOREWORD

Shortly after he took office as United States Commissioner of Education, James E. Allen, Jr., proposed a comprehensive national effort to achieve universal literacy throughout the country. It was his hope that if the necessary resources of knowledge, skill, manpower, and money could be committed and effectively marshaled, the goal could be attained during the 1970s. As a seasoned school man, James Allen was not misled by the naïve certitude of the popular "solutions" periodically put forward, for he knew that the so-called reading problem is in fact a complex of many different problems. He was aware that many students would learn to read if only they were given access to teaching of the quality already available in thousands of American schools. But he recognized also that for large numbers of others in the nonreading population, both children and adults, the mere multiplication of present programs would not be enough. Needs ranged from the preparation of better materials, through a wide spectrum of pedagogical and administrative improvements, to the basic interdisciplinary studies that might produce more promising theories of the reading process.

In developing the strategy for his project, Commissioner Allen sought help in government, industry, and the academic world. Late in 1969 he asked the National Academy of Education to create a task force on reading to address the following questions:

What scientific knowledge do we have and what scientific knowledge do we need in order to make the time-honored American dream of universal literacy a reality by the end of the 1970s?

What will be a reasonable conception of functional literacy for the kind of America that will come into being during the 1970s?

What technologies do we have and what technologies do we need to design to make universal literacy a reality, given the heterogeneity of the American population, and assuming the increasing availability of educational institutions other than the formal school system?

How can research and development provide a more effective base for reading program efforts in education?

What are the political and economic dimensions of an all-out effort to achieve universal literacy during the 1970s? What will be the cost in dollars? What commitments will be needed on the part of the various professions and publics that will necessarily be involved? And what contributions will be needed from local, state, and federal agencies?

The Council of the Academy authorized a committee on reading, which was promptly appointed. It consisted of Academy members and other men and women experienced in various aspects of the subject. The committee widened its own resources by commissioning papers from a number of distinguished scholars and key participants in new approaches to the teaching of reading. These papers provide much of the substance of this report.

Changes in the Office of Education, alterations in the form of the federal reading program, and difficulties encountered by the committee in the course of its work have delayed this report, but we believe that it has been improved by the refinements and additions that the extra time has made possible.

The final character of the volume reflects the insight, industry, and experience of its principal authors, Dr. John B. Carroll, who was at Educational Testing Service during the preparation of this report but who has now moved to the University of North Carolina, and Professor Jeanne S. Chall, of the Harvard Graduate School of Education. To them the committee, the National Academy of Education, and the users of this report are heavily indebted. Appreciative acknowledgment is also due Frank Jennings, secretary of Teachers College, Columbia University, who served as secretary to the committee and organized its working sessions.

This project has produced no final solution to the reading problem, but those who have been associated with it hope that it will cast a few rays of fresh light upon the nature of the reading process, the state of the art of teaching reading, and the possibilities for productive inquiry and action in moving toward the goal James Allen set before us.

John H. Fischer

PREFACE

The Committee on Reading was appointed by the Executive Council of the National Academy of Education in response to a letter, dated December 5, 1969, from the then Assistant Secretary (HEW) for Education and United States Commissioner of Education James E. Allen, Jr., to Dr. Lawrence A. Gremin, then President of the Academy, asking for basic guidance in the conduct of the Right-to-Read program, which Commissioner Allen had first announced in an address to the National Association of State Boards of Education on September 23, 1969.

The first meeting of the committee, chaired by Dr. John H. Fischer, President of Teachers College, Columbia University, took place in New York City on January 22, 1970. The undersigned were privileged to have been invited to serve as members of the committee, along with Kenneth B. Clark, James S. Coleman, John I. Goodlad, Harry Levin, and Mark R. Shedd.

At this first meeting, it was decided to respond to Dr. Allen's request by commissioning a number of experts to write papers on selected aspects of the reading problem as it had been delineated in the commissioner's letter, subsequently convening a conference at which these papers would be considered in order to formulate a final report. Since a report was desired by the summer of 1970 at the latest, steps were promptly taken to commission these papers, to be available by the time of the conference, which was scheduled for June 12 to 14.

In the spring of 1970, however, events took place in Washington which cast in some doubt the future of the Right-to-Read program. Dr. Allen was dismissed from his posts in the Department of Health, Education, and Welfare by President Nixon, ostensibly for "poor administration," but more probably because of Allen's outspokenness against the country's involvement in the war in Vietnam. The June meeting of the Committee on Reading was held as planned, nevertheless, because its organizers felt that it was important that progress be made toward the aims of the Right-to-Read program, regardless of who might be in place as Commissioner of Education. During the first two days of this conference, the commissioned papers were presented by their authors and discussed; on the last day the committee met in executive session to develop the substance of its final report, at least in skeletal form.

Even though a sense of urgency in the production of a report continued to be felt, various delays and difficulties prevented this. It did not become possible to prepare and circulate among members of the Committee a semifinal form of the report until late in 1971, shortly after James Allen's tragic death in an airplane accident. (Two days before his death, in a conference with one of us, Allen had reviewed and made suggestions about a portion of the report.) Since that time, further revisions were seen to be desirable. The present form of the report prepared by the undersigned has been endorsed by all members of the Committee who have been able to respond to the request that they examine it.

In the meantime, it was foreseen that publication of the report would be delayed so long that it would be desirable to have the commissioned papers revised and updated. Nearly all the papers printed here were revised by their authors during 1973; because of other commitments, Eleanor Gibson was unable to revise her paper, which is consequently printed here in the form in which it was presented at the June 1970 conference. The paper originally prepared by T. A. Ryan has been extensively revised with the help of William Furlong; a paper originally prepared by Oliver Brown and Donald Rappaport was revised by Mr. Brown with the help of Guilbert Hentschke, and Donald Rappaport withdrew from authorship of the paper. An entirely new paper on current practices in the teaching of beginning reading was commissioned in 1973 from Helen M. Popp. In revising their paper on the work of Children's Television Workshop in the reading field, Samuel Gibbon and Edward Palmer brought in a third author, Barbara R. Fowles. Author Popp and coauthors Furlong, Hentschke, and Fowles were not involved in the 1970 conference.

The commissioned papers are published here as having been useful background resources for the work of the committee. Statements made or views expressed in these papers are not necessarily endorsed by the committee.

As editors of the committee report and of the accompanying materials, we are grateful to the other members of the committee for their many contributions, and to the authors of the commissioned papers, especially to those who graciously consented to bring their papers up to date after a lapse of three years from original publication.

The work of the Committee on Reading, including the holding of meetings and the commissioning of the papers from experts, was supported from general funds of the National Academy of Education, funds that were provided in part by the Carnegie Corporation of New York. Proceeds from the publication of the present book will contribute to the support of further activities of the Academy.

Even though this report was occasioned by a specific request from James Allen for assistance to his office, we are confident that we are carrying out his intentions in addressing it to the public at large. We have the assent of the National Academy of Education in so doing, and in dedicating the work to the memory of the man who had the vision to initiate the Right-to-Read effort.

John B. Carroll
Jeanne S. Chall

For the Committee

PART ONE

Report of the Committee on Reading, National Academy of Education

REPORT

THE READING PROBLEM

CASE STUDY NO. 1

Thomas Robinson is in the third grade of an inner-city school. He is poor and black, and he has not learned to read. It is not his fault that he cannot read, for he has never really been taught to read. When he entered the first grade, his teacher soon decided that he was so "sleepy" and slow in his reactions that there was no use trying to teach him; she let him sit in the back of the room while she worked with the more promising children. This is the way it was during most of Thomas's first year in school. Toward the end of the first grade, Thomas and his grandmother had to move to another part of the city because the building where they lived was to be torn down. Thomas found himself in another school with a teacher who shouted at him when he seemed not to respond to her. After a few encounters of this sort the teacher decided she had no time to waste on him. Again, he was put on the sidelines. In the second grade Thomas became more and more of a discipline problem. Far from being slow and "sleepy," he became overactive, restless, and at times defiant. He resisted any attempt to get him to learn to read, or to learn anything, for that matter. There were quite a few others in his class who couldn't read, either, and Thomas soon became one of the ringleaders of a group that continually created disturbances in the classroom—disturbances that the teacher was completely unable to cope with. So Thomas's second year at school was pretty much of a loss. Thomas's third-grade teacher is a stern disciplinarian who sends him off to the principal's office whenever there is sign of trouble. Thomas is not learning to read in the principal's office, either.

CASE STUDY NO. 2

Maria Florez is also in the third grade, and she cannot read. Her family came to an East Coast city from Puerto Rico when she was four. Nothing but Spanish is spoken at home—and hardly any English is spoken in her neighborhood. Her family sent her to school with high hopes that she would learn not only to speak English but also to read it. This didn't work out for Maria. Forty-two children, nearly all of them Puerto Rican, were crowded into her first-grade classroom. The teacher, who spoke only English, paid attention only to those children who had been lucky enough to learn some English before coming to school. At the end of her first year, Maria was able to understand only a little of what the teacher said, and the squiggles on the blackboard and in the reading primers made no sense to her whatever. She found her playmates among the children who spoke only Spanish. By the end of the second grade Maria could understand most of the English spoken in the classroom, but she was seldom moved to speak English except in brief responses to the teacher. She (and many of her classmates) were so far behind in reading, however, that the teacher thought it best to ignore her, rationalizing that her time was better spent in helping the few "bright" boys and girls whose reading ability was up to the standard for the grade and whose progress she could "show off" whenever the reading supervisor came around to visit. In fact, this second-grade teacher was regarded by her principal as one of the really outstanding teachers in Maria's school. Maria's third-grade teacher, this time a Spanish-English bilingual, found that Maria knew only few letters of the alphabet and that she could recognize (if not always correctly) only about 50 words in a first-grade primer.

CASE STUDY NO. 3
Bob Countryman lives in a well-to-do suburb of a large Midwestern city. He is white and in the third grade, but he can read no better than Thomas Robinson or Maria Florez. In fact, his test scores are not even up to Maria's. With his normal physical development, excellent command of English (in fact, he is one of the most talkative boys in his class), and a superior, sympathetic home background, he is nevertheless the despair of his parents and his teacher. Something must have gone wrong in the first grade. Unlike all the other children in his class of twenty-one, Bob failed to respond in the usual, expected way when he was first introduced to reading. Ample, brightly printed reading materials from one of the country's best-known educational publishers were at hand, and his first-grade teacher had just acquired a master's degree in elementary education from the state university. From what she had been taught at the university, the teacher decided that Bob was not "ready" to learn to read; she wisely (or so she thought) decided to wait until she saw signs of readiness. This might have been a wise course with some children, but in Bob's case it had an unexpected effect. He became at first extremely negative, then emotionally upset. He would burst out crying at unpredictable times, whining that he hated the teacher, the school, and "all those books." He got into the habit of boasting to his classmates that he didn't need to learn to read, even if he could and wanted to. In the second grade Bob was referred to a physician who diagnosed him as a case of minimal brain

damage and suggested that he be put in a special class. His shocked parents objected, however, insisting that he was so bright in everything but reading that they were sure he would eventually succeed in the regular class. Unfortunately, his second-grade teacher disliked overtalkative boys and regularly passed him by when it might have been his turn to read. Thus it went, and when Bob entered the third grade he could "read" only his name and a few street signs.

CASE STUDY NO. 4

Sandy Faulkner, an eleventh grader, is a tall, good-looking boy whose father was a blue-collar worker in the aerospace industry near Seattle before he was laid off. Sandy can "read," if you define the word generously enough. He could manage to read aloud an item in the newspaper, but he would do so haltingly and with little semblance of normal expression. He would understand very little of what it said and would not be able to answer any sharp questions about it. The process of reading is so arduous for Sandy that he avoids reading whenever possible. The star of his high school basketball team, Sandy has pushed through to the eleventh grade merely by timeserving. Like Bob Countryman, he hadn't learned to read by the third grade, but somehow, because of the long dreary exposure to printed materials through the rest of the grades, he has learned at least to "decode" print to the point of being able to express some of it audibly. Sandy talks and understands ordinary conversation as well as his peers, He is outwardly well adjusted and popular with his classmates—even idolized by some for his athletic skills. Sandy has worked summers on construction jobs, but at the moment he has no idea of what he might do after he graduates from high school. For guidance purposes he was given a reading test in the fall of his junior year; it showed that his reading skill was at the fifth-grade level, or at the third percentile for the eleventh-grade norms. The themes he writes in English class are almost unintelligible, although they occasionally show flashes of insight. When asked to explain his poor grades and test scores, Sandy says that somehow none of his teachers ever got him interested in reading, or showed him how to read, and anyway, "the stuff in most of my books is too hard to understand." He likes sports broadcasts on radio and TV, though, and he can tell you much about the history of sports.

CASE STUDY NO. 5

John Rejiak is a thirty-five-year-old welder in the Detroit area. He came to the United States when he was five and went to school until he was fourteen, when he had to get work in order to support his ailing mother. He was never able to make much progress in school and had attained only about a third-grade reading level when he dropped out of the seventh grade (which he was then repeating). Since he liked to work with his hands, he learned welding from his uncle. When he was twenty he was drafted by the Army but was rejected because of his low test scores. When his uncle died, he tried to take over the business, but he soon found it impossible to keep up with the paperwork, and so he sold it. He never married and has supported himself for some years with a succession of jobs in body-repair shops. He had saved up a little money and decided to use it to go to a night school in order to learn to read better. After a week of trying, however, he dropped out because he was ashamed to reveal to the other members of the class—all younger than he—the fact that he can hardly read at all.

Multiply these cases by some indefinite factor of several millions, and you will have some impression of the nature and extent of the "reading problem" in the United States. These cases are fictitious, of course, and perhaps somewhat overdrawn, but they reflect real, true-to-life conditions that are repeated over and over across the land in almost infinite variation. They have been devised to illustrate and suggest some of the causes of the reading problem. The reading problem is not just one problem; it is many problems, with a multiplicity of causes and manifestations that are beyond any cold statistical reckoning. Merely to know that there are some millions of our citizens who cannot read, or who as schoolchildren are not learning to read to a level sufficient to satisfy their personal needs, and who are thereby precluded from full participation in our society, should make us pause to wonder why this is so and to speculate on what could be done to remedy this tragic situation. It is not only from a sense of sympathy or high-minded altruism that we should show concern. To the extent that illiteracy is significantly present in our nation, the options and resources available to the literate citizen are thereby abridged.

Levels of Literacy

What does "literacy" mean? What does it mean to say that a person is "able to read"?[1]

It is not satisfactory to define literacy as something that is either present or absent, as some legal or census definitions might lead us to believe. "Illiteracy" does not necessarily mean the complete absence of ability to read, and "literacy" covers a wide spectrum of capabilities—all the way from, say, being able to decipher a want ad in a newspaper to being able to enjoy a novel by Thomas Mann or read a scientific treatise with understanding.

Every commission or investigating body that has been charged with defining the extent of the literacy problem has been confronted with the

---

[1] For an extended discussion of the definition of literacy and problems in measuring different levels of literacy, see Chapter 1 by Bormuth (pp. 61–100).

facts that there is no generally accepted definition of functional literacy and that statistics on literacy are generally based on unsatisfactory data and criteria. The figures given in some sources concerning rates of literacy in various sectors of the population are generally not comparable. Statistics for the "literacy" rates of various foreign countries as compared with the United States are well-nigh uninterpretable, because they are nearly always based on people's own reports or upon indirect estimates derived from information on years of schooling.

Many people who consider themselves literate mean only that they can render print into spoken language. If given a simple text, they can read it aloud, even if such reading is very laborious and inaccurate. This is a level of literacy, however, that is very low—in fact, it is minimal. Normally it is attained around the third or fourth grade of school, and even earlier by a considerable proportion of children. But it is common knowledge that not all third or fourth graders can read even this well. And not everyone who can read a printed text aloud will understand what it says. Whether or not the text is understood depends on the difficulty of its phraseology and content and often, also, on the reader's prior familiarity with its subject matter.

The average fourth grader can read with satisfactory understanding only those simple stories and textbook explanations that are characteristic of the material written for the fourth grade. Such material contains a rather limited, nontechnical vocabulary of perhaps three or four thousand of the commonest words of the language, and it tends to be couched in short, syntactically uncomplicated sentences.[2]

The reports of fires and scandals that are written for typical daily newspapers, and many articles in digest magazines, are composed at a degree of vocabulary difficulty and language complexity that is understood only by the average child at the eighth-grade level or above. Journalistic accounts and editorials covering the more complex social, political, economic, and technological developments in current events are frequently written at a level that requires a much higher reading skill—twelfth-grade or even college level.

Of course, children differ in reading ability. Some eighth graders can satisfactorily comprehend newspaper editorials that are written at the level of the average college-educated person. But even college-educated

---

[2] There are, of course, conceptual difficulties in ascribing grade levels to reading material, since such grade-level designations reflect the average reading abilities that in practice may be found to be associated with these grade levels in the schools of the country at large. Grade-level designations may even perpetuate the questionable belief that any child who can read material whose reading-difficulty level corresponds to his grade is necessarily making satisfactory progress. Despite the objections to the grade-level concept, we know of no other practical and readily understandable way of indicating the difficulty of reading material and hence we will employ this concept here.

persons differ in reading ability; some college graduates have difficulty following editorials in papers like the *New York Times* or the *Washington Post.*

The important point is that a great deal of the reading material to which our citizenry is exposed is written at levels of difficulty that are far beyond the comprehension of one who possesses only that minimal level of literacy manifested by being able to read a text aloud. And it is impossible to rewrite this material down to the level of a minimally literate person. Many government bureaus, publishers, industries, business organizations, and trade unions have retained consultants to help them simplify prose, but even when this is done, the *lowest* grade level of difficulty at which complex subject matter can be written about is often found to be around, say, the ninth or tenth grade. The instructions for the 1970 federal tax returns, even though claimed to have been "simplified," are at about the twelfth-grade level of difficulty. Fortunately, a person who can't understand them can get help in filling out his return, but he can't always rely on getting help in reading materials like manuals of traffic rules for drivers, mail-order catalogs, insurance policies, rental agreements, and so on. The literacy requirements for satisfactory functioning of an individual in our society are not known with any precision, but they are certainly far above the level of minimal literacy.

We take the position that the "reading problem" in the United States should not be stated as one of teaching people to read at the level of minimal literacy, but rather as one of ensuring that every person arriving at adulthood will be able to read and understand the whole spectrum of printed materials that one is likely to encounter in daily life. In terms of grade levels of difficulty, a meaningful goal would be the attainment of twelfth-grade literacy by all adults—roughly, the ability to read with understanding nearly all the material printed in a magazine like *Newsweek.* As one member of our committee has pointed out, our national educational policy is that every child is expected to complete at least the twelfth grade; we ought then to expect every child to attain twelfth-grade *literacy.*

To be realistic, we must grant the possibility that not every adult has the mental capacity to attain such a level of literacy. Just what level of intelligence is required to attain twelfth-grade literacy at adulthood is not known with any precision. There are "custodial" and "trainable" mentally retarded groups, constituting about one-quarter of 1 percent of the population, who (at least according to the common opinion in the field of mental retardation) cannot be expected to attain even minimal literacy at adulthood. But most "educable" mentally retarded persons (about 5 percent of the population, with IQs of 50 to 75) can and do attain minimal literacy, achieving from about grade 3 to grade 7 levels on standardized reading tests given in adulthood. From this point on up to the "normal intelligence" defined as an IQ of 100, it is believed that a person can attain twelfth-grade literacy at adulthood in proportion to how near his IQ approaches 100. Any such statement is based on many assumptions concerning the degree to which a person of a given measured IQ can or cannot be taught. The educational ideal, at any rate, should be to bring each individual up to his maximal level of attainment.

The Need for Literacy

The opinion is sometimes expressed, and seriously argued, that in our modern civilization with its advanced technologies the ordinary citizen does not have to be able to read. It is claimed that he can get all the essential information he needs from word-of-mouth communication and from the nonprint media—TV, films, and the like. Certain critics have charged that teaching a person to read is a form of political control because the person is made to read and believe whatever is printed by the "Establishment."

Such claims strike us as fatuous, illogical, and absurd. Possession and use of a system of writing has been one of the marks of civilization for more than 5,000 years, and the use of writing in the form of printed materials has increased rather than decreased, even along with the introduction of "nonprint" media like television. In fact, many television presentations presuppose considerable literacy on the part of the viewer. It is not generally true that information can be gained more quickly, efficiently, and accessibly through word-of-mouth communication and "nonprint" media.

As for the argument that the teaching of reading is a form of political subjugation, one need only remind oneself that most revolutionary movements have capitalized on literacy to promote their causes; witness the "underground" newspapers of contemporary social movements. The last thing an Establishment would do to consolidate its position would be to promote literacy, unless it were in order to dictate what should and should not be read.

The simplest and, to us, the most persuasive argument for literacy is that an individual cannot fully participate in modern society unless he can read, and by this we mean reading at a rather high level of literacy. The options available to a nonliterate person, or even to a person with "minimal literacy," are much more limited than those available to one who can read, and read *well*, at the twelfth-grade level of difficulty or higher.

We have met few persons who would not prefer literacy to illiteracy. It is well to set full literacy, and all that it implies, as a national goal, but it is even more appropriate to let illiterates set their own goals. Most of them have already done so; it is a national responsibility to allow them to achieve those goals.

A national Right-to-Read program need not be regarded as a Machiavellian scheme to divert attention from other pressing national issues.

Nor should it be regarded as providing a panacea for solving those problems.

True, the mounting of a Right-to-Read program of sufficient size might create some tens of thousands of jobs for those who would conduct the program, but there is little hope, at least in the short run, that teaching illiterates to read would significantly decrease the overall unemployment rate. In the present state of our economy, we cannot offer an adult illiterate any guarantee that if he learns to read he will be able to get a better-paying job, or any job at all; we can only say, perhaps, that his *chances* of bettering himself economically will be increased. Thus is posed a difficult problem in motivating illiterates to put in the amount of effort required to learn to read. As Rose-Marie Weber's chapter (pages 147–164) suggests, the road to full literacy for an adult illiterate is a long and arduous one. Nevertheless, we believe there are ways in which people can be motivated, even when the eventual rewards are uncertain.

In the *long* run, raising the nation's level of literacy, however defined, could indeed bring social and economic benefits to the nation. At the very least, it would yield more options as to the way the nation's human resources can be utilized for the benefit of all. But there are grounds for greater optimism than this. Increased literacy *could* promote fuller employment, a more equitable distribution of wealth, and better utilization of talents. It could bring greater satisfactions to larger numbers of people. Even if it brought greater awareness, to some, of reasons for being dissatisfied with their condition, society would benefit.

The ultimate justification of a Right-to-Read effort, however, is of a moral or ethical nature. Article 26 of the United Nations Declaration of Human Rights states, "Everyone has the right to education." If literacy is one of the primary objectives of education, it would follow logically that literacy is a fundamental human right—to be pursued even if only for its own sake. We are under no illusions that a Right-to-Read effort will make our entire population readers of great literature, but we do think literacy is a matter of survival, both for the individual and for society.

The National Deficit in Literacy

In a sense it is fortunate that literacy is not something externally visible, like length of hair, type of clothing, or color of skin. One cannot tell how literate a person is by looking at him. To the literate person in our society, it may seem almost unbelievable that the nation's population contains some millions of people who cannot even read a simple printed sentence aloud. We have only indirect evidence concerning the numbers of these people, but the evidence is compelling enough to permit the statement that something like one adult in every twenty has not attained minimal literacy. We could push this further, without too much fear of contradiction, by asserting that something like one adult in every two or three has less than a twelfth-grade literacy level. Here we are considering the total adult population of upward of 125 million—whites, blacks, Orientals, American Indians, people with English, German, Italian, or Spanish surnames; in short, everybody. And these are conservative estimates.

In school populations, the figure of 15 percent has been cited over and over again as reflecting the number of children who have serious deficiencies in reading. Although the bases on which this figure is founded are controversial, in the absence of truly reliable and immediately meaningful statistics from nationwide surveys we have no alternative but to accept it. At least, it is not seriously out of line with what data we have from standardized reading tests given in many localities throughout the country. For example, in the national norms for the STEP Reading Test published by Educational Testing Service, from 10 to 15 percent of the pupils tested at any given grade level from 7 to 12 are below the *median* score for the grade three years behind. Although these figures might cynically be regarded as reflecting merely "normal variation," we believe that they represent deficiencies that in a large number of cases could have been avoided.

The picture is not all bleak. The data cited above from the STEP Reading Test were collected about 1954. Recent restandardizations of this and other tests show that national averages have been moving upward.[3] We are making progress, but very slowly. We believe that a national effort to improve reading levels would have measurable and significant outcomes that would show up on reading tests.

It is known that reading deficits in certain minority groups—particularly among poor blacks, Chicanos, and Puerto Ricans—are much greater than in the population at large. In fact, it is likely that deficits are increasing in some of these groups. While other sectors of the population should not be neglected, it is probable that most progress in moving national literacy levels upward could be made by concentrating efforts on those groups where the need to improve literacy is greatest.

A national program for improving literacy would have to be based on the best possible information as to where the deficits are and how serious they are. The information we now have is limited, although the surveys conducted by the National Assessment of Educational Progress (Denver, Colorado) are beginning to broaden our information base. To make possible the collection of accurate information, there is a pressing need for instruments that are properly standardized and calibrated to measure reading levels in functional terms—that is, in such a way as to indicate what levels and types of reading materials can be comprehended meaningfully by students, whether they be children or adults. Most currently avail-

---

[3] See W. S. Schrader. *Test data as social indicators*. Princeton: Educational Testing Service, Statistical Report SR-68-77, September 1968. 32 pp.

able instruments measure these levels only in terms of grade equivalents, but these grade equivalents are difficult to interpret and may be said to constitute moving standards, since they could change over periods of time as national averages move up or down.

At the lower levels of reading competence, a variety of such tests would be needed, adapted to the characteristics of the many special groups to which the tests might be applied. For example, conventional reading tests are in some respects unsuitable for assessing the reading competence of lower-class blacks and children who do not speak English as their native language because the language used in the tests does not correspond to the language used by these groups, and the content of the tests bears little relation to their interests and experiences. However, beginning in the upper grades of the elementary school, when the student must be able to read in standard English material of a more abstract and general nature, there is little need for tests designed only for special groups. If minority-group children are to compete with the majority in secondary and higher education, by the time they arrive in the upper grades they should be taught and tested in the same way as the majority.

A DIAGNOSIS OF THE NATIONAL
READING PROBLEM

It would be folly to mount a national Right-to-Read program without some notion of why the enormous efforts that have regularly been devoted to the teaching of reading to children and adults have not been as productive and successful as might have been reasonably expected. Why is it, that is, that we have large deficiencies in literacy when our schools have presumably been emphasizing the teaching of reading, and when considerable sums of money from federal and state sources have been made available to supplement local funds for both in-school and out-of-school reading programs?

The fact should not be overlooked that the literacy levels of large sectors of the population are already fairly high. Many children *do* eventually learn to read well, and the median literacy level of the adult population is probably higher than at any other time in the nation's history. Evidence mentioned previously suggests that the average reading level of the school population has increased significantly over the past 10 years. It is doubtful whether the present level of the nation's ability to read could have been attained without the supplementary funds that have been committed to the teaching of reading and to education generally.

Nevertheless, we believe our national literacy level is not high enough, and in that sense there is a national reading problem.

The causes of the reading problem are complex. They cannot be reduced to any simple formula. In this section, we present an analysis of these causes. For convenience, they are discussed under a number of categories, but the order in which they are taken up should not necessarily be interpreted as indicating their relative importance. In fact, there is no sure way of estimating their relative importance.

Particularly to be avoided is the notion that any *one* cause or factor is at the root of the reading problem. We emphatically decry the tendency of some critics to focus attention on some one factor, e.g., teaching method, classroom organization, dialect differences, or the use or nonuse of "phonics," as if it were the sole variable that is critical.

Teaching Methods, Procedures, and Materials

CASE STUDY NO. 6[4]

Arlene Jones is in the middle of her first-grade year. She is black, and she can read well. In fact, upon her entrance to the first grade it was noticed (with much surprise) that she could read, and a researcher from a nearby university was called in to test her. The test gave her a reading level score of 2.9, though her IQ proved to be only 91. Arlene was the youngest of three children in her lower-class family; her two brothers were much older. Her mother, when interviewed, mentioned with pride that she (the mother) was an avid reader, being from a "family of teachers," although she had never been a teacher herself. She had had two years of college when she married. Arlene's father had been a poor student in school and now works as a laborer in a tire factory. Long before Arlene went to school she had spent a great deal of time with her mother, who frequently read to her, always doing so in such a way that Arlene could see the pages. Even at age two, Arlene started to ask questions about the words being read. Mother and daughter also frequently "played school." In this way the mother taught Arlene the names of letters and colors and identified the words in various alphabet books. She taught her child something about the sound of letters, using a phonics workbook she had seen advertised in a parents' magazine. Soon Arlene was reading on her own; she had a good supply of children's books at home, and she had access to more at a nearby branch library. Before going to school she never learned to print, however, because her mother was not sure how to teach this skill correctly. The mother was proud of having been able to help Arlene in the pre-school years. The two older brothers, she reported, had had trouble in learning to read at school, probably because (the mother thought) their teachers didn't have enough time to give them. She said she was sorry she

---

[4] Adapted from a case study in Dolores Durkin's *Children who read early* (New York: Teachers College Press, 1966), pp. 59–61.

had followed the advice of these teachers, who had warned that she would only confuse them if she tried to help them at home. She was highly pleased with Arlene's progress in school, particularly since Arlene had also now easily learned to print.

In the minds of most parents, and of many teachers and trainers of teachers, the most important aspect of teaching methods has to do with the relative emphasis, at different stages of the learning process, on "phonics" as opposed to the recognition of words at sight. In a strict "phonics" method, children are taught the sounds of letters and letter combinations as a basis for word recognition, whereas in the pure form of the sight-word method, they are taught to recognize whole words without analyzing them into letters and their sounds.

Over the last 100 years or more, there have been swings of opinion as to which of these methods is superior, and the content and organization of reading primers have reflected these swings. During most of the period when the present adult population was in primary school, a sight-word method was generally in vogue, but in the last decade opinion has gradually shifted toward favoring a phonics or "code-emphasis" approach. A boost to the phonics approach has been given by the widespread belief that it is supported by recent advances in the science of language. Also, a series of empirical research studies sponsored by the U.S. Office of Education indicated that children taught by methods emphasizing letter-sound relationships learned somewhat more quickly, on the average, than children taught by sight-word methods. The differences, however, were slight and by no means uniform; moreover, they tended to disappear by the time the children reached the upper grades.

Jeanne Chall (a member of our committee), reviewing earlier studies on these issues in her book *Learning to read: The great debate,*[5] concluded that the evidence favored methods that had an early "code-emphasis"; that is, methods in which quite early in the teaching process children are taught the letters of the alphabet and the sounds they represent in words. Many readers of her book neglected to notice that she was very cautious in drawing this conclusion and that she drew attention to many other important aspects of teaching procedures.

To the extent that it has been assumed that a teaching method must be oriented exclusively toward *either* phonics *or* sight-word recognition, the concern with this controversy has been misguided. From research on the reading process, we know that *both* "phonic" and "sight-word" approaches must be included in any comprehensive teaching procedure. Children learning to read need both a knowledge of letters and their sounds and an ability to recognize words at sight. A teaching procedure

[5] New York: McGraw-Hill, 1967.

may fail with a child if in the long run it plays down either of these aspects of learning to read. What is important is a proper balance between them.

Above all, the teacher needs to be flexible in her approaches. If one approach fails to yield results with a particular child at a particular stage in his learning, another approach will frequently pay off.

In the large majority of reading classrooms in this country, some series of primers and "basal readers" is used. Until the middle 1960s, most of these series had a heavier "sight-word" emphasis, while those produced since the late 1960s have tended to have relatively more "code-emphasis." It is too early to say whether this change in emphasis will have any marked effect on reading levels being achieved by elementary school children.

The teaching of beginning reading in the United States has been marked by much anxiety about what "method" is correct. The use of reading series and the strict adherence to the teachers' manuals accompanying them has tended to make for excessive rigidity in teaching procedures. Even when teachers feel comfortable in departing from the procedures laid down in the materials, their supervisors frequently discourage them. All this concern with "method" is somewhat ironic in view of the fact that, as the case study preceding this section suggests, some children learn to read before they go to school; they learn from mothers or older siblings whose minds are uncluttered with strict rules and doctrines about how to teach reading and who do not ordinarily use any formal sequence of teaching materials such as is provided in classrooms.

This is not to say that teaching method is unimportant. There are good approaches and poor approaches, and teachers need to know what the good approaches are, even if these latter have much in common with the relatively straightforward but apparently unsystematic methods that are sometimes intuitively arrived at by untrained persons. Many failures in the teaching of reading are undoubtedly caused, in part, by the use of inappropriate methods—methods (and the materials associated with those methods) that fail to give the child adequate opportunity to notice and learn the relationships between letters and their sounds, and between printed words and their meanings.[6]

But there are many other aspects of the teaching process that are quite as important as "method." One of these is the amount of time a child actually spends in reading practice or in receiving direct instruction in reading. Although superficial observations of primary school classrooms would seem to indicate that the majority of class time is devoted to reading instruction and reading activities, it is not necessarily the case that every child spends the amount of time in active attention to reading tasks that he or she needs to spend; nor is it the case that every child gets the amount of individual guidance that he or she needs.

[6]For a discussion of current practices in the teaching of beginning reading, see Chapter 2 by Helen M. Popp (pp. 101–146).

Another important aspect of the teaching process is the teacher's system of beliefs about how well different kinds of children can learn to read. Possibly because they have been misled by some of the literature about the poor performance of certain groups, many teachers are under the impression that because a child shows himself to be a "slow learner," or is from a certain minority group, or is poorly dressed, or whatever, he cannot learn to read. In Chapter 8 (pages 257–277), Lauren Resnick and Betty Robinson point out some of these unfortunate attitudes and give suggestions as to how these attitudes may be changed—often by an experienced supervisor's concrete demonstrations that these children can indeed learn.[7]

But even when the teacher is convinced that the child can learn, she may not be able to motivate him adequately, and this is another major source of reading failure. From psychological studies of reinforcement techniques, we know much more than we used to about methods of reliably maintaining the attention of children and of motivating them to learn. Some of these methods are discussed both in the Resnick-Robinson chapter and in Chapter 9 by Norris Haring (pages 278–287). We are inclined to agree with Resnick and Robinson that in the normal classroom situation the use of "intrinsic" rewards arising from the child's feeling of satisfaction with his accomplishments is to be generally preferred over the use of "token economies" and similar procedures described by Haring; nevertheless, these latter procedures, which emphasize the use of "extrinsic" rewards, will help in some situations and with some children.

Lastly, a major source of reading failure that stems from poorly directed teaching techniques is the failure of the teacher to make wise use of what have sometimes been called "feedback and correction procedures." When a child makes an error, his learning can be helped if (a) he knows that he has indeed made an error, and (b) he is informed why he made the error and how he can correct it. Teachers tend either to neglect the correction of errors completely or to spend too much time in the correction of errors without adequately explaining to the child why he made an error or how he could avoid it in the future. Much of the time, there is a reason why an error occurs: the child is using a false hypothesis or a wrong cue. The skilled teacher knows how to diagnose and correct such errors and do it so unobtrusively that the child is not annoyed or discouraged.

Essentially the teacher should be thought of as a manager of learning. The teacher must be aware of what each child has been able to achieve at a given stage of his learning, what the sources of his difficulties are, and

---

[7] See also Ray C. Rist, Student social class and teacher expectations: The self-fulfilling prophecy in ghetto education, *Harvard Educational Review*, 1970, **40**, 411–451, where it is shown that unfortunate social-class attitudes are not confined to white teachers.

what he is ready to learn next. This means that instruction must as far as possible be tailored to the learning rates of individual children—whether children are taught in groups, or, literally, individually, as by an individual tutor. In too many classrooms adequate individualization of instruction is not practiced, but skilled teachers do manage somehow to pay adequate attention to children as individual learners.

From this discussion, it will be evident that we believe that a major solution to the problem of reading failure can come from improvement in teaching practices in the classroom. The methods and materials play a role, as was discussed above, but may in fact be of less importance than how these methods and materials are used and applied. A good teacher of reading can teach effectively regardless of the type of materials she may be required to use; a poor teacher can fail even with the "best" materials.

Unfortunately, it is very difficult to obtain systematic and scientifically valid observations of actual teaching practices as they affect children. Systems of classroom observation that have been devised generally fail to capture the continuous, long-term transactions between a teacher and individual children that are the real basis of success of failure in teaching.[8]

What has been said here about the necessity of individualizing instruction, providing adequate feedback and correction, and motivating students applies not only to the teaching of reading to young children but also to the teaching of more advanced reading skills to older children and to the teaching of literacy to adults. But teaching advanced skills of reading comprehension and interpretation requires a methodology of its own—a methodology that is almost nonexistent. Little is known about how to diagnose and treat students' deficiencies in language knowledge; most teachers rely mainly on asking questions, conducting group discussions, and the like. Modern theory and research on language comprehension should make it possible to develop a more adequate methodology of teaching.

Factors in the Learner

As far as is known, the sensory and mental capacities of the normal child mature soon enough for him to be able to attain minimal literacy at an age considerably earlier than the age of normal school entrance. Some children learn to read at a simple level as early as three years of age, and there are reports that some aspects of reading can be taught at this age

---

[8] Less systematic, more impressionistic observations, carried out over long periods, seem to provide better evidence of the real dynamics (or lack thereof) of the classroom. See, for example, Philip Jackson, *Life in classrooms* (New York: Holt, Rinehart and Winston, Inc., 1968), and John Goodlad, M. Frances Klein et al., *Looking behind the classroom door* (Worthington, Ohio: Charles A. Jones, 1974). These writers stress that most teachers fail to individualize instruction, even though they may believe they are doing so by creating "homogeneous" groups.

such as recognition of signs, letters, and the like. It is not certain whether such early teaching is of any real or long-lasting advantage to the child, although there seems to be some evidence that on standardized tests the advantage holds through the elementary school years.[9] The fact that the biological maturation necessary for learning to read occurs fairly early does, however, lend support to the desirability of introducing informal experiences with simple reading activities during the preschool years as preparation for the formal teaching of reading.

It may be of incidental interest, and of some importance in planning instruction, that it is no longer believed, as it was during the 1930s and 1940s, that a mental age of at least 6.5 is required for the teaching of reading and of letter-sound relationships. This idea was based on a mis-interpretation of certain research studies.

Starting too early is therefore unlikely to be a major source of reading failure. There are, however, children who seem to be unready to learn to read even at the age of normal school entrance. A variety of factors needs to be considered to account for this, such as below-normal intelligence, slow maturation, lack of adequate preschool language experience, emotional blocks, and lack of orientation to school life.

Apart from cases of obvious, severe, and confirmed mental retardation, below-normal intelligence should not be regarded as a major source of reading failure, since, as has already been mentioned, individuals in the "educable" and "borderline" ranges of intelligence can eventually acquire at least a minimal level of literacy; often they go much further than this. But since below-normal intelligence tends to reflect a retarded rate of biological maturation, the age at which a minimal level of literacy can be attained by a child of below-normal intelligence may be higher than for the normal child.

There have been unfortunate incidents in which children have been wrongly classified as mentally retarded. For example, a number of Spanish-speaking children in California were found to have been placed in classes for the mentally retarded because of their low scores on an intelligence test given in English. A court order obtained by a group of their parents directed that they be given a test in Spanish.

Malnutrition, poor vision, poor hearing, and other kinds of less than normal physical conditions can be listed as among the causes of reading failure, but they can be remedied or counteracted by suitable programs of physical care and treatment. Cases of severe blindness or deafness will, of course, be recognized and treated accordingly. Minor visual and hearing problems sometimes fail to be recognized early enough, however, and any Right-to-Read effort should make provision for services that will ensure

[9] Dolores Durkin. *Children who read early* (New York: Teachers College Press, 1966).

that these problems are detected and corrected. On the other hand, there has been a tendency to regard a visual problem as a major cause of reading failure when the true source of that failure may be of a completely different character.

Much has been written about whether or not various kinds of deficits or deficiencies in the child's home background and experience before he comes to school can be sources of reading failure. Inadequate language experience (resulting in retarded language development), lack of care and affection at home, overcrowding and excessive noise in poverty areas, and the like, have been suggested as factors predisposing children to reading failure (and often to school failure generally). It is difficult to assess the relevant evidence, however, because it is practically impossible to isolate the precise causes of failures in such cases. Retarded language development can too easily be confused with dialect differences. Nevertheless, the evidence suggests that there can indeed be cases of true language retardation arising from inadequate stimulation at home and that such cases are likely to present reading problems.[10]

Parents and others in the home background may have either positive or negative influences on reading success. On the positive side, sometimes children are able to learn some elements of minimal literacy at home from parents or other persons who are able to teach them by informal methods. Studies have shown that such children tend to advance more rapidly in their school work, even several years after entering school, than children who do not read when they come to school and that most of these children are in the normal range of intelligence. On this basis we feel that parents should be encouraged to give their children help in reading before (and after) they enter school—by reading to them, by teaching them such things as the names of the letters of the alphabet and the sounds of letters, and by helping them learn to recognize a small vocabulary of words. Parents should not force this teaching on their children; they should give it only if a child seems to show interest in letters and words, and in reading generally—interest that parents can promote by showing that reading is a pleasurable and meaningful activity. We are aware that, on the basis of widely held but poorly supported views in the reading profession, reading teachers have frequently discouraged parents from giving help in reading on the grounds that it would "confuse" the child and produce conflict with teachings in school. We believe this is unlikely to happen.

It cannot be said, on the other hand, that the failure of parents to give help in reading is truly a source of reading failure, because the teaching of reading is and should remain fundamentally the responsibility of the

---

[10] This is shown even in studies done in other countries. See, for example, Renate Valtin, *Legasthenie—Theorien und Untersuchungen* (Weinheim: Julius Beltz Verlag, 1970).

school. Of course, various kinds of parental neglect and mistreatment (either physical or psychological) have sometimes been observed to be factors contributing to poor adjustment at school; such cases should be provided for through social work and similar services.

It is well now to consider the issue of "dyslexia." There is little agreement about this term even among professionals. Indeed, a literature search by the National Advisory Committee on Dyslexia and Related Reading Disorders[11] revealed so many senses in which it was used that the committee decided not to employ the term in its report. The definitions ranged from those that simply referred to defective reading (thus covering all children and adults with reading problems) to those that pointed to a serious reading problem that cannot be attributed to defective vision or hearing, limited intelligence, emotional problems, limited cultural background, or inadequate schooling. Most definitions assumed the cause to be neurological—either a neurological defect, a dysfunction, or a maturational lag.

To complicate the matter even further, there has been a growing tendency to use other labels that overlap to a greater or lesser degree with the term "dyslexia" and with the older term "reading disability." Among these are: "perceptually handicapped," "language disability," "specific language disability," and "learning disability." Again, as with "dyslexia," these "newer" terms are not always clearly defined, and there is much overlap among them.

The growing popularity of these "newer" terms can best be understood as a reaction against an older view of reading problems as stemming primarily from inadequate teaching, lack of student motivation, or emotional problems. This was, of course, a highly simplified conception of the problem. Yet it seems to have influenced the practices in schools sufficiently to prompt dissatisfied parents to join with professionals—such as neurologists and others in medicine, and teachers, particularly teachers of special education—to petition state legislatures and the federal government for needed resources. Thus, although a decade ago only a few hospitals and university clinics recognized the existence of children with special reading problems, such institutions, along with many public school systems, now have diagnostic and remedial services for them.

How many children are so affected? Estimates range anywhere from 3 percent to 15 percent, predominantly boys. How are such children screened and diagnosed? Again, there is great variation, ranging from an hour or so of testing by a learning or reading disability specialist to 10 or more hours of individual testing in a clinic by a multidisciplinary team. There is similar variation in treatment. In some clinics and schools it

---

[11] Appointed by the Secretary of HEW, Wilbur Cohen, in 1968. The report of this committee, *Reading disorders in the United States*, is available from Developmental Learning Materials, 3505 North Ashland Ave., Chicago, Ill. 60657.

consists mainly of intensive remedial teaching that often resembles simply good classroom reading instruction. In others the treatment concentrates on the child's diagnosed weakness as shown in poor performance on visual perception, auditory discrimination and sequencing, and visual-motor tasks. Some programs combine these treatments with instruction in reading; others do not.

As might be expected, there are strong proponents for these different labels, diagnostic procedures, and (especially) different treatments. Often, too, particular groups of specialists tend to exaggerate the extent to which their ideas and procedures differ from those of other groups. The level of discussion tends sometimes to verge on the fanatical. Yet one must under-stand that such a situation would not be unexpected in a field that is as limited as it is in solid research evidence and where the numbers of chil-dren needing help are large. Such a confusing situation cannot be a comfortable one for the professional; it is even sadder for the child with a reading problem and for his parents who seek help for him.

Nevertheless, recent work on early prediction seems to indicate that children who fail in reading at the end of grade 2 can be identified as early as the kindergarten year. Their problems in kindergarten tend to fall in the areas of language and perceptual-cognitive skills. It has been found that among children predicted to fail, those taught by competent teachers (as judged by their principals) had a lower percentage of failure than those placed in classes of teachers judged to be poor.[12]

Thus, there appears to be evidence that some children, predominantly boys, have certain characteristics that make it more difficult for them to learn to read. The research, although meager, also seems to indicate that the earlier these children are identified and treated, the better they are able to achieve. Although their problems stem primarily from their indi-vidual characteristics, competent teaching in the regular classroom appears to cut down considerably the number of failures and the extent of the difficulties. There is also evidence, however, that in spite of highly com-petent teaching, some of these children need long and consistent individual help if they are to achieve on a level commensurate with their general mental ability.

We recommend, therefore, research and development programs for the prevention, diagnosis, and treatment of the reading problems of such children. We also recommend that the Right-to-Read effort provide support for systematically upgrading the diagnostic and remedial services that now exist in school systems and in university- and hospital-based clinics.

We have reason to hope that the research programs will bring about clarity and order in the use of labels and foster consensus among the

---

[12] Jeannette Jansky and Katrina de Hirsch. *Preventing reading failure* (New York: Harper & Row, 1972).

various professionals serving children with reading problems. Such research programs could also bring clarity to the children themselves, and to their confused parents, for often the very fact of labeling a child gets communicated to the child, or to his parents, thus engendering difficulties that might not otherwise occur.

Special Problems of the Child Who Speaks a Language Other than English

Children in many minority groups in our population are failing to learn to read because they are confronted with the almost impossible task of learning to read in a language they know only slightly, if at all. Mexicans in California and the Southwest; Cubans in Florida and the Southeast; Puerto Ricans in New York and the Northeast; American Indians in various parts of the country; and assorted groups of children whose native language is French, Chinese, or any one of a dozen other languages—all have special problems. These are in general not immigrant groups (although some are) whose parents are seeking to be assimilated into American culture; they are groups which have chosen to maintain their own cultural traditions and language.

Long-standing educational policies of this country have tended to isolate and alienate these groups by requiring that they get their schooling solely in English, even from the earliest grades. These policies have had the unfortunate effect of making many of the children in these groups "illiterate in two languages," to use a phrase from Vivian Horner's chapter (pages 190–199) on problems of bilingual literacy. Statistics show that the reading levels, in English, of the majority of these "other-language" children are substantially below the norms for English-speaking children. The deficits in reading ability that they display tend to increase with age—whether because of some type of cultural resistance, because of an increase in the complexity and difficulty of the English-language materials with which they are confronted, or because of some other cause or combination of causes.

The national conscience with respect to these groups has finally awakened with the passage of the Bilingual Education Act of 1968.[13] It was designed to support programs of education for speakers of other languages that would, among other things, permit the teaching of reading and other subjects in the child's native language along with the gradual introduction of oral and written English as a second language. The theory that would underlie such programs is well founded: experience in other countries has suggested that children are much better prepared to study a second language and will make more progress in it if they have a solid

---

[13] Actually, as Title VII of the Elementary and Secondary Education Act as reenacted in 1968.

foundation in their own language. They are also better motivated to remain in school.

If fully carried out, these programs would entail the development of a broad range of suitable materials and the preparation of an adequate cadre of specially trained teachers.

One advantage of these programs arises out of the circumstance that nearly all the native languages involved (e.g., Spanish) have systems of writing that are much more regular than that of English. Children taught to read in these languages find that the transition to reading English is relatively simple once they have mastered the orthography of their native language. Thus, these bilingual education programs have some of the same virtues that are claimed for the Initial Teaching Alphabet, a special alphabet for approximating a regularized spelling of English to help English-speaking children learn to read in the beginning stages before a necessary transition to normal English orthography.

A national Right-to-Read effort should, we believe, join forces with programs supported under the Bilingual Education Act because their ultimate objectives would have much in common, so far as minority-group children are concerned.

The Organization of Reading Programs

One of the more interesting and illuminating findings in the U.S. Office of Education (USOE) Cooperative Reading Studies was that some schools and school systems had consistently better results than others, even when the types of communities were similar, and when similar methods and materials were used. The chief factor that seemed to be responsible for the superior results in these schools was the amount of interest and attention given to the organization of the reading program by the school administration. Teachers of reading need understanding and encouragement from their superiors—supervisors, principals, school superintendents, and school board members. They need to work in a climate that supports and rewards their efforts, gives them help when they falter, and allows them freedom to try out new approaches that seem reasonable to them.

An indirect cause of reading failure, we believe, is the demoralization of teachers that may occur when school authorities do not fully understand their problems or do not give them the material and psychological support they need. Those of us who have visited many schools sense that schools vary very much in this respect. At one end of the spectrum there is the school where the principal closely watches test results, makes provision for reading specialists or consultants to help teachers, organizes remedial classes for failing readers, and arranges workshops and in-service training courses for all teachers who are in any way concerned with the teaching of reading. At the other end of the spectrum there is the school where the administrator shows little or no interest in the reading program and leaves teachers to solve their own problems. The amount of interest in reading programs shown by higher administrators can be quite independent of the amount of financial support that is given to provide materials, remedial services, and the like.

Failures in Funding

Considerable sums of money have been spent by the federal government in various types of efforts directed toward the improvement of reading levels in the population. For example, through the Cooperative Research Program money has been spent on research on the reading process and on the effectiveness of different reading programs and teaching procedures. Through several titles of the Elementary and Secondary Education Act (ESEA) of 1965, large sums have been allocated to schools for the support of educational programs that in many cases included reading programs. Have these allocations of money had any effect? Whether they did or not, in what ways did these funding efforts fall short of their goals?

It can be definitely stated that the research funds made it possible to obtain much useful and needed information. Never before have we had such abundant knowledge concerning the nature of the reading process, the ways of measuring reading skills, and the effectiveness of a variety of procedures in the teaching of reading. In fact, many of the statements made in this report about teaching procedures and reading failures could not have been made with our present degree of confidence if the federally supported research of the past 15 years had not been performed. But this research has thus far had its greatest benefits only among professional educational research workers and those who shape professional opinion concerning reading problems.

The linkage between what is found in research and what goes on in schools and classrooms throughout the land is very loose and tenuous. It takes a number of years for research findings to be well confirmed, interpreted, and disseminated, and the network through which these findings must be disseminated in order for them to be applied is exceedingly complex. The first stage of this process takes place almost solely through the professional journals and professional contacts of educational researchers. A second stage is that in which these findings are interpreted and disseminated through the publications of those who train teachers in universities and teacher-training institutions. A third stage occurs when the findings are discussed in publications (journals, textbooks, and the like) that are read by such persons as reading specialists and supervisors in the schools. A fourth stage of the dissemination process occurs when the findings of research, in much watered-down form, reach the classroom teacher who is "on the firing line." The probability that research findings become known immediately even among teacher trainees is quite low, and the likelihood is even smaller that they will reach at an early date and affect the behavior of teachers who have been on the job for a number of years since receiving formal training. Under the present system of disseminating research findings, it is unrealistic to expect that there will be any appreciable direct effect of research on classroom procedures, before a considerable time lapse, except possibly through the implementation of research findings in the textbooks, readers, teachers' manuals, and the like that are used in the classroom.

The process whereby research findings are reflected in instructional materials is slow and precarious for the "development" phase of educational research in the field of reading is long and frequently very costly. The persons who have prime responsibility for this process are the authors and publishers of the basal reading series, teachers' guides, standardized tests, and other materials actually used in schools. The major reading programs carry the names of leading figures in the field of reading, many of whom participate in research work or are at least aware of the work of others, and there has been some progress in revising these programs in such a way as to reflect the research findings of the past 15 years. There needs to be, however, better developmental research and formative evaluation of these programs so that there can be more assurance that the revised programs are in fact more effective than previous programs. This is a matter in which publishers have a particular responsibility.

It is extremely difficult, then, to assess the effects so far of recent federally supported reading research on the way in which reading is taught or upon the literacy levels of the population, even if we consider only the population currently in school. But we would now be in much worse straits if this research had not been done.

It is difficult also to assess the overall effects of the sums of money that have been allocated toward the support of reading programs in schools and other educational centers throughout the nation. The uses of ESEA funds were exceedingly diverse. All sorts of curricular enterprises were supported, from art education to trips to the zoo. Nevertheless, it has been stated by USOE officials that about 70 percent of ESEA Title I funds were expended on reading programs, almost exclusively in poverty areas. We are not aware of any information that would allow us to make confident general statements as to the effect of these programs. There are indications, however, that the added funds did indeed make a difference where they were used to provide improved reading teaching, services, and materials. For example, it has been reported that in poverty areas of New York City, reading test performance improved in the *early* grades, where the funds were applied generously, although not in the later grades— where the funds were not distributed as generously, or where perhaps it would be more difficult for the funds to have an impact. Throughout the country, we believe, ESEA funds tended to make for improved reading performance wherever they were intelligently and conscientiously applied. Even where instructional materials and teaching procedures were not significantly improved, many children learned to read who might not have done so if the funds had not been provided.

Illiteracy in Adults

Up to now, we have been discussing the failures of the schools. Despite these failures, most young people do eventually become readers in the course of their schooling, although their level of literacy may remain lower than what they could achieve with better teaching.

But the failures of the schools often produce adult illiterates. We have no way of knowing how many such people there are, but we are certain that there are large numbers of them—people who drop out of school before reaching school-leaving age or high school graduation, even people who somehow graduate from high school without attaining minimal literacy. One long-range solution to the problem of adult illiteracy is to improve the teaching of reading in the schools and to require *at least* minimal literacy for graduation from high school.

In the meantime, we are faced with the fact that we have in our population some millions of adults, of all ages, who have not attained minimal literacy or whose level of literacy falls far short of what they require and have a right to attain. Some of these people are in low-level jobs; others are unemployed. Still others are in penal institutions. Some adult illiterates are persons who for one reason or another have *never* had the benefit of schooling in English.

In recent years a number of special programs have been established to promote adult literacy. One of these is the Adult Basic Education program of the Office of Education. Another has been the so-called Project 100,000 established by the Department of Defense whereby persons with low test scores and poor reading ability could be made qualified for military service. The Job Corps provided literacy training for trainees who needed it. Private industries and labor unions have attempted to provide literacy training for certain classes of employees and workers.[14]

The amount of success in raising literacy levels through these programs has not been impressive. The programs do not by any means reach all those who need literacy training. Trainees generally make slow progress and frequently drop out of training before their literacy goals are achieved. The programs have suffered from a shortage of well-trained instructors. Some of the programs have been expensive to operate.

The chapter by Rose-Marie Weber (pages 147–164) identifies some of the reasons for the failures of these programs. In part the weaknesses

---

[14] Further information on these and other programs is given in Chapter 4 by T. A. Ryan and William Furlong (pp. 165–189).

are ones that have already been cited in connection with reading programs in schools—ineffective teaching techniques, inadequate procedures for motivating students, and the like. But adult literacy programs also have certain unique problems: teaching materials that in content and style are inappropriate for adults, and the greater need for protecting the privacy and dignity of the learner. We believe these problems can be solved if they are properly recognized.

One of the major obstacles to progress in eliminating adult illiteracy is the general lack of concern about it in the public at large. The literate adult does not see illiteracy as making for any abridgment of his security, well-being, or prospects. He is inclined to think of illiteracy as just one more of those ills that beset society, but a less threatening and less critical one than, say, heart disease or air pollution. He may pity or scorn the illiterate, but he sees no pressing need to help the cause of literacy.

The fact is that illiteracy is very much bound up with other social problems and that the long-range plans for dealing with crime, poverty, etc., must include a concerted attack on illiteracy.

A NATIONAL STRATEGY FOR ATTACKING THE READING PROBLEM

It is plain that while there have been many achievements in our teaching of reading in which we can take pride, there have been many failures, at all levels. A strategy for correcting those failures can and must operate simultaneously in a number of directions and at many levels.

Research and Development

We begin our discussion with a statement concerning research and development, not because it is necessarily the first order of business in an action program, but because it takes logical precedence over many aspects of such a program.

The committee was asked to assess the present state of our knowledge about reading and its teaching. We believe that actually a great deal is known about reading and its teaching. The statements made in the previous discussion are based partly on an analysis of the wealth of research literature that has poured out in recent years, much of it supported by federal research funds. At least, there is enough knowledge about the reading process and its teaching to serve as the foundation of the program of action that will be recommended here.

Further basic research on the psychology of the reading process, such as is described in Eleanor Gibson's chapter (pages 288–321), may add to our understanding and contribute insights that will be useful to the refinement of instructional materials and the elaboration of teaching techniques. In addition, linguistic research on letter-sound correspondences and more generally on the properties of languages can possibly lead to more efficient kinds of teaching presentations. More information is needed on how adults learn to read and on the role of bilingualism and bidialectalism in reading.

With so much of the previous research focused on the teaching of the "decoding" processes involved in attaining minimal literacy, more research and development is needed on teaching higher levels of literacy; i.e., on how persons can be taught to understand language that involves progressively more difficult vocabulary, syntax, and ideas than are found in simple reading material.

Fundamental research should also be supported on ways of motivating learners of different ages (both children and adults) and from different backgrounds.

Intensive, carefully conducted research is needed on problems relating to those children who fail to learn to read even when they are taught by methods that are effective with most children. Research on whether, in fact, there is any such category of children who need special teachers and special teaching techniques needs to be provided to the point where there can be general agreement on the answer. Further research on instruments that might identify such children before they encounter failure might lead to a reduction in the number of children who become labeled as "retarded readers" or "dyslexics."

Basic research on teacher training and teacher effectiveness should include attention to the education and training of reading teachers—both those whose primary subject matter is reading and those who are to become involved in it through the teaching of other subjects. Much evidence indicates that although most teachers would like to do a better job in teaching reading, they are inadequately prepared.

Immediate research tasks. One problem that calls for immediate attention, and for which the technology is now available, is the development of a series of instruments or tests—devices that will measure stages or levels of literacy in meaningful, directly interpretable terms. These instruments are needed in sufficient variety to be used in the evaluation of many different kinds of reading programs—programs for adults as well as those for children, and programs for speakers of nonstandard English as well as programs for speakers of standard varieties of English. They should include diagnostic tests that would readily reveal what aspects of the learning process are causing difficulty for a given learner.

Instructional materials for the teaching of reading now exist in enormous profusion, although the basal reading series of a few major publishers dominate the field. School personnel who have the responsibility of selecting textbooks do not now have any firm basis on which to make their decisions; they are justifiably hesitant to rely on the claims of the respective publishers. They need access to evaluations that could be made by systematic procedures employing content analysis and empirical try-outs. We believe that research leading to the development of such procedures should be undertaken at an early stage in a national Right-to-Read effort. This research would yield the kind of information needed to operate a kind of "consumers' bureau" that many believe should be established for the field of reading.

Since presently available instructional systems may be less than adequate to serve the needs of all learners, support should concurrently be given to projects that are directed toward improved and more comprehensive systems. Of course, any evaluative procedures that are developed should be applied as much to these new systems as to those in common use.

Since we feel that teaching procedures are of crucial significance in the success of teaching programs, improved techniques are needed for observing, evaluating, and modifying teacher performance as it relates to the promotion of reading skills.

Measures to Be Taken in Schools

The committee is convinced that regardless of any other measures that may be proposed, the first line of attack on the reading problem is in the schools themselves. This section is therefore addressed to teachers, principals, school superintendents, parents, school board members, legislators—and in fact to all those whose actions can have a positive influence on school programs.

Probably every school would claim to have a "reading program," or at least some kind of language arts program under which reading would be subsumed. Many schools, especially in the suburbs, have reading programs that outwardly appear to be excellent, and these schools can point to high median grade achievements on standardized reading tests. Other schools, especially in the inner city, have reading programs that are obviously in trouble. But there are "success stories" in the ghettos, just as there are "horror stories" in the suburbs. What are some of the critical elements of a reading program? In our opinion, they include the following:

1. *Attention to the reading program.* A successful reading program is one that engages the continued attention of all concerned—particularly the teachers and the school principal. The school principal and his staff are alert to allocate sufficient class time to the teaching of reading, to note the progress of all children, to judge whether the methods and procedures being followed are producing the desired results, and to modify those methods when necessary. Good reading programs require both strong leadership and "tender, loving care."

2. *The conviction that all children can learn to read.* It is pointed out

in the Resnick-Robinson chapter that many teachers seem to have the self-defeating attitude that some children cannot learn to read, and therefore they fail to devote themselves to teaching such children. Successful reading programs are conducted by teachers who know from inner conviction or from actual experience that all can learn to read at a minimal literacy level and that once in possession of this minimum literacy level they can go on to higher levels.

3. *Individualized attention to individual children.* Although many children can be taught with group-teaching approaches, some children need individualized attention because of the special difficulties they encounter. Successful reading programs are successful in recognizing such children and in making provision for them to be given the special help they need, in the first instance from the regular teacher or a teacher aide (preferably with the advice of a reading specialist), or, if such help does not avail after a reasonable length of time, from a special teacher or reading clinic. There needs to be an intensive period of diagnosing and correcting reading disabilities, preceded by assessment and preventive measures between the ages of 5 and 8. Where necessary, additional personnel and resources should be provided for this level in each school.

4. *Flexibility in the use of teaching methods and materials.* If reading research has shown anything, it has shown that no one method or set of materials is uniformly more successful with all children, all teachers, or all schools than any other. A successful reading program has a variety of teaching approaches at its disposal and adapts their use to the problems and needs of individual children. This is not to suggest that there can be no standardization of the reading program at all. Some successful reading programs employ mainly a series of basal readers; others base their teaching on fairly specialized materials. In nearly every case, however, it is found necessary to supplement the regular materials with other materials appropriate for individual children.

5. *Avoidance of anxiety about apparent reading failures.* It may seem contradictory to recommend, on the one hand, that school people should give attention to the reading program—be devoted to it and show concern for it—and, on the other hand, that they not be anxious about reading failures. The fact is that overanxiety, if communicated to the child, can itself be a cause of reading failure—failure that may be more difficult to remedy than what is found in the normal course of things. Even under optimal conditions, some children may be delayed in learning to read. It should not be an occasion for alarm if a child enters the second grade with a reading level below beginning second grade, as long as there is assurance that he is making progress in the light of whatever shortcomings or handicaps he has. Under the guidance of a sympathetic teacher such a child can make better progress in the second grade. The point is that parents should not become overanxious about slow progress, and teachers,

provided they use their best professional judgment and skill, should not become guilt-ridden over apparent failure. Because of differences in children's rates of intellectual maturing, even "performance contracting" systems should not be expected to get every child up to some fixed standard of performance at stated times.

6. *Proper coordination of the reading program with other aspects of "language arts" teaching.* It would be tragic if so much attention were given to the teaching of reading that writing, spelling, composition, literature, listening, and speaking skills were slighted. In fact, we believe that such an emphasis would be counterproductive. A good reading program teaches literacy in the context of other language skills.

7. *Follow-through of the reading program throughout the school years.* Because the attainment of minimal literacy is only an early stage in the development of higher levels of literacy, a successful reading program is one that shows continued concern with all these levels—up through the high school years. Protracted emphasis on the attainment of high levels of reading comprehension and speed with materials that are increasingly difficult and specialized in vocabulary, syntactical construction, and conceptual content should be a feature of a good reading program. This will usually mean that the reading program must extend into the specialized content areas, such as literature, social studies, and science.

8. *Where appropriate, recognition of the special problems of minority groups.* It is our assumption (an assumption that seems commonly agreed upon) that in a nation where "standard English" is the norm in nearly all forms of verbal transaction, every child should eventually attain the highest possible level of literacy in standard English. Nevertheless, it is not necessarily the case that every child should be introduced to standard English in the earliest stages of his schooling. The evidence suggests, as pointed out in Vivian Horner's chapter (pages 190–199), that children who come to school speaking a language other than English are better served if they are first taught literacy in their own language. Then, later on (provided they are also given training in spoken English), they can easily transfer this literacy to English. While there are practical problems in applying this generalization in all cases (as where there is considerable linguistic diversity among the children in a given school), we recommend greatly expanded support for efforts in bilingual education. Children who come to school speaking some form of nonstandard English (such as "Black English") present a somewhat different case. While such nonstandard dialects must be respected as viable forms of language, it must be recognized that inasmuch as these children are usually much exposed to standard English (e.g., through television), there should be no great difficulty in teaching them to read standard English, even if their oral rendition of standard English is of a dialectal character—just as, for example, Scottish children read standard English in a Scots dialect. While

there have been some experiments in developing instructional materials in nonstandard dialects, we have little hard evidence, thus far, that teaching with such readers makes for greater success than with more conventional materials. We believe that some of our recommendations, e.g., those in favor of more positive teacher attitudes and of giving individualized attention, are more appropriate to emphasize in the case of children with nonstandard dialects. In any case, teachers can be helped if they are made more knowledgeable about consistent differences in the dialects of their children with regard to phonology, syntax, and vocabulary.

Many schools and school systems are in urgent need of help in improving their reading programs along the lines indicated above. They may need help in any one or more of the following ways:

(*a*) Securing outside advice and consultation

(*b*) Securing better-qualified teachers, reading specialists, librarians, and other staff personnel for the reading program

(*c*) Purchasing newer instructional materials and devices

(*d*) Developing and expanding school libraries

(*e*) Setting up and conducting in-service training programs

(*f*) Establishing and maintaining adequate systems of testing, evaluation, and record keeping

We believe that a national Right-to-Read effort should make legislative provision for grants to schools and/or school districts that would enable them to obtain help in these categories to the extent that their own financial resources are inadequate. The criterion for awarding such grants should be need that is demonstrated by significant amounts of reading failure or pupil dropout, for example, or by other conditions indicating inadequacies in the reading program. Possibly these inadequacies should be evaluated and verified by independent agencies.

Measures Having to Do with Teacher Training[15]

In-service training. We begin with in-service training because, regardless of how much we might improve pre-service training, the large majority of children will continue to be taught by teachers now in service. There is abundant evidence, from common observation as well as from many research surveys, that teachers differ enormously in their success in the teaching of reading. As matters now stand, whether a child will readily learn to read appears to depend to a considerable extent on who his teacher is. It is not that some teachers are willfully unsuccessful; it is simply that some teachers are less capable, less creative, and less well trained than others. We believe that much can be done to improve the teaching skills of teachers in service.

---

[15] An appendix to this report, by Jeanne Chall, considers in further detail problems of the availability and training of teachers of reading as well as of other specialists in reading. See pp. 45–57.

Teaching skills can be improved through the establishment of good in-service training programs, and there are many ways in which in-service programs can be improved:

1. By allocating sufficient time for conducting these programs. Two or three days during the whole school year are hardly enough. More or less regular sessions throughout the year are advisable.

2. By encouraging all teachers of reading to participate in the programs, either as "instructors" or as "students." Experienced teachers known to be successful should describe and demonstrate their methods for the benefit of the less experienced, less successful teachers.

3. By establishing curriculum centers where teachers can keep abreast of new material and promising developments in the teaching of reading.

4. By providing special in-service training in the teaching of advanced reading skills for teachers in the upper grades and in the junior and senior high schools.

5. By having classroom demonstrations, by videotaping and subsequently discussing teacher performance, and by having "clinical" sessions devoted to the teaching of "problem cases."

6. By scheduling occasional sessions with reading specialists from other schools or from local university resources and by establishing closer ties with universities and with reading and learning disability clinics.

7. By testing teachers' knowledge and skills in the teaching of reading.

In some localities and regions of the country, there exist organizations specially equipped to conduct in-service training.

Pre-service training. Surveys have repeatedly shown that, whatever the reasons, teacher-training institutions have in general failed to provide adequate pre-service training. State certification requirements have not been stringent enough, or specific enough, to ensure that prospective teachers are well prepared to teach reading. Courses in the teaching of reading are not intensive enough and do not provide enough practicum and clinical training. Textbooks on the teaching of reading, with few exceptions, have been full of bland generalizations and have failed to offer detailed knowledge about the nature of the reading process or about the learning process—knowledge that is presently available and that is probably desirable for the teacher to have if he or she is to do his job competently.

Fortunately, this situation is now changing rapidly. Certification requirements are being strengthened in many states; teachers' organizations have adopted standards for the preparation of teachers of reading; and courses in teacher-training institutions have been improved and updated. Some of our newly gained research knowledge on the nature of the reading process in relation to language development is getting into textbooks on reading and its teaching. Further progress in these directions, however, is needed and should be encouraged.

The training of reading specialists. The training of reading specialists has, we believe, been much more thorough and adequate than that of beginning teachers, partly because of the standards that have been established for these categories of personnel and partly because the training of these specialists has been concentrated in a smaller number of the better institutions. There is, however, a shortage of qualified reading specialists, and it may be necessary, in a national reading effort, to make provision for scholarships or other financial arrangements to ensure a greater supply.

The training of school administrators (principals, superintendents). It has been stressed above that a good reading program requires understanding leadership. It is our impression that prospective school administrators are not made sufficiently aware of the characteristics of good reading programs. This is a matter that should be forcefully brought to the attention of institutions where school administrators are trained.

The training and use of paraprofessionals. There are at least three types of paraprofessionals who might be used in different capacities: (1) adults from the local community; (2) college students, particularly those planning to become reading teachers; and (3) high school students, including dropouts, who might be especially useful in reaching certain categories of primary school pupils. Each of these types of paraprofessionals needs certain specific training. We would emphasize, however, that all should be trained and should work under the supervision of professional teachers (whether within the school or under other auspices). Although in the case of the majority of children the process of teaching reading may be easy and straightforward, the variety of problems that can be encountered over the whole range of children makes it illusory to believe, as some have proposed, that large numbers of paraprofessional tutors can be quickly trained to become completely independent teachers of reading.

Possibilities Outside the Schools

Up to this point, our report has presented what we feel can and should be done within the regular school establishment—in elementary and secondary schools, in teacher-training institutions, and in the universities. We are quite aware that to many our recommendations may have an excessively familiar ring—being in many respects the same kinds of recommendations that have been made many times in previous years. We insist on making these recommendations, nevertheless, for two reasons. (1) For lack of funds, enthusiasm, knowledge, or whatever, these recommendations have never been adequately acted upon—with a broad enough base to encompass all schools everywhere. (2) We see as yet no good reason to weaken or abandon the present school establishment, despite contrary voices, and every reason to strengthen it.

We recognize, however, that by no means does all education take place in schools—and certainly it need not. The committee is not as much concerned about *where* and *how* children learn to read as it is about *whether* they learn to read. Agencies and institutions outside the regular schools should be exploited for their maximum possible contribution to a Right-to-Read effort.

The most promising possibility now on the scene is television. The success of the original *Sesame Street* program in promoting certain pre-reading skills is already well known and well documented. The sequel to this program (*The Electric Company*), designed among other things to teach a limited range of actual reading skills, appears to be equally successful.[16] The committee applauds these efforts and believes that they are worth continued support, including support from federal funds. If programs such as these prove effective in the long run, they must not be regarded as "one-shot" enterprises but should be made regular features of the educational environment and coordinated with school reading programs. The many possibilities inherent in educational television have been admirably discussed in the chapter by Markle, Markle, and Maccoby (pages 200–214) and are by no means limited to the teaching of minimal literacy and "decoding skills." In fact, we suggest that thought be given to special educational television programs and series designed to promote higher levels of literacy; many efforts should be made to encourage viewing by the audiences for which they would be designed.

Other media, such as radio and the press, can play a part in a national Right-to-Read effort. In the first place, they can promote the effort itself by alerting the public to the nature and urgency of the national reading problem and to the measures needed to alleviate it. They can report progress in achieving the goals of the Right-to-Read effort and bring new opportunities for learning to the attention of their audiences. They could expand their present efforts to inform parents about ways of promoting the reading skills of their children.

In the second place, these media could make a greater conscious effort to promote reading and other language skills by presenting actual instructional materials. The daily syndicated columns on word study found in some newspapers could be expanded to include, for example, instructional materials on other aspects of reading such as idiom and syntax. Materials labeled as being at designated levels of readability could be published in newspapers and magazines to encourage adults to gauge their reading ability and strive to improve it. (Techniques are available for estimating readability levels directly from the process of typing or composing an article for printing.)

Some of the chapters, particularly those by Saxe and de Lone (pages

---

[16] See Chapter 7 by Gibbon and Palmer (pp. 215–256) for a description of these programs and an account of the research on their effects.

322–332) and Brown and Hentschke (pages 333–351), argue that reform within the present school system may be very difficult to bring about and that therefore certain innovative systems that could provide reading instruction outside the regular schools should be envisaged. One of these is a system whereby parents are given "vouchers" permitting them to send their children to whatever kind of educational institution seems to offer the best instruction, whether it be a regular school, an independent school, or even a profit-making education center established under commercial auspices. The vouchers would in effect pay for such education. Presumably, most children would still be sent to regular schools, but the competition provided by independent schools and centers would lead to the improvement of the standard of instruction at regular schools. Many arguments can be marshaled against a voucher system, and we are skeptical as to whether or not a nationwide or even a statewide voucher system would be feasible. Nevertheless, certain localities are currently experimenting (in some cases under federal auspices) with voucher systems. The consequences and effects have not been fully evaluated as yet. The most that the committee can recommend at this point is that these experiments should be closely watched for their specific effects on the improvement of reading skills.

A much more reasonable procedure for encouraging reform within the schools, the committee believes, would be the operation of some sort of external agency that would enforce the concept of "accountability" in the schools; that is, the concept that the schools should make themselves accountable for delivering educational services that meet established criteria in terms of pupil achievement. There are, to be sure, many technical problems associated with the concept of accountability. For example, there is the matter of establishing standards of literacy and accurate tests for measuring them. The committee believes, however, that with adequate research and development, employing presently available technology, these problems can be relatively easily solved in the case of reading.

One form of external agency for enforcing accountability would be one that accepts, approves, and coordinates reports from schools or school systems. Another form of agency would be one that is actually responsible for administering tests and other evaluation instruments in schools. Some states (for example, Iowa) already have agencies that go far toward serving such a purpose. In either case, the agency would be responsible to the public at large through its non-school-connected political representatives. The committee recommends that such bodies be set up within at least statewide or regional boundaries.

Of course, such bodies may be unnecessary. Present trends indicate that public opinion and pressure are forcing the schools themselves to accept the concept of accountability and to act on it.

Adult Literacy Programs

In a previous section (pages 26–27), the possible reasons for the lack of success of adult literacy programs were discussed. The actions suggested there may be summarized as follows:

1. Programs need more adequate funding, organization, and leadership. Such programs could be organized in community centers, churches, libraries, and other local entities, and the teaching could be done either by professionals or by paraprofessionals who are trained and supervised by professionals.

2. Special efforts should be made to recruit and train effective instructors of adult literacy.

3. Further development of instructional materials that are specially appropriate for the needs of various types of adult illiterates should be encouraged and supported.

4. New developments in educational technology, such as programmed and computer-assisted instruction and "talking typewriters," should be exploited for use in these programs because they offer the possibility of circumventing the problems of student motivation that are particularly acute in such programs.

5. New tests and evaluation procedures, as suggested elsewhere in this report, are needed to establish standards of literacy that can clearly and meaningfully inform both students and teachers about progress in meeting these standards.

6. A variety of incentive systems for attracting adults to literacy programs and for ensuring that they remain in them long enough to achieve reasonable goals should be investigated, and the more promising ones should be developed and disseminated. If such incentive systems require outlays of funds—toward monetary rewards for achievement, for example —such funds should be provided to the extent feasible.

LEGISLATIVE AND ADMINISTRATIVE ACTIONS

Despite occasional assertions that newer means of communication have rendered print obsolete, literacy remains a personal and public necessity. Because it is the key to formal education and a vast variety of other learning tasks, the ability to read has become an essential requirement for active membership in modern society. How to cultivate that ability widely and well among our people is today an important question of public policy.

The structure that gives our system of universal education stability and the processes that give it vitality extend far beyond the institutions that constitute its public sector. But the residual responsibility of the public parts, to say nothing of their actual and potential power to produce the results required, lays upon governmental agencies at all levels quite special obligations to attend to the reading problem and to act upon it. In approaching these tasks it will not be enough to confine efforts to existing mechanisms, although they should be used to their maximal capability. Wherever they will not or cannot adapt with sufficient speed or effect to the needs now being recognized, they will have to be supplemented or, where necessary, reformed or replaced.

Administrative Action at the Federal Level

The report of the National Advisory Committee on Dyslexia and Related Reading Disorders[17] called for the establishment of an office within the U.S. Office of Education to stimulate and coordinate all actions that might be taken at the federal level with concern for the national reading problem. Fortunately, Commissioner Allen saw the need for such an office when he announced his Right-to-Read program, and an office was in fact set up in the spring of 1970.[18]

The Right-to-Read office started rather modestly. As described in early press reports,[19] it had a relatively small staff and a budget of only $1.5 million for its first year. Since then, under former Commissioner Marland, it has grown in staffing and fiscal support, with an annual budget of approximately $10 million for the past 2 years.

Under the direction of Dr. Ruth Holloway, the major objective of the office is "to insure that by 1980, 99 per cent of those under 16 will have the skills to read to the full limits of their desires, and 90 per cent of those over 16 will possess and use literacy skills." This objective is being met, according to a communication to deans of schools of education from the

[17] See fn. 11.

[18] At about the same time, the National Reading Council was established. With Mrs. Richard M. Nixon as honorary chairman, its members were some fifty to sixty distinguished citizens appointed by the Secretary of Health, Education and Welfare; the members came from industry, labor, government service, sports, the media, and the major reading associations. As envisioned by Commissioner Allen, the National Reading Council was to be concerned primarily with the private sector, although initial funds came from grants from the Office of Education. The National Reading Center, the administrative arm of the Council, was established soon afterward, in 1970, and maintained offices and a staff in Washington through 1972. The Council was terminated in 1973, along with the Center.

Among the projects undertaken by the Council and implemented by the Center were extensive volunteer tutoring projects, programs for training volunteer tutors, brochures for parents and laymen, the sponsoring of two national surveys on "survival" literacy, and the dissemination of information on the extent of functional illiteracy in the United States.

Throughout their tenure, the efforts of the National Reading Council as well as the Center were primarily involved in the private sector, while the Right-to-Read office in the U.S. Office of Education was and is concerned primarily with the public sector.

[19] *Educate*, November 1970, pp. 14–19.

office dated May 30, 1973, primarily through demonstration projects in schools and community centers and through the identification and dissemination of exemplary reading programs. As of 1973, there were 244 Right-to-Read projects in operation or in the planning stage—170 school centers (of which 21 were in large cities) and 74 community centers. Each of these centers reaches some 500 persons per year. Among the Right-to-Read projects are an in-service training project for teachers of Indian and Eskimo children in Alaska, a reading program to meet the diverse literacy needs of 2,200 Indian reservation residents, a special program for women prison inmates, a special program for upgrading the reading skills of welfare mothers, and a diagnostic-prescriptive program in sixteen elementary schools in a large city school district.

The office has identified five exemplary reading programs and has disseminated them in multimedia kits. It cooperates extensively with existing reading organizations. It hopes to move into several new areas of activity, such as working with teacher-education institutions through the development of improved training programs for teachers of reading and developing an adult version of the *Sesame Street* program to reach functional illiterates.

The work of the Right-to-Read office is admirable, and we support fully its objectives and its various projects. We believe, however, that the office is not sufficiently large, and sufficiently funded, to meet the national reading problem as described in this report. This committee, therefore, agrees essentially with the recommendations of the National Advisory Committee on Dyslexia and Related Reading Disorders to the effect that, ultimately, a large and powerful office concerned with the reading effort should be established at the highest possible level in the Department of Health, Education and Welfare. A high level of authority is required partly because this office should coordinate its activities with the many activities of the federal government in the field of reading, not only in the Office of Education itself but also in the Armed Forces, the Department of Labor, the Bureau of Prisons, the Bureau of Indian Affairs, the Office of Economic Opportunity, and so on. The office might become in a sense the operating arm of those divisions of the National Institute of Education concerned with research and development in the teaching of reading and related basic skills.

Although such a high-level office concerned with reading could be established by administrative action at the Secretarial or Presidential level, passage of special legislation, as discussed below, could facilitate such action, particularly if the legislation made provision for supplying the necessary funds.

We can be more specific concerning the desirable amount of authority for an expanded Right-to-Read office.

Initially, such an office would help to prepare and promote the necessary legislation under which it would ultimately operate, making recommendations as to the required budgetary allotments over extended periods.

Once in control of adequate funds, it would administer the corresponding legislation that would involve support of programs in schools, teacher-training institutions, research organizations, and elsewhere, awarding contracts and grants. It would have the power to redirect some of the efforts that have heretofore been administered under various bureaus in the Office of Education and to channel funds to other agencies such as the Office of Economic Opportunity. In addition, it would attempt to coordinate the efforts of many federal, state, and local agencies in the cause of improved literacy through persuasion, information services, and similar activities.

Legislative Action

The committee submitting the present report is convinced that if a Right-to-Read effort is to be successful, it must be supported by special legislation that would provide massive amounts of funds, over a period of years, for the various activities and programs that would make it successful.

The exact nature of this legislation and its timing are matters of debate. In the chapter by Saxe and de Lone (pp. 322–332), some of the factors that must be considered in projecting legislative action are discussed. Among these are the following:

1. The necessity of addressing the legislation to benefit relevant constituencies. The authors point out that the most powerful constituency looming in the future is that of the "suburbs." Certainly there is concern in the suburbs for the reading problem, and the suburbs deserve consideration for their own immediately perceived needs, e.g., help with reading failures and increased teachers' salaries. But close and continuing attention must also be directed to the inescapable relationship between the well-being of the suburbs and the quality of inner-city education. The evidence grows daily that neither district boundaries nor zoning laws can permanently protect outlying communities from the consequences of urban neglect and deterioration. The most relevant constituencies, though perhaps not the most powerful, are of course those of the inner city and of minority groups. Whatever is done, the legislation must bring effective aid to the currently disadvantaged as well as to those who are more fortunately situated.

2. The desirability of securing the support of educators and school authorities. Such support would be hard to get for legislation that would bypass the regular schools. The committee takes the position that the first line of attack on the reading problem should be through the schools, and it considers it imperative that the legislation be framed in this way. Educators must be brought in to assist with its framing.

It is important that we use and profit from our experience during the last decade with curriculum programs in the sciences, mathematics, and other fields that became the focus of attention under the NDEA and the National Science Foundation projects. In many cases these efforts were retarded, and some fell far short of their promise, largely because they were designed without sufficient regard for the realities of schooling or for the school officials in positions of responsibility and power. Whether this pattern of procedure was due to impatience or to unintended failure to use available resources, the results were unfortunate. They were wasteful and in the long run deprived large numbers of students of benefits they might have received had the strategies and tactics of change been planned more thoughtfully. Too frequently program changes were designed and introduced with insufficient attention to the experience and the concerns of the people who had long been on the scene and who would continue to carry responsibility for years after the enthusiastic reformers had departed. No institution can survive without the relatively stable core of persons who maintain its continuity. By definition, they are the "establishment" of the institution. If it is to be reformed from within or from outside, the group must necessarily be involved in the process, unless the changes are so drastic as to include its displacement. Where that happens, future continuity is possible only if a new "establishment" can be formed to replace the old one and to assume the functions of providing the stability required for survival. Effective reform, in brief, can be achieved only if we are as attentive to long-term consequences as we are to creative innovation and vigorous stimulation.

3. The desirability of by-passing the church-state issue. The committee believes that in view of the necessity of reaching all sectors of the population with the Right-to-Read program, the pattern set by the ESEA legislation, or a similar one, should guide the design of new legislation. The major consideration here is that the right to read not be limited to pupils in public institutions.

4. The desirability of conforming to current policies concerning state aid and categorical legislation. By its very nature, legislation for a Right-to-Read effort must be recognized as categorical. Despite many arguments for general aid to education, the committee believes that there is enough urgency and specific need for a Right-to-Read effort to justify categorical legislation. It can be argued, too, that reading is so central to education that a Right-to-Read program would virtually constitute a form of general aid. At the same time, the necessity of decentralizing at least some of the administration of this program would make legislation involving block grants to the states (rather than to individual school districts) not only possibly more effective but also more accommodating to current policies of the administration. Certain constraints on state action, possibly through guidelines to implement the intent of the Congress, should nevertheless be provided for in the legislation.

Since considerations concerning the proper timing of the introduction of legislative proposals to the Congress depend on rapidly changing political conditions, the committee makes no recommendation on this point other than to suggest that careful attention be given to it. There must be an adequate period of time to formulate the legislation in order to secure the benefit of various points of view and to profit from the experience that is being gained from current exploratory activities directed by the Right-to-Read office.

The committee does not wish to be highly specific in its recommendations concerning what should be covered by legislation for a Right-to-Read effort. The previous section of this report sets forth numerous recommendations as to what is needed to promote higher levels of literacy. Many of these recommendations are addressed to professional educators and other concerned groups rather than to legislators. Among the measures that might be covered or supported by federal legislation, however, are the following:

1. Funding for the adequate staffing of central and field offices that would administer the Right-to-Read effort.

2. Increased funding for research and development in the area of reading and the language arts. About 10 percent of these funds should be allocated to a grant program for basic research on the reading process, teaching methods and procedures, systems of motivating students, and problems of retarded readers. The bulk of the funds should be allocated for contracts for the development and field testing of practical tools, such as reading achievement and diagnostic tests; methods for describing and evaluating instructional materials and teaching procedures; and complete teaching systems for various types of pupils, including systems utilizing computer-aided instruction, television, and other newer educational media.[20]

3. Increased funding for the training of high-level specialists, such as trainers of teachers, curriculum developers, curriculum evaluators, and educational researchers.

4. Funding to enable schools, school districts, and educational institutions generally to

   (a) Secure expert opinion and consultation, either in technical aspects of the teaching of reading or in related problems of school management and organization.

---

[20] Since the preparation of the present report, the National Institute of Education has been assigned responsibility for conducting and supporting basic research in education, including research on reading and related problems. This is all to the good, but there still exists a concern that research on reading may not be adequately funded even under the National Institute of Education. The above recommendation, therefore, may be allowed to stand.—Eds.

(*b*) Secure better-qualified teachers and staff personnel for the reading program.

(*c*) Purchase newer instructional materials and devices.

(*d*) Set up and conduct adequate in-service teacher-training programs.

(*e*) Establish and maintain adequate systems of testing, evaluation, and record keeping related to reading progress.

5. Funding of programs designed to recruit and train teachers of reading, reading specialists and supervisors, and persons in other categories of school personnel.

6. Funding to aid adult literacy programs conducted by federal or state agencies, colleges and universities, schools and school districts, or business and industry.

7. Funding of miscellaneous support activities, such as

(*a*) A system of establishing and maintaining accountability standards and procedures.

(*b*) Field tests of voucher systems and other innovative procedures.

8. Provision of tax incentives for publishers and other profit-making organizations concerned with educational development, under the condition that products be adequately field-tested and validated.

The specification of the budget that should be attached to this legislation is a matter outside the expertise of the committee. We call attention, however, to the chapter on this subject by Brown and Hentschke (pages 333–351), without necessarily endorsing its detailed recommendations.

Local and State Action

Since under the American system basic responsibility for education lies at the state level, the most that federal legislative or executive action can accomplish is to stimulate, facilitate, and lead state action. But these things federal intervention can indeed do, often with crucial and far-reaching results. The history of federal intervention in education, from the establishment of land-grant colleges to the creation of Head Start programs, offers abundant evidence that federal initiative, assistance, and funds have repeatedly strengthened the hands and the resolve of local authorities. The direction of schools remains in state and local control, but the quality and effect of that direction are significantly enhanced when old goals are more sharply defined, new purposes validated, and better means of education made possible. Like the success of any national undertaking in education in the United States, gains in the field of reading instruction will depend upon the quality and strength of federal, state, and local collaboration.

It cannot be too strongly emphasized that whatever may be done through federal action, much initiative must be taken at state and local levels. State education authorities can give overall direction; establish and enforce standards; organize statewide programs; collect and disseminate necessary information; monitor, measure, and evaluate results; and give support through funds and personnel. The results ultimately produced, however, will reflect the ability and willingness of local authorities to use state and federal services and to bring the total pattern of resources to bear upon the individual school.

The evidence is growing that substantial help in education can be provided, particularly to young children, through television. The results attained among the preschool and kindergarten groups by watching *Sesame Street* and the early-stage reports of the effect of *The Electric Company* are impressive. But where these uses of the mass medium are highly illuminating and encouraging, the task of the traditional institutions remains fundamental and formidable. The major responsibility for building popular literacy still resides in the public school system, and within that system the key unit is the individual school. Data on relative success in reading among school systems are inconclusive, but much that we know indicates that the most significant variation in the effectiveness of programs may be attributed less to differences in district-wide patterns than to distinctive leadership and ingenuity in particular schools. Much remains to be done in identifying such schools and analyzing the reasons for their success.

It should not be assumed, however, that the cultivation of literacy can be left to the schools alone. Especially in furthering adult literacy, local communities can do much to help themselves by organizing literacy programs in local centers. Community organizations of many kinds, social clubs, political organizations, labor unions, and religious groups can all participate usefully in establishing activities under their own auspices and lending support to others. Business and industry have unusual opportunities to join in the effort by organizing programs for their employees. These may be developed in connection with in-plant programs for new employees or as a means for enabling employees already on the job to upgrade their skills. Employers and unions can also play influential roles by encouraging employees to use opportunities offered by local adult education agencies.

Not least among the actions that can be taken locally is the support of literacy programs—and the general endorsement of individual efforts toward literacy—by local news media. Specific and competently conducted teaching activities are essential, but they are far more likely to flourish if the leadership elements of the community deliberately undertake to create a public climate that favors the cultivation of literacy and appropriately recognizes those who improve their own literacy or help others to do so.

PERSONNEL FOR THE TEACHING OF READING AND ITS IMPROVEMENT: PREPARATION AND AVAILABILITY

Jeanne S. Chall

Do we have sufficient personnel adequately trained and available to implement the recommendations of this committee? Various surveys conducted during the 1960s and early 1970s indicate that to a large extent we do not. The situation is improving somewhat, however, particularly at the elementary school level.

The problems of training and availability of manpower will be discussed under the various categories of personnel: classroom teachers, reading specialists, school administrators, faculty in teacher-training institutions, reading researchers, and paraprofessionals.

CLASSROOM TEACHERS

We start with classroom teachers on the assumption that they, more than any other group, are responsible for the teaching of reading. While some children may at some point require individual diagnosis and remediation from a reading specialist, most will not. But should a reading specialist be needed, it is the classroom teacher who must contact that person for the necessary help and work with him or her in carrying out the special program. Thus, the classroom teacher must be knowledgeable enough to make the initial screening. And even if the child receives remedial help from the specialist, the classroom teacher is still responsible for the child's work in the other curriculum areas. With the help of the specialist, the teacher makes the necessary adjustments in the child's assignments.

To what extent has the classroom teacher's preparation been adequate in order to accomplish these tasks? According to a widely circulated study of teacher education in reading (Austin & Morrison et al., 1961), it has not been adequate. A questionnaire survey of 371 teacher-education institutions revealed that only 50% required a separate reading methods course for those preparing to teach in elementary schools. An additional 43% required some form of instruction covering the teaching of reading, but only as part of a course in language arts or in general methods. The time devoted specifically to the teaching of reading in these courses was quite limited. Seven percent of the institutions had no requirements with regard to reading methods.

A second study by Austin and Morrison (1963), a survey of the content, conduct, and practices of elementary reading programs in 1,023 school systems in the United States, essentially confirmed their earlier findings. "Interviews and observations of two thousand teachers revealed that their college preparation in reading had been seriously deficient" (Austin, 1968, p. 361).

A recent attempt to follow up these studies by analyzing 347 catalogs of teacher-education institutions seems to show a small improvement for elementary school teachers, for 64% of these institutions required a separate course in reading methods. However, 33% were still requiring it only as a part of a language arts or general methods course, and 3% had no requirements (Harsh, 1971).

In what ways has the preparation of teachers been deficient? According to the above surveys, the time given to the teaching of reading was insufficient for gaining the skills and understandings needed. Also, most readings methods courses for elementary school teachers concentrated primarily on methods of teaching reading in the primary grades. Not enough time was devoted to the more advanced reading skills needed for the intermediate and upper elementary grades. In addition, both teachers in training and teacher educators surveyed during the 1960s and early 1970s repeatedly reported "that there was insufficient time given in the education program for adequate preparation in the diagnosis of pupils' reading problems and in the use of individualized or special techniques for the remediation of reading difficulty" (Harsh, 1971, p. 165).

State certification requirements with regard to the teaching of reading seem to be even more limited than those of teacher-education institutions. Although it was difficult to determine with any precision the state certification requirements, Harsh concluded the following from an analysis of existing reports: "In 1970, as in 1960, the majority of institutions preparing teachers had requirements that exceeded the certification requirements of the state in which the institution was located" (Harsh, 1971, p. 165).

In short, it appears that the elementary school teachers educated during the 1960s and early 1970s were not receiving adequate instruction. For most, it was one course in reading methods or some limited work in reading as part of a course in language arts or general methods. This seems hardly enough. Indeed, Conant (1963), in his study of teacher education, recommended more—a minimum of one course (3 semester hours) for all elementary school teachers and two courses (6 semester hours) for teachers of kindergarten and the first three grades. The second course was to emphasize the identification and correction of reading problems.

There appears to be a trend toward stronger requirements for the teaching of reading by states and by colleges and universities. The state of New York, for example, as of January 1972, requires a minimum of 6 semester hours of courses in the teaching of reading for all persons seeking elementary certification on an individual basis. For the large majority who are accredited through the various institutions of higher learning within the state, provision for a stronger background in the teaching of reading is made by requiring that, as of January 1972, the institutions provide evidence to the State Education Department that persons recommended for certification have demonstrated specific competencies in the teaching of reading (*Report of the New York State Commission on the Quality, Cost and Financing of Elementary and Secondary Education*, Vol. 2, 1972, p. 6-4).

Since as late as 1971 the vast majority of colleges and universities in New York State required work in the teaching of reading only as part of a general methods or language arts course, we can assume that considerable revisions have been taking place. It seems reasonable to assume that the changes are in the direction of giving more emphasis to reading beyond the beginning stage and better preparation in diagnosing individual reading problems and providing remedial instruction, as well as cooperating with reading and learning disabilities specialists (*Report of the New York State Commission on the Quality, Cost and Financing of Elementary and Secondary Education*, Vol. 2, 1972, p. 6-15). The diagnostic and remedial skills can be acquired only through supervised clinical practice. Thus, carrying out an effective program for the preparation of elementary school teachers may involve considerably more than substituting one course for another or merely adding a second course in reading to the education requirements. A clinical practice course requires more instructional time per number of students, and it often needs special facilities and materials.

Therefore, in this time of shrinking finances, colleges of education may need state and federal support to provide prospective teachers with this very much needed experience.

Is there a similar trend toward improved preparation in the teaching of reading for high school teachers? The evidence seems quite mixed. While 9% of institutions required a reading methods course in 1960, only 6% required one in 1970. However, it appears that teacher-education institutions are becoming increasingly aware of the need for reading instruction in the high school, since 59% offered such a course in 1970 as compared with 27% in 1960 (Harsh, 1971).

Two recent surveys suggest that there is no trend toward a better preparation of high school teachers in the teaching of reading. A national survey of high school English teachers by McGuire (1969) revealed that 84% had not taken a course in the teaching of reading at the undergraduate level. In addition, of those teachers who had taken an English methods course, 79% indicated that the course treated the teaching of reading "to little or no extent." Only 8% indicated that the teaching of reading was treated "to a considerable extent." Also, 54 percent indicated that they received no form of in-service education in the teaching of reading in their school during the last 5 years. When years of teaching experience was crosstabulated with preparation, the results indicated that no improvement had taken place in the preparation of new English teachers for reading instruction (Harsh, 1971, p. 182).

A study by Farr, Laffey, and Brown (1970) of Indiana secondary school reading programs found that in 73% of the programs the basic responsibility of reading instruction was assigned to regular English teachers. And yet, the authors observed, secondary English teachers were not required to take graduate courses in the teaching of reading. Sixty-nine percent of the teachers responding in the Indiana survey had taken no courses in the teaching of reading as undergraduates; 58% had no courses in the teaching of reading as graduate students; 12% were enrolled in a reading course. Only 10% of the schools employed teachers who had completed graduate programs in elementary and secondary reading (Harsh, 1971, p. 183).

It seems quite clear that the preparation of secondary school teachers, including English teachers, is inadequate with regard to the teaching of reading. Although there seems to be a trend toward improving the preparation of elementary school teachers, there are few indications that such a change is taking place for secondary school teachers.

Overall the current status of state certification requirements and the preparation given by teacher-education institutions in the teaching of reading indicates the need for considerable improvement. Every effort must be made to assure that new teachers being prepared for the elementary schools possess the knowledge, skills, and attitudes toward the teaching of reading that are required to help all children, particularly those who have difficulty in learning. Since reading continues to develop and grow through the high school and even college years, it is essential that all junior and senior high school teachers, especially English teachers, be equipped to help their pupils advance in reading skills, particularly those pupils whose reading level is below that required for reading the regular assignments.

Further evidence for the need for improvement comes from a recent USOE national survey of school principals to ·determine the incidence of pupils with reading problems and the availability of special reading assistance. Each school was asked to report the number of pupils with reading problems and whether or not these pupils were receiving special assistance. About 15% to 20% of the pupils were designated as having reading problems, but of this population, 63% of the elementary school pupils and 53% of the secondary school pupils received *no* special instruction or assistance. Where those students with reading problems did receive special assistance, 55% of the schools provided this as part-time instruction in special classes, while 40% provided the assistance in the regular classes, and 5% in a full-time special class (Dwyer, 1971; see also Harsh, 1971, p. 181).

Thus, most of the work with "problem readers" is carried out essentially by the classroom teacher. Indeed, the same study found that 80% of the teachers who provided special instruction and assistance to pupils with reading problems did so in the regular classroom, while about 20% provided such instruction in separate classes. In addition, 29% of the elementary schools and 30% of the secondary schools had no special reading personnel regularly assigned or on call (Harsh, 1971, p. 181).

The need for in-service education for teachers at both the elementary and secondary levels is clear. Since surveys continue to find that most problem readers are given special assistance only in the regular classroom, it is imperative that classroom teachers have the skills to give this assistance.[1]

READING SPECIALISTS

There seems to be no disagreement about the need for reading specialists. "All surveys are consistent in reporting a need for more reading specialists than are currently available" (Harsh, 1971, p. 183).

A survey of twenty major cities (seventeen responded) regarding certification requirements for reading specialists revealed that all employ

[1] A decade ago, the International Reading Association (IRA, 1965) published its minimum standards for the professional preparation of classroom teachers of reading.

some type of special reading teacher. But wide variation was found in the pre-service requirements for the special teachers of reading. Seven cities required no formal pre-service preparation beyond that required for regular teacher certification. Five others did not require special preparation for some of their special reading teacher categories but required it for others. Three cities required a master's degree with special courses in reading. About 10 percent indicated that the International Reading Association's minimum requirements for reading specialists were followed closely, but they were not specific about the degree, course, or competency requirements (Harsh, 1971, p. 167).

The local regulations regarding the preparation and competency of specialists in reading do not consistently mention the reading certification of the states in which the city is located. When the reading specialist certification requirements of cities are compared to those of the states in which they are located, it appears that at least one-half of the cities do not require the state special reading certification for their categories of reading teachers and reading specialists. However, in states with special reading programs created by the legislature, special certification for teachers is required by each local district. Forty percent of the major cities required 1 to 5 years of successful teaching experience for specialists in reading or reading teachers. About one-third of the cities required in-service courses for the several kinds of specialists.

Overall, there appears to be little consistency in the certification of reading specialists across states, across large cities, and for cities and the states in which they are located. The titles for reading specialists under state certification do not always include the variety of special reading teachers and reading specialists in the large school districts. There is a marked discrepancy between the state-certified categories and those of the large cities. This situation led Harsh to conclude, "The analysis of these data from the major cities suggests that even when the city is within a state having certification for reading specialists, some (if not all) of the local positions for reading teachers and reading specialists have other requirements than those of the state certification" (p. 179).

An earlier report by Austin (1968) reveals a similar picture: "In reviewing the requirements for teacher certification in reading, the lack of agreement among states concerning operational definitions of 'reading teachers,' 'remedial reading personnel,' and 'reading consultants' is evident. Until state departments and professional associations establish criteria for these levels of competence and define the roles of responsibilities of reading personnel, data cannot be collated in a meaningful manner." According to a study by Donalson (1965), only twelve states certified reading specialists—i.e., persons "prepared to perform duties associated with the detection and correction of reading difficulties and/or supervision of a remedial reading clinic" (Austin, 1968, p. 372).

It appears, then, that although the International Reading Association's standards for professional training of reading specialists (International Reading Association, 1968) have been in existence for some years, little change with regard to certification has taken place on the state or local level. The IRA standards cover four types of specialists: special teacher of reading, reading clinician, reading consultant, and reading supervisor. To qualify on the first level, special teacher of reading, the standards suggest a master's degree, including 12 semester hours in graduate-level reading courses, such as foundations of reading and diagnosis and correction of reading disabilities, and a clinical or laboratory practicum, as well as at least 3 years of successful teaching experience which includes reading instruction.

A second year of graduate study and additional courses and experience in reading and reading-related areas are required for the more advanced levels of specialization—reading clinician, consultant, and supervisor.

During the past 10 years another related group of specialists has become involved in the diagnosis and remediation of children with reading problems. In some states the specialists are referred to as "learning disabilities specialists." In others they may be called "specific language disability specialists," "teachers of the perceptually handicapped," etc. Their professional preparation is usually in a department of special education, while the reading specialists referred to above tend to receive their professional preparation in departments of curriculum and teaching, elementary education, or educational psychology. "Learning disabilities specialists" may work with children who have other problems besides a reading problem, but much of their work involves the diagnosis and treatment of reading problems, usually where the problems are severe. (See the section on "dyslexia" in the committee report, pages 20–22.)

Certification requirements for remedial reading specialists differ somewhat from those of learning disabilities specialists. Because of the differences in titles and in certification requirements, it is not inconceivable that a situation may arise that prevents the best-qualified persons from working with those children who need their help most. It is essential, then, that some agreement is reached regarding types of specialists, the minimum professional standards they are to meet, and the kinds of positions they may hold.

SCHOOL ADMINISTRATORS

A recent study of inner-city schools that were successful in teaching reading found strong leadership to be one of the eight characteristics common to these elementary schools. Indeed, four additional factors fall more within the realm of administrators than of teachers: good atmosphere, strong emphasis on reading, additional reading personnel, and careful evaluation of pupil progress (Weber, 1971).

In the Austin-Morrison study (1963), 776 school principals were surveyed on the roles they filled in matters relating to the reading program. Most frequently reported was the selection, distribution, and use of materials. Conferences with teachers rated next, concerning grouping children for instruction, selecting children for special programs, and advising those whose pupils had specific reading problems. Also listed as a main responsibility was the evaluation of test results or the administration of tests to groups of children or to individuals.

Yet it appears from a survey completed a few years later (Bryant, 1965) that certification requirements for elementary school principals in fifty states made no mention of the need for a formal course in reading. It should be noted, however, that the Department of Elementary School Principals of the National Education Association developed guidelines in 1961 for the preparation of principals that included work in curriculum, with special emphasis on reading instruction (Austin, 1968).

It appears that the responsibilities of elementary school principals for the reading program are considerably greater than what is implied by the professional training generally required of them. If they are to exert strong leadership, make appropriate selections of reading materials, interpret reading test scores properly, and guide teachers in the various other ways that are expected of them, a thorough knowledge of these responsibilities should be part of their professional preparation. In addition, inservice courses and workshops should be provided for those who are already in their positions or who have not had such work in the last 5 or 10 years.

FACULTY IN TEACHER-TRAINING INSTITUTIONS

Inevitably we come to the question—are there enough fully qualified teachers on the college level to offer the kind of professional training needed by reading specialists as well as by regular classroom teachers?

It appears that there probably are not. In 1960 Austin found that most college reading faculty members had majors in elementary and general education. Of 638 instructors, 96% held master's degrees, but only 4% of these were in reading. Of the 38% who held doctor's degrees, 11% had majored in reading in their doctoral program. "It appears, then, that undergraduate courses in reading instruction were being taught by those whose own preparation had been in education generally rather than in reading specifically" (Austin, 1968, p. 383).

Some improvement may have taken place since the 1960s. A survey in 1970 found that 44% of teacher-education institutions were offering graduate programs for reading specialists, compared with 23% in 1960 (Harsh, 1971, p. 162). A more recent survey by the International Reading Association, *Graduate programs and faculty in reading*, lists 66 universities as giving an Ed.D. and/or a Ph.D. with a specialization in reading (Wanat, 1973). Most of these institutions also give master's degrees, and some give a post-master's sixth-year certificate as well. An additional 124 colleges and universities give a master's degree only, or post-master's work not including the doctorate. An examination of the educational backgrounds of the faculties of these institutions, particularly those institutions giving doctoral degrees, indicates that the great majority received their doctorates after 1960, and their graduate work was in reading and related areas, such as educational psychology or curriculum.

Whether there are now a sufficient number of college and university teachers knowledgeable in the psychology and teaching of reading to train all the prospective teacher trainers, reading researchers, clinical directors, program developers, reading specialists, and classroom teachers is difficult to tell.

My impression is that the shortage may continue for some time to come, particularly if most states follow New York in amending their elementary teacher certification requirements to include at least two courses (or the appropriate competencies) in the teaching of reading. The shortage will continue also if most states require at least one course in reading methods for prospective high school teachers, and if they adopt the minimal standards for various reading specialists sponsored by the International Reading Association.

If this occurs, the colleges and universities offering advanced degrees in reading may find themselves short of the highly qualified faculties needed. To prevent such a circumstance, it is recommended that assistance be given by appropriate government agencies (OE, the Bureau of the Handicapped, etc.) to further develop and expand high-quality graduate study. Fellowships and stipends will also be needed to attract the most able and imaginative people to the field.

READING RESEARCHERS

Considerable dissatisfaction with the quality of the research in reading was prevalent in the early 1960s. A study by Wilder (1966) of the research activities of reading experts found that the experts were not given the institutional support that scientists need if they are to produce definitive research. The schools of education in which they studied and worked were isolated from research activity in the basic sciences. Further, reading research did not receive the financial support on the scale and over the period of time required to yield reliable answers to questions that needed answering. Altogether only 1.6 percent of reading experts queried in 1963 received half or more of their income from research bureaus or projects (Chall, 1967, p. 88).

Since then, there have been several large-scale attempts, with government support, to develop researchers with a strong commitment to reading. Among these were Project Literacy, directed by Harry Levin of Cornell University. For about 5 years, through series of consortiums for various social scientists—psychologists, linguists, sociolinguists, psychiatrists—basic research on various aspects of reading was undertaken. A summary of some of these studies is included in Levin and Williams, *Basic research on reading* (1971), and in the chapter by Eleanor Gibson in the present volume (pages 288–321).

Other large-scale research studies on reading have been undertaken at the Research and Development Centers at the University of Wisconsin, Stanford University, and the University of Pittsburgh. Many of the researchers on these projects were trained in one of the basic disciplines, usually psychology or linguistics.

The question occurs as to the best way to train reading researchers. It would appear from the Wilder critique and from the later work by Cronbach and Suppes (1969) that the best way to develop prospective educational researchers is through a thorough grounding in disciplined research and only later in a specialization. Cronbach and Suppes wrote:

> The person concerned with reading, for example, may find his supporting disciplines in linguistics, or perceptual and even physiological psychology, in sociology, in communication research, or elsewhere. But he must be selective; to try to become expert in all these areas is to guarantee mastery of none. . . . Such proposals depart radically from the tradition of training the reading specialist . . . under a senior specialist in that applied field. The history of that type of training has not been encouraging. We of course do not advise that the researcher attack an applied problem without informing himself of the traditions and past work in the field. Our position is that the investigator should be a disciplined inquirer first and a topical specialist second; those with experience in his topical area have much to teach him (pp. 218–219).

Thus, to develop future researchers in reading it will be necessary for the various departments and faculties in a university to coordinate their work. It is questionable whether a reading faculty in a school of education can by itself turn out highly qualified reading researchers. By the same token, a psychology or a sociology department cannot do it alone.

There are indications that more well-qualified reading researchers are now being educated than in past years. It is important that this training continue and be expanded, since much needs to be learned about reading and its development.

PARAPROFESSIONALS

There are many tasks in the teaching of reading that can be undertaken, with constructive results, by those who have received little formal training. Indeed, reports of the effectiveness of student volunteers, adult volunteers, and teacher aides have been encouraging. What is usually overlooked, however, is that the successful programs have provided considerable preparatory training as well as regular supervision by professional teachers. While paraprofessionals can share some of the responsibilities of regular teachers and reading specialists, it is questionable whether they can do the work independently. Indeed, the results can be disastrous if a pupil who has a serious reading problem is assigned to a volunteer who has received no special training or supervision. If the pupil fails to learn, he will become more frustrated. No matter how willing or pleasant the paraprofessional, the pupil will have experienced one more failure to learn, from one more person.

When given the proper training and supervision, paraprofessionals can be extremely helpful in a classroom and in special remedial programs. Adults from the community can be paraprofessionals; some of them may become regular classroom teachers through career ladder programs. College students majoring in elementary or secondary education may become paraprofessionals before they do their student teaching. College students majoring in psychology, sociology, or other fields, may also work as paraprofessionals. Often this kind of experience attracts them to teaching as a profession.

Still other paraprofessionals can be found among high school and even upper elementary students, including those who themselves may be having difficulty in reading (Gartner, Kohler, & Riessman, 1971). Indeed, it appears that in some projects that use these student paraprofessionals, the tutors make even greater gains in reading than the tutees (Cloward, 1967).

REFERENCES

Austin, Mary. Professional training of reading personnel. In Helen M. Robinson (Ed.), *Innovation and change in reading instruction,* the 67th Yearbook of the National Society for the Study of Education, Part II, 1968, pp. 357–396.

Austin, Mary C., & Morrison, Coleman. *The first R: The Harvard report on reading in elementary schools.* New York: The Macmillan Company, 1963.

Austin, Mary C., Morrison, Coleman, et al. *The torchlighters: Tomorrow's teachers of reading.* Cambridge, Mass.: Harvard University Press, 1961.

Bryant, Bill. Academic and professional education requirements for elementary administrative credentials. *Journal of Teacher Education,* 1965, **16,** 74–76.

Chall, Jeanne. *Learning to read: The great debate.* New York: McGraw-Hill Book Company, 1967.

Cloward, Robert. Studies in tutoring. *The Journal of Experimental Education,* Fall 1967, **36**(1), 14–25.

Conant, James B. *The education of American teachers.* New York: McGraw-Hill Book Company, 1963.

Cronbach, Lee J., & Suppes, Patrick (Eds.). *Research for tomorrow's schools.* New York: The Macmillan Company, 1969.

Donalson, William R. A comparison of certification requirements for the reading specialist, for the elementary teacher in reading, and for the general elementary teacher. Unpublished Master of Science thesis, Florida State University, 1965.

Dwyer, Carol Anne. Tables prepared from unpublished documents from the National Center for Educational Statistics (DHEW). Berkeley, Calif.: Educational Testing Service, 1971.

Farr, Roger C., Laffey, James, & Brown, Rexel. Secondary reading programs in Indiana: Status and needs. *Journal of Reading,* 1970, **13,** 269–274.

Gartner, Alan, Kohler, Mary, & Riessman, Frank. *Children teach children: Learning by teaching.* New York: Harper & Row, Publishers, Incorporated, 1971.

Harsh, J. Richard. Nature and extent of current practices in educating those who teach reading. In Reginald Corder (Ed.), *The information base for reading: A critical review of the information base for current assumptions regarding the status of instruction and achievement in reading in the United States.* Final Report, Project No. 0-9031, DHEW. Berkeley, Calif.: Educational Testing Service, 1971, pp. 138–219.

International Reading Association, Professional Standards and Ethics Committee. *Professional preparation in reading for classroom teachers: Minimum standards.* Newark, Del.: International Reading Association, 1965.

International Reading Association, Professional Standards and Ethics Committee. *Roles responsibilities, and qualifications for reading specialists.* Newark, Del.: International Reading Association, 1968.

Levin, Harry, & Williams, Joanna (Eds.). *Basic studies on reading.* New York: Basic Books, Inc., Publishers, 1970.

McGuire, George K. *The teaching of reading by English teachers in public high schools: A national survey.* Interim Report. Urbana, Ill.: Illinois State-Wide Curriculum Study Center in the Preparation of Secondary English Teachers (ISCPET), June 1969. BR5-0789. Contract OEC-5-10-029. 96 pp. ERIC: Document ED 031 498.

Report of the New York State Commission on the Quality, Cost and Financing of Elementary and Secondary Education, Vol. 2, 1972.

Wanat, Stanley F. (Ed.). *Graduate programs and faculty in reading.* Newark, Del.: International Reading Association, 1973.

Weber, George. *Inner-city children can be taught to read: Four successful schools.* Washington, D.C.: Council for Basic Education, 1971.

Wilder, David. The reading experts: A case study of the failure to institutionalize an applied science of education. Unpublished doctoral dissertation, Columbia University, New York, 1966.

PART TWO

Commissioned Papers

CHAPTER 1

READING LITERACY: ITS DEFINITION AND ASSESSMENT

John R. Bormuth

CONCEPTIONS OF LITERACY

Let us begin by examining some of the earlier efforts to define and assess literacy. We hear claims that there remain large numbers of illiterate people in the United States, a nation that has experienced free and compulsory public education over several generations. The late James E. Allen, Jr., former U.S. Commissioner of Education, cited these figures (1969):

1. One out of every four students nationwide has significant reading deficiencies.

2. In large city school systems up to half of the students read below expectation.

3. There are more than 3 million illiterates in our adult population.

4. About half of the unemployed youth, ages 16 to 21, are functionally illiterate.

5. Three-quarters of the juvenile offenders in New York are 2 or more years retarded in reading.

6. In a recent U.S. Armed Forces program called "Project 100,000," 68.2 percent of the young men fell below grade 7 in reading and academic ability.

EDITOR'S NOTE: A version of this chapter has appeared earlier (*Reading Research Quarterly*, 1973–74, 9, 7–66). For the present publication it has been further modified by the author and considerably shortened. The reader interested in the details of the author's proposals is advised to consult the version previously published.

If these statements indicate that there are large numbers of illiterate citizens within the United States, they may also be taken as evidence that educational institutions have failed tragically to achieve one of our most deeply rooted aims—that all people should have equal opportunities to develop and attain their ambitions. Reasoning similar to this seems to be what prompted Commissioner Allen and others to advocate massive research and development programs aimed at developing literacy instruction that could remedy this problem.

The Need for Better Literacy Assessment Procedures

Certainly, if the illiteracy level is so high, such programs would seem urgently needed and large expenditures of public moneys justified. Unfortunately, however, it is impossible to put much faith in these or in any other literacy statistics currently available, for none of them is based either on a careful analysis of the concept of literacy itself or on suitable methods of measurement. It may be worthwhile to examine some of the more commonly used procedures for assessing literacy and to describe briefly some data indicating that the literacy problem may be even far more serious than these procedures would lead us to believe.

Functional literacy. The Bureau of the Census attempts to assess the literacy of the population by tabulating the number of people fourteen years of age or over who have not completed 6 years of schooling. This constitutes the criterion for what is called *functional literacy.* In order to accept figures based on this criterion, it is necessary to make several dubious assumptions, but just one needs to be examined here.

There is no evidence to support the assumption that 6 years of schooling are sufficient to raise all students' abilities to the point where the students can deal competently with ordinary reading tasks. One study (Bormuth, 1969a) showed that the assumption is probably false. A fairly representative sample of eight articles was drawn from news publications. A cloze readability test was made over each,[1] and the tests were administered to students in grades 3 through 12. These children were from middle-class homes in a residential suburb of a large Midwestern city. The average percentage of students who were able to answer at least 35 percent of the cloze questions on the tests was calculated. On the average article, only 33 percent of the students in grade 6 and only 65 percent of those in grade 12 reached this criterion.

In other studies (Bormuth, 1971) it had been shown that students who are unable to answer at least 35 percent of the items in a cloze readability test can gain little or no information from materials at that level of difficulty. Consequently, there seems to be little basis for claiming that a person completing 6 years of schooling is literate. Even graduation from

[1] The cloze readability procedure will be discussed in some detail later in this chapter (pp. 84–86).

high school does not appear to be a very certain criterion of literacy. The fact is that the number of years a person has been in school is a very poor index of his ability to read, for within any grade level it is common to observe very wide variations in the reading abilities of the students. But even if grade level were an accurate index of literacy, the small amount of evidence that is now available would indicate that the grade 6 criterion is far too low and that the illiteracy rate is probably much higher than the Census Bureau would lead us to believe.

Achievement level. Others have tried to get around this problem by using, in some way, a person's reading achievement grade level instead of the years spent in school. This is a number found by giving a reading test of some sort to students who are in various grades in school, say at the 5.2 grade level. Their mean test scores are calculated, and thereafter students who get a score equal to the mean of this group are assigned a grade level at which, on the average, students are able to answer that number of questions on that test.

But, again, it is hard to tell what these grade-level scores mean. Commissioner Allen cited a study reporting that 68.2 percent of the men in an Armed Forces study had grade scores of less than 7.0. It is difficult to say, with any certainty, what this means. Can students at reading grade 7.0 read newspapers, college textbooks, or even the text in comic books competently? A grade-level score does not provide us with any information on just what kinds of real-world reading tasks a person can perform competently. Consequently, we learn little about the level of illiteracy in the population when grade-level scores are used to tell us either that some proportion of the population falls below a certain grade level or that some proportion is 2 grade-level years below their current grade in school.

Data from a study already cited (Bormuth, 1969a) shed some light on the matter. By performing a series of statistical regression analyses between scores on cloze readability tests made from each of the newspaper articles and a test that gave grade-level scores, it was possible to calculate that the grade-level score of the average person who answered 35 percent of the items on the cloze readability test was 10.5, indicating that the average person is literate with respect to half of the newspaper articles only after 10.5 years in school. This shows that the study cited by Allen employed a criterion that was far too low and also that the illiteracy rate may be very much higher than estimated by that study.

Grade-level expectancy. The third major way in which people attempt to assess literacy is by using the "expectancy" concept. According to this concept, a person has some level of aptitude for learning reading. This aptitude is usually measured by a verbal aptitude or verbal intelligence test score that is converted to a grade-level score. This grade-level score is said to be the person's reading expectancy, meaning that if he were working "up to his capacity," he would probably get a similar grade-level score when he is given a reading achievement test. Hence, a person whose achievement score is, say, 2 years below his expectancy score does not seem to be profiting very well from his instruction.

It is possible to cite several strong statistical reasons why the studies that have reported this kind of data in the past must be viewed with suspicion. But these can be put aside for an even stronger reason: The expectancy score is based on two grade-level scores, neither of which tells us anything about whether a person can perform competently on real-world reading tasks. In passing, it may be worth mentioning also that if every student were working exactly up to his capacity, and if the tests now used to measure capacity and achievement were slightly unreliable (as all tests are), then exactly half of the students would appear to be working below capacity at all times, a phenomenon Allen cited as evidence of extensive illiteracy in large city schools, but one that may be merely an artifact of the random error that is a component of test scores.

Proportion below grade level. One occasionally reads a report that such and such a percentage of the students in some school system falls below grade level and that these students are, therefore, destined for a life of illiteracy. If this prediction were true, it would not be because the children fell below grade level. The grade-level scores represent nothing more than the mean scores of the students in a given grade level. Hence, even if the achievement test were well made and fairly recent, we could always say with very good accuracy that half of all children are always below grade level at all times. But, because we are dealing only with grade-level scores, we still have no idea whether all, some, or even none of those children whose scores fell below grade level can respond competently to real-world reading tasks. Even if the percentage refers to the children whose reading scores fall, say, 2 years below grade level, the same difficulties of interpretation apply.

These remarks should not be interpreted as a criticism of Allen or of anyone else who has attempted to deal with the literacy problem at the policy-making level. He, and other people of good will, sense that something is amiss in literacy training—that large numbers of people probably never reach a level of reading ability sufficient to cope with even the common reading tasks confronting them daily. In order to rally the support needed to remedy the problem, these men require evidence. It is extremely unfortunate that there is as yet no adequate evidence to place in their hands.[2] But the fact is that we have not yet analyzed exactly what

[2] Since this was written, there has been issued the report of a survey based on a measure of reading skill, the Brief Test of Literacy, that is in some ways more adequate than those reports previously available. According to this report, it is estimated that "4.8 percent of the approximately 23 million noninstitutionalized youths 12–17 years old in the United States are illiterate, i.e., they cannot read at the beginning fourth grade level" (*Literacy among youths 12–17 years, United States.* DHEW Publication No. (HRA) 74-1613, Washington, D.C., December 1973).

is meant by literacy and then devised appropriate methods for measuring it.

The Nature of Literacy

The term "literate" may be used to refer to a number of different kinds of behavior, ranging from the ability to employ basic reading or writing skills to the knowledge of some body of literature. The term will be used here to refer to the ability to respond competently to real-world reading tasks. To define the term further, however, requires that we give detailed specifications of four parameters: (*a*) the skills we wish to observe and the way in which we measure them; (*b*) the criterion level of performance we expect a literate person to demonstrate on tests of those skills; (*c*) the kinds of materials on which we test the skills; and finally (*d*) any characteristics of the person tested, such as his age, his aptitude, and his practical needs (goals), that may be relevant to an evaluation of his level of attainment in literacy. Each of these four parameters is discussed in subsequent sections of this chapter.

Artifactual Nature of Literacy

An effort to define literacy is not apt to produce credible results unless it begins with the realization that the main task of the definition is to design a product that must thereafter be adopted as a social goal.

Many discussions of literacy attempt to approach the definition of literacy in the same way as a naturalist would study natural states and events such as corn and its growth. The naturalist's job is to discover the inner workings of such states and how their processes relate to environmental factors. He would need to consult his personal and social goals in only the most indirect fashion, for the composition, structure, and growth processes of corn are largely independent of what he might imagine is the ideal food crop. If we were to take a naturalistic approach to the definition of literacy, we would *not* concern ourselves with what is the most desirable process for transmitting information to a reader. Rather, we would identify instances of reading and then attempt to describe how that process takes place. Our emphasis would be not on if and how we *want* people to read but rather on how people *do* read.

However, this naturalistic approach to the definition of literacy ignores a fundamental fact: *Reading is an artifact of man and not a product of nature.* Reading is based on language and therefore is simply a special adaptation of general language processes. Some tend to view these language processes as being products of nature. This view may arise partially from the fact that the processes come down to us from prehistoric times and partially from the fact that they are so well adapted to our innate learning mechanisms that children learn languages at an early age with little or no conscious instruction from adults. But the fact is that languages must be learned by humans from other humans. At some point, humans must have invented and developed language as a tool to serve their needs. Therefore it is as much an artifact of man as is a clay pot, a symphony, or a Ford. And its special form, reading, must be seen in exactly the same way, as a structure of processes that we design and build in people to suit our needs.

Employing a naturalistic approach to the definition of literacy misses the point that this definition must serve as a goal statement, a statement of what literacy skill a person ought to have. To attempt to define literacy by describing the skills possessed by some group of people is to beg the question of what skills they ought to have. Answering this question could conceivably lead us to describe a set of skills very similar to those possessed by some group of people, but it could instead lead us to describe a set of skills that no one at present possesses. Thus, when we seek a definition of literacy, we are not seeking a description of nature. Rather, we are formulating an ethical judgment that society's values would be best served if its members acquired a particular set of literacy skills—which is to say, the definition would explicitly claim that acquiring these skills would consume the least amount of our resources while simultaneously enabling us to maximize the attainment of our goals.

Viewing literacy as an artifact of man should also lead us to demand that a definition take into account both of the major determinants of literacy. Most efforts to define and teach literacy have been placed exclusively in the hands of educators, so it is not a bit surprising that their definitions have dealt primarily with specifying what types and amounts of reading skills a person acquires. Nor is it surprising that their literacy programs have been aimed primarily at teaching literacy skills to people. This is the only determinant of literacy over which the educator has much direct control. *But the kind and amount of reading skill that a person has is just one of the factors that determines his literacy.* The other major factor is the readability of the materials the person is confronted with. Imagine a person who has a certain level of skill. If we provided him with materials that were written in very complex language, he would probably not get the information that he needed from them, and we would classify him as subliterate. But if we were to provide him with other versions of those materials that were written in simple language and that required many fewer and more common skills, we might find that we could classify him as literate or even as overliterate. Thus, since literacy is an artifact of man, printed language not only constitutes a problem that man must deal with; it also constitutes a problem that he creates.

Publishers constitute the group that is most acutely aware of the influence of readability on literacy. People will generally avoid buying materials that they cannot comprehend; therefore, the sales of newspapers, books, and magazines and the profits obtained from their sale can be sharply reduced if they are written in language that is obscure and complex. Consequently, editors are usually careful to hire only writers who can write in comprehensible language; the editors also provide style guides to aid in this writing. Similarly, a standard item in the curricula of schools of journalism is the study of the technical aspects of readability; that is, the study of how the comprehensibility of printed language can be altered to suit various audiences. Thus, it is possible to choose any one of a large number of levels of reading skill as representing the level that a person must achieve in order to be considered literate. If a very high level of skill is chosen, then much effort and expense must be directed toward teaching people greater numbers of reading skills, and little effort and expense need to be expended on the training of writers and the editing of materials. But if a low level is chosen, less needs to be spent on reading instruction, and more must be spent on readability control in order to achieve essentially the same effect.

It is extremely unlikely that we could obtain much support for a definition of literacy that fails to take this relationship into account. Support for this definition would depend on whether a convincing case could be made that the level of skill specified by the definition was, in fact, the most desirable level. We have just seen that, within fairly broad limits, we can achieve essentially the same effects by trading off instruction in reading against editorial adjustment of the language in materials. So the credibility of our definition is likely to hinge to a very great extent on whether the level that it specifies represents the most economical allocation of resources between these two factors that determine literacy.[3]

KINDS OF LITERACY SKILLS

The first component of a literacy definition is a set of statements describing the kinds of skills a person must be able to exhibit in order to be classified as literate. Pertinent to this are discussions of (a) the range of skills that must be considered (though not necessarily included) whenever a definition of literacy is formulated; (b) the need to limit the range of skills included in a particular definition intended for practical use in research, development, or instructional programs and the more important criteria for selecting those skills to be included; and (c) some of the major measurement problems involved in designing tests for assessing literacy.

---

[3] The trade-off that I have just described is not as simple as I may have made it sound. For example, not all printed language can or *ought* to be controlled for readability. Poetry, aesthetic writing, and technical writing each present special problems. Unfortunately, space does not permit us to examine these problems in any detail here.

Range of Skills Involved in Literacy

At first glance it would not seem to be a particularly difficult task to say just what behaviors are implied by the term "literacy." To say a person is literate seems to claim that he can perform some set of reading tasks competently. So all one would have to do to arrive at the sought-after literacy skills is to analyze those tasks to see what skills they require. But this first glance is deceptive, for this problem is closely associated with another problem containing several complexities that have led to heated and emotionally charged controversies. These controversies arose out of the question of whether the reading act involves just *word* recognition *behaviors*—those skills involved in decoding written words into spoken words—or whether it *also* includes such skills as comprehending that language, critically evaluating its truth and relevance, appreciating its aesthetic qualities, and so on. When this problem is properly analyzed, it reduces not to an either/or question but merely to a series of questions about priorities which can be rather easily (but not painlessly) resolved on the basis of values shared by the protagonists on both sides of the argument.

Controversy. Although this controversy has existed for a very long time in the area of reading instruction, it surfaced and became a full-blown public controversy with the publication of *Why Johnny can't read* by Rudolph Flesch (1955). Flesch noted that substantial numbers of children were unable to perform competently even the most rudimentary reading skill—decoding written words into spoken words—and he attributed this fact not only to a lack of phonics content in the reading curricula used in schools but also to the presence of a considerable amount of instruction designed to teach students the higher-level skills commonly referred to as "comprehension," "critical reading," "literary appreciation," and the like. It was not his contention that these were unimportant skills to learn. Rather, it seemed to be his belief that these higher-level skills were of secondary priority in the sense that they could not be learned until the decoding skills had been mastered and that their early introduction into the curriculum interfered with word recognition instruction by diverting energy away from the acquisition of decoding skills.

A confused controversy, however, has continued in other forms among psychologists, linguists, and educators, centering, among other things, on the issue of whether or not reading curricula should include instruction in the higher-level skills. Some psychologists and linguists have argued that reading can be conceptualized as consisting of only those skills uniquely involved in decoding written language into spoken language and that everything else in the reading curriculum does not really teach reading skills at all, but rather something often vaguely lumped together and labeled "thinking skills." A number of others, mostly reading specialists, have taken the position that the reading act could not really be broken up in this way. They argue that there is an underlying continuity in the reading act, that such a distinction is arbitrary, and that omitting instruction in the higher-level skills would cripple children's potential for performing useful reading tasks.

This argument would have long since evaporated had the protagonists begun by addressing themselves to the same issue. The group that wishes to define reading as being conterminous with the decoding skills has included largely scientists in linguistics and psychology. To them, identifying reading behaviors primarily involves breaking them down into small classes so that they can plan and carry out manageable scientific analyses. A scientist simply cannot perform useful theoretical work until he has obtained rigorously defined classes of phenomena to study; thus, for their purposes, these scholars were absolutely correct in placing the decoding skills in a class by themselves in order to have a fairly natural and manageable phenomenon that they could analyze from existing linguistic and psychological theory.

On the other side of the argument one finds mainly the specialists in reading instruction. Their objective is to teach a complete system of behaviors that would permit students to cope effectively with the reading tasks encountered in the real world. When the specialists analyze these real-world reading tasks, they see that the students must learn not only the decoding behaviors but also the higher-level skills, which their opponents *seem* to oppose teaching. The reading specialists then label all these skills "reading skills," but without making it clear to others that they use this label merely as a convenient method of referring to *anything* that is taught during the period labeled "reading" in the schedules which appear in curriculum guides. To them, the label includes instruction in how to turn the pages of a book and in how to find and read page numbers, along with the teaching of decoding skills and any other skill that they think (*a*) is functional in coping with real-world reading tasks and (*b*) can be more conveniently taught during that time period than, say, during the period labeled "mathematics." Both groups, then, were apparently led into thinking that they are talking about the same thing because they both wish to use the same label. And since each side had developed its definition through careful reasoning, it seemed to feel the need to zealously defend its usage against anything that appeared to be a rival definition. Yet since each definition was designed to serve quite different purposes, they are in no way rivals.

Seen in this light, the problem of choosing the skills to be included in a definition of *literacy* is not a problem of identifying what is truly a reading skill. Rather, the selection of the skills to be included in a given definition depends upon the consideration of the purpose that definition is to serve. If its purpose is purely scientific, then the criteria of conceptual and theoretical tractability seem appropriate for identifying those skills. But if the definition is to serve as the statement of the objectives of an instructional program that purports to develop a system of skills having utility in the real world, then it is appropriate to apply stringent social, political, cultural, and economic criteria in the selection of those behaviors.

What is important to note at this point is that there is no *true* definition of literacy. Rather, each definition must be designed for the purpose to which it is to be put, and its correctness may be judged only in terms of how well it serves that purpose. Thus, when a definition of literacy is being developed, it would seem rational to state clearly the purpose of that definition, to derive from this statement a set of criteria for selecting and excluding skills, and then to select skills using these criteria. It seems likely that had rational procedures of this sort been followed in the earlier formulations of the concept of literacy, we might have been spared much pointless and often destructive controversy, as well as the need to make this rather lengthy digression.

Taxonomy of literacy skills. Much effort has gone into the matter of identifying the skills a person must have in order to deal with a variety of reading tasks. Collecting these categories has been largely the work of curriculum specialists in reading, but much of the content itself has been contributed as a result of analyses in the disciplines of psychology, history (in its study of manuscript criticism), linguistics, library science, and others.[4]

First, there are the "decoding" skills, which enable a person to map letters, letter groups and patterns, and typographical features of print onto oral language units. Normally this includes the phonics skills, which entail mapping the smaller graphic units onto language sounds; the word structure skills, which entail mapping whole syllables and affixes as units onto their corresponding sounds; the sight recognition skills, which entail mapping whole words onto their corresponding sounds; the context recognition skills, which utilize the context surrounding a word to map the word onto its sounds; and the dictionary skills, which enable a person to locate, pronounce, and grasp the meaning of a word from its entry in the dictionary.

Second, there are the "literal comprehension" skills, which enable a person to learn the information explicitly signaled in a reading task. This normally includes the vocabulary meaning skills, which enable a person to assign the correct meanings to words in their contexts; the sentence comprehension skills, which enable a person to combine the meanings of

---

[4] At this point it would be inappropriate to attempt either exhaustive listings or precise definitions of these skills. More extensive listings may be obtained from other sources, such as Betts (1954), Bond & Tinker (1967), or Harris (1962). The problem of defining complex cognitive skills will receive separate treatment below. The brief discussion presented here is provided merely to give the reader a general impression of the range of skills that must be considered for inclusion when a definition of literacy is being developed.

words in sentences according to patterns conforming to the syntax of the sentences; the anaphora comprehension skills, which enable a person to identify the recurrences of concepts in a reading task so that the appropriate concepts are modified when they reoccur in sentences; and the discourse comprehension skills, which enable a person to combine the meanings of sentences in a passage according to patterns signaled by the discourse syntax of a reading task.

The remaining classes of skills have generally been less well analyzed than the two just named. The third might be described as the "inference" skills, which enable a person to derive information not explicitly signaled by the reading task. These skills might be described impressionistically as those that occur when a person "reads between the lines" or somewhat more formally as being logic-like processes in which statements in a text might be substituted into logical algorithms and true sentences not in the text computed using predicate calculus.

The fourth set of skills is generally called the "critical reading" skills; these skills conform roughly to the procedures known as manuscript criticism in the study of history. They consist of applying tests of the consistency of the logic of a text, verifying its factual claims, verifying the authority of the writer, and detecting and evaluating propaganda devices.

The fifth set is the "aesthetic appreciation" skills. These are difficult to characterize because they are typically discussed in terms that do not readily lend themselves to behavioral analyses, including phrases such as "detecting the tone and mood of the story," "seeing the deeper meanings," and "detecting the pacing or rhythm of the prose." This set of skills seems to be largely appropriate for just those reading tasks that have aesthetic pretensions.

The sixth set of skills has been traditionally known as the "reading flexibility" skills. They are the processes that enable a person to speed up or slow down his reading, depending on the nature of the task. They also enable a person to focus on just the parts of the text containing the types of information tested by some set of questions or described in some set of instructions and to switch his attention to conform to a wide variety of such instructions. More recently, some of these skills have come to be known as "mathemagenic behaviors" (Rothkopf, 1966).

The seventh and final category comprises the "study skills," which include an assortment of skills that enable a person to use various reference devices to locate information and then to judge its relevance to some problem. This category also includes skills that enable a person to interpret special devices for presenting information, such as maps, graphs, outlines, charts, and diagrams.

Obviously a complete listing of all the skills implied by these seven categories would constitute a work of its own. It should be noted, also, that other classes of skill could be added—the primitive reading readiness skills such as those studied by Gibson (1970), for example. However, these rather brief descriptions should be sufficient to enable the reader to get some sense of the full range of skills that are included in at least some instructional programs labeled as "literacy" or "reading" programs.

Limiting a Definition

In the broadest sense of the word, "literacy" is the ability to exhibit all the skills a person needs in order to respond appropriately to all possible reading tasks. However, it is unlikely that a definition of literacy that specified all these skills would have much utility. "A definition of literacy," as that phrase is used here, represents a detailed and explicit statement of the goal of a research, development, or instructional program; and all such programs must contend with limitations on funds, time, adequacy of scientific knowledge, access to skilled personnel, and so on. And they must state a reasonably believable goal in the first place even to be granted the use of any resources at all. As a result, they invariably face the need to limit the scope of their goal statements.

One convenient and often necessary way to limit the definition is by including in it only some of the skills normally regarded as literacy behaviors. However, this must be done with considerable care in order to avoid serious mistakes. If certain scientific considerations are ignored, for example, the definition may only appear to be sufficiently limited to be useful when in fact it may implicitly commit the program to an impossibly large task. Or, if the definition includes only socially trivial skills the program may fail to win either the financial or scientific support essential for its success. Hence, the matter of selecting skills to include in a definition deserves some examination.

Utility. Selecting and validating educational objectives involves problems peculiar to reading instruction. The first has already been discussed in another context. This is the problem that reading behavior can either be viewed as a phenomenon that can be studied usefully to make scientific contributions to basic linguistics, psychology, history, and other areas of study, or regarded as a system of skills having considerable economic, social, cultural, and political value both to the individual who has learned them and to the society of which he is a part. While from many points of view this coincidence that reading skills have value in both respects may be a happy one, it also occasions some confusion and controversy.

For example, one psychologist (Gibson, 1970) has been conducting an interesting series of investigations of how children learn to recognize printed letters, and she was awarded special recognition by her fellow psychologists for her contributions to the understanding of the *reading process.* This has occasioned a considerable amount of wonderment among educational psychologists, who regard the work as trivial on the grounds that the processes she was analyzing have seldom been the source of much difficulty in instruction. If the results of this research and all other research of the same type were to be applied conscientiously to the design of reading instruction, the consequence would be almost no improvement in the rate or degree of children's mastery of reading skills.

It is not important to note here whether the academic or the educational psychologist is correct, since, in a certain limited sense, both are. Two different value systems can be and have been applied to this single set of reading or literacy behaviors, with the result that the final judgments were quite different depending on which value system was applied. The same is true of most of the other literacy behaviors. For example, the historian would undoubtedly place a high value on research that contributed to a better understanding of the so-called critical reading skills because of the vital role those skills play in the development of his theories, and the specialist in literature would undoubtedly place a high value on the analysis of aesthetic responses to literature; yet in the context of instruction these two classes of skills might be assigned considerably different values. Again, different values can be applied to the same literacy skill, because each skill functions differently in different areas of activity. Hence, one can identify and include a skill in a definition of literacy on the basis of its utility, but not without a considerable risk of confusion, unless the purpose of the definition and the criteria used for selecting and rejecting skills have been made explicit.

This is not to say, however, that scholars from academic disciplines have nothing to say about the utility of skills for instructional purposes. Quite the contrary, they often have an excellent grasp of how the literacy skills with which they are concerned function in real-world reading tasks. The historian, for example, would likely severely judge a program that omitted instruction in the critical reading skills. He would point out that such a program might produce a population of credulous dolts who could be counted on to learn and believe almost anything they read but who would be continually subject to the manipulation of demagogues.

Finally, when a definition is used to identify the goals of an instructional program, not only must whole classes of literacy skills be selected on the basis of economic, social, cultural, and political criteria; the specific skill within each class must also be subjected to criteria of utility. For example, some phonics rules apply with very high frequency in commonly encountered words, and so they would generally be regarded as having high social utility. Other rules apply in only one or two words, and those words occur rarely in English, and so these rules are judged to be of low utility.

Hierarchical entrainment of skills. Since the cognitive processes underlying reading behaviors are not directly observable, their relationships are not always immediately apparent, and the results can have serious conse quences. One of these consequences is that even though the literacy defini- tion specifies that only one set of skills will be taught in an instructional program, it may in fact prove to be necessary to teach many additional related cognitive skills before acceptable performance on the target skills can be obtained.

Such skills are said to be hierarchically related (Gagné, 1965). The simplest case of a skill hierarchy may be represented by a diagram, $a \rightarrow b$. Here the letters a and b represent two skills; skill b is the more complex of the two and depends upon skill a. An example of a hierarchy of this sort might be knowing the phoneme corresponding to the letter f, which would correspond to skill a, and being able to assign a correct pronunciation to the nonsense syllable *FOD*. The latter skill, of course, depends upon or entrains skill a but also involves unique components. It follows, then, that skill a must be mastered before b. A somewhat similar relationship can hold between classes of skills. These hierarchies are symbolized with capital letters, $A \rightarrow B$. In this case, every skill in class B depends upon at least one skill in class A. An example of this kind of hierarchy is that the skill of assigning meaning to printed words depends upon the skill of assigning sounds to printed words.

If a literacy definition lists a complex class of skills, it is implicitly listing the simpler skills entrained by that complex class. This fact presents a potentially serious problem when literacy definitions are developed for use in instructional programs in reading. These hierarchical relationships remain only partially understood, and so it is unclear just what may be entrained in complex processes like the critical reading skills or the aesthetic appreciation skills. It is possible that when they are subjected to careful analysis, they might prove to be quite simple and easily taught. On the other hand, it is also possible that they could turn out to be ex- tremely complex so that a definition that included these skills might implicitly commit the program for which it serves as a goal statement to a course that is quite beyond the resources allocated to that program.

Interactions among skill classes. There are very good reasons to doubt that it is possible to draw sharp distinctions between classes of skills that are hierarchically related to one another. In those processes that have been carefully studied, we seem to fiind hierarchical relationships running in both directions. The main evidence for this is that there is no set of decoding skills that, taken by itself, is sufficient to permit the pronuncia- tion of all the words a person is likely to encounter. The phonics skills, for example, have often been offered as the word pronunciation skills *par excellence*. And, indeed, they probably do represent one of the most useful sets of skills one can employ to pronounce words.

It is now clear, however, that the phonics skills cannot be employed to pronounce many words unless those skills are coupled with certain of the literal comprehension skills. An obvious example is the printed word "read" in the clauses "they read it yesterday" and "they read it now." One cannot apply the appropriate phonics rule to the vowel letters until he has read the rest of the sentence and comprehended it well enough to determine the tense of the verb "read." The printed word "lead" in the sentences "They lead their dogs" and "It is made of lead" presents a somewhat different situation in which the application of the correct phonics rule to the vowel letters depends on the person's having assigned the word to the appropriate part of speech—a process that is thought to be an essential component of the language comprehension processes (Osgood, 1963).

Venezky (1967) has reviewed this matter in some detail and has pointed out that there is a class of words to which the phonics rules can be applied only after each word has been assigned to a part-of-speech category. The printed words "suspect," "relay," "imprint," and "permit," for example, are pronounced differently depending on whether they are employed as verbs or nouns. Although this constitutes a fairly small class of words, Goodman (1969) has been able to provide a substantial amount of evidence to show that the comprehension skills are employed extensively by children to aid them in the word recognition processes.

Ordinarily, the reading comprehension skills are analyzed as hierarchically entraining the word decoding skills. Relationships of this kind must be taken into account in selecting behaviors to be included in a literacy definition. The foregoing discussion demonstrates that a *reverse hierarchy* of a sort operates to connect the same two sets of skills. Furthermore, it seems likely that these two-way hierarchies may prevail among a number of classes of skills. Research by linguists shows that while language at a higher level of analysis, say the morphological level, is built up out of units from a lower level of analysis, the phonological level, many of the phenomena at the lower levels cannot be explained except in terms of the theory employed at the higher levels.

MEASURING LITERACY SKILLS

Deciding what types of skills one ought to expect of a literate person presents one type of problem, but deciding how those skills should be observed and measured presents problems of a completely different order. The former is primarily a matter of social policy making in which one decides what social, political, cultural, and economic values are affected by each class of literacy skills, weights each class of skills according to the weight given each value affected, and then includes in the definition of literacy as many of the most valued skills as practical circumstances will justify. Measuring and observing those skills, on the other hand, is a scientific and technical problem that involves constructing a theory of the processes underlying those behaviors and then identifying test tasks that can be performed by all, and only persons who have actually acquired those skills. Consequently, discussion of the latter must deal primarily with the logical and scientific issues involved in testing literacy skills.

The argument pursued here has this general form: First, it is economically and logically desirable to use verbal questions as the primary mode of testing literacy skills. Second, traditional methods of deriving verbal test questions are primitive; they do not provide us with the explicit rationale that seems essential for tests that operationally represent research and development programs, especially for those programs which have either serious scientific pretensions or a responsibility for accounting for the effectiveness with which their funds were used. Finally, techniques have become available for developing adequate rationalized literacy tests.[5]

Although it is necessary to restrict our consideration to the problems of testing the more complex literacy skills, omitting the word decoding skills and the study skills, the arguments presented apply self-evidently and with equal force to the areas eliminated. The problems involved in testing the more complex literacy skills are complicated and have only recently been subjected to analyses that are scientifically adequate, making it more important to focus specifically on them.

Necessity of Observing Only Overt Behaviors
In discussions of literacy assessment, as in most discussions of the operations involved in testing cognitive processes, it seems necessary to begin with an apologia of two rather elementary but very important facts about testing. The first is an explanation of the function of a test item or test task, and the second is an explanation of the problems presented by the necessity to observe only overt behaviors.

Function of the test item. Literacy skills, like nearly all cognitive processes, are not just a set of overt and stereotyped behaviors that a person repeats over and over in nearly identical form, like turning a key in a lock or throwing a ball. People simply are not expected to read the same passage over and over. And when they read, the activity of major importance is not even observable directly. Rather, a person is expected to exhibit literacy performance in response to passages he has never seen before. Thus, a person is literate only when he has learned and can apply

---

[5] Each component of this argument represents a complex set of issues, and so the discussions presented here are necessarily brief. More detailed treatments may be found in Anderson (1972), Bormuth (1970, 1969c), Bormuth et al. (1970), Finn (1973), and Hively et al. (1965).

a set of *mental processes* that enable him to respond with the appropriate set of performances to passages that are new to him.

But a mental process is an event that occurs internally, where it is not directly observable or interpretable. To determine whether a person is literate, we are forced to observe only objects and events external to the individual. We may observe the materials placed before him, the instructions, the questions he is asked about those materials, and the responses he makes. What we are forced to observe is not the processes that we really would like to observe but merely objects and overt behaviors that we take as being signs of the presence or absence of the processes that in fact determine whether a person is literate. To be specific, in order to determine if a person is literate, we must have (*a*) a theory about the nature of the mental processes that constitute literacy and (*b*) a secondary theory that connects overt behaviors in certain situations to the various mental processes that constitute literacy.

The test task or test item is a product of this secondary theory. It functions as a set of circumstances in which a person is forced to exhibit some sort of behavior; the nature of that behavior is interpretable within the theory as evidence that the person does or does not possess the mental process being studied.

Problems with observing only overt behaviors. Quite aside from the purely scientific problems encountered in developing the theories of processes and the secondary theories of testing, there is the troublesome problem of whether it is possible to test all the important literacy processes merely by observing overt responses to tests. For example, the critical skills might include a set of processes that we might label "the ability to sense ulterior motives of an author." If a very large number of test items testing these processes were devised, it would still be possible for someone to claim that many of the processes that he thinks fall under that label will remain untested by any of the items in the set and by any other items derived in the same way. This type of assertion may be used as the motive for developing new types of items. But sometimes it is used with destructive intent as the basis for the claim that testing is worthless because all testing must rely on the observation of only overt behaviors, and some mental processes can *never* be observed in a person's overt behavior.

This assertion can be answered at three levels. First, at the pragmatic level, we can point out that the roles performed by testing are not merely peripheral to instruction but are actually essential components of it. From the point of view of the student, test tasks represent the only effective way he has of determining what it is that he is supposed to be learning and whether he is learning it. The instruction may contain many exhortations directed to him, telling him to strive to attain many things, but in the final analysis the only things he *has* to learn and the only things about which he can *find out* whether he has learned or whether he needs to seek further instruction are just those processes required by the tests he is given. Also, from the point of view of the instructor, the only evidence he has of what he has taught or failed to teach is obtained from the tests he uses. Consequently, at the pragmatic level, the argument against testing has little force, since there remains a need to learn those processes that *can* be tested, and tests are an indispensable element in that instruction.

Second, a somewhat more general argument can be built on the fact that operationalism is a fundamental prerequisite for accurately communicating scientific knowledge. A verbally expressed concept is subject to almost as many interpretations as there are people to interpret it unless that concept has been defined in terms of publicly observable events, objects, and operations. Thus, the processes underlying literacy behaviors are defined jointly by the form of the written language to be read, the form of the questions or test tasks, the relationships among the test tasks and the passage, and the conditions under which the tests are given.

At the third level, the proposition that mental processes can never be measured with overt behavior may be refuted in arguments claiming that a process cannot be taught to people unless it can be tested, and thus the untestable process cannot possibly be given attention at a research, development, or instructional level. A proposition that there is some important and untestable process might indeed be interesting, but it requires evidence before it can be fully believed. That evidence would probably have to be in the form of a task that would evoke an overt behavior that served to index the process in question. Finding this evidence amounts to a refutation of the original proposition that the behavior was untestable. Hence, the claim seems devoid of any substantive meaning. The principal philosophical question at issue seems to be this: *Of what consequence can a mental process be if it has not yet been demonstrated to have any manifestations in a person's overt behavior?* We cannot even make a convincing claim that such a process exists, without refuting that claim.

Selection of a Testing Mode

There seem to be just two major classes of test tasks used to measure literacy skills. The first is the *performance task*: a person is required to read some passage and then to demonstrate a literacy behavior by performing a task that involves either concrete objects and events or pictures of objects and events. One such task might require a person to read instructions for assembling a bicycle and then have him either actually assemble a bicycle or discriminate among pictures depicting correct and incorrect methods of assembling it. The *verbal test question* consists of a sentence requiring a response; both are derived from the language in the passage. The person is required to read the passage and then either write, speak, or select the response from a group of alternative responses. This type of item may range from those that ask a person to pronounce a word to those that ask him to induce and describe the moral principles that govern the behavior of the hero of a story. It should be noted that the principal distinction between the verbal question and the performance task is not whether or not one employs language in the test task. Both invariably do, at least in the instructions for the task. Rather, the distinction is that a verbal test question involves only language in both the question stem and the response.

Evaluation of performance tasks. Superficially, the performance task seems to provide the most valid type of literacy test. Perhaps the ultimate criterion of literacy would be obtained by giving a person a passage to read and then following him about as he went through his normal life routines and observing whether the passage had the appropriate effects on his behavior. This, of course, is a preposterous proposal, if for no other reason, because of the enormous expense involved. Consequently, it is necessary to employ some artificial but more convenient testing procedure and then demonstrate and subsequently infer that a correct response on this artificial task may be taken as valid evidence that the person would be found to respond correctly in his normal life routines if we were to follow him about. This can be referred to as the *pragmatic validity* of a test task.

The performance task attempts to gain its validity by simulating situations the person might encounter in his normal life routines, and it gains considerable practical usefulness because these simulations can be performed at the convenience of the tester. Still greater economy is obtained by using pictures instead of concrete objects and events. However, it should be recognized that this may reduce the item's apparent pragmatic validity, which depends on the apparent quality of the analogy between the performance task and the normal life situation. Yet, whether or not a type of item is actually pragmatically valid depends solely on its experimentally demonstrated ability to predict appropriate behaviors in the person's normal life routines. Since there have been no studies attempting to demonstrate the pragmatic validity of performance items as a class, it must be said that the pragmatic validity of any performance item is apparent only, and not demonstrated.

The second limitation (as was mentioned above) of the performance item is the rather obvious one of expense.

The third limitation is a severe one. It is impossible to use the performance item to test the full range of literacy behaviors. A substantial amount of language is used to refer to impossible and unobservable events and objects, such as "The elf thought hard about the loss of his magical powers" or "God is a disembodied power," and some language refers to observable but extremely abstract notions, such as "The search for truth is the quest for power." It becomes difficult to imagine a way the performance task could be used to assess a person's literacy with respect to printed language of this sort. Unless it could somehow be shown that the processes underlying responses to statements of these types were identical to the processes underlying responses to statements about real and concretely observable things, it must be recognized that performance tasks are applicable only to language that deals with concrete and observable things.

Evaluation of verbal questions. The verbal test question seems to escape most of these problems. It seems entirely possible to determine experimentally the pragmatic validity of verbal items. It is possible to develop algorisms that produce whole populations of items (Bormuth, 1970) in such a way that it is possible to either generate or select unbiased samples of items, and it is therefore possible to conduct experiments to determine the pragmatic validity of verbal items. It is also at least conceptually possible to develop similar definitions for *any* verbal question that is relevant to a passage.

On first analysis the verbal test question seems to involve a circularity that has an undesirable effect on certain classes of questions. The verbal task tests a person's responses to language merely by giving him a question that is also language and then observing his response, which is still more language. At no time is it necessary for the person to make a response to the objects and events referred to by that language, demonstrating that he actually understood it.

That this is not only a possible but even fairly common phenomenon can be seen from a consideration of these sentences:

1. All daxes have wobs.
2. We have daxes in our dorf.
3. Do we have wobs in our dorf?
4. What has wobs in it?
5. Who has a dorf?

Although questions 3, 4, and 5 are fairly easily answered by most speakers of English, one could hardly say that the answers reflect comprehension of sentences 1 and 2, since several of the lexical morphemes in them are nonsense syllables.

However, there are many classes of verbal questions that can be defined, and *this effect* seems to be limited only to a few of those classes. Consider, for example, this sentence set:

6. The youth mounted the steed.
7. Who climbed on the horse?
8. Who mounted the steed?

It is much less likely that verbalism could occur on 7 than on 8, and each of these represents different classes of items that can be rigorously defined. Anderson (1972) has explored the evidence on this matter in some detail. Consequently, while the apparent pragmatic validity of some types of verbal questions may be questionable, those classes of items can be defined and separated from those classes of items that appear likely to be shown to have acceptable pragmatic validities.

The verbal question is fairly inexpensive to construct and use. This is not to say that the verbal questions generated by just any speaker of English would suffice for testing literacy skills. It requires the skills of a person highly trained in linguistics and item-writing theory to prepare acceptable items. Nor is this the claim that we already know how to write every type of item that might be employed in literacy definitions. To reach this point of development will require considerable investment in research. Rather, the claim is that the verbal question will generally cost less to prepare and use than its major rival, the performance item.

The verbal question is further recommended by the fact that it is equally applicable to all language. Questions are, in fact, nothing more than transformations of the syntactic and semantic structures underlying the language in passages. Sentences 4, 5, 7, and 8 are each examples of questions derived through applying semantic and syntactic transformations to the sentence to which each, respectively, is relevant. Number 3, on the other hand, is derived from the syntactic relationship underlying and connecting the continuous discourse represented by sentences 1 and 2. Some of the details of these question transformations have been examined elsewhere (Bormuth, 1970).

Finally, regarding verbal questions as transformations of the structures of the language in a text provides the verbal question with numerous advantages. Of greatest importance in the immediate context is the fact that these question derivation transformations enable us to give exact definitions of classes of items[6] and subsequently to use these definitions of item classes to give equally exact definitions of literacy skills. With respect to the performance item, it is extremely difficult to define classes of items in an exact manner because doing so requires that we possess well-developed semantic theories and theories that relate physical situations to each other—theories that are presently so poorly developed as to be almost nonexistent. As a result, it is impossible to say with objective certainty that two different performance items are members of the same class or of different classes. And when one cannot even say that two collections of items are at least formally different, there is no logical justification what-

---

[6] The author (1970) suggested that the question transformations defined by Chomsky and others could serve as a prototype for these definitions. However, this proposal turned out to encounter several difficulties because of deficiencies in transformational grammar. Finn (1973) has since found that algorisms based on a case grammar seem to overcome most of these problems.

ever for claiming that the mental processes tested by each population of items are in some respect homogeneous within the populations and systematically different from the processes tested by other populations. In the case of the verbal question, however, differences among classes of items can be denoted by differences in the transformational procedures by which they are derived, thereby providing at least the first logical basis for operationally defining different classes of literacy behaviors. Moreover, there is now strong evidence that the classes of questions that are generated by syntactic transformations do, in fact, test homogeneous categories of behavior (Bormuth et al., 1970).

One implication of this last statement is that the rationale and technology that underlie all educational test writing fall short of what might be considered scientifically acceptable. Thus, the benefits of treating verbal questions in a scientifically acceptable manner can be attained only after considerable effort has gone into the research necessary to lay the scientific base for the required technology.

Tests Made by Traditional Procedures

Having noted the verbal question as the best mode of testing literacy behaviors and having acknowledged that its value is only potential because the methods by which verbal questions have traditionally been made are not reliant on the rational procedures of a science, we should examine traditional test-making procedures and some of the problems that have grown out of them.

Classical test-writing procedures. The classical method of writing tests involves four steps (Bloom et al., 1956). First, the test writer lists each of the mental processes he wishes to test. These processes form a set of column headings in a table or matrix. Second, he lists all the different types of subject matter he perceives as being taught by a passage and that he wishes to test. The list is placed in the left-hand column of the table, and each item on the list serves as a row label. This forms a table of the type illustrated by Table 1, where the items of content are represented by the symbols $C_1, C_2, \ldots, C_m,$ and the mental processes are represented by the symbols $P_1, P_2, \ldots, P_n.$ Third, he then attempts to write for each cell of his table the type of item that permits him to test a person's knowledge of a given item of content by having him exhibit it using whatever mental process serves as the column heading. For example, suppose that P_1 stands for the mental process involved in comprehending the main idea of a paragraph and C_2 stands for content dealing with the structure of atoms, then the item written for cell C_2P_1 would be written in a manner that appeared to the test writer to force a person to demonstrate his ability to comprehend the main idea of a paragraph that dealt with the structure of an atom. The test writer is not provided with any definite set of operations

TABLE 1
Illustration of a Test Writer's Matrix

Mental Processes

	P_1	P_2	$\cdots$	P_n
C_1	C_1, P_1	C_1, P_2		C_1, P_n
C_2	C_2, P_1	C_2, P_2		C_2, P_n
$\vdots$				
C_m	C_m, P_1	C_m, P_2		C_m, P_n

(Content Items)

for deriving the wording of the item. Rather, most writers on this topic (see Davis, 1964, p. 262, for example) regard the actual formulation of the item as an informal and subjective writing task. Finally, a jury reviews his work to see if it agrees with the work or if revision is necessary.

Lack of operationalism. This conceptualization of item writing laid the basis for all modern test theory. Particularly important was the insight it gave us into the dual nature of the test item. That is, an item not only tests knowledge of some information, it also tests a person's competency to perform the processes necessary to derive that information from his instruction. However, it left a number of problems to be resolved. In one way or another, virtually all the criticisms that can be leveled at this procedure grow out of its heavy reliance on the personal judgments and intuitions of the test writer. Stated another way, the criticisms grow out of the absence of operationalism of the procedure—the absence of specific instructions for carrying out each step.

The test writer is told that he should test a mental process only when it is appropriate for the passage, but he is never told by what rules one decides if it is appropriate. The test writer is also told to write items that test those mental processes, but he is never given explicit rules that specify the form of those items. He is told to list the content topics he thinks the passage deals with, but he is never given explicit rules that instruct him how to identify these topics or that tell him how grossly or narrowly he should analyze these topics.

As a result of looseness in the classical procedure, it seems doubtful that a test made in this way could meet the ordinary requirement of operational replicability, which is imposed on all activities laying claim to scientific status. Before an activity can be regarded as useful for making verifiable statements, we ordinarily demand that it be operationalized to the point that others working independently can perform the same operations and verify the results. Classical test-writing procedures can only loosely meet this requirement.

Somewhat the same demand is placed on the evaluation of programs that employ public funds and represent matters of public policy, only in this context it is phrased as a demand for accountability, understandability, and freedom from personal bias. If two test writers cannot independently replicate each other's work—and it is extremely unlikely that they could—it becomes immediately suspect that the concepts of the mental processes, the subject matter topics, and the question-writing procedure mean different things to each test writer and are therefore not expressed in a form that is understandable and can be communicated. Instead of being regarded as demonstrably impartial, the results of a test cannot easily be defended against the suspicion that they were biased by whichever test writer happened to prepare the test.

At this point it may be appropriate to note that test writers themselves have long been aware of and concerned about the problems inherent in their procedures. But they have also been faced with the urgent ongoing need for tests in the schools. Consequently, they have had to do as well as they could using methods which are less than scientific until some way was found to develop better test-writing methods.

Operationalizable Test-Writing Procedures

While verbal questions made by classical procedures are of dubious value, this is not a property of the item itself but merely of the way it is derived. That is, the items ordinarily produced by classical test-writing procedures are good items in the sense that they do test some sort of behaviors which at least intuitively appear to be important behaviors. What is required, however, are item-derivation procedures that can produce populations of items in a replicable fashion. There are now two such procedures that may be useful for testing literacy behaviors—the cloze and the *wh-* question procedures.

Cloze procedure. The cloze procedure is a way of making tests by mechanically deleting the words in a passage of written language and replacing each word with an underlined blank of a standard length. People taking the tests are expected to guess what word was taken out of each blank and write it in that space. There are a variety of ways to select the words to be deleted. One can delete every *n*th word, every second noun, all adjectives, and so on. What distinguishes a cloze test from an ordinary deletion test, though, is the fact that in a cloze test the words may be selected for deletion only by a completely replicable set of rules. Using introspective concepts like "key words" is ruled out.

The advantages of such a procedure are primarily that the tests made in this fashion are completely replicable, making true validity studies possible. One can define the population of all items where predicate adjectives are deleted. This makes it possible to draw a random sample of such items, study their properties, and then attribute the results to that population of items. It can also be claimed that items made by these procedures do not reflect the biases of the test maker. In these respects the cloze procedure satisfies some of the most basic requirements necessary for an acceptable test of literacy.

However, cloze items have a rather serious shortcoming because it is difficult to relate the items to a theory of language comprehension. In this theory (Osgood, 1963; Mowrer, 1954) comprehension is regarded as taking place by a series of events through which the meaning of one word or phrase is combined with or modified by the meaning of another word or phrase. The character and order of these modifications are regarded as being controlled by the syntax of the text. Thus, in sentence 9 the word "boy" might be thought to be modified by "the," "hill" by "the," "climbed" by "the hill," and "the boy" by "climbed the hill," in that order. Ordinary

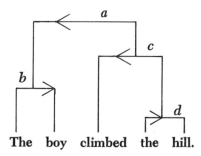

9.   The boy climbed the hill.

verbal questions that begin with *wh-* words like "who," "what," "where," and so on can be directly related to this theory since, unlike the cloze procedure, whole words, phrases, clauses, and even sentences may be deleted. For example, "What did the boy do" is derived by deleting the whole predicate "climbed the hill." And thus the verbal question can be regarded as testing associations at each of the various points at which modifications occur in a sentence. The question "What did the boy do" tests the modification marked *a* in sentence 9, and the question "What did the boy climb" tests the modification marked *c*. Modifications *b* and *d* can be tested with questions such as "Which boy climbed the hill," questions that test anaphorically related constituents of discourse.

On the other hand, because only single words are deleted in the cloze procedure, only the lowest-level modification can be directly tested.[7] Some of these may primarily test structural modifications, as when the

---

[7] Some people have interpreted this fact to indicate that the cloze procedure tests only the short-range constraints in a passage. This can be equated to testing only the simplest factual information in the passage. It is true that the short-range constraints have a powerful effect on the response (MacGinitie, 1961), but they are by no means sufficient to fully explain cloze responses (Taylor, 1954).

word "the" is deleted. Possibly the most serious disadvantage of the cloze test is the fact that the individual test items are difficult to interpret. When we use questions, it is a fairly simple matter to relate the test item to the structure of the text and thereby interpret what process the question tests. An inspection of cloze items, however, shows that responses to most of them depend on a variety of processes, and it is difficult to identify those processes. However, reviews of the rather extensive research literature on this type of test seem to show that what cloze tests measure is indistinguishable from what is measured by ordinary comprehension questions.

Wh- question procedure. As just noted, the verbal questions that generally begin with *wh-* phrases such as "who," "what kind of," and "what did" do have the desirable property that they can be related directly to a theory of comprehension. And, although in the past it was possible to derive them only by classical test-making methods, it is now possible (Finn, 1973) to derive them using procedures that make it possible for one test maker to independently replicate another's work and for one to give precise definitions of a number of populations of items.

This is accomplished by regarding the question as being derived from the language in a passage through a set of semantic and syntactic transformations. For example, each of the questions mentioned in the paragraphs immediately above can be derived by a set of transformations that can be crudely described as deleting one branch of a modification, replacing the deleted branch with an appropriate *wh-* phrase, and then, if the *wh-* phrase is not already there, shifting it to the front of the sentence. This description, of course, neglects many of the details of the transformations, but what is important is the fact that *it is possible to devise rules* that exactly describe how each of the various classes of *wh-* questions can be derived. This fact makes it possible to anticipate that *wh-* questions derived in this way will have all the basic properties necessary in order to develop them into fully satisfactory tests of literacy skills, such as "ability to get the important points," "ability to get the main ideas," and "ability to comprehend the structure of the knowledge or material." The definition of such items depends on being able to assign a syntax to a passage that connects its sentences and larger segments of discourse to each other in an explicit and replicable fashion. Such an analysis seems feasible to develop at this time, and some segments of it have been developed. This syntax is then used to define various classes of questions. Bart's (1970) work strongly suggests that it is also possible to employ the syntax of Aristotelian logical algorithms to texts in order to define classes of items that test what have been known in traditional terms as the "inference" skills and many of the "critical reading" skills. This recent research provides fairly good grounds for the claim that all important tests of literacy skills may eventually be derived by this type of procedure.

However, one fact should be made plain. The great benefits that can be attained through this procedure of test writing cannot be gotten without a very considerable amount of research, a type of research that the educational research community is only partially prepared to undertake. The research deals primarily with the calculi of linguistics and logic, areas of research for which only a few educational and psychological researchers have been trained. Consequently, getting research of this type under way will necessarily involve a considerable amount of interdisciplinary research and training programs. Although tests made by classical procedures fall far short of being wholly desirable, fortunately they are not wholly inadequate for the tasks presently required of them. They will have to be used until better procedures have been developed.

CRITERION OF LITERATE PERFORMANCE

The second parameter that must be specified in a definition of literacy is the level of performance a person must exhibit on a test before he may be regarded as literate. In literacy assessment we wish to perform binary classifications of people as being either literate or subliterate. Being able to employ an either/or classification is vital, for we can then use the person's classification for making decisions that are important for him and for the society as a whole. When the individual becomes literate, he can stop using up irreplaceable fractions of his life learning literacy skills and turn those skills to more directly productive activities. And society can stop spending money for expensive instruction in literacy skills and turn its resources to other tasks. In both cases the criterion should provide a rational procedure for deciding to terminate one type of activity and to commence different activities. Unfortunately, groups of people have an annoying tendency to exhibit a continuous range of scores on tests rather than a tendency to fall into two well-separated clusters of scores. Consequently, there is no natural or immediately obvious way to make the binary decisions required.

Problem

Thus it can be seen that what we are really dealing with at this point is the classic problem of *how good is good enough*—where goodness is measured along a continuous scale having no natural boundaries that would facilitate metrically clean and logically neat binary decisions about when a person's performance on literacy tasks is good enough to warrant his being labeled as literate. Or, stated operationally, the problem is to assign personal social values to test scores and then to identify the score that has the greatest value to a person and to society. This problem can be solved when it is properly conceptualized. But first it may be instructive to look at previous approaches to its solution.

Earlier criterion scores. At various times a number of criterion scores have been advocated. Each has been the subject of some skepticism, for both technical and philosophical reasons. Let us begin by noting three of the better-known criterion scores. One of the earliest and most widely used criterion scores was proposed by E. L. Thorndike (1917). He recommended that a student should be able to answer at least 75 percent of the questions on a test made from a sample of instructional material in order that the material be considered suitable for use in that student's instruction. Another criterion is the so-called 90-90 criterion whereby instructional programmers attempt to revise and improve their materials until 90 percent of their students can answer 90 percent of the questions given them at the termination of instruction. Finally, some have interpreted (probably erroneously) the writings of Bloom (1968) and Mayo (1970) as advocating that a student's instruction in a body of content be continued until he can demonstrate perfect performance on a test of that content.

Nearly all proposals of criterion scores, including these three, have assumed that tests made by the traditional procedures would be used to measure attainment of the criterion level of performance. Lorge (1949) pointed out that the absolute magnitude of scores on tests of this type are usually subject to biases introduced by the idiosyncracies of the people who wrote the tests. Test items testing different content and processes often differ widely and systematically in difficulty. In addition, even slight variations in the phrasing of a test item can sometimes lead to wide variations in the difficulty of the item. Thus, a test writer can have a great deal of influence on the difficulty of the test. In classical test-writing methodology, the test writer is only partially constrained with respect to the content and processes that he may test and almost completely at liberty to phrase his items to suit his personal preferences. Hence, two different test writers might be expected to produce tests of quite different difficulties to test exactly the same instruction. Thus, Lorge reasoned that these criterion scores do not represent a standard level of competence.

Few advocates of a criterion score have advanced a rationale to justify their preference for the scores they chose. Bloom (1968) appears to have been the exception. He pointed out that students required to reach a high (but not necessarily perfect) level of performance on each unit of content tend to exhibit similar levels of final achievement, overcome initial deficiencies in aptitude, and master succeeding units of content in less time. Bloom did not specify a particular level of performance as a criterion. He simply advocated using a high level of mastery as a criterion. However, many have interpreted his concept of mastery to mean perfect performance. A critique of this misinterpretation is highly relevant to the problem we are considering here.

There are at least three reasons why perfect performance is unlikely to be considered the most desirable level of performance. First, using such a criterion is likely to drive some of the costs of instruction to preposterous levels. Almost every learning study shows that mastery of a body of content increases rapidly on the first few repetitions of the material and then flattens almost to the horizontal well before perfect performance is reached. Hence, attempting to reach perfect performance is likely to be a time-consuming and expensive undertaking. Second, since efforts to reach this criterion are likely to involve much repetition and drill, we could anticipate adverse effects on the students' attitude toward the content of instruction. That is, students find much repetition boring and unpleasant, and they could transfer those attitudes to the content and thereafter try to avoid its further study and use. Third, attempting to reach perfect performance on a unit of content implies that all the items of content in that unit are essential to learn. This may be true of a few isolated units, such as the one dealing with the multiplication tables, but most units of content deal with collections of content items that differ greatly in their utility to the individual.

Reformulation as a rational problem. This critique of the criterion of perfect performance now puts us in a position to reformulate the problem of identifying criterion scores.

Let us start with the proposition that neither literacy skills nor any others are taught for the pure hedonistic pleasure of learning. Rather, they are placed in curricula because they are valued for the tangible and intangible things that they enable individuals and society to attain. But, even then, their placement in curricula is decided only after these positive benefits have been weighed against the negative benefits, that is, the costs associated with learning the behaviors. Second, an individual can acquire varying numbers of literacy skills, and this fact can be accurately indexed by his scores on an appropriately made achievement test. Third, each level of an individual's performance produces effects on each of the various benefits, both positive and negative, that he is likely to gain. The problem of identifying a criterion score, then, consists of finding the level of performance at which the overall benefits are greatest.

This problem can be approached at two levels—either through an analysis of the operations required to attain what might be thought of as the "ideal" solution, or through an attempt to describe how one might establish a performance criterion right now, using practical procedures presently available to us.

In the ideal solution to the problem of establishing a performance criterion, one should be able to attach a cost and a benefit weight to each literacy skill separately, select those behaviors whose learning seems likely to produce a net positive benefit for the learner, and then determine what level of performance on a test of these behaviors is associated with the greatest expected benefit to the learner. In the present state of knowledge, such an ideal solution cannot be carried out because we do not have adequate information about the nature of literacy skills, their interrelationships, and the processes that underlie them, and because consequently it would be impossible to assign cost and benefit values to each.

Outline of a Practical Solution
In the context of research that I am conducting, an attempt has been made to establish rational performance criteria for at least two of the major categories of literacy skills and to incorporate these criteria into literacy assessment procedures that will be substantially better than those in current use.

This problem, as I saw it, was essentially one of working out an ethically acceptable procedure for deciding what test score people like most, where the test score is a measure of the extent to which a person comprehends a given material and where the decision is so complex that it is not obvious to people how their values will be affected by the choices that they might make. In order to be consistent with the earlier definition of literacy, it was necessary to start from the proposition that a person's literacy can be judged only with respect to a particular reading task. And then his literacy on that material can be judged by whether he is able to comprehend it at a *desirable* level. Thus, in order to classify people as being literate or illiterate on any given material we must first solve a general theoretical problem by devising an acceptable way to decide what level of comprehension is best from the point of view of a legitimate decision maker. And then we may solve the specific operational problem that is of direct interest: finding this most desirable level on a type of comprehension test that can be made in a comparable fashion from any reading task.

As it turns out, the general theoretical problem is just a complicated version of the procedure that people commonly use when they try to make other kinds of complex decisions. While our immediate problem calls for us to help a decision maker identify the comprehension test score he likes best, it could just as well call for us to help him arrive at any other complex choice, such as the choice of a new family car. Each is a complex decision that is apt to leave him uncertain about the wisdom of his choice unless he approaches the decision systematically. And the systematic approach to each would employ essentially identical rationales and very similar practical operations. If he were trying to select a car, he would probably begin by listing every car that he could conceivably select as his final choice. Next, he would try to anticipate each of the effects that any one of these cars could have on his future satisfaction with it, effects that might be indexed by variables such as the cars' prices, their gas mileages, their prestige values, or their leg room in the rear seat. Then he would study these measurements to try to decide how he felt about the amounts on each variable considered separately and in combination with amounts of the other variables. For example, he would decide how much more he preferred paying only $3,000 for a car over paying $8,000 when all other things were equal and then again when other things were unequal. And, finally, this process would, if done systematically, lead him to say how much value he attached to each car, to rank the different cars that he was considering, and to select the car that he preferred most. Selecting the best comprehension test score involves the same reasoning: The alternative scores are listed, 0 percent to 100 percent; the effects associated with these scores are anticipated and measured; the decision maker states his preferences for these effects; and these preferences are then used to rank each of the possible scores on a test of this kind.

The basic strategy in solving the operational problem in my recent studies was to determine what score level on a test of reading skill for a particular passage was associated with the maximum weighted sum of a variety of "effects" and values that reading that passage would have for the individual. The test of reading skill is the cloze procedure described earlier—that is, the score is determined as the number of deleted words that the individual can correctly fill in. Such a score seems to measure most of the word recognition and literal comprehension processes involved in literacy skills. Four "effects" of reading a passage were measured: (1) the amount of information gained from the passage, measured by comparing the individual's state of knowledge before and after reading the passage; (2) the rate of reading; (3) the suitability of the conceptual difficulty of the passage to the individual, measured by having students rate the degree to which the passage was "about right" for them, as opposed to its being too easy or difficult; and (4) the students' willingness to study the passage, measured by having them rate it on a scale from *dislike* to *like very much*. The weights assigned each of these effects were determined on the basis of teachers' judgments. The criterion cloze score for a passage, i.e., the score representing the minimum "literate performance," was then chosen as that cloze score associated with the maximum weighted sum of the effects over a group of students at a given grade level. The procedures were applied to 32 passages representing 8 levels of difficulty, tests on which were administered to 1,600 students drawn in equal numbers from grades 3 through 12. Full details of the study are to be found in a report by Bormuth (1971).[8]

---

[8] The reader may also be referred to the extended version of this chapter that has been published previously. See editor's note on page 61.

Before we leave this topic, it should be noted that research on this problem is still in progress. In the research project just described, I assumed that the value that teachers placed on an effect depended just on the general nature of that effect. However, this assumption may not always be sufficient. Their preferences could show a complex relationship to various amounts of a single effect and to the amounts of other effects associated with an alternative. Although it is mathematically complicated to take these relationships into account, it is perfectly feasible to do so within the scope of modern utility theory. My present research is directed at devising a way to perform the appropriate measurements of a decision maker's preferences.

IDENTIFICATION OF POPULATIONS OF READING TASKS AND A CORPUS LITERACY CRITERION

The third parameter that must be described in a definition of literacy is the kind of language and reading tasks with respect to which people should be literate. The goal of a literacy program would be hopelessly vague unless the definition on which it was based contained such a description. Language is used for many areas of discourse and for many different purposes within those areas. The language employed in each area differs materially in vocabulary structures, in sentence structures, and in discourse structures; and each of those different structures presumably requires a different literacy process or level of skill to cope with it. Thus, if a definition failed to specify the corpus or population of reading tasks it dealt with, it would implicitly commit the program to deal with all possible corpora of discourse—a task of overwhelming magnitude.

Presumably, the sample of reading tasks upon which a criterion of literacy would be based would be selected, by certain criteria, from the population of all possible reading tasks. An example of an attempt to define such a population was that by Kučera and Francis (1967) in the course of assembling a corpus of 1 million words for statistical and linguistic studies; they used systematic sampling procedures to select texts from all prose materials written by Americans and first printed in the United States in the year 1961. Similar procedures were employed by Carroll, Davies, and Richman (1972) in assembling samples of text materials to which children in grades 3 through 9 are exposed. Neither of these corpora, however, might be appropriate for selecting reading tasks for a criterion of literacy. Whatever procedure is used, its details and its rationale must be made as explicit as possible. Literacy skills may be employed in a number of important political, social, cultural, and economic activities in our society, and having or not having those skills has direct implications for a person's rights, responsibilities, and opportunities to participate in those activities. For example, it is not uncommon to hear of people who failed to receive job promotions because they could not acquire the information necessary to carry out their new duties. Since situations of this kind are traceable, at least in part, to those people's failures to acquire certain literacy skills, it must be recognized that both society and the individual have the right to know exactly what literacy skills are selected for or excluded from instruction and the reasoning by which these decisions were made. Or, stated another way, these decisions ought not, as they have been up to the present, to be left obscure by allowing them to be treated as the creative acts of individual teachers or as the unexplained technical decisions made by publishers of instructional materials.

This matter has not previously received the careful analysis it deserves, and the present discussion will merely pose the problem and demonstrate the need for its further analysis. At least five criteria seem relevant to making decisions about whether or not to include or exclude a particular type of reading task: (1) monetary cost, (2) economy of time, (3) goal-achieving utility, (4) commonness, and (5) frequency.

The monetary cost of a reading task refers to the resources necessary to teach literacy for that task; teaching literacy for some types of tasks might be so expensive as to exclude them from consideration. The criterion of economy of time refers to the amount of time necessary to teach literacy for the task. The criterion of goal-achieving utility refers to whether or not the task can be employed to achieve some sort of social, political, cultural, or economic goal for the individual. The criterion of commonness has to do with whether the task is commonly needed by all people or whether it is associated only with special occupations and hobbies. Finally, the criterion of frequency, which should be used with caution, has to do with how frequently a person is likely to encounter the task.

Criterion of Corpus Literacy

Suppose, then, we had followed some rational procedure and had selected a corpus of reading tasks. Suppose also that, by procedures outlined earlier (pages 90–92), we had arrived at a criterion score for each of the tasks that would specify the performance that would be regarded as "literate." There would still remain the familiar question: On what proportion of the passages should a person be literate—or how good is good enough? The answer again seems to rest on the development of a decision theory that permits us to consider simultaneously the relevant negative and positive benefits associated with each level of literacy and to obtain a criterion score that maximizes the values we wish to derive from literacy instruction. This will be referred to here as the "corpus criterion score."

This procedure should utilize the criterion identification model and be carried on in much the same way as in the previous illustration. First, we would identify the negative and positive benefits associated with being able to read various proportions of the corpus at a desirable level. These might include estimates of a person's expected income level and other measures of his occupational success, estimates of the costs associated with raising people to each level of literacy, and estimates of the degree to which people can and do participate effectively in political-civil affairs and in cultural activities. These measures would be assigned relative values.[9] And finally, the data would be entered into the model. The model would thereupon identify for some hypothetical average person the most desirable level of performance on that corpus of materials.

The reader is again reminded that the notion of a corpus criterion score cannot be fully acceptable unless certain characteristics of individuals and populations of people are taken into account. The treatment given here was intended only to develop the concept of corpus criterion scores and to illustrate a rational procedure by which they can be identified using whatever form of test might be suitable and available.

IDENTIFICATION OF CHARACTERISTICS OF INDIVIDUALS IN THE POPULATION

The fourth parameter of a literacy definition consists of a set of characteristics of the people who are the subjects of the literacy program. It is almost a cliché to point out that there are individual differences among people—differences in their native endowment, environmentally acquired assets, and motivations. Hence, there is every reason to believe that their instructional needs will differ, not just in how instruction should be administered, but in which literacy skills they should learn and how many of those skills should be mastered. While the preceding sections have not entirely ignored the characteristics of the individual, neither have they examined them systematically. The present section will examine why individual characteristics must be represented in a model, identify the major variables, and then present the outline of the model as far as it will be developed by this investigation.

Inclusion of Individual Characteristics

The objective of a criterion model is to help us make decisions about the instruction of people, decisions that will help people to realize their aspirations while simultaneously conserving their resources. It is doubtful

---

[9] Presumably these values would be appropriately adjusted by the usual accounting procedures so that they would accurately reflect the trade-off between immediate and deferred benefits.

that a model that omitted individual characteristics could reach this objective satisfactorily. To omit them would have the effect of forcing us to apply the same criterion to everyone or, worse, to allow only a select few to acquire literacy skills. And these skills would be the ones that were found to be appropriate for the *average* person. This would force us to waste an enormous amount of personal and social resources and to achieve results that have little correspondence to the aspirations of individuals and society. Consider the obvious case of the severely mentally retarded child who cannot possibly aspire to accomplishing much more than bare self-sufficiency in the simplest kinds of occupations. Almost any criterion that is appropriate for the average person in a broad segment of the population would certainly include many skills that the mentally retarded person would have little occasion to use. Moreover, because he learns very slowly, his instruction would be very prolonged, expensive to society, and expensive to him in terms of the proportion of his life that he would have to devote to the learning task. Conversely, consider the mentally gifted person who can aspire to occupations of great complexity and of great benefit to himself and society. He could attain this criterion rapidly and at little cost to anyone, but his instruction would be terminated well before he could realize his aspirations. Hence, it should be clear that the cause of neither justice nor efficiency is served by applying the same criterion to everyone.

Identification of Relevant Characteristics

Three factors seem particularly relevant in identifying a literacy criterion for an individual—his native capacity to learn, his environmentally acquired capacity to learn, and his motivations.

Native capacity for learning. The primary reason for including capacity in the model is that it is a major determinant of what it costs the person and society for him to master a given body of content. Carroll (1963) has shown that aptitude can be operationalized in either of two ways, by measuring the amount that a person is likely to learn with a fixed amount of instruction or by measuring the amount of time required for that person to reach a criterion level of performance in learning some body of content. From the point of view of this model, we are most interested in the conceptualization of capacity to learn as *time to reach a criterion.* Time spent in instruction can be translated directly into costs. The instruction costs the student an irreplaceable fraction of his life, a fraction of his life that has value to him to the extent that he could be using it to produce other things that would also be satisfying to him. Similarly, the time spent in instruction is a major source of the costs of education to society. Thus, we cannot very well identify a criterion without considering the individual's native capacity to learn.

Acquired capacity. A person's acquired capacity to learn affects costs in much the same manner as biological capacity. But acquired capacity must be weighted differently in the model, since deficits of this kind can be overcome through instruction, and since society is willing to allocate a considerable portion of its resources to overcoming them.

Motivations. People differ in the kinds of occupational choices they make and in the kinds of cultural and political activities that they engage in. Each of these pursuits involves different kinds of reading tasks and different amounts of reading. Consequently, if this factor is not taken into account, much could be wasted by teaching people skills that they neither wanted nor would ever use or by failing to teach them skills that they needed. Let us refer to this concept of motivation as the individual's "intentions" and distinguish it from another sense in which the term is used.

The term "motivation" is also used to refer to the extent to which a person perseveres in attending to a learning task. This is an important consideration in the model, since it also helps to determine the costs of the instruction. If a person perseveres in attending to the instruction, the costs will be lower than if he does not.

These two concepts of motivation should probably be represented quite differently in the model. Intentions should probably be represented in the boundary conditions, for two reasons. First, a person's choice of pursuits is not a continuous variable. Rather, it is simply the choice of whether or not to enter each of a number of different pursuits that have no obvious dimensional continuity. Second, this variable undoubtedly interacts with the weights assigned to the effects that are associated with various levels of mastery of literacy skills. That is, the weight that we would assign to, for example, information gain depends to some extent on the reason that motivated us to read in the first place. On the other hand, a person's perseverance is a continuous variable and can be treated much as any other variable.

Form of the Model
Thus, when we formalize the model as it now stands, we obtain the expression

$$V(C_{si}|I_j) = f(N, A, P, E_d)$$

which is to say that the value (V) that a person is likely to accrue as a result of achieving a given level of performance (i) on a criterion test (C) measuring a given set of comprehension skills (s)—and given that he intends (I) to elect a particular pursuit (j)—is some weighted function (f) of, each, his native capacity to learn (N), his acquired capacity to learn (A), his ability to persevere on the learning task (P), and the appropriate discounted (d) effects (E) associated with this level of performance on the criterion test.

The weights are the values assigned by those people affected by where the criterion score is set. This would include a broad spectrum of people, including the individual himself or his legitimate representative. The effects are discounted in the customary way to balance the advantages of immediate benefits over deferred benefits. The effects, themselves, are variables of the type mentioned in connection with establishing task and corpus criterion scores.

It should be explicitly understood that neither the symbols nor the preceding discussions prescribed any particular method of measuring the factors in the model. I have been deliberately vague on these matters because they raise questions that are logically subsequent to the ones we are addressing here, namely, what should be the general content and form of the model. However, it should be noted that the results of this model can never be any more valid than the tests and measurements employed to apply it.

A Rejected Model

Before we leave this topic it seems important to examine briefly an alternative model that was explored and then rejected on ethical grounds. In recent years we have seen a marked increase in the study of the manpower needs of the United States and of the developing countries of the world. These investigations have dealt mainly with projecting the needs for personnel who are trained in the highly specialized skills involved in some occupation that is essential to the economies of those nations. But a few, particularly those addressed to the economic problems of developing nations, have also dealt with education in basic areas such as literacy. These studies attempted to build models for identifying how many people should be trained. These are models that are analogous to the corpus criterion model in which we sought to determine what portion of materials people should be able to read.

In our society this type of model is ethically unacceptable for deciding whether reading instruction should be given to an individual. When it is suggested that we might like to know what proportion of people in our society should be literate, we are actually indulging in a euphemistic phrasing of the question of what proportion of the people in our society should be forced into illiteracy. And this implies that the policy makers have the right to decide who should learn to read and who should not. It is true, of course, that our educational resources are limited and that we may not be able to raise everyone to the level of literacy that we would ideally prefer. However, it seems unacceptable to allocate resources in this way. Suppose that it is partially true that the ability to read competently is an essential prerequisite to the exercise of our rights and responsibilities as citizens and to participation in the social, economic, and cultural benefits of our society. And suppose that there is also some truth to the proposition that cultural advantage and disadvantage tend to perpetuate themselves. It seems that with this model we would be delegating to policy makers the right to create a caste system in our society.

Now, it remains true that our society and every other society can make the most of its resources by forecasting its future needs and by setting goals for meeting them. And we need information in order to do this. But that information is useless if it is cast in a form that is unacceptable to society. In our society we are willing to accept differences in the allocation of resources among people and differences in people's eventual levels of attainment. But we prefer that those differences be explicitly determined by the personal choice of the individual himself and by biological factors. Hence, we must reject this type of model.

A FINAL COMMENT

In essence this paper has been seeking a useful way to *ask* the question how well a person should learn to read. We quickly rejected the arbitrary criteria previously used and then went on to reject models based on simplistic notions such as "more is better" and "perfect mastery is ideal." We also rejected partial solutions to this problem by recognizing that a person's literacy was jointly determined by both his reading ability and the readability of the materials that he needed to read. We chose to think in terms of models that regarded a person as literate when he could perform well enough to obtain the maximum value from the materials he needed to read. Consequently, we thereupon set out to examine, on the one hand, models that might tell us when a person was literate with respect to a single material or a corpus of materials and, on the other hand, models that might tell us when a person could read well enough to achieve his aspirations. Each of these models could probably be used with present techniques and produce modestly believable results, although each would be greatly improved if it received the benefit of further conceptual analysis and research. However, we must realize that these models, no matter how well they may be developed in the future, provide only preliminary and partial answers to the central question—how well should a person learn to read, given that literacy is jointly determined by reading ability and readability. The ultimate purpose of investigations of this sort is to help us make maximum use of our resources in realizing our goals, and this cannot be fully achieved until we have developed a model that permits us to *jointly* identify a criterion of literacy and readability.

REFERENCES

Allen, J. E. The right to read—target for the 70's. Address delivered before the National Association of State Boards of Education, September 23, 1969.

Anderson, R. C. How to construct achievement tests to assess comprehension. *Review of Educational Research*, Spring 1972, 42, 145–170.

Bart, W. M. A construction and validation of formal operational reasoning instruments. Paper read at the American Educational Research Association Convention, March 1970.

Betts, E. A. *Foundations of reading instruction.* New York: American Book Company, 1954.

Bloom, B. S. Learning for mastery. *Evaluation Comment*, March 1968, 1 (2), 1–8.

Bloom, B. S., Engelhart, M. D., Furst, J., Hill, W. H., & Krathwohl, D. K. *Taxonomy of educational objectives handbook I: Cognitive domain.* New York: David McKay Company, Inc., 1956.

Bond, G. L., & Tinker, M. A. *Reading difficulties: Their diagnosis and correction.* New York: Appleton-Century-Crofts, Inc., 1967.

Bormuth, J. R. *Development of readability analyses.* (Report of Project No. 7-0052) University of Chicago, 1969a. (ERIC Document No. ED 029166)

Bormuth, J. R. Factor validity of cloze tests as measures of reading comprehension ability. *Reading Research Quarterly*, Spring 1969b, 4, 358–367.

Bormuth, J. R. An operational definition of comprehension instruction. In K. S. Goodman & J. F. Fleming (Eds.), *Psycholinguistics and the teaching of reading.* Newark: International Reading Association, 1969c.

Bormuth, J. R. *On the theory of achievement test items.* Chicago: The University of Chicago Press, 1970.

Bormuth, J. R. *Development of standards of readability.* (Report of Development Project No. 9-0237) University of Chicago, 1971. (ERIC Document No. 054 233)

Bormuth, J. R., Manning, J., Carr, J., & Pearson, D. Children's comprehension of between and within sentence syntactic structures. *Journal of Educational Psychology*, October 1970, 61, 349–357.

Carroll, J. B. A model of school learning. *Teachers College Record*, November 1963, 64, 723–733.

Carroll, J. B., Davies, P., & Richman, B. *The American Heritage Word Frequency Book.* Boston: Houghton Mifflin Company, 1972.

Davis, F. B. *Educational measurements and their interpretation.* Belmont, Calif.: Wadsworth Publishing Company, Inc., 1964.

Finn, P. J. An algorithm for deriving operationally defined comprehension questions from written texts. Unpublished doctoral dissertation, University of Chicago, 1973.

Flesch, R. *Why Johnny can't read, and what you can do about it.* New York: Harper & Brothers, 1955.

Gagné, R. M. *The conditions of learning.* New York: Holt, Rinehart and Winston, Inc., 1965.

Gibson, Eleanor J. The ontogeny of reading. *American Psychologist*, February 1970, 25, 136–143.

Goodman, K. S. An analysis of oral reading miscues: Applied psycholinguistics. *Reading Research Quarterly*, Fall 1969, 5, 9–30.

Harris, A. J. *Effective teaching of reading.* New York: David McKay Company, Inc., 1962.

Hively, W., II, Patterson, H. L., & Page, Sara H. Generalizability of performance by Job Corps trainees on a universe-defined system of achievement tests in elementary mathematical calculation. Paper read at the American Educational Research Association Convention, February 1965.

Kucera, H., & Francis, W. N. *Computational analysis of present-day American English.* Providence: Brown University Press, 1967.

Lorge, I. S. Readibility formulae—an evaluation. *Elementary English,* February 1949, **26,** 86–95.

MacGinitie, W. H. Contextual constraint in English prose paragraphs. *Journal of Educational Psychology,* January 1961, **51,** 121–130.

Mayo, S. F. Mastery learning and mastery testing. *NCME, Measurement in Education,* March 1970, **1,** 1–4.

Mowrer, O. H. The psychologist looks at language. *American Psychologist,* June 1954, **99,** 600–694.

Osgood, C. E. On understanding and creating sentences. *American Psychologist,* March 1963, **18,** 735–751.

Rothkopf, E. Z. Learning from written instructional materials: An exploration of the control of inspection behavior by test-like events. *American Educational Research Journal,* November 1966, **3,** 241–249.

Taylor, W. L., Application of "cloze" and entropy measures to the study of contextual constraint in samples of continuous prose. Unpublished doctoral dissertation, University of Illinois, Urbana-Champaign, 1954.

Thorndike, E. L. Reading and reasoning: A study of mistakes in paragraph reading. *Journal of Educational Psychology,* October 1917, **8,** 323–332.

Venezky, R. English orthography; its graphic structure and its relation to sound. *Reading Research Quarterly,* Spring 1967, **2,** 74–103.

CHAPTER 2

CURRENT PRACTICES IN THE TEACHING OF BEGINNING READING

Helen M. Popp

INTRODUCTION

Beginning reading[1] instruction in the United States remains a subject of great concern to professional educators, parents, scholars from other disciplines, and interested lay people. This chapter presents an overview of developments in initial reading instruction over the past 5 years,[2] reflects briefly on what the future might bring, and raise several points of concern.

Three forces influencing beginning reading instruction are discussed. First, current research and writing on the teaching of reading are considered. Educators and psychologists, linguists and psycholinguists, and other scholars at universities and research centers are all contributors. Technological developments are considered in the second section. A discussion is presented of their influence on research, the development of curricula, and modes of instruction. The third section is devoted to a

---

[1] As a definition of beginning reading, I should like to adopt a slight revision of one given by Downing and Thackray (1971) as reported in Downing (1973): the recognition of the auditory and semantic significance of printed or written words in familiar syntactic structures.

[2] Reviews by Matthews (1966) and Chall (1967) give due consideration to the historical perspective up to their time, and Chall's description of programs current in 1967 is excellent.

consideration of the impact of a growing social and political awareness. A final section presents a summary and suggested implications for the future.

There is certainly a constant interaction among these forces, and it is unrealistic to attribute changes in reading instruction to any single influence. Other forces not mentioned interact as well. Nevertheless, specific reading programs are described within each of the separate sections as examples of changes in instruction relevant to the influence or factor under discussion. Table 1 (at the end of the chapter) summarizes the relevant characteristics of the programs described as well as several other programs.

Only a few of the many approaches to beginning reading instruction which have recently appeared on the market are described. Readers wishing to select among the newer programs for their own use should base their decisions on the needs and values important to them. No attempt has been made in this chapter to assess which approach is "best," as that question is meaningful only in the context of a particular school in a specific community with a certain teacher working with children whose strengths and weaknesses have been assessed. A further resource for new developments has been compiled by the ALERT Information System of the Far West Laboratory for Educational Research and Development (Henrie, 1972).

Historically, the methods of teaching beginning reading have been categorized into one of four approaches: learning letter-sound correspondences (often called the "phonic" method); learning whole words (the "sight" method); learning words in meaningful context (the "sentence" method); and, more recently, learning correspondences between spelling patterns and oral word patterns (the so-called linguistic method).[3] Recent developments in beginning reading schemes might still be so classified, but it has become more difficult to do so for several reasons. (1) Within a single program the emphasis of instruction may shift frequently; i.e., letters in words may be emphasized in several lessons and then a shift made to words in sentences before considering letters in words again. (2) Authors and publishers are now emphasizing other characteristics such as programming, individualization, formal prompts, writing, literature, etc. within the structure of their programs. Therefore, no attempt has been made to categorize the programs in the traditional way.

---

[3] Each of these approaches is variously defined by different authors, and not all definitions are accepted by proponents of the different methods. Perhaps the greatest disagreement is found over the linguistic method; however, the reader may find it convenient to accept the above arbitrary definitions.

RESEARCH AND WRITING ON THE
TEACHING OF READING

Educators and Psychologists

Educators and educational psychologists have continually expressed interest in the process of learning to read, particularly the beginning stages of that process. In this part of the first section the current writing of eight individuals or teams is considered, and materials or practices which seem to reflect their concerns are noted.

Jeanne Chall (1967) wrote *Learning to read: The great debate,* a definitive study of beginning reading instruction. Her conclusions and recommendations are carefully stated, and she reminds the reader that they are relevant to the time in which the book was written:

> I write in a period when excellence in academic work is highly valued, when intellectual precociousness is viewed as a promise of later accomplishment, and when "normal" achievement is not enough. I write at a time when automation is making obsolete abilities that once were indispensable, and when there is a desperate push to "up" the standards of literacy. This is an ambitious age for knowing and for doing [p. 305].

During the years that have followed, existing school conditions and goals of education have probably not changed to any great extent. There has been an increased interest in the "progressive" or "cognitive developmental" philosophy of education (see Kohlberg & Mayer, 1972). However, in spite of the fact that more schools seem to be establishing "open classrooms" and more teachers and administrators show an interest in the progressive philosophy, the value placed on achievement in schools and in society is still predominant. Educators and parents tend to seek ways of influencing a child's development from the earliest moments of his life, and the direction of that influence, to a great extent, is toward achievement. And so, the comments presented in this chapter are written in a time characterized similarly to that of Chall (1967).

Three major lines of innovation in reading instruction evident in 1967 are set forth in Chall's book:

> 1. Innovations to bring about earlier acquisition of the alphabetic principle.
> 2. Innovations to bring about greater individualization of instruction.
> 3. Innovations to bring about more vital, realistic, and imaginative content or to underplay content altogether [p. 48].

Conclusions which she reached and recommendations she advanced for improving the quality of beginning reading instruction were based on her theoretical analysis of the probable course of development of reading skills and her review of the research evidence on various instructional approaches. It is likely that her first major recommendation has given strong support to the first of the three lines of innovation quoted above. Chall recommended that we "make a necessary change in method." Her recommendation was for a code emphasis method as a *"beginning* reading method—a method to *start* the child on—and I do *not* recommend ignoring reading-for-meaning practice" (p. 307).

Several publishers of the conventional basal reader series[4] seemingly have adjusted their programs in light of Chall's recommendations. Even prior to the publication of the Chall study, publishers had begun to incorporate changes in method; however, since 1967 the changes have been more dramatic, more obvious. Among the publishers of basal programs who have responded to the challenge are Ginn and Company with *Reading 360* (1969) and Holt, Rinehart and Winston, Inc., with *The Holt Basic Reading System* (1973).

The "code emphasis" aspect of instruction in these basal readers represents a change. The first reader of the previous edition (*Ginn Basic Readers,* 1961) included under objectives for "Phonics" only initial and final single consonants, digraphs, and consonant blends. The major emphases of that program were on comprehension, word meaning, word recognition (there is a sight vocabulary of 171 words in the first reader), reading habits, and attitudes and appreciations. The current edition of Ginn's *Reading 360* (1969) program claims three emphases for the series: decoding, literature, and creativity. The "phonemic and structural skills of decoding" for levels 1 through 5 (level 5 approximates the end of reader 1 in the older series) include initial and final single consonants, digraphs, consonant clusters, vowel correspondence, and CVC, CVVC, and CVCC spelling patterns.[5]

Levels 1 through 8 (grade 1) of *The Holt Basic Reading System* (1973) include phoneme-grapheme correspondences for single consonants; digraphs; consonant clusters; and initial, medial, and final vowels, including digraphs and vowel plus *r*—as well as CVC, CVCC, and CVVC patterns.

[4] Basal reading programs provide a system for teaching reading and usually include the following components: a set of children's readers for each level (usually prereading, several at the first-grade level, and two each for the remaining five grades) containing a variety of reading selections, workbooks or exercises to complement the readers, and a teacher's manual for each level. Often teaching aids such as charts, tapes, films, etc. and supplementary books for the children are included in a basal or total reading program. Instructional materials, projects, and similar items mentioned in this chapter are listed in alphabetical order following the "References" section.

[5] C represents "consonant letter," and V represents "vowel letter." Thus, words such as "bat," "dim," and "hop" exemplify the CVC pattern; "maid," "heat," and "seek" follow the CVVC pattern; and "mast," "task," and "milk" follow the CVCC pattern.

Thus the recent editions of the Ginn and Holt systems have included more decoding skills in their initial instruction. However, publishers may still find support for not emphasizing decoding skills initially in the writings of other educators.

Goodman (1969b) emphasizes the comprehension aspect of initial instruction:

> Instead of word attack skills, sight vocabularies, and word perception, the program must be designed to build comprehension strategies. . . . Children learning to read should see words always as units of larger, meaningful units. In that way they can use the correspondences between oral and written English within the semantic and syntactic contexts [p. 32].[6]

As one of several authors for Scott, Foresman's new series, his point of view probably has had considerable influence. The 1971 edition of the *Scott Foresman Reading Systems* retains an emphasis on comprehension and, in fact, indexes "letter-sound relationship cues" under "comprehension strategies." Lessons to teach such relationships are always in the context of words in meaningful sentences. Level 4 (first grade) includes the recognition and use of letter-sound relationship cues for consonants and vowels.

The Ginn, Holt, and Scott, Foresman basal reading series are described more fully after consideration is given to several groups of research studies.

Bond and Dykstra (1967) compiled the data and reported on the twenty-seven individual studies on first-grade reading instruction sponsored by the U.S. Office of Education (USOE). One of the basic questions asked by the study was, "Which of the many approaches to initial reading instruction produces superior reading and spelling achievement at the end of the first grade?" A real answer to that question then might have made the writing of this chapter quite a different and much easier task. But the question was more complex than anticipated. The design for such a study, maintaining adequate controls, would have to be more intricate than the one used, and it may, in fact, not be possible to carry out such a study. The diversity of the twenty-seven studies, argues Stauffer (1966), and the fact that the methods were not sharply defined and clearly different leads one to the conclusion that "any attempt to compare method with method or study with study could produce gross misunderstandings and false conclusions . . ." (p. 564).

---

[6] It is interesting to note here the summary of educators' views of his day presented by Huey (1908, reprinted in 1968): "The mechanical reading is thought to come from learning reading as mere word-pronouncing; the stumbling and hesitation, from the over-attention to form as against content, especially from the early and too constant analysis of the reading process in phonics . . ." [p. 303].

Nevertheless, the one conclusion or indirect answer to the question posed by the study that is constantly reiterated is that no method is outstanding. Suggestions are made that the teacher and the characteristics of the learning situation, rather than methods and materials, might "make the difference." Several other conclusions from the USOE first-grade studies have probably influenced the direction of the new basal series also. These conclusions were (1) that "word study skills must be emphasized and taught systematically" and (2) that "combinations of programs, such as basals with supplementary phonics materials, often are superior to single approaches" (Bond and Dykstra, 1967, p. 122).

The USOE first-grade studies (and Chall's [1967] study also) are discussed in a most comprehensive review of studies pertaining to methodology discussed below.

Corder (1971) and his group prepared a report as part of the Targeted Research and Development Program on Reading, funded by the USOE. Their tasks included not only a "census of instructional materials, but also a determination of the convergence or disparity in the conceptual bases of the variety of instructional methods utilized in reading instruction. A further area of investigation was to determine whether or not documentation existed for the assessment of the time and resources expended in utilizing the several methods" (p. 7). In this broader context, the Bond and Dykstra (1967) report was evaluated:

> How was Bond able to reach these conclusions based upon the reports of the twenty-seven studies? If, as Stauffer has pointed out, any attempt to compare method with method is not justified, then how can one conclude that no method is outstanding? If reading instructional time is not controlled, how can one decide that adding components is not just adding additional practice? If the measurements used are not adequate, how is it possible to distinguish differential outcomes from inadequate testing? If non-randomly selected groups differ at the end of instruction, how is it possible to attribute that to differences in teachers rather than to differences in groups? [Corder, 1971, p. 127]

With reference to the adequacy of any of the investigations on methodology already existing, Corder (1971) said, "The conclusion is that the present literature on methods of reading instruction cannot be used, except in special circumstances, to justify decisions involving millions of children and, possibly, if adequately funded education becomes a national priority, billions of dollars" (p. 134).

Since these studies, several researchers have worked on other methods, and the methodology of one team of researchers is described briefly below.

Gleitman and Rozin (1973) have designed reading instructional materials which begin with the syllable as the unit of instruction. They base this work on the premise that the "fundamental conceptual problem in reading acquisition is psychoacoustic: it has to do with awareness of phonological segmentation, and it has very little to do with the writing system itself (with the visual input)" (p. 452). Their instruction begins with learning to associate oral syllables with a few pictures and a few written one-syllable words; these are combined to form words of more than one syllable and to form sentences. Their earlier research indicated that the rebus-syllabic system (a more appropriate term than "syllabary," incidentally) is learnable, even by populations that have not shown significant progress with traditional methods. Learning that the orthography does, in fact, track the sound stream and learning the correlations between written symbols and pronunciations appear to be more easily taught at the level of the syllable. A base curriculum including sixty syllables is now being tested with kindergarten and first-grade children. The introductory materials may be followed by a range of instructional materials, including those that focus on phonemic concepts or basic spelling patterns.

We turn now from writers interested in methodological issues to those who are concerned with the content of the readers. Here, too, the research is not conclusive, but philosophical and theoretical issues are raised.

Busch (1972) advocated reading material that is more interesting and relevant to the children. He asserted that we generally take it for granted that children will be motivated to learn to read. The child's need for mastering his surroundings is characteristic of his developmental stage when reading is formally taught. However, Busch cautioned that publishers and teachers should also look at motivational qualities inherent in the reading process and should not regard learning to read as an autonomous process, unrelated to anything else. In television viewing there is no boundary between the *how* and the *why* of it. But *how* to learn to read is taught, and *why* seems left to the child's previous experiences—experiences that may be much less rich than they were in former days. A child, claimed Busch, perceives reading as an activity of intrinsic interest only through models, in his home and in school, of others who enjoy reading, and through the quality of the material he is reading or having read to him.

As to the relevance of content, Busch turned to theory in the writings of the psychoanalytic workers. He refers to Erikson (1959) as pointing out that "the child needs to have the feeling of mastery of conflict at this stage of development. Most important is that the child's normal developmental concerns during this period lead him to be both interested and involved in mastering his inner as well as his outer world." From other psychoanalytic writers he gleaned that "the key for these writers, as with Erikson, is the development of healthy mechanisms (i.e. ego functions) for the child's ability to cope with what is going on inside of him and with the realities of the external world, as well as the interaction of these two" (Busch, 1972, p. 23). He then mentioned work by Friedlander (1942) and

Peller (1958) concerning books that have endured. Two important factors are revealed: The lasting stories are related to the developmental concerns of preadolescent children, and at the core of each story there is a universal daydream containing within it the conflicts with which each child must struggle. Therefore it seems that the child is drawn to stories that include the conflicts of the type he is experiencing. Busch expressed the concern that this type of conflict is avoided in the first-grade texts he examined.

Rose, Zimet, and Blom (1972) conducted a study of children's preferences. Pairs of stories were read to children, and the pairs were controlled for content variable as well as length, reading difficulty, and environmental setting. In their sample ($N = 76$) a clear preference was shown for stories of pranks over Pollyanna stories and for stories of peer interaction over child-parent interaction stories. They found that boys preferred stories about boys and girls preferred stories of girls.

An impression gained from looking through the newer basal series is that there is more diversity in the types of stories included and that authors and publishers are attempting to make the stories more relevant to children's interests and activities. An extensive analysis of the content of these materials should be undertaken to confirm this impression and thence to note the children's responses to the stories.

Basal series remain a very popular mode of instruction, and newer editions have been created with some of this literature on content and the recommendations for methodology as background for a stated rationale. Three such series are described quite briefly below to give the flavor of their content and structure.

In *Reading 360* (Ginn, 1969), nine strands are emphasized by the authors throughout the K–6 program: comprehension (inferential and literal), creativity development, decoding (phonemic and structural analysis), acquisition of knowledge and information, language, literary understanding and appreciation, sensitivity to social-moral values, study skills, and vocabulary. Reading is defined by the author as (1) decoding, (2) understanding the author's message, (3) making a critical evaluation of that message, and (4) incorporating the author's ideas into one's thinking and actions. The claim is made that a systematic and sequential development of all four aspects is provided. In order to go beyond (2) above, the guided discussions before reading and after reading each story are directed toward aspects (3) and (4). Decoding skills are systematic and are introduced in the very first level. This series now has a set of children's literature to accompany it (Magic Circle books), and the authors stress moving children into these books as soon as it is feasible.

Authors of *The Holt Basic Reading System* (1973) have selected a very broad range of content organized around unit themes thought to be relevant to the emotional needs and varied backgrounds of children. Situations where reading was necessary, children and their pets, fantasy, urban events, suburban events, friendships, family situations, and trips are first-grade themes. The program is described as a "total-language approach," and objectives for each lesson (or story) are very explicit. For the first grade they include gaining skills in characterization, demonstrating specific grapheme-phoneme correspondences, using context clues, inferring motives, giving multiple meanings of specific words, stating some phonic generalizations, constructing titles for selections, identifying quotation marks, and constructing contractions. Such objectives do indeed reflect the definition of reading offered: "Reading is essentially the interpretation of the patterns, structures, and meanings of written English and the sounds we bring to it."

Each lesson may be preceded by a suggested activity involving the children in some aspect of the story. Model lessons provide activities, games, and exercises for teaching specific skills. Appropriate questions—some asking for specific recall, some inferential, and some asking for creative and evaluative answers—are given in the teacher's manual on the pages where the student's text is reproduced. Paperback "Satellite Books" which parallel the themes developed in the basic books are available, as well as other enrichment materials, such as filmstrips, music and story recordings, games, and A-V kits. The quality of the design of the books and the illustrations (including some children's drawings, as well as paintings by Renoir and other masters) make them very appealing and far from stereotyped.

The *Scott Foresman Reading Systems* was not available for detailed analysis, but sample materials from the program indicate that there are a great many components included. Read-Aloud library books (one for each of the first six levels of the program), pupils' books (four to nine different softbound books at each of the first six levels), study books for each level for each pupil, further independent practice books with exercises paralleling the study book, "Magneboard" and "Magnepieces" (magnetized pictures, color cards, sentences, phrases, words, letters, etc. for teacher presentation), and numerous other supplementary items are recommended. The authors' definition ("Learning to read is the extension of a child's natural language development. Reading itself is a search for meaning—the active reconstruction of a message from written language.") and the content of the lessons indicate a strong emphasis on meaning. The authors introduce the use of sound-letter relationships but admonish the teacher not to have pupils concentrating on the correct identification of individual words.

These new basals reflect the current literature on initial instruction. Each has an emphasis (meaning or decoding), but that emphasis is not as forceful as in previous editions. A wide variety of instructional techniques and content is offered. While these basals initially use content created specifically for reading instruction, children's literature is also incorporated.

Another team of educators has renewed interest in using content created by the child; these educators have devised a scheme for doing so. MacKay and Thompson (1968) at the University College, London, have advanced the notion that beginning reading instruction should be more consciously incorporated into a broader language arts program.[7] The Schools Council Program in Linguistics and English Teaching at the University College, London, led by David MacKay, developed *Breakthrough to Literacy*, an initial literacy program for primary-grade children incorporating reading and writing. It is now published in the United States by Bowmar.

Breakthrough materials are designed to teach reading and writing by prompting children to express themselves orally and to create printed language for themselves about themselves. Emphasis is placed on having the children learn that they can communicate their own ideas in writing, just as they do in speaking. Each child has his own "reading book" which is composed by him (transcribed at first by the teacher and later by the child), and he has his own "sentence maker and stand" modeled after a larger one which the teacher uses to introduce words and language concepts. The child's "word maker" is used to gain knowledge of word endings and information about sound-symbol correspondences. Also, little books (sixteen pages long, in full color) written on three broad levels of difficulty are read by the teacher initially and later by the children as a precursor to reading children's literature. A teacher's resource book provides lesson suggestions and activities and also describes the purpose of each of the components of the program. From the publisher's introduction we read:

> . . . some children will need to have many oral language experiences—to retell stories, make them up, explain events, sing and sing, and talk and talk and talk—over a longer period than other children. Similarly, some children will need to work for a longer time with the teacher using the teacher's materials before they work alone. All children, regardless of their readiness, will, in due course, have the opportunity to use all the materials, but the time they spend developing skills and consolidating them and their readiness for another step will depend upon their individual needs [MacKay et al., 1970].

MacKay's statements reflect a view common to other English educators as well: that of delaying formal reading instruction. Of the two types of approach to reading found in the English infant schools, formal and in-

---

[7] See also R. McCracken and M. McCracken, *Reading is only the tiger's tail* (1972), and J. Moffett, *A student-centered language arts curriculum, grades K–13: A handbook for teachers* (1968).

formal, most American authors importing English ideology concentrate on the latter wherein reading is considered to be mastered best by incidental learning (see Southgate & Roberts, 1970). The "progressive" philosophy here in the United States advocates allowing children the freedom to grow and explore for a longer period prior to any concern over formal reading instruction.[8]

In addition to the research on materials and methods, some notice is being given to teacher training.

Ruddell and Williams (1972) have turned their research efforts to in-service teacher training. A basic assumption of their *Project DELTA* is that the most significant agent for effecting educational change is the classroom teacher who assumes the final instructional responsibility for curriculum implementation with individual youngsters. In Ruddell's study, factors thought to be of importance for teachers working with young children in beginning reading were emphasized in a training program. Perhaps the most unique feature of the teacher training was the effort directed toward making teachers aware of their level of questioning and the level of questions and answers used by the children, i.e., the interactive strategies used in the classroom. A "comprehension taxonomy" was developed for analyzing these interactive strategies, and definitions were established for three levels of meaning: "factual," "interpretive," and "applicative." For categorizing strategies of questioning within these levels they defined and used the following terms: "focusing" (maintaining attention on the discourse unit), "ignoring" (not responding to the question posed or response given), "controlling" (dominating; the teacher handles the cognitive task rather than giving the children an opportunity to do so), "receiving" (merely acknowledging; no elaboration), "clarifying" (making explanatory comment), "extending" (seeking additional information at the same level of comprehension), and "raising" (seeking additional information at a higher level of comprehension).[9]

Strategies of questioning were categorized for classes in grades 1, 2, and 3. It was reported that during the time when the classes were videotaped, 68 percent of the teachers' questions were "factual," and 32 percent were "interpretive." The report stresses the need for teachers to consider the level of questions used in the classroom. The authors suggest the need for additional use of "clarifying" and "raising" strategies in developing comprehension at the interpretive level. Focusing on very specific skills

[8] Again, it is interesting to note Huey's comments of 1908 expressing the same underlying philosophy of his day. "It is believed that much that is now strenuously struggled for and methodized over in these early years of primary reading will come of themselves with *growth*, and when the child's sense organs and nervous system are stronger; and that in the meantime he should be acquiring own experiences and developing wants that will in time make reading a natural demand and a meaningful process, with form and book always secondary to own thought" (p. 303).

[9] Several of these categories are adopted from Taba and Elzey (1964).

could influence instructional techniques, particularly if these skills are shown to be effective in increasing children's comprehension. However, Ruddell's research is one of the few that deal with specific teaching skills.

The educators/psychologists cited above have contributed greatly to our thinking about current practices in beginning reading instruction. Their views are not all consonant with each other, and diversity remains in the instructional materials and methodologies. Their impact on teacher training techniques ought to be more noticeable in the near future.

Linguists and Psycholinguists

Publishers of reading materials are now including linguists as authors or consultants for their programs. The reading profession has turned to linguists and psycholinguists in seeking answers to problems of beginning reading instruction, and the linguists have extended their theoretical work to encompass the concerns of the practitioner. Perhaps this is one reason why "the great debate" (Chall, 1967) has refused to die, for the "linguistic" answers are quite diverse. As an example, two linguists most recently addressing themselves to beginning reading are Frank Smith and Richard Venezky, each with a different opinion.

Smith (1971) has hypothesized that for the fluent mature reader, comprehension may precede word identification rather than follow it: ". . . the three aspects of reading in which a reader may engage—the reduction of letter, word, or meaning uncertainty—are quite independent." Thus, a reader "may reduce his meaning uncertainty without making any prior decisions about words." The most efficient identification of meaning is *immediate* (or direct) rather than *mediated* (or indirect). The three aspects of reading (or reducing the uncertainty of letters, words, or meaning), Smith claims, cannot be conducted simultaneously. An attempt to identify "words when the aim is comprehension, must inevitably result in delay and disruption of both identification processes" (p. 213).

Smith asserts that in the process of learning to read, the child must "learn what are the distinctive features of written language and their relations to letters and words and meanings; . . . establish 'categories' for letter and word identification as well as establish all the visual-semantic associations required for comprehension" (p. 227); learn "how the rules of syntax are related to the written aspect of language together with the relation of visual configurations and semantic interpretation" (p. 228); and also become a fast or fluent reader almost immediately in order to comprehend. Consequently, Smith postulates that the child should learn from an initial exposure to a very large sample of "evidence" or data at the letter, word, and meaning levels, rather than at any one of these levels only. Since we do not know "enough about the distinctive features of print, for example, to give a child the knowledge that he really needs in order to be able to distinguish letters or words," he must be given enough information to establish the feature lists for himself [p. 225]. Parallel arguments are made for establishing acoustic and semantic category associations, and for learning the sources of redundancy in the written language. He characterizes the learning process as one of testing his hypotheses by making responses and getting feedback ("about whether the supposition upon which the response was founded is appropriate"). Thus the teacher's role is to give the child *information*.

> A child has to be given the information as to whether two configurations are the same or different. . . . A child has to be told the "names" that are conventionally associated with letters, and should not be left too much to work out for himself the names of words by phonic methods. Once again, an overdependence on mediated reading places an almost intolerable burden on the visual information-processing system. Similarly, a child has to be given examples where differences in meaning lie, so that he can establish the necessary visual and semantic relationships [p. 228].

The most extreme aspect of Smith's position is that he advocates that even the beginning reader should establish visual-semantic relationships, or print-to-meaning associations.

Venezky (1972) offers the following definition of reading: "Reading is the translation from writing to a form of language from which the reader is already able to derive meaning" (p. 1). He goes on to characterize the initial reading process as encompassing the ability to decode, but not confined to that skill. In addition, he places a strong emphasis on the learner *utilizing* his existing language and comprehension abilities, which are *not* to be confused with being able to translate from writing directly to meaning. Venezky (1967) states,

> Learning to read . . . requires primarily the translation from written symbols to sound, a procedure which is the basis of the reading process and is probably the only language skill unique to reading. (Comprehension, for example, while a necessary criterion for reading, is a function of both speech and writing [p. 102].

In the same article: "Learning to read is to a great extent learning to relate orthographic forms to already existing phonological forms" (p. 104). In this article Venezky questions the pedagogy of sequencing materials from simple to complex (specifically, from one-to-one grapheme to phoneme correspondences instead of one-to-many where a child would learn, for example, that *a* corresponds to /æ/ in some graphemic environments and /ey/ in others: "hat," "hate").

The Wisconsin Research and Development Center for Cognitive Learning, where Venezky is a faculty member, has designed an outline of reading skills. While other investigators are responsible for the outline (Otto & Peterson, 1969), it does respond to Venezky's questions of sequence.

> Since there is as yet no definitive proof that one teaching sequence of skills is inherently better than another, we achieved approximation of skill placement by consensuality. Our intent is not to be prescriptive; rather we expect that the local schools will adapt the Outline to fit their local needs, and further expect that teaching will be to the needs of the pupils regardless of the grade placement of the pupils or the level placement of the skills [p. 9].

Blumenthal (1972) questions the relevance of much of the work in linguistics and psycholinguistics to reading instruction. From the field of linguistics it is reasonable to expect knowledge of the

> constituents of language, their rules of formation and the logical relations among them. . . . Knowledge of linguistic structure is indeed important, but it is *not criterial* in the task of understanding how people talk or read. Now I think we can go a step further and say that an understanding of how people talk or read may similarly be valuable but again not criterial in the task of understanding how to *teach* people to talk or read [Blumenthal, 1972].

In the same paper Blumenthal reminds us of the classical mistake, recognized from the early days of psychology, referred to as the "stimulus error." He uses it in a different context, but it is perhaps appropriate here to restate it.

> The stimulus error is the search for an understanding of psychological capacities by means of studying the structure of stimuli (the 'stimuli' here need not be just those things external to the organism but may include certain internal phenomena as well).

Such an "error" could easily occur in the development of reading programs (and in research in reading pedagogy) if we depend too heavily upon descriptions of the structure of *what* is taught (the written form of the language and its association to the spoken form) or descriptions of the performance of the mature reader. While extensive knowledge of both are essential, observations and analysis of the performance of the beginning reader and cues from the expert teacher of beginning reading are also true sources for insights into the process and how it might be better taught. "Perhaps the field of reading pedagogy might become more concerned with its own independence and unique problems" (Blumenthal, 1972).

Diversity in the so-called linguistic programs then on the market was discussed by Chall (1967). Some programs marketed since then are also called "linguistic," and other programs have been influenced by linguists[10] who served as consultants. Again, the difference in the focus of various linguists, their research, and the application of this input to reading instruction are a clear indication that the use of the science of linguistics for reading pedagogy is, at best, quite variable. A description of the *Miami Linguistic Readers* is therefore not representative, but it is included here as one example of the newer "linguistic" programs.

The *Miami Linguistic Readers* (1970), published by D. C. Heath and Company for grades 1 and 2, concentrate on teaching the sounds and structure of standard American English before as well as during the teaching of basic reading skills. The readers were developed in Dade County, Florida, for bilingual (English- and Spanish-speaking) children and were strongly influenced by structural linguistics. In this carefully sequenced program, only a few sound-symbol relationships are presented in spelling patterns at each level. Writing activities begin with tracing, copying, and finally actual production. The stories at the beginning of the program are about animals, followed by myths and folklore, and finally by stories which deal with realism and adventure. There are twenty-one paperbound readers and related workbooks, and the developers have included placement tests which may also serve as a measure of achievement.

Regional Research and Development Centers

Are the regional research and development laboratories under government sponsorship affecting changes in initial reading instruction?

The Pittsburgh Learning Research and Development Center (LRDC) has developed an Early Reading Program (ERP) designed to teach isolated letter sounds and the blending of these sounds into words. As part of its Individually Prescribed Instruction (IPI) system in several experimental schools, it has also worked on other reading curricula. Commercially available materials, such as McGraw-Hill's *Programmed Reading,* and components of several basal series have been modified for programmed sequences of instruction.[11] In addition to these adapted materials, LRDC has created materials such as diagnostic and evaluative instruments and correlated curriculum materials. Specific skills are taught in a hierarchical fashion, and alternative modes of instruction in mastering these skills are

[10] For example: Roger Shuy for *Reading 360,* Andrew Schiller for *Scott, Foresman,* Bernard Weiss for *Holt,* Theodore Glim for *Palo Alto Readers.*

[11] A history of LRDC's involvement in reading instruction and a description of the reading system under development is given in Beck & Mitroff (1972).

encouraged. Access to library and trade books is incorporated, and management schemes are designed to guide students through the program. In field trials, use of these materials effected an increase in mean reading achievement, but the percentage of students who still performed below grade level prompted LRDC to consider the creation of a new system.

A New Primary Grades Reading System (NRS), oriented toward city children aged 5 to 9, is now under development. Each component is to be designed to interrelate with all other components, and effective implementation procedures are also to be developed. Individualization in terms of different strategies for adapting instruction to varying abilities and motivations as well as student rate of learning is to be incorporated into the system. Preliminary plans seem to suggest that alternative strategies would be tutorial help in the same skill or adjusting the direction of the approach; e.g., "symbol to sound" would change to "sound to symbol," and synthetic blending of sounds into words would change to an analytic extracting of sounds from whole words. The initial approach to reading is to have a heavy decoding emphasis, but meaning will also be incorporated. These materials are still in the development stage, and so naturally they have not had an impact on materials available commercially.

Analyzing major components of reading (e.g., decoding and comprehension), breaking these into subskills, and further breaking the subskills into specific behavioral objectives is a useful scheme for research. It allows one to look at the efficacy of particular methods in achieving those objectives. However, there is an inherent danger in getting locked into a sequence of mastering objectives; it is possible for the objectives themselves to be thought of as absolutely necessary for all students who wish to master initial reading. Already in commercially available materials there are instances where the objectives assume such an all-important role that normal reading behavior seems to be thought of as unattainable except by the prescribed route.

Rosner, also at the Pittsburgh LRDC, has been developing an individualized perceptual skills curriculum to train children in abilities commonly thought to be prerequisites for reading and arithmetic instruction (Rosner, 1972). The curriculum trains children to recognize both visual and auditory constructions (words, sentences) as being made up of a finite number of elements that are interrelated in a specific manner. A pretest for individual differences among children is given to determine which training program will be assigned, and then children work through a carefully sequenced program. Rosner has presented evidence to indicate that auditory-motor training does have an impact on the children's reading skills.

The Pittsburgh LRDC has also completed the development (Frankenstein, 1971) and field testing (Popp, 1972) of another beginning reading program which emphasizes decoding. As part of the instructional strategy, each of eleven vowels is associated with a color, and the various letter representations of each vowel are introduced simultaneously. Thus, for example, the variant spellings of "long *i*" (*igh, y, ie,* and *i*) are introduced together and are all colored purple, followed by a story incorporating many instances of that element in addition to other elements previously taught. The program, with some revisions, will be published as *Color Keys to Reading* by Appleton Century Crofts, and the revised version will be field-tested again in 1973–74.

The Wisconsin Research and Development Center has developed a "design" for reading instruction as a part of its Project on Individually Guided Instruction: Elementary Reading. Other projects contributing to knowledge on the initial reading process are Project on Basic Pre-Reading Skills, Project on a Structure of Concept Attainment Abilities, and Project on Variables and Processes in Cognitive Learning.[12]

The Wisconsin Design for Reading Skill Development represents a new trend in reading instruction, as it is really a management system for determining students' needs, planning and organizing instruction, and assessing progress in the reading skill areas of word attack and study skills. The staff members at the Wisconsin Research and Development Center for Cognitive Learning provide behavioral objectives and tests for measuring them to aid the teacher in becoming an "effective diagnostician." While resources or programs are suggested for each skill area and objectives, none are incorporated into the system. The teacher determines areas of need for students, temporarily groups students for instruction in the needed skill areas, and, using the resource file or his or her own materials, provides instruction and materials for the students. The objectives emphasize word attack skills at the earliest level. The center plans to add objectives and resources for self-directed, interpretive, and creative reading skills in 1974 and comprehension skills in 1975.

The Southwest Regional Laboratory for Educational Research and Development (SWRL) has also made a sizable contribution to research in beginning reading. Studies on children's language structures and on vocabulary development, comprehension, kindergarten reading, the cloze procedure, etc. are available for reading researchers or curriculum developers. The laboratory has completed its development of and research on a program for teaching beginning reading skills to young children.

The *Beginning Reading Program,* developed by the Southwest Regional Laboratory for Educational Research and Development over a period of 6 years, was published by Ginn and Company in 1972. It is intended for very young children (part of a kindergarten program), and the objectives are to teach the child to read approximately 100 words by

---

[12] Technical reports from these projects are available from Wisconsin Research and Development Center for Cognitive Learning, The University of Wisconsin, Madison, Wisconsin.

sight and to master beginning word attack skills (twenty-three initial and ending word elements and any one-syllable words composed of those elements) and comprehension skills. For each of the ten units there are criterion exercises to check mastery, four practice exercises for children who do not master the criterion exercises, "good work badges" for adequate performance, comprehension sheets (for the last three units only), tiny paperback storybooks which may be taken home, guides to the teacher for activities and materials, alphabet cards, word flash cards, and animal cards.

The developers state that words used in the program were selected by linguists and learning psychologists to meet the following criteria: "(1) They are common in the vocabulary of beginning school children; (2) they include a combination of regularly spelled words and high usage function words; (3) their component sounds combine to form many additional words; and (4) their sound combinations facilitate the efficient learning of the word attack process" (Henrie, 1972). The students learn individual words, sound associations for several consonants (e.g., *m* and *s*), and VC patterns (e.g., *at, it, eet*); they then "sound out and read" words combining these elements and continue to learn several more consonants, VC patterns, etc. The related storybooks are integrated into the teaching sequence. The books are about animal characters and their imaginative antics. Each little book of animal character stories is read as soon as the vocabulary contained in it is mastered.

The Far West Laboratory has developed a self-instructional teacher-training sequence.

Minicourse 18: Teaching Reading as Decoding provides practice for teachers of beginning reading (specifically in teaching decoding) through microteaching. The trainees are videotaped while teaching a few students who are deficient in a particular skill, and then they observe and evaluate themselves. *Minicourse 18* contains about fifty selected strategies for teaching five different levels of decoding skills, each of which is justified, explained, and demonstrated. The course materials include a teacher handbook, videotapes of demonstration lessons, diagnostic tests for the pupils of the teachers-in-training, and materials for teaching. "Results to date have shown it to be more successful in training intern teachers than conventional training" (Henrie, 1972, p. 351).

The Center for Research in Human Learning at the University of Minnesota has a Reading Research Project funded by the National Institutes of Child Health and Human Development. During its first year of research it has initiated studies in beginning reading, and its technical reports span perceptual learning, information processing, associative learning, visual recognition memory, focal attention, decoding, and other components of the reading process. Eventually these studies may have an effect on instructional materials, particularly as the authors have drawn practical implications from them. For example, in a report by Samuels and

LaBerge (1973) we find advice for teaching letter names. Or again, in an experiment on focal attention, "Efficiency in learning to associate responses to graphic stimuli is significantly greater when the word is presented in isolation than when presented in sentence context or in association with a picture, or both" (p. 5).

The contradictory points of view expressed in the research and writing on the teaching of reading by educators, psychologists, and linguists have reinforced the diversity in approaches to beginning reading instruction. These groups have drawn attention to content also, and they have given an indication that teacher training deserves more emphasis. The research and development centers have undertaken a formidable quantity of research for their own programs, and considerable quantities of data are available for reanalysis as questions of "Which skills? For whom? And in what sequence?" are reconsidered.

The impact of this work has been more evident in the development of instructional materials than in the development of in-service and pre-service teacher training. Likewise, when we consider the influence of technological developments and the influences of a social and political awareness, changes in materials are more visible than changes in teacher training.

TECHNOLOGICAL DEVELOPMENTS

In addition to the influence of educators, psychologists, linguists, and other researchers on initial reading instruction, we are certainly aware of the influence of advances in technology.

Computers are being used in the actual instructional process (e.g., *Stanford CAI Program in Initial Reading*, Atkinson & Hansen, 1966) and in the management of systems as well (e.g., *Project Plan*, Flanagan, 1971). These two projects are currently operational, and Ginn and Company is now working out a management system for *Reading 360* which would have a teacher/computer option. As a part of Westport's *Cooperative Individualized Reading Project*, individual lessons or exercises concerned with decoding from various published reading programs have been categorized according to specific behavioral objectives. In order for the teacher to use the available materials for individualized diagnosis and instruction, a cross-referenced index between the objectives and the materials was constructed. The computer played a significant role in its development, but the project directors opted for printing the reference/index in manual format rather than recommending the use of on-line computers for coordinating the student's needs (objectives) and the materials.

The computer provides rapid access to stored information; however, achieving "rapid access" to the computer in an educational setting presents real problems for the teachers. In the actual teaching situation, teachers may opt to manage the day-to-day very specific objectives (such as those associated with word analysis skills) in less sophisticated ways and to relegate questions (issues) of broader scope to computer management. Longer-range educational objectives are probably more susceptible to computer management than the behavioral objectives we are familiar with in beginning reading instruction.

In addition to computer technology, technological advances in instruments for audio, visual, and audio-visual presentations have been made. These have resulted in the incorporation of such materials in reading systems more frequently in recent years.

Books with accompanying records or tapes[13] are now available for beginning readers. A child may select a book and listen to it being read while he follows the text in the book. These materials are not advertised yet as constituting a beginning reading instructional method, but some children may learn to read in this manner. We are reminded that in 1908 Huey wrote of the imitative method:

> In the Orient, children bawl in concert over a book, imitating their fellows or their teacher until they come to know what the page says and to read it for themselves. Many an American child cannot remember when reading began, having by a similar method pored over the books and pictures of nursery jingles and fairy tales that were told to him, until he could read them for himself. Miss Everett, writing in the *New York Teachers' Monographs*, thinks that some day the debris and obtrusive technique of reading methods may melt away into the simplicity of some such practice as this [Huey, 1968, p. 274].

Printed and auditory material may be presented simultaneously in programs designed for machines such as the EFI machine,[14] Bell and Howell's *Language Master*,[15] Grolier's *Reading Machine*,[16] and EDL's various machines (*Listen Look Learn*; see below). Borg Warner's *System 80* presents audio-visual programs which provide for student responses and immediate feedback. Several supportive "systems" or programs offering individualized instruction in the area of beginning reading were

---

[13] *Weston Woods*; McGraw-Hill's *Listening Time*; ICT/Taylor Associates, *Story Library*; Scott's *Children's Heritage*; etc.

[14] *Patterns in Phonics* and others. Electronic Futures Inc., North Haven, Conn.

[15] *Phonics Program, Word-Picture Program, Autosort Language Arts Program,* and others. Bell and Howell Co., Audio Visual Products Division, Chicago, Ill.

[16] *Grolier Creative Reading Program*. Grolier Educational Corp., New York. (A remedial or developmental program using cards and an audio component color-keyed to the cards. Storybooks using the words taught are also incorporated.)

developed by Donald Durrell.[17] One program which emphasizes the use of machines is described below as an example of how materials may be coordinated.

Listen Look Learn is a program developed by Educational Developmental Laboratories, Inc. (now a division of McGraw-Hill), which incorporates audio-visual techniques. Performance objectives for the *Listen Look Learn* system are categorized as (1) visual and auditory perception, (2) vocabulary (sight vocabulary), (3) word study (phonic analysis, structural analysis, dictionary skills, and word attack strategies), (4) comprehension (literal comprehension, interpretation, evaluation, organization, and location of information), and (5) reading fluency. These strands run through the seven levels of the program, and a teacher may locate the basic skill development activities and skill reinforcement activities within each of the seven levels by referring to the Scope and Sequence Bulletin.

Listen Look Learn introduces and maintains concepts and skills systematically through the use of various audio (recordings) and visual (tachistoscopes, controlled reader, filmstrips) media as well as standard reading materials. Teacher-directed learning, teacher aide–directed learning, and autoinstruction are involved in the four-part cycle of instruction. (1) Instruction in perceptual accuracy and visual efficiency involves use of the Tach-X[18] and Controlled Reader.[19] (2) Experiences pertaining to relevant concepts are built through discussion, story writing, or story listening. (3) Skill building involves the Aud-X[20] presentation of words, word study and stories, Tach-X word recognition exercises, Controlled Reader "processing training,"[21] and story reading for fluency. (Stories contain only words previously encountered, with emphasis on those taught within the same cycle.) (4) Individualized reading and related language arts activities include guided as well as independent reading, listening, speaking, observing, manipulating, and study skills kits for reading in the content areas. Phonic analysis skills are introduced slowly in this program, with only initial consonants being considered by cycle 20 (of 100 cycles); simple vowels are taught after cycle 40.

And, of course, **television** must be included also in this section on technological advances. *Sesame Street* and *The Electric Company*, pro-

---

[17] *Learning Letter Sounds and Pre-School Concept Development: Beginning Language Concepts.* Borg Warner, Niles, Ill.

[18] Tach-X is a tachistoscope: a quick-exposure device for displaying small amounts of visual material, usually words or phrases.

[19] Controlled Reader is a filmstrip projector which makes use of a moving slot to project printed material in a left to right manner at a predetermined rate.

[20] Aud-X is a sight-sound synchronized instrument.

[21] "Process Training" is a continuous tachistoscopic training whereby stories are projected on the screen one word at a time on the same spot on the screen at an exceptionally high rate.

duced by The Children's Television Workshop, are seen on a nationwide basis, and several other programs have been produced by local educational TV stations. (See the chapter by Gibbon, Palmer, and Fowles, in this volume, pages 215–256.)

SOCIAL AND POLITICAL AWARENESS

In this section, I shall briefly discuss the influence of our growing social and political awareness on initial reading instruction. In a recent publication of the International Reading Association, *Social perspectives on reading,* Callaway set forth the premise that issues and problems regarding reading should be studied and viewed from a political perspective. He claimed that educational decision making is a critical activity and that educators have ignored that fact. "Thus a consideration of reading must reflect an awareness of the use of power and existence of conflict as elements of the political reality involved" (Callaway, 1973, p. 6). The stance taken is that the emphasis on reading in our society is a function of cultural elitism used to keep our subcultures in America divided; that for political purposes, it is a critical element in social mobility; and that the reading establishment and industry are caught up in a self-fulfilling prophecy, the specific direction of which is to lead others to hold values and attitudes about reading which they hold. Thus Callaway viewed the Right-to-Read effort as an unnecessary infringement on a different right: the Right-Not-to-Read. He further argued that the decisions about reading programs have been political decisions rather than decisions based on knowledge: ". . . because of what is known about child growth and development, reading should not be taught until the chronological age of ten or eleven." That we do otherwise, he postulated, is because the importance of reading has been overemphasized.

What is it that is known about child growth and development that leads Callaway to conclude that reading should not be taught until age ten or eleven? He makes general reference to Gesell and Piaget but does not refer to empirical data available on the question.

Very early acquisition of reading has been found for some three- or four-year-olds (see Durkin, 1966), and most six- and seven-year-olds can and do learn to read. Durkin and others have presented evidence that there are greater achievement gains for early readers:

> . . . the average achievement of early readers who had had either five or six years of school instruction in reading, was significantly higher than the average achievement of equally bright classmates who had six years of school instruction but were not early readers [p. 41].

There are suggestions from her data as well that "an earlier beginning in reading might be of special value for the slower child" (p. 40).

Reading is an important tool for the young child in his years of formal education as learning is cumulative. Bloom, in his book *Stability and change in human characteristics* (1964), concluded from his "results on general achievement, reading comprehension and vocabulary development that by age 9 at least 50% of the general achievement pattern at age 18 has been developed" (p. 105). While these results naturally reflect the current school curricula, they also reflect the more basic growth and development in individual students. As we remain sensitive to the total development of the child, we must not negate the power implicit in the *use* of properly taught reading skills, including interpretive and evaluative components. Surely these studies and others strongly suggest the value of earlier reading as opposed to delaying instruction.

An awareness of political and social issues surrounding decisions about reading programs has also generated concern over the value implications in the content of programs and in the organization or operation of the programs. We have been made aware that the beginning reading programs in the past have been designed with middle-class children in mind and have mirrored a middle-class society with all its attitudes, values, prejudices, and struggles. Educators can no longer claim ignorance of the fact that their decisions do reflect a political perspective. They therefore have attempted to gear their efforts toward more than the predominant culture. Four specific directions which these efforts have taken in initial reading instruction are (1) an increased attention to the content of the beginning readers, (2) an attention to dialect differences as a potential problem area, (3) a concentration on teachers' attitudes, and (4) a continued request for government funds for research and evaluation. Very much like other attempts by society itself, these attempts have been faltering and have met with varying degrees of success.

1. Content of Instructional Materials

Ours is a pluralistic society, and various cultures within that society as well as "proponents of educational change" have been steadfastly influencing changes in reading instructional materials. Prior to 1967 some changes in the content of beginning reading texts had taken place. Follett's *City Schools Reading Program* (1966) made one of the first attempts to portray youngsters in a racially mixed neighborhood. However, critics of the program have argued:

> What they did do was to present characters of several ethnic backgrounds living in an almost completely white, middle-class neighborhood. [they presented] series of stories that focused on children who were often unable to succeed in whatever they attempted to do [Blom et al., 1970, p. 201].

These same critics also analyzed *Bank Street Readers* (1966) and the *Chandler Language-Experience Readers* (1966). Their conclusions were as follows:

> First, what may appear on the basis of its cover and promotional literature to be a multiethnic first-grade reading book may, on closer inspection, contain few significant characters of ethnic background other than white Anglo Saxon. Second, including other ethnic groups does not necessarily imply that the environmental setting of the stories is any different than that of the traditional, suburban-oriented series. Third, although multiethnic series are not generally characterized by stories in which the main activity ends in failure, some authors may have a tendency to emphasize lack of success to a greater extent in their multiethnic series than they do in their traditional first-grade reading books. . . . Waite (1968) approached this problem through a clinical analysis of some character types in one multiethnic urban reading series. He focused on comparisons of white and Negro six-year-old boys and their fathers, in terms of their behavior characteristics displayed in all the stories of the series. Waite found that the Negro boy was depicted as athletic, less intelligent, impulsive, distractible, and as the object of humor. In contrast, the white boy was presented as reflective, more intelligent, and socially secure. The fathers of these two boys also showed definite individual characteristics. The white father had greater economic resources, displayed consistent masculine behaviors, and offered assistance to the Negro father. In comparison, the Negro father had fewer economic resources, performed feminine tasks or assumed feminine responsibilities in nearly half of his appearances, and accepted help from the white father [Blom et al., 1970, p. 206].

A quick look at the newer basal series from Ginn (1969), Scott, Foresman (1971), and Holt (1973) reveals the inclusion of more minority-group members than in previous editions. The concern for minority groups has also influenced the look of the trade books for students learning to read. Some of the most relevant stories are those created by black authors and published by newly formed minority-owned publishing houses.[22] *Ebony Jr!*, for instance, promises to be a very successful periodical directed to the needs and interests of black readers. Perhaps basal texts will also incorporate stories *by* minority-group members as well as stories *about* minorities. We do not all hear the beat of the same drum, but increasingly there is an awareness that different drums are, in fact, beating. Bringing

---

[22] For example, Ray Shepard, John Steptoe, and Eloise Greenfield are popular authors, and minority publishers include Associated Publishers, Washington, D.C.; Johnson Publishing Co., Inc., Chicago, Ill.; New Dimensions Publishing Co., New York; and Quinto Sol Publications, Berkeley, Calif. The Council on Interracial Books for Children, 29 West 15th St., New York, N.Y. 10011, reviews books and maintains an up-to-date list of minority publishers.

that fact to a conscious level has meant that there has followed both an opportunity and an obligation for people to determine how the materials they are developing grapple with issues relevant to the young readers in today's society. In addition, authors and publishers now realize that their materials are viewed as reflections of what the author/publisher holds to be of value. A question still unanswered empirically is: To what extent does a change in content influence the achievement and attitudes of the students?

2. Dialect Differences

Roger Shuy is well known among the linguists who have concerned themselves with the mismatch of materials to a child's culture. He has been associated with the Center for Applied Linguistics, which is concerned with finding ways to apply language research to practical situations, particularly in the area of education. (The center has, for instance, undertaken policy studies and surveys in the area of Indian education; sponsored conferences, published studies, and developed teaching materials for other specific populations; and conducted research, identified research needs, and served as a clearing-house to coordinate research from other individuals or groups.) One focus of attention for the people at the center is the concern that "the linguistic system of the ghetto Negro is different in a number of identifiable features from that of standard English" (Shuy, 1969, p. 37). The mismatch that occurs is thought by some to be serious enough to interfere with the initial processes in learning to read. Several solutions have been offered where such a mismatch occurs.

One solution is to teach standard English as a second dialect before literacy skills are introduced. This approach is advocated by Venezky (among others), and he stated that beginning reading materials should, in content, vocabulary, and syntax, be as dialect free (and culture free) as possible (Venezky, 1970).

A second solution is also offered. In this solution the dialect speaker is taught reading in standard English, but if his responses are in his own dialect, they should be accepted as correct by the teacher. Goodman advocates this strategy: " . . . children must be permitted, actually encouraged to read the way they speak" (Goodman, 1969a, p. 27).[23] Here the onus is on the teacher to learn the child's dialect in order to assess the correctness of the response. Venezky also concludes that children should be allowed to translate from writing to that form of language from which they already obtain meaning; that is, dialect differences should not be considered reading errors.

A third solution to the problem would be to present to the child

---

[23] Surely this is one reason why Goodman is a strong proponent of initial reading as translating writing to meaning directly, rather than as decoding.

materials written in his own dialect. Joan Baratz (1969) advocated this position and created materials in the vernacular for a research project (*Lester. Ollie. Old Tales.* Education Study Center, Washington, D.C., 1970). This view is also reflected in *The Psycholinguistic Reading Series* (1969) published by the City of Chicago Board of Education. A bidialectical approach is taken, and two forms of each of the little readers are printed: one in "school talk," one in "everyday talk" (dialect): The modifications made in the "everyday talk" readers are of grammatical forms only, and spelling is standard. The books are Afro-American and child-centered, dealing with the child, his family, his home, his school, and common activities. Natural language patterns are used, and each lesson is focused on a verb form. Positive attitudes are stressed, and oral discussion is encouraged.

A thorough discussion of the mismatch and the solutions offered is given by Wolfram (1970) in his article entitled "Sociolinguistic alternatives in teaching reading to non-standard speakers," and a number of relevant articles are also found in *Teaching black children to read,* edited by J. Baratz and R. Shuy (1969).

A mismatch between the speaker's oral language and the written text ranges all the way from the most extreme case of the student who speaks only a foreign language, to the case of the dialect speaker (a category which includes a broad range of differences in itself), to the case of the standard English speaker (does such a child exist?) who naturally speaks differently from the oversimplified and/or restricted language found in his first readers. Even for this latter case, some authors have urged a modification. Reid (1970) advocated that writing in beginning texts for all children should avoid literary forms of the language and use only the forms which are familiar to the beginning reader. Where, along this continuum of mismatches, it is efficient to introduce any one of the "solutions" (let alone which one) is not clear. Authors and publishers have themselves responded variously, and we have materials that address the problem quite differently: The Chicago *Psycholinguistic Readin_ Series* (with the two written forms): *DISTAR* (which teaches language forms to children to aid them in developing simple concepts); and the *Miami Linguistic Readers* (which were designed to provide students with oral-aural control of English before they proceed with the mechanics of reading). The Chicago *Psycholinguistic Reading Series* and the *Miami Linguistic Readers* were described earlier in this chapter. *DISTAR* is described below.

DISTAR Reading is a highly structured program in which groups of children respond to the teacher's questions, which are explicitly stated in the teacher's guide and coincide with the spiral-bound presentation books. Students use "take-home" worksheets and read in short story books written on eight levels of difficulty to reinforce the skills taught in the lessons. The emphasis of *DISTAR* is definitely on decoding skills, and it is suggested as a complete beginning reading program for K–2 or K–3. Mastery tests are embedded in the reading materials, and teachers must monitor student progress carefully. Siegfried Englemann and Elaine Bruner at the University of Oregon are the authors of the materials. Their instructional approach is one of high teacher control, teacher-directed presentations, frequent oral responding by the children, and reinforcement by the teacher. Isolated letter-sound correspondences are taught, and blending skills follow.

There is increasing realization that both emotional-motivational and cognitive factors are operating in the learning-to-read process, and particular attention should be given to those factors for the children whose dialect creates a mismatch with standard English. We have been made sensitive to the problem of the mismatch in recent years, but our ignorance of what to do about it has diminished only slightly. The one point of agreement among those who offer advice to the teachers is that the teacher must be careful not to reject children on the basis of their language or consider them stupid; nor should the teacher consider their language inferior, confront or attack their language, or discriminate against them because of their language. This admonishment takes us directly to the next concern.

3. Teachers' Attitudes

Any discussion of the methods and materials of beginning reading instruction cannot avoid the relevant teacher variable. A teacher's influence on any adopted method and/or materials is, of course, acknowledged. But in this section we are concerned with the attitudes and values held by teachers and promulgated by them; attitudes toward the materials in use, attitudes reflecting approval or disapproval of life as portrayed in the texts, and attitudes toward the learners themselves. Whereas story content may be influential, one well might ask if the teacher's attitude with regard to that content is not equally as important. What about the kind of questions the teacher asks? Are children guided to make evaluative judgments for themselves, or do they learn early to respond in a manner pleasing to the teacher? And what comes through to the children as "pleasing the teacher"?

The young people I see going into teaching today are concerned for the children they teach, concerned for their entire development. The teaching of reading can provide children with a tool to further their development. Interpretation, evaluation, and assimilation are common to reading *and* other modes of communication as well. Communication and thinking skills are developed through reading, writing, discussing, experimenting, experiencing . . . living in an environment of active inquiry, an environment which can be enriched by the world of books, papers, magazines, etc. to be read and interpreted, read and evaluated, read and enjoyed. When teachers respect children enough they will assume a responsibility for finding a way to reach each of them and teach each of them to become literate in the broadest sense of the word. It is possible that higher expectations and a belief in the capacities of children may make a difference in initial reading instruction, particularly if they go hand in hand with a sense of responsibility for teaching reading.

Among the visible changes in instruction which have surfaced on this wave of positive attitudes is the increased involvement of parents and the community in the education process. For example, the IPI program developed by the University of Pittsburgh has built in the relationship very systematically, as did the SWRL program.

Another change is in the *emphasis* on the teacher's attitude in some programs, e.g., *Action-Reading*. Though this is only one aspect of George Cureton's program, a description of this program is included at this point, for it was developed specifically for inner-city children of mixed racial and ethnic backgrounds, and it emphasizes parent involvement and positive teacher attitudes.

Allyn and Bacon, Inc., published the *Action-Reading* (1973) approach developed by George Cureton, whose philosophy, as much as method, pervades the program. The first basic assumption is that "children, without regard to their racial or economic background, can learn to read if they are effectively taught," and the first steps in the program are directed toward success for the children. Teachers and children literally act out the relationship between the visual stimuli of letters and a variety of sounds; they act out the combining of sounds into words. The class is taught together "as a gang," and it is a noisy, active situation with a lot of positive reinforcement from the teacher. The approach is defined by physical involvement, pace, high expectations, and positive reinforcement.

Each sound is cued to an object which is pictured on the "alphamobile." (E.g., "aah" is cued to "apple," "buh" is cued to "book," and "kuh" to "can."[24]) The isolated sounds and/or their pictured objects are then combined to make a word. Thus a picture of a book ("buh"), an apple ("aah"), and a tooth ("tuh") would signify "bat." Comprehension and functional sight words are also incorporated into the program, to which 3 hours every day are to be devoted. Reading orally every day is recommended, and material slightly above the gang's level incorporating many different types of literature is suggested.

In *Action-Reading* parents are prompted to participate both in school and at home, and specific teaching suggestions are given to them.

The *Action-Reading Kit* includes a teacher's guide, an alphamobile

---

[24] "Aah," "buh," etc., represent the manner in which these sounds are expressed (i.e., written out) in the teacher's guide. The alphamobile consists of twenty-six plastic ovals (12 inches long) with these picture cues printed on both sides (no letters). They are attached to hooks and hung from a cord where they may easily be rearranged.

with cord and hooks, sound cards, word cards, duplicator masters for worksheets and parents' letters, and student profile sheets.

4. Government Funding

The U.S. Office of Education sponsored a series of first-grade studies in reading discussed earlier in this chapter. Since the expenditure of that large sum of money, reading has acquired government support in numerous other projects. Penney and Hjelm (1970) report that over the several years prior to 1970, the USOE allocated nearly $12 million for 257 separate reading projects. Title I funds and Title III funds have been used to finance reading and reading-related activities. Several of the Research and Development Laboratories (Pittsburgh, SWRL, Wisconsin) have ongoing projects in initial reading instruction, as mentioned earlier, and the Targeted Research and Development Program on Reading was also funded by the USOE. While no instructional issue has been completely resolved by these projects, there is an abundance of research to be looked at again and data to be reanalyzed; there are new programs/practices whose effectiveness may be examined critically; there is experimentation proposed that should further our knowledge; and there is a growing communication between disciplines which should be enlightening. Any and all of these efforts may find support from government funding.

The national Right-to-Read effort has been funded by the federal government. A description of the Right-to-Read office and recent developments is given on pages 38–40 of this volume. Its influence on beginning reading instruction will become apparent as the model programs gain more publicity and as the materials developed for tutoring programs are disseminated.

The National Institute of Education (NIE) has funded $10 million for its Field Initiated Studies program for 1973. The studies represent a wide range of educational problems and issues, and "reading" came in for a fair share of the funding (Welsh, 1973, p. 9).

On a local level, considerable amounts of money are spent on materials, of course. Many of these materials are unproved, in the sense that there is little data to support their effectiveness. One manner in which school systems have elected to cope with this situation is to underwrite "performance-based contracts." Publishers and other independent firms supply to the school all reading materials, consultants, and/or training for teachers, and they guarantee a particular level of reading achievement in a given time. At the end of that period, usually an academic year, school districts are reimbursed a certain amount from the original payment to the publisher for each of the students who have failed to achieve the stated goals. The goals are usually expressed in terms of grade levels on standardized achievement tests. There are many unresolved issues surrounding

"accountability" in general. Though not considered here, of great importance are questions pertaining to the design and implementation of the
evaluation procedures to be used.

It is perhaps appropriate to suggest also that research efforts and
government funding might be used in another way. An orientation toward
improving existing programs in the schools might be considered as an
alternative to continually changing programs on the basis of questionable
data. Close monitoring of programs and materials, day to day and week to
week, to determine how they might be made more efficient or used more
effectively would provide an opportunity for the teachers and students to
participate in the evaluation as well. Such "formative" evaluation can
easily take place after a curriculum has been adopted and could help to
direct the school's efforts toward those goals which it feels are most important (Bloom et al., 1971, p. 117).

SUMMARY

Table 1[25] provides a summary of some of the relevant characteristics of
beginning reading programs discussed in this chapter. It is my purpose in
presenting this table to indicate how these particular newer programs
appear to reflect some of the influences from educators, psychologists,
linguists, and researchers; from technological developments; and from a
growing social and political awareness as discussed in the major sections
of this chapter. Variables are limited to those which could be rated by
inspection of the programs. Most programs on the table were initially
included in the chapter as illustrations of an effect of one of these influences. And although as a group they constitute only a small sample of the
many materials recently published, inspection of the data in Table 1 does
suggest certain trends.

Before considering these trends, I wish to make more explicit the
relationship between the variables in Table 1 and the influences considered earlier. Chall (1967), Goodman (1969), Bond and Dykstra (1967),
and Corder (1971) all raised the issue of the initial emphasis of programs;
variables related to that issue are found in Table 1 in the section entitled
"Initial Emphasis." Other variables related are "Vocabulary control" under
"Reader Content" and the type of words introduced in the "Word Attack
Skills" section where the actual techniques of teaching are summarized.
Issues of the relevance of the story content expressed by Busch (1972)
and by Rose, Zimet, and Blom (1972) are rated in the section "Lifestyle

[25] Table 1 is a modification of the more technical classification scheme presented
in Chall (1967).

and values portrayed." MacKay and Thompson's (1968) concern with reading as a part of the total language arts is reflected in the section "Initial Emphasis" and also under "Child's Behavior." Ruddell and Williams's (1972) attention to the level of teacher questioning is considered in "Cognitive level of questions in teacher's guide" under "Teacher's Role." The contradictory points of view of Smith (1971) and Venezky (1972) are reflected in judgments made on the variable "Vocabulary control." Blumenthal's opinion on the relevance of linguistics and psycholinguistics to reading pedagogy cannot be translated directly to an evaluation of the data in Table 1.

The effect of the work at the research centers is sprinkled throughout the data, but perhaps most applicable is the consideration of "Behavioral objectives," "Tests," and "Teacher-training kits" under "Components," as well as "Illustrations" under "Reader Content."

Technological developments are reflected in the section "Components."

The issues arising from a growing social and political awareness are reflected in the section "Reader Content." Two concerns, teacher attitude and government funding, are beyond the scope of this table, except that "Parental Involvement" does, to a certain extent, set the stage for an expected teacher attitude of concern for the child.

With the above guide to connecting the table variables to the influences presented, I should like to present a further guide to the interpretation of the symbols used in Table 1. A check mark ($\sqrt{}$) indicates that a program incorporates a given feature, and a blank cell indicates that the program has not included that feature or has paid little attention to it. A check plus ($\sqrt{} +$) indicates that the variable has received very strong emphasis, and a "T" indicates that the teacher must exercise her option in including or emphasizing a particular variable. Other abbreviations are self-explanatory.

Although I have inspected only a small sample of recent programs, consideration of the individual variables might suggest some apparent trends. The reader could thus be alerted to look for evidence in other materials to confirm or refute my summary statements. Each set of variables is discussed as data from Table 1 are interpreted below.

Components

Several large publishing houses have continued to invest in complete basal series with many components intended for levels K–6 or K–8. However, many of the programs sampled begin with kindergarten materials and are confined to the primary grades. Apparently publishers are not feeling compelled to produce only programs which extend to the upper levels, and beginning programs are seen to have a viable market. Teacher training in intermediate and advanced reading skills becomes more crucial if teachers are apt not to be following a teacher's guide in a published program.

TABLE 1

Thirteen Reading Programs Analyzed in Terms of Selected Variables

	Action-Reading (Allyn and Bacon, 1973)	Alpha One (New Dimensions in Education, 1969)	Breakthrough to Literacy (Bowmar, 1973)	Chicago Psycholinguistic (Chicago Board of Education, 1969)
COMPONENTS				
Grade levels included	K,1	1,2	K,1,2	1
Teacher's guide	√	√	√	√
Children's readers		√	√	√
Programmed texts				
Workbooks, dittos, etc.	√	√		√
Audio: records, tapes		√	√	
Visual: films, transparencies, charts	√	√	√	
Supplementary books (literature)			T	
Teacher-training kits				
Tutoring program				
Behavioral objectives and/or criterion measures†	√	√		
Tests (placement, diagnostic, summative)		Sum		
READER CONTENT				
Selections				
From literature				
Created for readers		√	√	√
Lifestyle and values portrayed				
White, black, Hispanic, Indian, mixed			Wh	Bl
Urban, suburban, rural, mixed			Sub	Urb/Sub
Low SES, mid SES, hi SES, mixed			Mid	Mid
Child-centered, community, nature, fantasy		Ch,Fan	Ch	Ch
Illustrations				
None, relevant, general		Rel	Rel	Rel
Vocabulary control				
Meaningfulness/frequency			√	√
Phonic regularity (grapheme/phoneme)	√	√+		
Word patterns	√			
WORD ATTACK SKILLS FOR EARLIEST READERS				
Isolated letter/sound	√	√+	T	
Word patterns	√			
Individual words	√		√	√
Blending sounds into words (synthetic)	√	√	T	
Abstracting letters/sounds from words (analytic)	√		T	√
Direction emphasized in introducing elements				
Symbol to sound		√		
Sound to symbol(s)	√+		√+	√
Set for "diversity" or "regularity"	Reg	Reg	Div	Div

Color Keys to Reading (Appleton Century Crofts, 1973) Exp. Edition	Holt Basic Reading System (Holt, Rinehart and Winston, 1973)	Listen Look Learn (Educational Developmental Laboratories, 1972)	Miami Linguistic Readers (D. C. Heath, 1970)	Palo Alto Reading Program (Harcourt, Brace & World, 1968)	Reading 360 (Ginn, 1969)	SWRL Beginning Reading Program (SWRL, 1972)	Scott, Foresman Reading Systems (Scott, Foresman, 1971)	Structural Reading Program (Random House, 1972)
K,1,2	K–6	K–3	1,2	K–3	K–6	K–1	K–8	K–3
√	√	√	√	√	√	√	√	√
√	√	√	√	√	√	√	√	√
√*		√	√	√				
√	√	√			√	√	√	√
	√	√			√	√		T
	√	√			√	√	√	
					√	√		
					√			
	√	√ +	√	√	√	√	√	
Sum,Pl	Pl,Sum, Diag	Sum	Pl,Sum	Sum	Pl,Sum, Diag	Pl,Sum, Diag	Pl,Sum	√
	√	√			√		√	√
√	√	√	√	√	√	√	√	√
Mix	Mix	Mix	Mix‡	Wh/Mix	Mix	None‡	Mix	Mix
Mix	Mix	Mix		Sub	Mix		Mix	Mix
Mix	Mix	Mix		Mid	Mix		Mix	Mix
Ch	Mix	Ch	Mix	Ch,Na	Mix	Fan	Mix	Mix
Rel	Rel	Rel	Rel	Rel	Rel	Rel	Rel	Rel
	√	√		√	√	√	√ +	
√			√	√ +		√ +		√
			√ +	√ +		√ +		√
√				√		√ +		
	√	√	√ +	√	√	√ +	√	√ +
√	√	√ +	√	√ +	√ +	√	√	√
	√	√	√	√	√	√ +	√	√
						√	√	
√ +								
Div	Div	Div	Reg	Reg	Div	Reg	Div	Reg

Table 1 (*Cont.*)

	Action-Reading (Allyn and Bacon, 1973)	Alpha One (New Dimensions in Education, 1969)	Breakthrough to Literacy (Bowman, 1973)	Chicago Psycholinguistic (Chicago Board of Education, 1969)
Other cues		People/		
Diacritics, color, other	Objects	letters		
Contextual: text or pictures		Pic	Txt&Pic	Txt&Pic
INITIAL EMPHASIS				
Comprehension	✓		✓+	✓
Decoding	✓+	✓	✓	
Writing		✓	✓+	
Communication (language arts)			✓+	✓
PACE				
Rapid, moderate, slow, flexible	Rapid	Slo	Flex	Mod
Controlled by teacher or child	Tchr	Tchr	Ch	Tchr
CHILD's BEHAVIOR				
Discussion		✓	✓	✓
Listening activities	✓	✓	✓	✓
Oral reading in readers		✓	✓	✓
Silent reading in readers		✓	✓	✓
Answering questions	✓	✓	✓	✓
Spelling	✓	✓	✓	
Learns phonic relationships	✓	✓		
Writing	✓	✓	✓	
TEACHER's ROLE				
Introduces new elements (words/letters)	✓	✓		✓
Reads daily with children			✓	✓
Follows routine of guide (for selections)	✓	✓		✓
Cognitive level of questions in teacher's guide				
Recall	✓	✓		✓
Problem solving		✓		✓
Creating ideas			✓	✓
Evaluative		✓		
Optional (teacher decision)			✓	
PARENT INVOLVEMENT	✓+	✓		

✓ = Variable is present to a significant degree.
✓+ = Variable is emphasized.
T = Teacher's option.
= Variable is not emphasized.
° Workbooks in Color Keys are semiprogrammed.
† A statement of skills taught is also included in this category.
‡ Animal characters are used throughout.

	Color Keys to Reading (Appleton Century Crofts, 1973) Exp. Edition	Holt Basic Reading System (Holt, Rinehart and Winston, 1973)	Listen Look Learn (Educational Developmental Laboratories, 1972)	Miami Linguistic Readers (D. C. Heath, 1970)	Palo Alto Reading Program (Harcourt, Brace & World, 1968)	Reading 360 (Ginn, 1969)	SWRL Beginning Reading Program (SWRL, 1972)	Scott, Foresman Reading Systems (Scott, Foresman, 1971)	Structural Reading Program (Random House, 1972)
Color	Txt&Pic	Txt&Pic	Txt&Pic	Txt&Pic	Txt&Pic	Txt&Pic	Txt&Pic	Txt&Pic	Txt&Pic
	✓	✓+ ✓ ✓	✓ ✓ ✓	✓+ ✓	✓ ✓+ ✓+	✓+ ✓	✓	✓+ ✓	✓ ✓
	Rapid Tchr	Mod/Rap Tchr	Flex Both	Mod Tchr	Mod Tchr	Mod Tchr	Slo Tchr	Mod Tchr	Mod Tchr
	✓ ✓ ✓ ✓ ✓ ✓	✓ ✓ ✓ ✓ ✓ ✓	✓ ✓+ ✓ ✓ ✓	✓ ✓ ✓ ✓ ✓ ✓	✓ ✓ ✓ ✓ ✓ ✓	✓ ✓ ✓ ✓ ✓ ✓	✓ ✓ ✓	✓ ✓ ✓ ✓	✓ ✓ ✓ ✓ ✓ ✓
	✓ ✓ ✓	✓ ✓ ✓	✓ ✓ ✓	✓ ✓ ✓	✓ ✓ ✓	✓ ✓ ✓	✓ ✓ ✓	✓ ✓ ✓	✓ ✓ ✓
		✓ ✓ ✓ ✓	✓ ✓	✓+ ✓	✓	✓ ✓ ✓ ✓	✓	✓ ✓ ✓ ✓	✓
	✓					✓	✓	✓	

SOURCE: Adapted from Chall (1967, p. 337).

Further developments in teacher training at the research centers will be very important.

Teachers' guides remain an integral part of every scheme, and children's readers have been created for all but one of the thirteen programs inspected, as have children's workbooks. Few self-instructional programmed texts have been produced for these young children, but audio and/or visual aids are increasingly available. Going beyond data in Table 1, it is surprising that the increased availability of instruments for presenting audio and visual materials has not made as great an impact as predicted in the mid 1960s. There are many materials marketed, but I don't believe this avenue of instruction has been anywhere near fully exploited. There may be some resistance on the part of teachers who feel their role has been usurped or who feel the teaching/learning process must be more "personal." Certainly automation incurs added expense; however, one would expect further developments to occur in this area.

Five of the publishers actually include supplementary literature books for the children, and one strongly suggests their use. Earlier (page 120) I mentioned the children's books available with records and tapes. In addition, attractive packages of children's books are being marketed. While the analysis of the reading programs indicates some increase in the use of children's literature, it is perhaps fair once again to go beyond these data and hypothesize a trend toward a significant increase in the use of children's literature in the reading programs.

Included only quite recently are such components as a teacher-training kit or a tutorial program, and one might hypothesize further developments here.

Behavioral objectives and tests are found in many programs. Behavioral objectives range from very specific statements such as "make the sounds for s and m (when shown each letter and asked to make the sound)" in Unit 1 of the SWRL program to more general statements of the skills taught.

Three publishers have included diagnostic tests intended to pinpoint the children's areas of weakness. Placement tests which give an indication of where a child should enter a given system are also prevalent. Tests designed to be used in these ways, if successful, should further promote a focus on individual children's needs. The apparent trend to use objectives and measures to "individualize" is one of great importance.

The "individualization" that arises from the use of objectives and measures has led to very precise specifications for instructional materials and for student performance. The reading process has been broken into subskills or components, and behavioral objectives have been sequenced within the programs. While this provides an excellent research mechanism and valuable data for the evaluation of both the child and the materials, there may be some danger in adopting specific sequences of subskills as a reading program. It is possible for children to be locked into working through subcomponents regardless of their own level of development in the learning-to-read process. Do we know, for instance, that the visual perception of isolated letters should precede perception of letters in context and that both should precede word identification for all (or any) children? Might the optimal sequence for certain children be the reverse of this?[26]

Reader Content

While all programs continue to create stories and selections for their graded readers, several have included excerpts from children's literature. All these newer programs have illustrations which are related to the content. These illustrations, as much if not more so than the story content, help to portray a wider diversity of lifestyles than what is shown in the earlier readers. Different ethnic groups and different environments are apt to be represented. A third of the programs portray mostly middle-class settings, but a wider range of socioeconomic levels has been introduced in many readers. We no longer find the white middle-class suburban child dominating all readers. One program (SWRL) avoids the issue of the representativeness of its characters and depicts anthropomorphic animal characters only, no people. While the stories in all of the programs are mostly child-centered, a wider array of story genre is present now than in earlier programs. Considerable emphasis has been placed on the importance of the literary quality of children's reading material for cognitive as well as affective reasons.

The vocabulary used in the beginning levels of most of these programs is very tightly controlled. Five of the programs introduce words on the basis of their phonic regularity and word patterns (see page 132). Two others sequence letter-sound relationships and introduce words which conform to the relationships taught. The programs of six publishers, with their primary emphasis on "meaning," control the vocabulary by systematically introducing words expected to have greater meaning for the children (words which are frequent in the children's oral vocabularies and frequent in most written material), and there is no attempt to control for

---

[26] One factor that was not considered in this chapter which is of considerable importance is that of the trend toward criterion-referenced testing instead of norm-referenced testing. If criterion-referenced testing becomes more common in reading, we will have to investigate the ramifications of defining specific criterion performance in subskills of reading. We might hypothesize that demanding criterion performance in certain subskills before allowing a child to go on in a specified sequence of instruction may, in fact, be hindering his own efforts to develop strategies quite different from what the program outlines. In my opinion, chances are very good that there is no one optimal sequence.

the regularity of letter-sound correspondences or for word patterns. However, three of these same six programs do teach word attack skills via word patterns as indicated below.

Word Attack Skills

Each of the reading programs is structured to teach the child to learn appropriate oral responses to the written words presented. Two of the programs teach only isolated letter-sound correspondences and the blending of these into words (*Alpha One* and *Color Keys*). Three others which also teach isolated letter-sound correspondences (*Action, Palo Alto,* and SWRL) combine this teaching with attention to the spelling patterns of the words, to blending (synthesis), and to abstracting letter-sound correspondences from known whole words (analysis) as well. Six programs that have their vocabulary introduction controlled for meaning teach individual words and later teach letter-sound relationships by abstracting them from the known words. A recent development in this type of program is the attention to word spelling patterns; this is found in four of these same six programs. Of the linguistic programs of the 1960s which taught solely through word patterns (Bloomfield's *Let's Read,* the *Merrill Linguistic Readers,* SRA's *Basic Reading Series,* and Stern's *Structural Reading*), only one has been revised and republished since 1967 (*Structural Reading*). Two new linguistic programs (*Miami Linguistic Readers* and *Palo Alto*) have emerged. The concept of teaching through spelling patterns ("linguistic" approach) has been incorporated into both the phonic programs and the meaning-emphasis programs, as each devotes some attention to word structure. The future direction in teaching children word attack skills appears to be one where the teaching techniques emphasized in any one approach may be considered eclectic. In particular, attention to letter-sound associations is generally given sooner and in larger doses, even in the meaning-emphasis programs, than in programs developed prior to 1968.

In actual teaching practice the direction for introducing elements in the reading program is somewhat ambiguous. Whether the sounds of the letters and words are presented first, followed by their written counterparts, or vice versa is not easy to discern. And while the philosophy of beginning with what the child knows (the sound) and moving to the unknown (the letters or words) is espoused in several programs, the degree to which that pedagogy is followed through must vary considerably. The "set for diversity" (in most of the programs) arises from the variation in sound/spelling correspondences when the initial vocabulary is selected on a basis other than phonic regularity. Therefore, if a "set for diversity" has been adopted, the vocabulary is likely to be introduced in either direction. In programs espousing a "set for regularity," it is easier for a teacher to choose whether the visual symbols shall be presented prior to or after the phonemes. But here, too, there is some ambiguity, as many teachers consciously attempt to do both simultaneously.

Usually pictures and text are used to aid the young readers in their first attempts at reading. *Action, Alpha One,* and *Color Keys* provide other aids as well for helping the children to remember symbol/sound associations. The "alphamobile" in the *Action* program (see pages 128–129) and the letter-people in the *Alpha One* program provide cues for the one-to-one correspondences. *Color Keys* codes the various letters or letter combinations representing nine of the vowels (sounds); each is given a different color (see page 117).

Initial Emphasis

An inspection of the data in Table 1 on the initial emphasis of the beginning programs reinforces the notion that there is a tendency to blur the lines of distinction between the meaning-emphasis programs and the decoding-emphasis programs. Within any one program relatively greater attention (than was the case some years ago) is now given to that aspect, comprehension or decoding, which is not considered the primary emphasis.

Writing and communication skills have gained greater visibility in several programs as well. It is interesting to note this trend toward a more global view of reading taking place almost simultaneously with another trend to isolate the components of reading for instructional purposes.

Pace

I rated the pace at which a program progresses as "rapid," "moderate," or "slow" according to how quickly the various elements or words were introduced. The ratings are relative to each other, and those programs rated "slow" (*Alpha One* and *SWRL*) spend the most time establishing each relationship taught. Two programs are rated "flexible" (*Breakthrough* and *Listen Look Learn*) because in both individual children have a greater influence on the rate at which new material is introduced. In the former the child actually asks for words as he finds use for them, and in the latter the instructional cycles are adjusted to the child's needs (pages 110, 121).

Child's Behavior

In examining the behaviors exhibited by the child within the various programs, we find that the array of responses to be made is quite diversified. Perhaps I should have designated some of the responses (e.g., spelling) as being included in more programs, but only those programs that specifically ask for the behavior have been marked. The *Action* program was most difficult to assess on these variables because there are no readers for the children. Therefore, oral and silent reading may be included in that program in other contexts. Variables in this section are self-explanatory, and the view that reading instruction should include speaking, writing, listening, and reading is revealed here also.

Teacher's Role

A teacher's role may be as predominant as she wishes it to be, no matter what the program specifies. However, certain teacher behaviors are made explicit in most of the manuals, and these are indicated in this section of Table 1. Of particular interest is my attempt to classify the level of questions given to teachers to use with their children. In Ruddell's study, classrooms were videotaped, and the questions asked by the teachers were categorized. Sixty-eight percent of the questions asked were factual (see page 111) or of the recall type. In examining these programs it is apparent that authors and publishers have become aware of the need to go beyond factual questioning. It is encouraging to find that in many of the programs they do so even at the earliest levels.

Parent Involvement

Perhaps the *Action* program (more than any other) consciously stresses the active involvement of parents. George Cureton (its creator) is currently in the first phase of an experimental program with inner-city children in Boston. He is spending the first few months demonstrating the program to parents of the children to be involved. The effects of this variable have not been singled out in any study of which I am aware, but one can hypothesize that they are not negligible.

This overview of the variables related to influences on initial reading instruction during the past 5 years indicates that the current materials, methods, and learning environments are greatly diversified. No one method, set of materials, philosophy, or theoretical rationale has been agreed upon. Even given an agreement upon a particular objective, the pathways taken to implement it are quite diverse. For instance, the trend toward individualizing instruction has different meanings for many of its advocates. Individualized instruction rarely means a differentiated approach to the process itself based on a child's ability, personality characteristics, modality preferences, maturity, or other factors. Apparently, it most often refers to "pace" within a sequence of highly structured instruction in the various subskills of reading.

Quite in contrast to the highly structured sequences are those programs which emphasize reading instruction as only one component in the area of language and communication, and language and communication as only one aspect of the child's development. Such programs tend to focus on examining the child's development in all areas and on responding to his individual progress in reading skills and his development in reading education. This trend signals the need for more in-depth training for teachers.

Materials that will be appropriate to a child's interests and his level of development at a particular moment must be made known. Profound familiarity with components of reading programs, knowledge of the process of learning to read, information on the effectiveness of various learning environments on different children, and a real acquaintance with the world of children's literature are essential. An awareness that reading education is an ongoing process and that many factors play an important role can better equip the teacher to cope with the daily problems in the classroom. Armed with as much information as is currently available (and that is not yet adequate), the teacher will make better judgments and rely less on prescribed instructional materials. Every time a teacher reads or writes a letter, a word, a sentence, or a story, some teaching/learning of reading is occurring for one or another child in the classroom.

In addition to the influence of the instructional materials and the teacher's expertise, there are other influential variables from the school, the home, the community, and society. Inquiry into these factors has been most brief in this chapter, but we must be aware of them as well.

Conclusions drawn from this overview must be considered as only a part of the larger concerns of reading education. As we continue to pose relevant questions, examine earlier answers to similar questions, and seek our own answers, we continually put the current trends in beginning reading instruction into a better perspective.

REFERENCES

Atkinson, R. C., & Hansen, D. N. Computer-assisted instruction in initial reading: The Stanford project. *Reading Research Quarterly*, Fall 1966, **II**(1), 5–25.

Baratz, Joan C. Teaching reading in an urban Negro school system. In J. C. Baratz & R. W. Shuy (Eds.), *Teaching black children to read*. Washington, D.C.: Center for Applied Linguistics, 1969. Pp. 92–116.

Baratz, Joan C., & Shuy, Roger W. (Eds.) *Teaching black children to read*. Washington, D.C.: Center for Applied Linguistics, 1969.

Beck, Isabel L., & Mitroff, Donna D. *The rationale and design of a primary grades reading system for an individualized classroom*. Pittsburgh: Learning Research and Development Center, University of Pittsburgh, 1972.

Bereiter, C., & Englemann, S. *Teaching disadvantaged children in the preschool*. Englewood Cliffs, N.J.: Prentice-Hall, Inc., 1966.

Blom, Gaston E., Waite, Richard R., & Zimet, Sara G. A motivational content analysis of children's primers. In Harry Levin & Joanna P. Williams (Eds.), *Basic studies on reading*. New York: Basic Books, Inc., Publishers, 1970. Pp. 188–221.

Bloom, Benjamin S. *Stability and change in human characteristics*. New York: John Wiley & Sons, Inc., 1964.

Bloom, B. S., Hastings, J. T., & Madaus, G. F. *Handbook on formative and summative evaluation of student learning.* New York: McGraw-Hill Book Company, 1971.

Blumenthal, A. L. On the relevance of language and cognition research to reading pedagogy. Address delivered to Pre-convention Institute, International Reading Association, Detroit, 1972.

Bond, G. L., & Dykstra, R. The cooperative research program in first-grade instruction. *Reading Research Quarterly,* Summer 1967, 2(4), 5–142.

Busch, Fred. Interest, relevance, and learning to read. In S. G. Zimet (Ed.), *What children read in school.* New York: Grune & Stratton, Inc., 1972. Pp. 19–26.

Callaway, Rolland. Social perspectives on reading: Politics. In James B. McDonald (Ed.), *Social perspective on Reading.* Newark, Del.: International Reading Association, 1973. Pp. 3–14.

Chall, Jeanne. *Learning to read: The great debate.* New York: McGraw-Hill Book Company, 1967.

Corder, R. *The information base for reading.* Final Report, Project No. 0-9031. Berkeley, Calif.: Educational Testing Service, 1971.

Downing, John. *Comparative reading. Cross-national studies of behavior and processes in reading and writing.* New York: The Macmillan Company, 1973.

Downing, John, & Thackray, Derek. *Reading readiness.* London: University of London Press, Ltd., 1971.

Durkin, Dolores. *Children who read early.* New York: Teachers College Press, 1966.

Erikson, E. H. Identity and the life cycle. *Psychological Issues,* 1959, 1, 82–88.

Flanagan, J. C. Project plan: Basic assumptions, implementation, and significance. *Journal of Secondary Education,* 1971, 46(4), 172–178.

Frankenstein, Roselyn. *A beginning reading program "Stepping stones to reading": Summary report.* Pittsburgh: Learning Research and Development Center, University of Pittsburgh, 1971.

Freire, Paulo. The adult literacy process as cultural action for freedom. *Harvard Educational Review,* 1970, 40(2), 205–208.

Freire, Paulo. *Pedagogy of the oppressed.* Translation by Myra Bergman Ramos. New York: Herder and Herder, Inc., 1971.

Friedlander, K. Children's books and their function in latency and prepuberty. *American Image,* 1942, 3, 129–150.

Gleitman, Lila, & Rozin, Paul. Teaching reading by use of a syllabary. *Reading Research Quarterly,* Summer 1973, 8, 447–483.

Goodman, Kenneth S. Dialect barriers to reading comprehension. In Joan C. Baratz & Roger W. Shuy (Eds.), *Teaching black children to read,* Washington, D.C.: Center for Applied Linguistics, 1969a.

Goodman, Kenneth S. Words and morphemes in reading. In K. S. Goodman & J. Fleming. *Psycholinguistics and the teaching of reading.* Newark, Del.: International Reading Association, 1969b. Pp. 25–33.

Henrie, Samuel N. (Sr. Ed.) *A sourcebook of elementary curricula programs and projects.* From the ALERT Information System. San Francisco: Far West Laboratory for Educational Research and Development, 1972.

Huey, E. B. *The psychology and pedagogy of reading.* New York: The Macmillan Company, 1908. Reprinted at Cambridge, Mass.: The M.I.T. Press, 1968.

Kohlberg, Lawrence, & Mayer, Rochelle. Development as the aim of education. *Harvard Educational Review*, 1972, 42(4), 449–496.

MacKay, David & Thompson, Brian. The initial teaching of reading and writing. (Some notes toward a theory of literacy.) *Programme in linguistics and English teaching, paper no. 3* (Communication Research Centre, Department of General Linguistics). London: University College, London, and Longmans, Green & Co., Ltd., 1968.

MacKay, D., Thompson, B., & Schaub, P. *Breakthrough to literacy: Teacher's manual.* London: Longmans, Green & Co., Ltd., 1970.

Matthews, M. M. *Teaching to read, historically considered.* Chicago: The University of Chicago Press, 1966.

McCracken, Robert A., & McCracken, Marlene J. *Reading is only the tiger's tail.* San Rafael: Leswing Press, 1972.

Moffett, James. *A student-centered language arts curriculum, grades K–13: A handbook for teachers.* Boston: Houghton Mifflin Company, 1968.

O'Neil, Wayne. Properly literate. *Harvard Educational Review*, 1970, 40(2), 260–263.

Otto, W., & Peterson, W. *A statement of skills and objectives for the Wisconsin prototype system of reading skill development.* Working Paper No. 23. Madison: Wisconsin Research and Development Center for Cognitive Learning, University of Wisconsin, 1969.

Peller, L. Reading and daydreams in latency, boy-girl differences. *Journal of American Psychoanalytic Association*, 1958, 6, 56–70.

Penney, Monte, & Hjelm, Howard F. The targeted research and development program on reading. Part I, History of the U.S. Office of Education's support of reading research. *American Educational Research Journal*, May 1970, 7, 425–434.

Popp, Helen M. *Test project for the LRDC beginning reading program, Stepping stones to reading.* Learning Research and Development Center, University of Pittsburgh, 1972.

Postman, Neil. The politics of reading. *Harvard Educational Review*, 1970, 2, 244–252.

Reid, Jessie. The most important R (Part I). *Teacher's World*, December 25, 1970, 3189, 20.

Rose, C., Zimet, S. G., & Blom, G. E. Content counts: Children have preferences in reading textbook stories. *Elementary English*, January 1972, 49(1), 14–19.

Rose, C., Zimet, S. G., & Blom, G. E. Children's preferences. In S. G. Zimet (Ed.), *What children read in school.* New York: Grune & Stratton, Inc., 1972. Pp. 39–46.

Rosner, Jerome. *The development and validation of an individualized perceptual skills curriculum.* Pittsburgh: Learning Research and Development Center, University of Pittsburgh, 1972.

Ruddell, Robert B., & Williams, Arthur C. *A research investigation of a literacy teaching model, Project delta.* EPDA Project No. 005262. Washington, D.C.: U.S. Dept. of Health, Education and Welfare, 1972.

Samuels, S. Jay, & LaBerge, David. Minnesota reading research project. Mimeographed unpublished report. Minneapolis: Center for Research in Human Learning, University of Minnesota, 1973.

Shuy, Roger W. Some language and cultural differences in a theory of reading. In Kenneth S. Goodman, & James T. Fleming (Eds.), *Psycholinguistics and the teaching of reading.* Newark, Del.: International Reading Association, 1969. Pp. 34–47.

Smith, Frank. *Understanding reading—a psycholinguistic analysis of reading and learning to read.* New York: Holt, Rinehart and Winston, Inc., 1971.

Southgate, V., & Roberts, G. R. *Reading—which approach?* London: University of London Press, Ltd., 1970.

Stauffer, R. The verdict: Speculative controversy. *Reading Teacher,* May 1966, **19**(8), 563–564 & 575.

Taba, Hilda, & Elzey, Freeman F. Teaching strategies and thought processes. *Teachers College Record,* 1964, **65**, 524–534.

Venezky, Richard L. English orthography: Its graphical structure and its relation to sound. *Reading Research Quarterly,* 1967, **2**(3), 75–105.

Venezky, Richard L. *Non-standard language and reading.* Working Paper No. 43. Madison: Wisconsin Research and Development Center for Cognitive Learning, University of Wisconsin, 1970.

Venezky, Richard L. *Language and cognition in reading.* Technical Report No. 188. Madison: Wisconsin Research and Development Center for Cognitive Learning, University of Wisconsin, 1972.

Waite, Richard R. Further attempts to integrate and urbanize first-grade reading textbooks. *Journal of Negro Education,* 1968, **37**(1), 62–69.

Welsh, James. FIS awards: Fund for one in fifteen. *Educational Researcher,* August 1973, **2**(8), 8–9.

Wolfram, Walt. Sociolinguistic alternatives in teaching reading to non-standard speakers. *Reading Research Quarterly,* Fall 1970, **6**(1), 9–33.

Zimet, Sara Goodman (Ed.) *What children read in school. A critical analysis of primary reading textbooks.* New York: Grune & Stratton, Inc., 1972.

INSTRUCTIONAL MATERIALS

(Programs, projects, machines, etc., mentioned in the chapter)

Action-Reading. Cureton, George. Boston: Allyn and Bacon, Inc., 1973.

Alpha One. Reiss, Elayne, & Friedman, Rita. Jericho, N.Y.: New Dimensions in Education, 1969.

Bank Street Readers. Bank Street College of Education. New York: The Macmillan Company, 1966.

Basic Reading. McCracken, Glen, & Walcutt, Charles C. Philadelphia: J. B. Lippincott Company, 1966.

Basic Reading Series. Rasmussen, Donald, & Goldberg, Lynn. Chicago: Science Research Associates, Inc., 1967.

Beginning Reading Program. Southwest Regional Laboratory for Educational Research and Development (SWRL). Boston: Ginn and Company, 1972.

Bell and Howell Language Master. Bell and Howell Co., Audio Visual Products Division, Chicago, Ill.

Borg Warner System 80. Niles, Ill.: Borg Warner Educational Systems.

Breakthrough to Literacy. MacKay, David, & Thompson, Brian. Glendale, Calif.: Bowmar, 1973.

Chandler Language-Experience Readers. Carillo, Lawrence W. (Ed.) San Francisco: Chandler Publishing Company, 1966.

Children's Heritage. (Records and storybooks.) Scott Education Division, Scott Graphics, Holyoke, Mass.

City Schools Reading Program. Writers' Comm. of the Great Cities School Improvement Program of the Detroit Public Schools. Chicago: Follett Publishing Company, 1966.

Color Keys to Reading (formerly *Stepping Stones to Reading*). Learning Research and Development Center, University of Pittsburgh (Paul Kjeldergaard, Robert Glaser, & Roselyn Frankenstein, Authors). New York: Appleton Century Crofts, in press.

Cooperative Individualized Reading Project. Lipp, Joe J. (Project Director). Westport, Conn.: LEA Westport Board of Education.

Council on Interracial Books for Children, 29 West 15th St., New York, N.Y. 10011.

DISTAR Reading. Englemann, Siegfried, & Bruner, Elaine C. Chicago: Science Research Associates, Inc., 1969.

Ebony Jr! Johnson, John H. (Editor and Publisher). Chicago: Johnson Publishing Company, Vol. 1, 1969.

Educational Futures Inc., North Haven, Conn.

Ginn Basic Readers. Russell, David H., et al. Boston: Ginn and Company, 1961.

Grolier Creative Reading Program. Creative Learning, Inc. New York: Grolier Educational Corp., 1969.

Holt Basic Reading System. Evertts, Eldonna L., Hunt, Lyman C., and Weiss, Bernard J. New York: Holt, Rinehart and Winston, Inc., 1973.

Learning Letter Sounds. Durrell, Donald. Niles, Ill.: Borg Warner Educational Systems, 1970.

Lester. Ollie. Old Tales. (Experimental readers in dialect for Baratz study.) Education Study Center. Washington, D.C.: Education Study Center, 1970.

Let's Read. Bloomfield, Leonard, & Barnhart, Clarence. Bronxville, N.Y.: C. Barnhart Inc., 1965.

Listen Look Learn. Educational Developmental Laboratories, Inc. Huntington, N.Y.: EDL, 1972.

Listening Time. Scott, Louise, & Wood, Lucille. (Books and recordings.) New York: McGraw-Hill Book Company, 1965.

Merrill Linguistic Readers. Fries, Charles C., Wilson, Rosemary G., & Rudolf, Mildred K. Columbus, Ohio: Charles E. Merrill Books, Inc., 1967.

Miami Linguistic Readers. Robinett, R. F., Bell, P. W., & Rojas, P. Boston: D. C. Heath and Company, 1970.

Minicourse 18: Teaching Reading as Decoding. Far West Laboratory for Educational Research and Development, Teacher Education Division. Berkeley: Far West Laboratory for Educational Research and Development, 1970.

Palo Alto Reading Program: Sequential Steps in Reading. Palo Alto Unified School District. New York: Harcourt Brace Jovanovich, Inc., 1968.

Patterns in Phonics. Singleton, Carlton, & Brown, Sandra. North Haven, Conn.: Electronic Futures Inc.

Peabody Rebus Reading Program. Woodcock, Richard, & Clark, Charlotte. Peabody Teachers College, Nashville, Tenn. Circle Pines, Minn.: American Guidance Service, 1969.

Phonics Program, Word-Picture Program, Autosort Language Arts Program, and others. Bell and Howell Co., Audio-Visual Products Division, Chicago, Ill.

Pre-School Concept Development: Beginning Language Concepts. Durrell, Donald. Niles, Ill.: Borg Warner Educational Systems, 1973.

Programmed Reading. Buchanan, Cynthia, & Sullivan Associates. New York: McGraw-Hill Book Company, 1966.

Psycholinguistics Reading Series. Chicago Board of Education (Lloyd Leaverton, Director, Psycholinguistic Project). Chicago: Board of Education, 1969.

Reading 360. Clymer, Theodore, Torrance, E. Paul, & Shuy, Roger W. Boston: Ginn and Company, 1969.

Scott Foresman Reading Systems. Scott, Foresman and Company. Glenview, Ill.: Scott, Foresman and Company, 1971.

Sounds of Language Readers. Martin, Bill. New York: Holt, Rinehart and Winston, Inc., 1966.

Stanford Computer Assisted Instruction Program in Initial Reading. Institute for Mathematical Studies in the Social Sciences (Richard Atkinson, Project Director). Stanford, Calif.: Stanford University, 1968.

Story Library. (Filmstrips of stories and tape cassette available for re-reading.) Instructional Communications Technology, Taylor Associates, Huntington, N.Y.

Structural Reading Program. Stern, Catherine, Gould, Toni S., & Stern, Margaret S. New York: Random House, Inc., 1972.

Weston Woods. (Books and records.) Weston, Conn. (Also has audio-visual cartridges of stories for the AVS-10 portable instruction machine, Viewlex Inc., Holbrook, N.Y.)

Wisconsin Design for Reading Skill Development. Wisconsin Research and Development Center for Cognitive Learning. Minneapolis: Interpretive Scoring Systems, a division of National Computer Systems, 1971.

CHAPTER 3

ADULT ILLITERACY IN THE UNITED STATES

Rose-Marie Weber

Americans by and large assume that people who hardly ever attended school or did not benefit from time spent there have lost their chance. Schools are for children or for adults who were successful students as children. If a person never learned to read with ease, there is no place for him to turn to. For a goodly number of citizens, however, the efforts of local and federal governments and innumerable volunteer agencies have belied this notion. Naturalization courses in the 1920s, the Civilian Conservation Corps in the 1930s, and the Army in the 1940s, for instance, provided literacy instruction, along with local schools, unions, women's clubs, and church organizations. In the 1960s, at least ten major federal agencies were authorized by nearly thirty laws to teach reading to adults (Greenleigh Associates, 1968a), while more than 600 nongovernmental agencies were engaged in adult basic education (Cortright & Brice, 1970). Still, many Americans do not know how to read at all, and even more find print obscure and unyielding. The fact remains that a comprehensive program to eliminate illiteracy in the entire population, although it has been envisioned (Allen, 1970), has never been fully mobilized, either by the lettered or the unlettered themselves.

There is much in the way of experience, talent, and resources for an intensive effort to build on. But adult basic education has always been a marginal enterprise in the educational system, receiving truly serious attention from only a few educators and political leaders. It includes much in its history that must be avoided if an intensive effort is to succeed. This chapter describes various aspects of recent English literacy programs for adults, concentrating in large part on efforts initiated by the federal government. The shortcomings rather than the successes of these programs are emphasized so that the difficulties inherent in the "Right-to-Read" goal will not be underestimated. In particular, questions about the fundamental aims and academic effectiveness of the instruction are raised. The educational resources now at hand—research to guide practice, materials, teaching expertise, and testing—are then briefly reviewed in order to assess the means for undertaking the academic side of literacy programs.

THE EXTENT OF ILLITERACY

Illiteracy, defined narrowly by the Bureau of the Census as the inability to read and write in any language, is on the the wane in the United States as the younger, more schooled generations replace the older ones. In the decade from 1959 to 1969, the incidence of illiteracy in this sense dropped from 2.2 percent to 1.0 percent (1.4 million) in the population aged fourteen years and older, although the size of this age group increased 18 percent in this time. By 1969, then, 1 of every 100 Americans was illiterate —1 of every 140 whites, but 1 of every 30 blacks. These tended to occur in the older age range; in the 14-to-24 range, in contrast, only 1 of 300 could not read and write (Bureau of the Census, 1971).

Illiteracy, defined more broadly as the inability to read or write on a level necessary to deal with everyday situations, is of course far more problematic to assess both for individuals and for the population as a whole. Any plan for attaining functional literacy, as skill commensurate with needs has come to be called, requires not only assessing the competence of individuals but also determining needs in a wide range of contexts. In describing the American population, functional literacy has usually been defined in terms of the number of school years completed. In most current discussions it has been set at 5 or 8 years. It is assumed that persons who have completed 8 years in school, for instance, would have the proficiency to confront most everyday reading tasks with ease and flexibility. By this criterion, about 13 percent (14.3 million) of the adult population aged twenty-five years and over are functionally illiterate; this figure is roughly equal to the proportion of the people who have completed the eighth grade and stopped there. Men illiterates in this sense outnumber women, and again blacks outnumber whites relative to their proportion in the population (Bureau of the Census, 1972).

The difficulty of describing functional literacy in terms of educational attainment deserves some attention. It is obvious that students who complete a certain number of years in school do not necessarily achieve or maintain the grade level established by standardized tests. It is possible that many with fewer years may progress beyond their grade level independently or with a little help after they leave school, as Gray reported for a group who had completed only 6 years or more (1956). In fact, the Bureau of the Census (1971) estimates that 43 percent of the people who have never gone to school at all have learned some degree of reading skill. But it may be more realistic to expect most adults with only a few years of schooling to lose their ability with time. In a study of urban residents, for example, only 7 percent had failed to complete 5 years in school, but half failed to score at the fifth-grade level when tested in reading (Hilliard, 1963), a finding roughly replicated in a current nationwide study of adult basic education students (Kent, 1972a). The number of school years completed, then, does not predict specific levels of proficiency, since it fails to account in particular for reading failure in school and loss in later years. Nevertheless, it turns out to be the factor most directly related to reading performance as tested, for instance, in national samples (Harris and Associates, 1970, 1971), as well as in small groups.

The fundamental problem of determining the level of proficiency that would make for a functionally literate person in our society defies easy answers. Describing reading materials in terms of school grade levels is a troublesome practice, in part because texts are ranked with respect to the average reading abilities of children. Analyses of texts show, at any rate, that much of the print that flourishes in our daily lives—from instructions on paint cans, to newspaper editorials, to safety manuals—surpasses the vocabulary and grammatical complexity of the eighth-grade level, not to say the fifth. The Harris studies (1970, 1971) attempted to assess functional literacy by testing the abilities of Americans across the country to deal with written information in such materials as classified employment ads, telephone dialing instructions, and application forms. A conclusion of both studies is that at least 4 percent of the adult population is functionally illiterate in that these people cannot cope satisfactorily with these sorts of materials. The studies do not suggest, however, the level or range of abilities that readers would need to succeed on such material. Other empirical research has attempted to assess functional literacy from just this approach in the narrow context of job performance. Project REALISTIC, for example, has undertaken analyses to determine the level of reading ability men need in order to use materials related to their jobs and the degree to which inadequate reading ability may interfere with doing a job well (Sticht, Caylor, Kern, & Fox, 1972).

The direction toward describing functional literacy in terms of making a living—*any* kind of living—is questioned by some as reflecting a limiting conception of people's needs and capacities. This position was recently expressed at the Third International Conference on Adult Education in 1972 in Tokyo, where the term "functional literacy" was rejected by many participants as suggesting that the aim of literacy was to subordinate people to economic mechanisms rather than stressing their potential for active involvement in their society (UNESCO, 1973). Whatever one calls it, the difference between the reading competence that some Americans have and the higher competence that they would benefit from remains great enough to be a matter of social concern.

THE AIMS OF LITERACY INSTRUCTION

The general objective of providing adults in this wealthy and technologically complex nation with the opportunity to learn to read well is hardly questionable. The reasons behind this objective nonetheless require serious consideration, since they determine the content and administration of programs, shape the interaction between teachers and learners, and raise promises of how lives may change.

For the most part, government agencies have stressed the importance of literacy skills for economic independence. This has been, of course, the main objective of projects authorized by such legislation as the Manpower Development and Training Act which have included reading instruction as only one aspect of training in vocational skills. It is also the dominant goal expressed in the legislation authorizing the Adult Basic Education program under the Office of Education (ABE-OE), by far the most extensive of the current federal efforts toward literacy education. The legislation specifies that basic education for adults is intended to help eliminate their inability to "get or retain employment," make them "less likely to become dependent on others," and improve "their ability to benefit from occupational training" (Title III of P.L. 91-230, Amendments to the Adult Education Act, Sec. 303c).

The principal question here is whether or not literacy skills, in and of themselves, are significant in qualifying adults for wider employment opportunities. There is little to suggest that they do. Basic education students, even though their numbers are small in relation to the job market, can rarely attribute a new job to their new reading skills (Greenleigh Associates, 1968b; Patten & Clark, 1968). Even the most conservative forecasts of manpower needs can give them little hope, since the demand for unskilled labor is decreasing even faster than the proportion of the unskilled in the population. As Dentler and Warshauer (1965) have pointed out, the difference between having a high school diploma or not, never mind having eighth-grade reading proficiency, hardly improves the job opportunities for young adults.

As has been shown elsewhere in the world, education does not create economic prosperity, but rather follows on it (Blaug, 1966). In their study of over a hundred large American cities, Dentler and Warshauer (1965) found that the more prosperous cities had the lowest proportions of dropouts and illiterates. The poorer cities had the highest proportions of dropouts and illiterates and also the most ambitious programs to keep youth in school and provide adult basic education, but the low economic opportunity in these cities determined job insecurity to a degree that the compensatory services could not overcome. Elsewhere in the world, the level of urbanization and industrial development may not demand a literate labor force, and so the promise of economic benefit from literacy campaigns cannot be fulfilled. In the United States the promise cannot be fulfilled either, but rather because our occupational structure has little room for the merely literate.

It is worth noting that a good proportion of the semiliterates who have enrolled in the ABE-OE programs do not share the concern for employability that the legislation expresses. Two-thirds of the students surveyed in ABE-OE programs in 1967 gave self-improvement as their main reason for taking a reading course, the same proportion of a nation-wide sample in 1972 who attended "to improve their educational status" (Kent, 1972a).

Traditionally, adult educators' main objectives in organizing literacy courses have been relatively modest: to help students fulfill their personal objectives toward self-improvement and cope with daily affairs. Old hands (e.g., Cass, n.d.) recommend bringing the learners' world into the class-room so that they, as new readers, will make greater sense of it. Providing enough instruction so that students may read the Bible on their own or overcome their shame in front of their children has brought satisfaction to teachers and students alike.

The articulation of broader educational objectives that would coincide with students' immediate objectives and would in turn build on them, however, has received little serious discussion in the field of literacy education in the United States. What little there is hardly constitutes an adequate basis for instructional practice. The literature, with few exceptions (e.g., O'Neil, 1970; Stanley, 1972; Crabtree, 1970), is silent on the implications of literacy for sharpening and extending memory, for making reasonable decisions, for distinguishing with precision the desirable from the undesirable, for seeing things from new slants, for discovering talents in oneself, for learning satisfying skills and enjoyable games, for reflecting on one's place in the world, and for undertaking enterprising and constructive change within and outside oneself. People do all these things without learning to read, and of course they can learn to read without taking any of them on. But the principles that would guide how and what a person should learn from basic education are restricted by and large to a concern for skills rather than for what a person can accomplish with them. They rest on a shallow image of the student, hardly taking into account that he or she is more than a worker who can learn to sound out words. An indication of this situation shows in the childishness and colorless content of materials designed for adults, to say nothing of the lingering use of materials designed for children in adult courses.

Of those educators who have pressed for humanistic objectives in elementary literacy education, the most provocative and currently influential is Paulo Freire (1970a, 1970b; for critical analysis, see Grabowski, 1972). Starting from the proposition that every educational practice implies a conception of people and their world, Freire presents his view that all people, even the unlettered, have the capacity for reflection and action by which they can transform reality. Drawing on his experience with illiterates in Latin America and an eclectic background of Western thought, he goes on to urge for a pedagogy directed toward "conscientization," the process by which people reach an ever-deepening awareness of the social context that shapes their existence and of their own potential for changing it. Learning to read, in his view, is action in this direction. Specific instruction in literacy begins with the word, which is generative in two senses. At the outset, a word such as *favela* (Portuguese for "slum") serves as the basis for dialogue through which learners analyze and interpret the reality of the object; this is a first step in conscientization. Then the generative word is analyzed into syllables and serves as the basis for building new words and sentences out of the given letters, allowing the learners to achieve an awareness of their own creative potential with written words. Freire, in spite of the inadequacies, convolutions, and dead ends in his writings, has successfully called into question the training objectives that motivate literacy programs by placing people at the center of a cultural context in which making a living is more than holding a job.

LITERACY EDUCATION PROGRAMS

As part of the War on Poverty in the 1960s, the federal government initiated a range of programs to meet the educational deficiencies of the poor and so complement its modest traditional commitment to military personnel, immigrants, and others. The most ambitious of these began with the Office of Economic Opportunity in 1964 and grew under the Office of Education with the enactment of the Adult Education Act of 1966 (P.L. 89-750, Title III) and subsequent amendments (P.L. 91-230, Title III). This act terminated in June 1973; the long-range future of the federal commitment to educational effort remains unclear.

The purpose of the Office of Education program (ABE-OE) has been to offer adults aged sixteen years and over the opportunity to attain reading, writing, and arithmetic skills up to the eighth-grade level and, in the case that this has been achieved in a state, to complete a high school equivalency course. To meet this purpose, the legislation provided for teacher training, for a range of special research and demonstration projects, and for a National Advisory Council to advise on and review the effectiveness of the efforts. The states, which had to meet 10 percent of the program costs, had the responsibility for planning and implementing curricula, administrative services, teacher training and evaluation. This has been an earnest effort; it has succeeded in bringing a needed service to many aspiring individuals. As a truly serious, comprehensive effort, though, it falls far short of the goal to raise the reading proficiency of large numbers of Americans.

Reaching the population. The most obvious shortcoming of the federal literacy program is that it has failed to reach a large proportion of the population that it was intended to serve. The number of students enrolled annually increased from 38,000 in 1965 to more than 800,000 in 1973. Nevertheless, this is a truly disappointing proportion of a population on the order of 15 million. The same number—nearly a million—drop out of high school annually. In contrast, more than 30 million other adults are enrolled in all sorts of continuing education programs throughout the nation. Clearly, the main limitation here has been insufficient interest, mobilization, and funds, not only for organizing programs but also for sustaining them. The actual funding for ABE-OE has always fallen far short of the amount authorized by the legislation. For instance, $225 million had been authorized by amendments to the Adult Education Act for fiscal year 1973, but only $61.3 million was appropriated. Furthermore, when the eligibility for ABE-OE programs was extended in 1970 to adults with less than a twelfth-grade education, the number of potential students more than doubled to over 40 million; funding did not.

Counting time. Another difficulty in literacy programs is that they tend to be implemented for only short periods of time, while they aspire to long-term goals. They are usually not funded for longer than a year and do not establish a sense of continuity that is necessary for students to persevere. On the other hand, few programs are set up for less than a year in order to meet immediate, short-term goals in a community.

One of the problems in working out a long-term curriculum toward a given level of performance is that it is hard to establish the optimal length and intensity of instruction for adults. There is some evidence that intensive courses are especially effective. During World War II the Army was successful in bringing men with minimal skills to fifth-grade competence within a few weeks of training under very special conditions (Houle et al., 1947). In their review of sixteen literacy studies, Anderson and Niemi (1969) point out that students in some of the shorter courses progressed farther than others in longer courses.

The length of time that learners must invest in order to progress depends on many factors, of course, but the literature generally fails to identify what these factors may be. A current study of nationwide ABE-OE students reports an average of a half-grade achievement over a period of 4 months; although a quarter of the students gained more than a grade in this period, fully a third made no gain or regressed (Kent, 1972b). Anderson and Niemi (1969) report mean achievement scores from 1.0 to 2.6 for programs ranging from 1 to 24 months. The lack of norms is reflected in the state requirements for completing ABE-OE programs. In fiscal year 1968, New Jersey required 144 hours to complete the beginning level of instruction, while New York required 415 hours (National Center for Educational Statistics, 1969). At any rate, it is clear that if an optimistic estimate for progress is two grade levels a year, short-term programs are inadequate to bring a student from primary level to eighth-grade proficiency—or any other modest degree of skill that he or she might want.

Implementing the programs. The academic record of many literacy programs is not impressive. The lack of administrative coordination at federal, state, and local levels, frequently complained about, must have its effects on the learning situation. Critics such as Anderson and Niemi (1969) and Barnes (1965) have commented on administrators' enthusiasm for setting up programs and filling classes, and also on their relatively mild concern for the quality of the curriculum, the excellence of teaching, or the need for critical assessment. Teaching materials too often reveal haste and carelessness in their preparation. On the other hand, there have been many steps taken to streamline administration and to upgrade instruction, most notably the teacher-training and demonstration projects sponsored by ABE-OE. With the growth of professional experience in the field, educators have become more ambitious and reflective.

Perhaps the most persistent weakness in literacy instructional programs is that, after all, few have hardly departed in any significant way from the objectives and curricula of children's reading programs. Establishing grade levels, measuring achievement, organizing classes, following a certain set of analytic steps in sound-letter correspondences, using a modified alphabet, and so on are generally derived from elementary school practices with only superficial adaptations for adults. Instruction through special devices such as teaching machines, furthermore, is based on essentially the same content. The conception of learning to read as a set of cumulative drawn-out steps is supported by the state of thinking about children's acquisition. In consequence, the reports of reading programs rarely suggest that the measured gains of hard-working students might be, after all, far below their potential abilities.

Serving the population. Low attendance and quitting are constant problems in adult literacy programs. Teachers frequently complain about the students' apparent lack of motivation, their negative attitudes toward learning, and their failure to recognize the long-term value of literacy skills. Fully one-third of the ABE-OE enrollees from fiscal year 1968 through 1970 dropped out annually (Osso, 1971); the proportion dipped to one-quarter in 1971 (National Advisory Council on Adult Education, 1973). A substantial proportion of students who leave give reasons relating to jobs, but another large group state lack of interest—13 percent in 1971. Many of the students do not continue from one year to the next. Some, of course, graduate from the eighth-grade level—in the neighborhood of 15 percent in recent years (Osso, 1971). Even so, only about half of the students continue on to the next year.

It is clear that illiterates in America have rejected the institutionalized patterns of education in large numbers by not joining, by withdrawing, or by participating only halfheartedly. Educated people tend to assume that illiterates turn away because of failure in their studies. But for some, going back to school may reflect a failure in other nonbookish areas of life that they may have aspired to and that, by the way, may even be considered illegitimate by their teachers (cf. Labov & Robins, 1969). Once enrolled, adults may be unwilling to suffer through tiresome exercises or show deference to the instructor. In courses designed to be more "relevant" to their own existence, they may face embarrassing ignorance of their life conditions and the suggestion of inferiority as well. They may further be struck by the inadequacy of literacy instruction to expand or redefine their social world so as to narrow the gap between their own lives and a better life. Haggstrom (1966), examining the obstacles to effective education for the poor, reports on the thirst for knowledge that grew when a religious or social movement communicated to the poor that their position in society warranted their own thought and action. Few contemporary students have been touched by such a movement.

EDUCATIONAL RESOURCES IN ADULT LITERACY

In the adult literacy programs of recent years, women have outnumbered men, although in the population they exceed men in educational attainment through the eighth grade. A substantial proportion of students live in hospitals and correctional institutions—about 15 percent of ABE-OE enrollees (Osso, 1971). Although they may be enrolled in elementary programs, many literacy students have already spent a long time in schools, as shown by an extensive survey of courses designed only up to the eighth-grade level; more than half the students had already completed nine grades of schooling, and almost 15 percent had completed high school (Kent, 1972a). Considerable attention and effort have been directed toward establishing a sound academic foundation on which to best serve these students. Toward this end researchers have tackled the demographic characteristics of students, the outcomes of programs, and the factors that contribute to these outcomes (see Jahns, 1970). The practitioners in the field have further worked toward developing a range of materials and tests and documenting thought and experience on methods and teacher training. In the sections below some of these resources for instruction in adult literacy education are briefly reviewed.

Further information on these topics can be sought through the ERIC system, as document in *Research in Education*; through the Adult Education Clearinghouse, now located at the ABE-OE–sponsored National Multimedia Center for Adult Basic Education at Montclair State College in New Jersey; in the professional journals *Adult Education* and *Adult Leadership*; and in guides to the field such as Cortright and De Crow (1970), ERIC Clearinghouse on Adult Education (1970), and Griffith and Hayes (1970).

Research on adults' learning to read. With the recent increase in literacy programs there has been a concomitant increase in the amount and quality of research efforts. To a certain degree, however, the definition of what constitutes research in adult education is still "exceedingly liberal," as Brunner and his colleagues remarked almost 15 years ago (1959, p. 6). Furthermore, interest in the perceptual and cognitive aspects of the reading process in adult learners has not been great, falling as it does between more general research on adult learning (e.g., Botwinick, 1967), which suggests few implications for learning to read, and theories on learning to read conceived with respect to children (reviewed by Williams, 1973).

The generalizations on adult learning that might guide instructional practice, for instance, include the finding that the time needed to perform certain tasks increases with age but that the level of performance does not change significantly through adulthood. This is supported by observations of adult learners, which is after all probably as reliable a source of information on the special characteristics of the undereducated as any laboratory studies. With respect to learning style, for example, Brazziel (1969) has remarked on the craftsman's concept of deliberate care that many adults bring to the learning task. The reluctance to take risks, often observed in reading classes, shows up on achievement test performances, where adults omit items that they are not sure of rather than guess the way high school students do (Karlsen, 1970).

The assumption that adults learn to read the same way as children has hardly been questioned. In fact, a serious effort to validate a specific skills approach for teaching adults to read is being undertaken with test data provided by children (Askov, Otto, & Fischbach, 1971). The handbooks on adult education exhort teachers not to treat their students as children, but out of respect for the student rather than for other pedagogic reasons. If adults, by virtue of their cognitive maturity, do have abilities that lead them to a particular strategy, they have not been examined in detail.

One relevant aspect of adults' abilities, their linguistic competence, can serve as an example here. Because this competence is more elaborate than children's, we might expect adults to deal with the writing system differently from children. Documented evidence on the way adults approach learning to read an unfamiliar alphabet, however, comes from an experiment with subjects already literate in English (Bishop, 1964); many of the observations on new literates dealing with print focus on a small aspect of the writing system such as tone-markings (Gudschinsky, 1959). Yet there is reason to believe that English-speaking adults' more elaborate vocabulary would affect how they learn the correspondences between sounds and print. Even a nonliterary vocabulary may allow readers to capitalize immediately on the underlying patterning in our spelling system that is obscured by matching individual letters. Thus they may handle sound differences but identical spelling patterns exemplified in "race"/"racial" or "industry"/"industrial" as easily as first graders handle "pin"/"pine." On another level of language, adults' more mature knowledge of the grammatical workings of the language and greater experience with a variety of types of discourse (e.g., narratives, descriptions, arguments) may give them an advantage in dealing with the way a written passage will unfold. As speakers of nonstandard English, they may not be so flexible as children in learning the bookish variety of English, but they may well benefit from explicit instruction on its differences from their speech. These sorts of questions—how sound-spelling correspondences are learned, the significance of underlying regularity in the writing system, the divergence between speech and written language, and the effects of explicit instruction on the relationship between spoken and written language—have been brought up and explored with respect to children, but they scarcely enter any discussion of the adult illiterate.

Materials and methods. Well over a dozen annotated bibliographies on materials on adult literacy have been compiled in the last 10 years; they reveal a moderate range of choice for adult educators (e.g., Ford & Nicholson, 1969; Nazzaro, 1971; Rancier & Brooke, 1970). A variety of handbooks (e.g., Otto & Ford, 1967; Cass, n.d.) as well as curriculum guides (e.g., Greer, 1966; Hollis, 1966) provide a good deal of information and counsel for teachers and administrators. The library profession maintains its traditional concern for the special needs of the undereducated adult (e.g., Stoffle, 1969; Casey, 1972). All in all, there is a substantial body of literature documenting the pedagogic efforts in adult education.

The teaching materials that are available include a range of approaches. For the most part, however, they are silent on the theory of reading acquisition which they rest on. The rationale for a particular approach or even a short exercise is stated, if at all, in objectives that are questionable and often remote; the principles that guide sequences or pacing are rarely made explicit. Some adult materials cover a span of development, while others cover just a small facet of instruction such as introductory phonics. As with children's materials, there are some that emphasize sound-spelling relationships from the outset and others that emphasize whole word recognition. Some stress comprehension by including tests in the materials rather than leaving it to be informally gauged by the instructor. Special practical skills for adults, such as writing letters and map reading, are often introduced early. Programmed materials allowing for various degrees of self-pacing are available, including several series with rather elaborate hardware. Instruction by television has been developed as well. In contrast, some adult educators propose to avoid prepared materials and urge that the subject matter come from the learners' environment or be written by the students themselves.

As might be expected, there is no clear evidence that any one set of materials is more effective than another in developing and refining reading skills in adults. Greenleigh Associates' (1966) study, for instance, showed no significant differences among four programs and only pointed up the usual difficulties of controlling all the variables as well as interpreting the effects of specific instructional procedures on gross achievement scores. Proposals in the literature regarding the suitability of materials for adults, the need for flexibility in format, and the inadequacy of materials for developing word analysis skills tend to be based on weaknesses that have been observed in programs rather than on their successes. One of the strongest convictions that comes across is that instruction should be through full sentences that make sense to adults. Another is that it should be individualized but yet buoyed by some group interaction. All in all, there are no clear directives for foolproof reading instruction for adults, either at the very beginning stages or later.

With respect to the context of learning, the formal classroom setting seems to have fostered fewer happy effects than other settings. In classrooms it is easy to maintain the unequal power relations between teacher and learner that nurture the stereotype of the adult literacy student as low in self-esteem, reluctant to take risks, and concerned either to use English correctly or not at all. In an effort to individualize instruction and to move away from fixed schedules, administrators have turned to programmed materials, allowing for greater privacy and self-pacing. In fiscal year 1970, half of the students in ABE-OE studied from them (Osso, 1971). Some programs have established so-called learning centers, where students can consult instructors and work through a range of different types of instructional aids at their own speed. The use of rather complex technology with adult learners, however, draws mixed results, not the least a lingering fear by some students that they will break the machines. Other programs have arranged for students to work at home and consult with tutors by telephone or by appointment. These efforts have given good results in some quarters. For instance, one center reports that achievement gains among adults studying at learning centers or at home are more than double those shown by those who attended traditionally structured classes (Scholes et al., 1972). Support, of course, is critical. The poor results of a TV course when shown at home as compared to when shown in class was attributable to the failure of home viewers to watch it (Anderson & Niemi, 1969).

Two suggestions for improving instruction that come up time and time again are to relate the objectives of adult literacy instruction to occupational and personal needs (e.g., Harman, 1970) and to design the instruction to fulfill larger social objectives. The full implications for instruction have not been followed through, at least on any large scale, except with respect to occupational needs. The experience with training programs has shown that in well-planned courses, when the demand for reading grows from the need to work out tasks and sharpen skills, achievement steadily increases (Gregory, 1970).

Teacher preparation. Next to financing, finding qualified personnel has been the most pressing problem faced by administrators of literacy programs. Ten years ago there was only a handful of persons professionally devoted to teaching adults. At that time courses dealing with adult literacy in education schools were practically nonexistent. Only a few states had special requirements for teaching adults, and these were rather lax. Most of the teachers in adult literacy classes, therefore, were moonlighting elementary or secondary school teachers, retired teachers, or people who had had no training at all in education.

The Adult Education Act of 1966 recognized the inadequacy of professional expertise for broad-scale programs by incorporating authorization for teacher-training programs. These have been set up for the most part as 2- to 4-week summer institutes for teachers and administrators who in turn are qualified to conduct pre-service and in-service programs at the state and local levels. In this way, 24,000 of the staff totaling 29,300 in fiscal year 1968 received something in the way of preparation (National Center for Educational Statistics, 1969). The Job Corps hired relatively inexperienced teachers and trained them especially for its largely self-instructional individualized program. It provided pre-service and in-service courses as well as consultants on request, thus giving support and guidance that few teachers of adult reading have had (La Plante, 1969).

In spite of the expansion of career opportunities in adult basic education in recent years, fewer than a hundred institutions offer courses in the topic; graduate programs, which tend to serve those who already have practical experience, are rare. The professional qualifications that a teacher might bring to adult classes, such as understanding the reading process or skill in managing a class, tend to be less valued in handbooks for teachers than the ability to get along well with students, to recognize their dignity as human beings, and to provide positive support for their awkward attempts to become fluent readers. In their evaluation of basic literacy programs, Greenleigh Associates (1966) concluded, although on rather weak grounds, that high school graduates were more effective than more highly educated teachers. Some programs have adopted the strategy of having recently advanced students teach their peers, trying to capitalize on the empathy among new learners.

Tests. Part of going to school is taking tests. Because students in adult basic education who have been away from school for a long time find paper and pencil tests particularly harsh, programs tend to rely on informal checks for placement and for assessing progress.

In the area of formal testing, instruments to measure the skills and progress of children are still widely used—a clearly questionable procedure. Several tests have been developed specifically for use with adults (Rosen, 1971). These have various technical flaws with respect to reliability, validity, and norms, and limitations with respect to content and range. Careful research on adult reading norms has yet to be done, but from it may come a cleaner picture of adults' development into fluent readers.

CONCLUDING REMARKS

The recent efforts toward providing adults with the opportunity to read better have resulted in a growth of expertise and knowledge on which to continue. But it is clear that adult basic education has continuously begged for recognition and support beyond rhetoric; the people it is meant to serve hold it in low esteem. For those who take up the opportunity to advance in book learning, the commitment requires patience, an integration of personal resources, and a strong belief in its value. As it stands in our society, the value of literacy education does not suffice to offset the arduousness of the learning task. The task itself has hardly been defined independently of the tradition in elementary education for children. Movement toward a literate socitey requires shifts in thinking about both the value of literacy and the way to achieve it.

REFERENCES

Allen, J. E., Jr. The right to read—target for the 70's. *School and Society*, 1970, **98**, 82–84.

Anderson, D., & Niemi, J. A. *Adult education and the disadvantaged adult.* Syracuse, N.Y.: ERIC Clearinghouse on Adult Education, 1969.

Askov, E. N., Otto, W., & Fischbach, T. Development of specific reading skills in adult education. In F. P. Greene (Ed.), *Reading: The right to participate. Twentieth Yearbook of the National Reading Conference,* 1971. Pp. 46–52.

Barnes, R. F. Problems facing teachers and administrators in adult basic education today. In *Teaching adults to read, Basic education handbook series,* 1. Galien, Mich.: Allied Education Council, 1965. Pp. 15–26.

Bishop, C. Transfer effects of word and letter training in reading. *Journal of Verbal Learning and Verbal Behavior,* 1964, 3, 215–221.

Blaug, M. Literacy and economic development. *The School Review,* 1966, **74**, 393–418.

Botwinick, J. *Cognitive processes in maturity and old age.* New York: Springer Publishing Co., Inc., 1967.

Brazziel, W. F. Teaching reading to disadvantaged adults. In J. A. Manzano (Ed.), *Strategies for adult education. Perspectives in reading II.* Newark, Del.: International Reading Association, 1969. Pp. 8–14.

Brunner, E. de S., Wilder, D. S., Kirschner, C., & Newberry, J. S. *An overview of adult education research.* Chicago: Adult Education Association of the U.S.A., 1959.

Bureau of the Census, Department of Commerce. Illiteracy in the United States: November 1969. *Current Population Reports,* Series P-20, No. 217, March 1971.

Bureau of the Census, Department of Commerce. Educational attainment: March 1972. *Current Population Reports,* Series P-20, No. 243, November 1972.

Casey, G. M. (Ed.) *Public library service to the illiterate adult.* Detroit: Wayne State University Office of Urban Library Research, 1972.

Cass, A. W. *Basic education for adults.* New York: Association Press, n.d.

Cortright, R., & Brice, E. W. Adult basic education. In R. M. Smith, G. F. Aker, & J. R. Kidd (Eds.), *Handbook of adult education.* London: Macmillan & Co., Ltd., 1970. Pp. 407–424.

Cortright, R. W., & De Crow, R. Resources for adult education. In J. A. Figurel (Ed.), *Reading goals for the disadvantaged.* Newark, Del.: International Reading Association, 1970. Pp. 327–339.

Crabtree, A. P. The strengths and weaknesses of the ABE program. In W. S. Griffith & A. P. Hayes (Eds.), *Adult basic education: The state of the art.* Washington, D.C.: U.S. Government Printing Office, 1970. Pp. 220–224.

Dentler, R. A., & Warshauer, M. E. *Big city dropouts and illiterates.* New York: Frederick A. Praeger, Inc., 1965.

ERIC Clearinghouse on Adult Education. *Adult basic education: Current information sources no. 27.* Syracuse, N.Y.: ERIC Clearinghouse on Adult Education, 1970. (ERIC Document ED 035 777.)

Ford, D., & Nicholson, E. Adult basic reading instruction in the United States: An annotated bibliography. *IRA Annotated Bibliography No. 15.* Newark, Del.: International Reading Association, 1967.

Freire, P. Cultural action for freedom. Cambridge, Mass.: Center for the Study of Development and Social Change and *Harvard Educational Review,* 1970a. (Originally published in *Harvard Educational Review,* 1970, **40**, 205–225, 452–477.)

Freire, P. *Pedagogy of the oppressed.* New York: Herder and Herder, Inc., 1970b.

Grabowski, S. (Ed.) *Paulo Freire: A revolutionary dilemma for the adult educator.* Syracuse, N.Y.: Syracuse University Publications in Continuing Education and ERIC Clearinghouse on Adult Education, 1972.

Gray, W. S. How well do adults read? In N. B. Henry (Ed.), *Adult reading. Fifty-fifth Yearbook of the National Society for the Study of Education.* Chicago: The University of Chicago Press, 1956. Pp. 29–56.

Greenleigh Associates. Field test and evaluation of selected adult basic education systems. New York, 1966.

Greenleigh Associates. Inventory of federally sponsored programs. Report to the President's National Advisory Committee on Adult Basic Education. New York, 1968a.

Greenleigh Associates. Participants in the field test of four adult basic education systems: A follow-up study. New York, 1968b.

Greer, E. (Ed.). *Guide for adult basic education: Beginning level.* Washington, D.C.: U.S. Department of Health, Education and Welfare, 1966.

Gregory, F. Preparation for employment as a motivator for Adult Basic Education. In W. S. Griffith & A. P. Hayes (Eds.), *Adult basic education: The state of the art.* Washington, D.C.: U.S. Government Printing Office, 1970. Pp. 142–149. (ERIC Document ED 051 475.)

Griffith, W. S., & Hayes, A. P. (Eds.) *Adult basic education: The state of the art.* Washington, D.C.: U.S. Government Printing Office, 1970. (ERIC Document ED 051 475.)

Gudschinsky, S. Toneme representation in Mazatec orthography. *Word,* 1959, **15**, 446–452.

Haggstrom, W. O. Poverty and adult education. In F. W. Lanning & W. A. Many (Eds.), *Basic education for the disadvantaged adult.* Boston: Houghton Mifflin Company, 1966. Pp. 142–160. (Originally published in *Adult Education,* 1965, **15**, 145–160.)

Harman, D. Illiteracy: An overview. *Harvard Educational Review,* 1970, **40**, 226–243.

Harris, L., and Associates. Survival literacy study. New York, 1970. (ERIC Document ED 068 813.)

Harris, L., and Associates. The 1971 national reading difficulty index. New York, 1971. (ERIC Document ED 057 312.)

Hilliard, R. Massive attack on illiteracy. *American Library Association Bulletin,* 1963, **57**, 1034–1039.

Hollis, J.-C. *Curriculum guide to adult basic education: Intermediate level.* Washington, D.C.: U.S. Department of Health, Education and Welfare, 1966.

Houle, Cyril, et al. *Armed services and adult education.* Washington, D.C.: American Council on Education, 1947.

Jahns, I. R. Adult basic education research. In W. S. Griffith & A. P. Hayes (Eds.),

Adult basic education: The state of the art. Washington, D.C.: U.S. Government Printing Office, 1970. Pp. 205–219. (ERIC Document ED 051 475.)

Karlsen, B. Educational achievement testing with adults—some research findings. In W. S. Griffith & A. P. Hayes (Eds.), *Adult basic education: The state of the art.* Washington, D.C.: U.S. Government Printing Office, 1970. Pp. 99–103. (ERIC Document ED 051 475.)

Kent, W. P. Interim report: Data on selected students in Adult Basic Education programs, 1971–72. Falls Church, Va.: Systems Development Corporation, 1972a. (Office of Education Contract OEC-0-71-3706.)

Kent, W. P. Second interim report: Test data on Adult Basic Education students. Falls Church, Va.: Systems Development Corporation, 1972b.

Labov, W., & Robins, C. A note on the relation of reading failure to peer group status. *Teachers College Record,* 1969, **70,** 395–406.

La Plante, W. The reading program—Civilian Conservation Centers. In J. A. Mangano (Ed.), *Strategies for adult education. Perspectives on reading,* II. Newark, Del.: International Reading Association, 1969. Pp. 48–54.

National Advisory Council on Adult Education. *Annual report.* Washington, D.C., 1973.

National Center for Educational Statistics. *Adult basic education program statistics.* Washington, D.C.: U.S. Government Printing Office, 1969.

Nazzaro, L. B. (Ed.) *Annotated bibliography, 1971.* Philadelphia: Free Library of Philadelphia, 1971. (ERIC Document ED 054 783.)

O'Neil, W. Properly literate. *Harvard Educational Review,* 1970, **40,** 260–263.

Osso, N. A. *Adult basic education program statistics: Students and staff data July 1, 1961–June 30, 1970 and summary of years 1966–1970.* Washington, D.C.: National Center for Educational Statistics, 1971. (ERIC Document ED 061 506.)

Otto, W., & Ford, D. Basic literacy programs for adults: A national survey. In G. B. Schick & M. M. May (Eds.), *Junior college and adult reading programs: Expanding fields. Sixteenth Yearbook of the National Reading Conference,* 1967. Pp. 240–246.

Patten, T. H., & Clark, G. E., Jr. Literacy training and job-replacement of hard-core unemployed Negroes in Detroit. *Journal of Human Resources,* 1968, **2,** 25–36.

Rancier, G. J., & Brooke, W. M. *An annotated bibliography of adult basic education.* Ottawa: Queen's Printer, 1970.

Rosen, P. Tests of basic learning for adults. Princeton, N.J.: ERIC Clearinghouse on Tests, Measurement, and Evaluation, 1971. (ERIC Document ED 058 274.)

Scholes, G. W., Eyster, G. W., & Hayes, A. P. Rethinking the Act: Progress toward meeting the goals of the Adult Education Act of 1966. Morehead, Ky.: Morehead State University, Appalachian Adult Education Center, 1972. (ERIC Document 068 799.)

Stanley, M. Literacy: The crisis of a conventional wisdom. In S. Grabowski (Ed.), *Paulo Freire: A revolutionary dilemma for the adult educator.* Syracuse, N.Y.: Syracuse University Publications in Continuing Education and ERIC Clearinghouse on Adult Education, 1972. Pp. 36–54.

Sticht, T. G., Caylor, J. S., Kern, R. P., & Fox, L. C. Project REALISTIC: Determination of adult functional literacy levels. *Reading Research Quarterly,* 1972, **7,** 424–465.

Stoffle, C. J. Public library service to the disadvantaged: A comprehensive annotated bibliography, 1964–1968. *Library Journal,* 1969, **94,** 141–152, 507–515.

UNESCO. Third International Conference on Adult Education. *Literacy: A newsletter,* 1973, No. 1.

Williams, J. P. Learning to read: A review of theories and models. *Reading Research Quarterly,* 1973, **8,** 121–146.

CHAPTER 4

LITERACY PROGRAMS IN INDUSTRY, THE ARMED FORCES, AND PENAL INSTITUTIONS

T. A. Ryan and William Furlong

In the 1950s and 1960s concern with improving the lot of minorities and of the poor led to numerous programs for increasing the employment opportunities of these groups. Literacy training was an important feature of many of these programs. In an earlier version of this report, the first author reported on an effort which had been expanding for a number of years. Experience had been gained, the problems defined, and the whole enterprise seemed to be reaching a stage of mature accomplishment—or at least the promise seemed to be there. The second author, however, has reviewed more recent events, and finds that little progress has been made. Many programs have been phased out, due to lack of support, and little further progress has been made toward making literacy programs more effective. Our account is therefore primarily an historical review of preliminary attempts to deal with the problems of literacy in relation to employment—preliminary investigations of ways and means which, unfortunately, do not seem to be leading to full-scale attacks upon the problem.

The efforts of the sixties were preliminary in the sense that they dealt with only a small fraction of the illiterate poor in pilot programs, and also because they were still trying to develop dependable methods. Nevertheless, from some points of view the total effort was very large. Some idea of the magnitude of the national effort in job training can be obtained from a report commissioned by the Committee on Administration of Training Programs and carried out by Greenleigh Associates (1968). The report contains a four-page table of acronyms for programs and agencies involved, and similarly extensive tables showing the activities of the various agencies. With specific regard to basic education and literacy training, there is a 176-page book entitled *Federal Support for Adult Education: Directory of Programs and Services* (Adult Education Association, 1969).

There was also a considerable body of literature on the magnitude of the problem to be solved. Labor economists and manpower specialists reported extensive statistics upon the number of unemployed and underemployed, their educational backgrounds, the extent of illiteracy and the like (e.g., Adair, 1964; Ferman, 1968; Ferman, Kornbluh, & Miller, 1968; Riessman, 1968; Zeller & Miller, 1968). Two examples will serve to illustrate the kinds of statistics available. In 1963 the Department of Labor estimated that 16.9 million workers had not more than an eighth-grade education, while another 12.2 million had some high school education but had not graduated (Manpower Administration, 1964). In a more detailed and localized study, Adair (1964) reported on functional illiterates in Texas, with illiteracy defined as less than fifth-grade education. He found that 13.4 percent of those twenty-five years or older were illiterate. He also showed geographical distributions and rates for various ethnic groups and age levels. Of course, the apparent magnitude of the problem depends upon the criteria of illiteracy. The 1970 U.S. Census put the figure for illiteracy at fewer than 2 percent in the adult population. Methods of defining illiteracy will have to be considered in greater detail below, because they affect not only our estimates of the size of the overall problem, but even affect the way we approach its solution. Nevertheless, even the lowest estimates of the rate of illiteracy point to a large problem for our society.

Literacy programs in industry. We consider together literacy programs within industry and those developed by private or governmental agencies for job training. The main emphasis will be on those designed for illiterates or those whose initial reading performance is below the eighth-grade level. There is less information available about basic education at the intermediate level, although there have been a few programs preparing for apprenticeship in the skilled trades which normally require high school graduation. There are also some reports of courses designed to increase the reading efficiency of executives or supervisors (Beck, 1967–68; Portman, 1966; Hastings, 1966). It is assumed, however, that the functionally illiterate constitute the major problem, and certainly this is the area to which the greatest concentration of effort and attention has been devoted.

Training carried on within industry has the same general purpose and many of the same problems as training carried on by external agencies concerned with unemployment. The motivational situation may be quite different in the two cases, and the clientele or students may be of different kinds. Ultimately, a systematic comparison may be possible and would throw light upon the role of these motivational and background variables. The most obvious motivational difference between the two types of program is the direct instrumental value of the literacy training within industry as a means for retaining a job and for advancement, together with the possibility of linking the training directly to specific uses on the job. Clearly we need systematic research comparing the different types of programs with comparable students and with prolonged follow-ups of their employment histories. It would also be desirable to study retention of the reading skills as a function of the type of program and also of the subsequent employment history.

In both cases, we are concerned with adult basic education and literacy training which is a part of a total program aimed at increasing the employability of "hard-core" unemployed. In general the program recruits the students rather than depending upon volunteer participation, and the students are paid for participation; some programs have even paid bonuses for rate of progress. It is because of the complex nature of the total program and its aims that there is frequently little information about the literacy component by itself.

Specific methods of teaching reading have varied over the whole range of possibilities within each general type of program. Some use the more standardized procedures such as those provided by the Board for Fundamental Education, Methods for Intellectual Development (MIND), and Laubach Literacy. A number use sets of materials put together by instructors in the specific program. Some use the "experience" approach; some use individual tutoring without specifying the method. There is one report of the use of the initial teaching alphabet (Patten & Clark, 1968).

Evaluating the outcomes. If we stress the functional value of reading skill in the life of the disadvantaged, we raise the question of what kind of reading is important and what levels of skill are critical for different purposes. The overall effect of a training program is usually reported in terms of job placement for programs developed outside of industry, or in terms of retention of workers by the company which develops on-the-job training. While this information is important, it does not measure directly the effect of the basic education and literacy training contained within the program. The success of the literacy training is usually measured by performance on standardized reading tests—gains in grade levels achieved at the end of the training period.

The meaning of changes in performance on tests of reading skill must be examined further. Although the results of these tests are often treated as the criterion for evaluating the program, it is obvious that the purpose of the program is not simply to change scores on standardized tests and that the scores are important only insofar as they relate to other criteria of the practical value of the program.

When we are concerned with comparing different specific methods of teaching, it is likely that differences in gain on standardized tests reflect the influence of the teacher as well as the materials used. Interpretation must be cautious, however, since most available tests are either standardized on children and/or scaled in terms of grade levels. We shall have to proceed with caution even in interpreting the tests as measures of immediate (or temporary) effect of the teaching on reading skill in adults.

It is not enough to evaluate the outcomes in relative terms, however. We also have to consider the absolute level of skill attained by the trainee in terms of the functional value of his reading outside of the classroom. Does the individual read well enough to be able to work at the job he is being trained for? Can he progress to the next level of job? What kind of information can he obtain from newspaper reading?

There is an important inconsistency in the aims of industrial literacy programs. On the one hand, the need for the programs is considered to be very great because there are so many "functionally illiterate" adults. Functional illiteracy is usually defined in terms of some grade level of skill—often the eighth grade—with the implication that reading levels below this point are of little use. On the other hand, a specific training program is often considered to be valuable because the trainees have been raised one or two grades in performance, even though they are still below the level of functional literacy. Here the implication seems to be that even such small gains in skill are of practical value, but we are given no indication of what the practical values are.

Of course it would be highly desirable to raise large numbers of individuals to the level of functional literacy or to whatever level is necessary to remove any restrictions on their promotion to higher level jobs, to learn skilled trades, to read newspapers and become informed voters and members of the community. As we shall see, however, there is no evidence that the programs so far developed can accomplish this goal. Even if they could be improved and extended in length, there is still the question whether large numbers of workers would be motivated to persevere long enough to reach the level of functional literacy. The ultimate goal needs to be broken down into a series of meaningful short-range goals, so that even the first step has practical meaning. To a child it is meaningful to progress from first-reader to second-reader level. Adults must be given a measure of accomplishment which is more than simply a numerical score.

We find only scattered observations bearing upon the question of literacy requirements of industrial jobs. One executive, reporting upon training the disadvantaged, mentions that the experience led to a reexamination of the real requirements for second-level jobs and the discovery that these requirements were actually lower than had been assumed (Van

Brunt, 1969). Others who have been developing training programs aimed at increasing minority-group entrance into apprenticeship programs feel that the literacy demands for entering the apprenticeship are greater than the requirements on the job itself. Often it is charged that the literacy requirements are designed to keep minority workers out of the trade. Some programs have emphasized coaching and practice in filling out application forms and taking entrance tests (Marshall & Briggs, 1967a, 1967b).

Such observations suggest that we need systematic analysis of jobs themselves to find out the extent to which they require reading and writing. The jobs need to be analyzed from two points of view: (1) are unnecessary demands made simply because literate workers have always been employed on the job, and (2) what do the necessary demands imply in terms of levels of performance on reading tests? Unlike many aspects of job analysis, this kind of research can use objective information. If reading is required for a particular job, the materials to be read must exist and must be available for sampling and analysis for level of difficulty. It should be possible also to separate the general vocabulary needed from the specialized vocabulary of the occupation, and provide for special training in the latter.

Analysis of the literacy requirements of jobs would seem to be essential to defining the problem and the goals of literacy training in and for industry. And yet very little systematic study has been devoted to it. Ohio Bell commissioned the Battelle Memorial Institute of Columbus to conduct a study of reading tasks related to company jobs (Battelle Memorial Institute, 1971). We shall also cite later a study of military jobs with civilian counterparts. These represent a small beginning on a task which should be pursued very widely. Until this is done, we do not know whether literacy training is playing an important or meaningful role in improving the employability of the trainees.

We referred earlier to general estimates of the magnitude of the literacy problem. "Functional illiteracy" has been given various definitions, usually quite arbitrary, and it is likely that we cannot agree upon a single definition. Even if we restrict our definition to reading ability, there are many levels of ability, and many different activities in which reading is used. Rather than trying to define a single dividing line between literacy and illiteracy, we should aim at a scale of demands made by various occupations and activities, and at a measure of ability which coordinates with the scale of demands.

General effects upon employment. The effect of literacy programs upon the ultimate criterion of employability is much more difficult to sort out, since the literacy training is embedded in a complex total program of job training. We know relatively little about the effect of the total training program, to say nothing of the specific contribution of the literacy component. We summarize below the information we have about the general evaluation of job training programs, but the approach by way of job analysis can be expected to give the more immediately useful results. The inclusion of literacy training in job training programs already implies a vague kind of job analysis—it is generally believed that the illiteracy rates among unemployed involve a causal relation between literacy and employability. This is probably true, but we need more precise information about the nature of the relationship.

Summary reports issued by specific training programs outside of industry often give optimistic reports of success in placing their students. Less frequently, they report difficulties in obtaining employment. There is little basis for a general evaluation, since the available reports may not be a representative sample. For what it is worth, the general impression is of relatively lower success in programs for apprentices in the skilled trades than in the programs which aim at employability in general. Among the more general programs success in placement is very strongly influenced by community support of the project, the relationship between the placement office and local industry, and so on.

Programs of on-the-job training within industry report on numbers of trainees who remain employed in the same company or in similar work elsewhere. Often, management considers that the programs are effective (Gassler, 1967; Drotning, Lipsky, & Fottler, 1969). The evaluations of management and supervisors are themselves important conditions for the success of these programs. It is impossible, however, to use these impressions for evaluating specific aspects of the training.

One more systematic attempt has been made at evaluating programs under MDTA (Manpower Development Training Act). A nationwide sample of 1,250 trainees who had completed a training program was questioned and compared with dropouts from the same programs and with a "snowball" control group (Main, 1966). (The controls were nominated by the trainees from among their friends.) In general, the respondents commented favorably upon the value of the training, and frequently mentioned the literacy training as an important component of the training.

In evaluating the economic effects of the training, it was found that the "snowball" control was not completely matched to the trainee group. One important difference was that the trainees had higher educational levels. Various statistical corrections had to be applied and the results were analyzed by multiple regression. Quoting the study:

> To put the entire research project in a very small nutshell: while some trainees said they learned little or nothing in their MDTA courses, most gave favorable evaluations; MDTA training apparently did not help get better paying jobs, but it did help them to obtain more full-time employment; the net effect of MDTA training on full-time employment is esti-

mated to be between 13 and 23 per cent of the period after training for "completers" and between 7 and 19 per cent for "dropouts" (Main, 1966. pp. 102–103).

Other studies have also obtained the students' own evaluation of the literacy training and its effects. They feel that it gives them confidence, helps them to deal with their children, and gives them prestige with their neighbors. In some cases these indirect effects are also relevant to employment. One student, for example, reported that she had never been able to take the bus before taking the reading course (Greenleigh Associates, 1966).

Measuring gains in reading skill. Although improving ability to read is not an end in itself, particularly in the context of job training, direct measures of reading performance would seem the best indicators of the effectiveness of methods of teaching. The tests should measure, however, the kind of reading skill which is relevant to the purposes of the training program.

Unfortunately, most tests commonly used have been standardized on children. Some reports point out deficiencies in the tests when applied to adults, while others do not consider this question at all. Some use several different tests, apparently in the hope that the deficiencies will cancel each other out. There are deficiencies in the tests which are immediately observable because adult trainees have difficulty in following instructions and find the tests frustrating.

There are also more fundamental problems which are seldom recognized. Evaluating the effects of adult training by tests standardized on children raises a number of technical questions:

1. What is the degree of equivalence of grade levels in reading derived from different tests in children? Do the same relationships hold for adults, or must the whole question be reconsidered using adult data? We have found only one piece of research on this question; this will be mentioned below.

2. To what extent do grade-level scores in children reflect sheer quantitative changes, e.g., in size of vocabulary, and to what extent do they depend upon the order of development of different component skills? If grade level depends upon the order in which components develop in children, is it possible that the order is different in adults and that scores standardized on children will have a different meaning? Since adults begin their training with a different oral vocabulary and different available concepts, qualitative differences in the process of learning would seem to be a possibility to be reckoned with.

3. Even leaving aside the question of precisely what kind of skill in reading is reflected in the tests, there is the further question of nonskill or external factors which are different for adults and school children. When

we see an adult training group which gains on the average one or two grades in reading test performance, how much of the gain is a gain in "test-wiseness," confidence, and lack of embarrassment? These are factors in the children too, but doesn't it seem likely that the changes are more marked in the adults who have had little or no previous schooling? Of course these gains are themselves of great practical value, but if we are trying to evaluate different methods of teaching reading, we should like to know whether differences reflect actual reading skills. The question also has bearing on our ultimate aims in training. Confidence in reading in classroom tests may or may not transfer to the uses of reading in the job situation.

In spite of these difficult questions about the meaning of the standardized tests as applied to adults, there are also very serious difficulties in developing tests specifically designed for adults. Children in the various grades provide a standardization population which represents, at least roughly, different levels of proficiency. If we were to try to standardize adult tests we would no longer have convenient reference groups representing different known levels of performance. The tests might be standardized on groups of adults with different amounts of previous formal schooling. Securing representative samples for each level would be an undertaking of major proportions, and would be especially difficult at the low levels of previous education. Moreover, we could expect extreme variability within each level because of the varied effects of postschool experience, so that very large samples would be required. Another possible approach would be to abandon grade-level scoring altogether. Instead, scores might be given only in terms of percentiles for a specified adult population. Again, however, we must face the question of what is the appropriate general reference population.

Some of the teaching programs specifically designed for adults do incorporate tests as part of the program. Insofar as they are standardized at all, these tests are based on adult students undergoing the specific training program. They can reflect progress within the program on a relative basis, but do not provide us with norms for adults in general. Most of the programs, however, measure progress by means of grade–level tests standardized on children.

Whatever the ultimate solution to these problems, it is clear that we do not now have the proper tools for evaluating the results of adult reading programs. One way to foster the necessary developments would be to establish a continuing committee or board made up of experts in literacy testing, those experienced in adult literacy training, and psychometric consultants. The purpose would be to develop recommendations on appropriate and informative methods of testing adults, and to foster research relevant to these problems.

Meanwhile, the bulk of the information available for evaluating methods of adult testing consists of reports in which we find that method A, used under condition B, produced average gains of (say) 1.3 grades on Test D after x weeks of training. The next study changes all these components at once. Both may report on the number of placements in industry, but they differ in the methods of placement, the industries available in the area, and the degree to which the industries themselves are involved in sponsoring the training programs.

Comparative studies of teaching methods. Most of the individual studies with their unique combinations of factors give optimistic reports. Gains in reading level are interpreted as real and practically meaningful, and job placements are believed to reflect useful outcomes and effective attacks upon the problems of unemployment. We do not mean to question this optimism, because it is quite possible that any kind of training and placement program is better than none. Even in older types of industrial training it seems that almost any systematic attention to training is useful, whether or not it is based upon scientifically established principles. Perhaps it means that the trainees adopt their own methods of learning anyway, while the principal function of the training program is to make information available to them and to give them time to practice with this information in the ways which the trainees find congenial.

Nevertheless, we would like to know what goes on in the training process in order to control and improve some components or variables in the process. For this, of course, we need studies which aim to isolate particular variables and control for the others. The only study approximating these requirements concerns adult basic education in a separate program, rather than as a part of occupational training. Nevertheless, we must consider it because it is directly relevant to the industrial training program, and its sponsorship by the Office of Economic Opportunity indicates its purpose.

A "Field Test and Evaluation of Selected Adult Basic Education Systems" was reported by Greenleigh Associates in 1966, and was based upon a total of 108 classes set up in three states. The 1800 students were welfare recipients reading below the fifth-grade level and recruited by welfare agencies. The variables were the type of published adult educational system and the type of teacher. Four basic educational programs were chosen on the basis of criteria set up by the Office of Education and were chosen as the only systems available at the time which were designed by their publishers to meet the criteria—i.e., they claimed to "take students from below the fifth grade through the eighth-grade level." The systems were: *Learning to Read and Spell* published by American Incentive to Read; *Reading in High Gear*, Science Research Associates; *The Mott Basic Language Skills Program*, Allied Educational Council; and *Systems for Success*, Follett Publishing Company.

The other main variable, type of teacher, involved: "(1) trained teachers, preferably experienced in adult education, (2) college graduates and (3) high school graduates." They were selected by the local school districts and the project staff on the basis of personal qualifications, and then assigned at random to the learning systems. All were given instruction in the use of the system by the project staff and by the publishers of the system.

We shall not go into further details of the design which seems to be well worked out within the practical limits of a field study. The most obvious limitations are: (1) Other systems are now available, some of them specifically designed as parts of industrial job training. (2) Recruitment was dependent on local factors and probably variable in method; even more important, the self-selection of the students with respect to motivation may be quite different from that in a job-training program, even though the students all came from the same general population of unemployed. (3) Another motivational factor is that the students were not paid for participation as they are in many occupational training programs.

Effects of the training were measured by the Gray Oral Paragraphs Test, and by the Iowa Test of Basic Skills. Limitations of these measures are explicitly recognized, and problems of administering paper and pencil tests in this population are described. The tests were intercorrelated and the authors conclude that the tests have "comparable ability to measure reading level in this population" (Greenleigh Associates, 1967, p. 18). On the other hand, the correlations were only .50 to .60, and hardly support the notion that the tests measure the same thing unless they are also quite unreliable. The authors mention that the teachers judge the progress of the students to be underestimated by the tests. In addition to test scores, qualitative data from student reports and analyses of the contents and characteristics of the teaching systems are included in the report.

The general results are easily summarized. No consistent differences either in test scores or student interest could be found among the teaching materials. In addition there was no interaction between the teaching program and the type of teacher. Most of the criteria also showed no differences due to the type of teacher. Some differences were found in the Iowa tests, but those that were significant favored the high-school-level teachers. (At one point in the report it is mentioned that gains are inversely related to starting scores and that high school teachers had a higher proportion of students with starting levels of 3.0 or below on the Gray test. The report does not seem to consider this finding in interpreting the average gains of different types of teacher.)

There are some interesting but puzzling regional differences. Gains in reading skill differed significantly from state to state with New York showing the highest gains. Moreover, among the black students, there was a significant interaction between type of teacher and state. The three groups of teachers had essentially the same results in New York but differed from each other in the other two states. In New Jersey the high school teachers were highest, the college graduates in the middle, and the certified teachers lowest. In California, the high school and college groups were equal and both exceeded the gains of the certified teachers. As the authors state, "These differences by state are not readily explained" (Greenleigh Associates, 1966, p. 62). Since the teachers were selected by local school administrations, there may be some differences in state educational "atmosphere" to be considered.

In considering the ultimate criterion of employability, the authors of the report are rather pessimistic. They imply that reaching eighth-grade level is barely enough to have a practical effect upon employment, while high-school level is needed for most jobs. ". . . in the final analysis, very few students really improved their qualifications for employment or job training, even if eighth grade reading is accepted as the criterion" (Greenleigh Associates, 1967). Whatever the functional meaning of the gains, it is true that the mean increases are from 1.5 to 2 grades, and that only 13 percent reach eighth-grade level in their final tests, while 26 percent reach sixth-grade level or higher.

Since the absolute magnitude of these gains seems to be typical of many literacy programs for the unemployed, the final solution requires much more effective teaching programs if we accept current literacy requirements for jobs. If we consider that such improvements are likely to be slow in developing, there is an urgent need to attack the problem from the other end as well—to try to adapt the job requirements to realistic possibilities in literacy training. As we have already suggested, this adaptation may be partially brought about simply by objective analysis of jobs to find out what their real literacy requirements are. We also need to know the extent to which literacy requirements could be modified without serious effects upon actual job operations.

Returning to the general variables which are studied in the report, the findings about types of teacher are, of course, of great practical importance. Effective solutions of the overall problems of employment of the disadvantaged must depend upon making the training available to large numbers of students. At present we are still in the stage of pilot programs, and it is not clear how many of these are continuing and expanding to meet the need. Unfortunately, a considerable number seem to be temporary trials; the reports urge continuation and expansion but we do not know whether these recommendations are heeded. If the recommendations are followed, the need for teachers will be very great, and the possibility of effective use of high school graduates is extremely encouraging.

Even the lack of differences among the educational programs is potentially important. Several interpretations should be considered. One is the possibility that the training materials are less important than the motivations of the students and teachers and the kinds of learning strategies adopted by the individual students. The studies do not eliminate the possibility that more effective new programs will be developed, but they also suggest that we should not rely entirely on this kind of development to solve the problem.

More recent developments. Some newer programs are specifically designed for industrial use and aim to reduce the participation of the teacher. The Board for Fundamental Education uses already available materials. It is based on a "team learning" method in which students help to teach each other. While there have been favorable comments on the part of industrial users (Gassler, 1967), we have no comparative studies. Where gains in reading scores are reported, they seem to be roughly comparable to those reported for the older methods in the Greenleigh study and in reports of individual projects. The Eastman program reported by Gassler, using the Board for Fundamental Education's material, produced average gains of 1.4 grades in reading and 3.0 grades in arithmetic. Another study in Dallas (Board for Fundamental Education, 1967) shows similar gains.

R. M. Stone of the Michigan Bell Telephone Company has reported some preliminary comparative data on the Method for Intellectual Development (MIND) program (personal communication). In that company in 1968-9, trainees were given basic educational instruction under the Detroit Board of Education at the McNamara Skills Center, using qualified teachers. In 1969, some of this education was transferred to "in-house" training centers, using the MIND programs administered by management people. Stone has supplied the following table of means, which he says have not been tested for significance.

TABLE 1

Michigan Bell Telephone Company—Stanford Achievement Test Results
(Grade Placement Levels)
McNamara Skills Center (1968–1969)

Population	N	Reading			Math		
		Pre	Post	Change	Pre	Post	Change
Females (1)	156	7.2	7.7	+.5	6.4	7.2	+ .8
Males (2)	65	7.1	8.0	+.9	6.1	7.4	+1.3
Total	221	7.2	7.8	+.6	6.3	7.3	+1.0
In-House Training Centers—MIND (1969)							
Females (3)	196	6.9	7.7	+.8	6.5	7.9	+1.4

(1) Telephone operators and switchroom helpers
(2) Splicer's helpers
(3) Telephone operators and general clerks

The MIND program began as a project of the National Association of Manufacturers. The pilot work attracted favorable attention from industry, and the work was taken over by a special company which is a subsidiary of CPC (Corn Poducts Company). Kline (1969) describes the general character of the program, but the only results we have been able to get are in Table 1. While preliminary and suggestive only, there is an indication that untrained teachers can use the program with results at least as good as those with experienced teachers. Note, however, that the training group does not consist of illiterates as defined in the Greenleigh study. We have not been able to get either quantitative studies or descriptive material on the actual content of the programs. The Board for Fundamental Education reported in 1970 that it had started a research department, but has not yet produced any comparative data.

In 1970, it was reported that several corporations were developing programs comparable to the MIND program, and this kind of industrial training was considered the "coming thing." What is the present situation with regard to industrial training for literacy? It is now easy to list the top 20 or 30 corporations, the public utilities in urban centers, and perhaps a dozen or so service industry institutions who have conducted or participated in literacy training. But the list is short, is now rather historical, and is now more wishful thinking than functional: American Telephone and Telegraph of New York conducts training for new employees recruited to serve in entry-level jobs, for example, for new information operators who are found unable to cope with their assignments. Polaroid, the Philadelphia Gas Works, Chrysler, Ford, Caterpillar Tractor, and General Electric—each conducts programs for the poorly educated (DeCrowe, Cogan, & Furlong, 1973).

Unfortunately, as one speaks with various officials, the conditions of the programs again color the picture. How many are served by any given program? It may be only from 100 to 150 per year. The Philadelphia Gas Works shepherds some 75 General Education Development (GED) graduates through their program each year. What about costs? Some are shared. Some are paid completely by employee. What is the payoff for the student? Sometimes it is a first job. There is usually a salary increase in terms of cents per hour. In some cases it means a promotion. What is the payoff for the company? Candid answers seem to indicate that the company profits little. It helps with community relations; it helps with unions; it creates new expenses which the company will bear only in times of good business.

In fact, more projects and programs die from effects of the economy than from any other factor. Student participation, achievement, etc., simply are recorded facts for the most part. As with the military, industry is faced with an increasing demand for highly skilled workers. Our society already produces a plentiful supply of educated workers—who needs to create special programs for the illiterate? The battle of the budget, in the military or in industry, usually forces decisions to be made about short-term necessity and long-term "social goals." The programs for the illiterate simply fall into the latter category.

Research needs and motivational problems. Even though literacy training in industry seems to be fading away rather than fulfilling its earlier promise, it is still desirable to assess our present knowledge of methodology. It will be useful to those who do continue the effort, and will be available if interest is rekindled by new events. Much more research will still be needed, but it is useful to know what direction it needs to take.

Since several new teaching methods and programs have been developed, the Greenleigh study will need to be repeated for these newer programs, but the scale will need to be very large. It will be necessary to compare different programs in industry, which will probably vary in the nature of the total training and in the initial status of the trainees selected for on-the-job training. It will probably be necessary also to set up extra-industrial programs in order to sample a wider range of trainees than is available in on-the-job training as compared to prejob programs carried on outside of industry. This would be an important variable to study, since there are claims that basic education given as part of an industrial training program is more effective. This claim seems plausible, but there is no firm evidence for it.

There is a strong possibility that motivational variables are more important than the particular method of teaching or the materials used. Teaching method itself has motivational effects, and experienced teachers stress the need for encouraging students, finding interesting material, and so on. Nevertheless, the teacher and the teaching materials provide only a small part of the general motivation to learn.

The most important motivational problem arises out of the time and effort required to learn and the length of program necessary to achieve "functional literacy." Adult learners, on the average, do progress faster than children if we can take the reading tests at face value. In a 16–20 week program, average gains of over one grade have been found. Nevertheless, the results also indicate definite limits on the rate of progress of the adult learner, even when he is interested and highly motivated to learn to read. Most of the programs so far reported have been of 16–20 week duration; occasionally one lasts 36 weeks. A few of the within-industry programs speak of the possibility of continuing instruction for longer periods, although actual results have not been reported.

It is unlikely that motivation to continue long enough to reach functional literacy from a low starting level can be maintained for large numbers of adults in programs outside of industry. If industry were sufficiently interested in solving the problems of the disadvantaged to maintain and expand the kinds of programs which have been started as pilot projects, incentives to continue progress beyond the first semester could be provided. We need short-range as well as long-range incentives. There should be practical effects of completing the first course, even if the gain is only a grade or two—practical effects in terms of eligibility for slightly higher levels of job or increases in pay. Then further advantages could be seen as the result of the next stage of training, and so on. As mentioned earlier, these short-range incentives could be made most effective if the reading skill developed in a 16-week course could be specifically related to actual requirements of a certain level of job. The aim should be a classification of jobs based upon degree of reading skill as well as upon specific technical requirements.

Although the main stress in this summary has been upon average results, there are also wide individual differences in the effect of training within the groups taught by a single method and teacher. This suggests another approach to problems of effective instruction. If we could discover the individual characteristics of those students who show substantial gains in reading skill, we might discover motivational variables which could be manipulated for the improvement of teaching. Some of the differences may involve personality or aptitudes which cannot be manipulated. Even so, we might be able to separate out those students who can profit most from a particular kind of training program. Even though our concern is with mass programs, research upon individual differences in personality, interest, and background can be of utmost importance.

Military programs. The new military establishment of the sixties seemed to indicate at least some interest in the problems of illiteracy. Programs of recruitment, training, and career development were planned. Of course, much of this happened in the light of interest in a peacetime army. A highly publicized (and still referenced) program was "Project 100,000" (Assistant Secretary of Defense, 1968). This program was designed as a significant effort to bring the illiterate into the military. Today the project is nothing but a memory.

Impressive results were recorded for the first 5,000 to 10,000 men. From that point on, and seemingly in relation to Vietnam manpower demands, the project ground to a halt. The reason, as now stated by the Department of Defense officials, was based upon reality. "Now we need a smaller number of talented people. We do not need, nor do we have the resources to recruit and educate and then train illiterates."[1]

---

[1] This statement was obtained in personal correspondence and conversations of W. F. Furlong with persons in the Public Affairs Office, Department of Defense, June and July, 1973.

Project REALISTIC is another interesting foray of the military into literacy programs. The project was designed "to determine functional literacy levels for selected military jobs having civilian counterparts" (Sticht, Caylor, Kern, & Fox, 1972, p. 424). Two interesting concepts related to functional literacy are studied in Project REALISTIC. First: "It suggests targeted skill level for adult basic training geared toward employment." Second: "An examination of the literacy demands of jobs indicates whether or not the stated literacy requirements of jobs are unnecessarily high" (Sticht et al., 1972, p. 427). The findings, which were not very startling, were:

1. Reading materials used by Repair and Supply personnel exceeded the average reading ability of the high-aptitude men by from four to six grade levels.

2. Reading activity was positively correlated with the reading ability of subjects.

3. Nonreading reception skills (listening) were as important as reading skills for some subjects, if not more so.

4. Standardized reading tests tended to be valid indicators of a subject's ability to perform adult-level reading tasks.

A most unsatisfactory picture of the military involvement in literacy training is presented here. It seems that the military is not currently attending to the problem of recruiting and educating the illiterate, and does not feel the need to. We do not intend to suggest that nothing is done for the illiterate in the military; rather, we intend to point out that the problem is treated with a low priority.

Dr. Thomas Sticht and others at the Human Resources Research Organization (HumRRO) have spent years working on projects for the military. Weighing the evidence, however, we feel that while dedication, interest, perseverance, and goals are clear, the final payoff is difficult to measure. Sticht himself suggests the true nature of the impact of military literacy training efforts in the following excerpts from his own writings:

> While no data bearing on the effects of *current* military literacy training programs on job proficiency have been found, there have been several attempts in the past by the Army, Air Force, and Navy to evaluate the effects of literacy training up to the 4th or 5th grade level on job training or job proficiency. These studies, summarized in detail in the book *Marginal Man and Military Service* (Department of the Army, 1965), failed to demonstrate benefits of literacy training on either job training or job performance, measured in various ways—supervisors' ratings, retention, pay scale achievement, conduct, and others. However, these studies also failed to demonstrate that the various literacy training efforts improved reading skills over those of control groups—where such comparisons were made. If proficiency in reading is not genuinely improved, it is meaning-

less to search for the effects of such non-improvement on subsequent measures of job training or job performance proficiency. . . .

He continues:

> If 8 or more weeks of formal *job training* may have little or no effect on subsequent job sample test performance in these types of jobs, is there any reason to believe that 4, 6, or even 13 weeks of *reading* training will be reflected in such measures? Probably not. Many job tasks can and will be learned by "show and tell"—especially tasks of high frequency and criticality—i.e., the types of tasks emphasized in task analyses and typically used to construct job sample tests.
>
> Furthermore, except for the *profoundly* illiterate (e.g., persons reading below the grade 2.0 level) which most of the military reading students are *not*, it seems unreasonable to expect 4 to 6 weeks of literacy training to meaningfully affect retention rates, rate of promotion, conduct (AWOLS; court martials), paper-and-pencil job knowledge proficiency test scores, or supervisors' effectiveness ratings. For the *profoundly illiterate*, improvement on any of these indices would be contingent upon successful literacy training up to some requisite level. The Air Force report by Zaccaria (1971) suggests that it is difficult to effect much reading improvement with such personnel in as much as 13 weeks of reading training. In this study, 85% of the men who entered reading at the 1st grade level exited reading at or below the 4th grade level. Ninety percent of men reading at the 2nd grade level on entry into the 13 week program exited reading at or below the 4th grade level. . . .
>
> It seems reasonable to argue that if reading training doesn't improve a person's ability to perform significant job reading tasks, then it is unlikely that the reading training will affect other, less directly reading-related indices of job proficiency, such as retention rates, supervisors' evaluations, job sample tests, etc. On the other hand, it doesn't necessarily follow that improved competency in performing job reading tasks will be reflected in other, non-reading-related indices of job proficiency. In fact, data from HumRRO (Vineberg, Sticht, Taylor & Caylor, 1971) indicated that job knowledge and job sample test performance for the four jobs mentioned earlier correlated only about .5, while supervisors' ratings were not at all correlated with either of the other indices of job proficiency. There is thus evidence to suggest that improvement on one index of job proficiency— e.g., the use of job reading materials—will not necessarily be reflected in improvements on other indices of job proficiency.
>
> Research evaluating the effects of Air Force and Army literacy training programs, and a special, experimental literacy training program being developed for the Army by HumRRO, on proficiency in performing Army job-related reading tasks for Cooks, Vehicle Repairmen, and Supply Clerks

has recently been reported (Sticht et al., 1973). This research indicates that all three literacy training programs resulted in improved job reading task test performance. Furthermore, the HumRRO program, which focuses reading training directly on the performance of job-related reading tasks, produced considerably greater improvement (1 to 2 grade levels) than the Air Force and Army programs, which provide general literacy training.

Thus, limited evidence suggests that relatively brief periods of literacy training can produce improved ability in performing job-related reading tasks *at the end of such training.* No research has been done, however, to determine if such improvement is retained. Nor has research been performed to determine if control groups of marginally literate men *not* submitted to literacy training acquire comparable levels of proficiency in job reading task performance as a consequence of their job training and work experience.

It does not seem unreasonable to suppose that the improvements effected by such relatively brief programs of literacy training as offered by the Air Force, Navy and Army (including HumRRO's experimental program) will be short-lived. This seems likely because: (1) the objectives of these literacy training programs appear to fail to meet the demands of the reading tasks encountered in even the least demanding jobs (even the experimental HumRRO program is targeted at producing ability to perform job reading tasks with the proficiency of a person having general reading skills of grade 7.0—and this meets the minimum requirements only for the Cook's job); for this reason men may be frustrated in trying to deal with reading materials which still exceed their reading skills, even after graduation from the reading program, and thus they may avoid job reading, resulting in a decline in reading skills to pre-literacy-training levels; (2) most job training programs which men attend after literacy training make little attempt to assist men in using their job training materials by providing usable glossaries, carefully sequencing new information, etc., and may even permit the less literate man to *avoid* reading by encouraging more literate men to do all of the "looking-up" of information and reading development after completion of literacy training; no job-related, developmental reading materials are provided, no encouragement or incentives to continue reading development are provided, and no officially scheduled time for continued literacy development is provided [Sticht, 1973, pp. 40–44].

The efforts of the military are commendable but probably of little significant consequence. All evidence seems to indicate that present levels of activity will have little long-run impact on literacy training.

Penal institutions. Prison programs aimed at rehabilitation rather than punishment are perhaps more likely to develop with long term "social goals" in mind. Of course, budgets will always influence programs. It seems that a growing interest in rehabilitation, however, gives viable hope to literacy programs in penal institutions. The Federal penal system has some thirty-four institutions operated by the Bureau of Prisons. In more than twenty-five of these institutions, programs for basic education, GED (General Education Development), and ABE (Adult Basic Education) are conducted. It is virtually impossible to obtain firm facts and figures on the status of illiteracy in these institutions.

A newly created Clearinghouse for Programs on Offender Literacy, created by the American Bar Association's Commission on Corrections with funding from federal sources, is attempting to spearhead literacy efforts. In a 1973 survey, some 300 penal institutions submitted program information. The Clearinghouse reports:

As best can be determined at this time and relying on scores self reported by the institutional education staff on a somewhat spotty regional distribution, the average reading attainment levels appeared as follows:

Regional Area	Average of Scores*	
	Adult	Youth
Southern States	6.1	—
North Central States	6.1	5.3
Mid-West States	5.5	5.3
Northeast States	5.5	3.7
Western States	5.1	4.5
Southeast States	4.5	4.6
Southwest States	3.4	—
National	5.1	4.6

* 6.1 means a reading performance of 6th grade, 1 month; 5.5 a reading performance of 5th grade, 5 months, etc.

If these data project a real situation (and they may not since the statistics are not fully relatable) there are probably a quarter million individuals, both adults and youth, incarcerated in this country on any one day, who cannot cope with reading tasks as well as the average sixth grade student. Such individuals would be classified as functional illiterates by virtually every agency that has studied or worked intensively with the problem in recent years (e.g., Job Corps, U.S. Army, U.S. Office of Education).

These statistics present a truly devastating picture. They suggest that around half of the population of all our correctional institutions read somewhat less proficiently than the average twelve year old. Pursuit of employment and/or continued schooling will, at best, be difficult to undertake. This is because future success, in no small part, will depend on the very skill which is most infirm and least developed—that of reading [Clearing-house for Offender Literacy Programs, undated, pp. 1–2].[2]

The Clearinghouse then reports on some programs that show promise in correcting the problems:

If literacy education can mean so much, what then should be done to combat the "reading blahs" within correctional institutions and increase the offender's chances for success upon release?

At present, there are some bright spots in a few institutions. Programs in reading geared to the diverse backgrounds and motivations of inmates are beginning to surface. Thus,

—the U.S. Bureau of Prisons, with federal "Right to Read" grants has launched demonstrations at two institutions specifically designed to strengthen reading skills and featuring specialists (graduate reading degrees), paid tutors, and individual diagnosis and prescription

—the Rehabilitation Research Foundation in Elmore, Alabama, has developed and field-tested an individualized programmed reading course for adult inmates (now being used nationally in a variety of correctional systems)

—the Fairfax County Jail in Virginia has a thriving reading program administered by community tutors using a simple but effective reading technology (Laubach Literacy Program)

—the Kennedy Youth Center in Morgantown, Virginia, has responded to needs of a short-stay population by a "quick movement program" bringing non-readers to minimum reading levels in only 10 organized workbooks supported by "token economy" incentives

—the Cook County Jail in Chicago has adopted a "technical management of reading approach," i.e., use of individualized materials and teaching machines along with contract agreements between staff and offenders on achievement of reading goals, all linked to job skill and job placement support

—the Lorton Youth Center serving D.C. offenders has a special program

---

[2] We have earlier (pp. 171–173) raised serious questions about the meaning of grade levels as applied to adult reading performance. We do not know, for example, that the adult who can "read somewhat less proficiently than the average twelve year old" really presents a "truly devastating picture" or that "pursuit of employment and/or continued schooling will, at best, be difficult to undertake." Nevertheless, while the functional meaning of grade-level scores obtained by adults still remains to be determined, it is good to have information about these scores as obtained by the populations of correctional institutions. The results also point up, however, the need for better research upon the measurement of reading proficiency in adult populations in all segments of the population. Project REALISTIC, mentioned above (Sticht et al., 1972) represents the beginning of the necessary kind of research; but it covers only four occupations out of thousands. Also, even that study does not compare grade norms with other possible approaches to adult norms.

for individuals under 7th grade reading levels which works with visual, perceptual, behavioral and auditory problems in addition to routine reading handicaps [Clearinghouse for Offender Literacy Programs, undated, pp. 8–9].

One must be encouraged by some of these efforts. Also, one must face reality. The military and industrial programs live and die by economics. So too do the penal programs. In each of the three cases cited, federal funds create or save the project. What happens when a new idea, a new priority, a new problem gains page one?

In each of the categories, military, penal, industry, it seems tragically apparent that literacy training is an idea which gains initial acceptance. Typically the federal treasury is tapped for demonstration funds, "seed money," or pilot projects, and yet whenever the program is to become institutionalized it quickly becomes a victim of expediency. This returns us to our original questions. Who cares about basic literacy? What is the basic motivation for basic literacy programs?

It is fair to say that the predominant attitude from leaders in all categories discussed is one of sympathy for the illiterate. They agree it is a perplexing situation. They point out, also, that their institution is not rightfully burdened with the failures of public education. Interest in the illiterate generally begins in necessity (i.e., recruitment) or "enlightened self-interest." In the former case the institution is forced to train the illiterate because he is the only one available. In the latter, the program just might have a positive residual or side effect. Finally, the "problem" of the illiterate really is not felt by many literates. Neither the social or economic effects are well-defined or promulgated. Thus it seems that not many people really care about the illiterate. That is, they don't care enough to do much about the problem.

CONCLUSIONS AND RECOMMENDATIONS

At first glance, it might be assumed that a committee on reading could limit its attention to the methods of teaching reading, and leave questions of overall effectiveness of occupational training programs to others. The very term "functional illiteracy," however, raises the question, "Functional for what?" We have argued that this is a problem for research, and that the research needs to involve specialists in reading. This general question implies several kinds of research, involving the following questions: (1) What are the literacy requirements of various occupations, and how can these be translated into levels of performance on reading tests? (2) Are the literacy demands really essential to the occupations, or could instructions, manuals, and reports be made less demanding? (This investigation requires the collaboration of job analysts and reading specialists.) (3) Are present tests of reading skill suitable for evaluating the functional value of adult literacy programs? If not, how can suitable tests be devised? These questions also imply a need for careful investigation of the process of adults learning to read.

While we need to know much more about the specific role of reading (and other skills such as arithmetic) in occupational performance, we must not limit our attention to these problems, and we must not assume that simplifying the reading requirement of a specific occupation would eliminate the need for literacy training for these workers. The "functionally illiterate" are handicapped off the job as well as on it, and we also need to know more about these handicaps. What do specific levels of skill as measured by tests mean about ability to read newspapers, magazines, etc.? What kind of information can be obtained by an individual with fourth-grade reading achievement? How much reading is actually done by individuals of low test performance?

We have suggested that a continuing committee should be formed for gathering and transmitting this information to those who are developing industrial and other adult training programs. Information in this field is scattered and much of it is not formally published, and so we may be unaware of information on these questions which is already available. If it is available, it has not yet had an effect on the evaluation of practical literacy programs.

The only comparative research on training methods deals with the effects of published "systems" of reading material and practice manuals and with the general qualifications of teachers. The results are discouraging, both because they indicate that the method factor is of little or no importance, and because the absolute changes in reading skill seem small. On the other hand, there is an optimistic note in the fact that untrained teachers with only high school education perform as well as those with higher educational background. The fact that newer programs, as yet unevaluated, make even smaller demands upon the formal training of the teacher suggests that really large-scale attacks upon illiteracy are not completely unrealistic.

Individual characteristics of both the teacher and the pupil are undoubtedly of great importance. Nothing has yet been done to sort out the effects of motivation and interest from those of aptitude. With the kinds of students involved in these training programs, it is doubtful if we yet know how to separate these variables. Some aspects of motivation could be investigated by relating effects of training to methods of recruiting the students, to the actual instrumental value of the program in providing opportunities for employment and advancement, and to the students' perceptions of this instrumental value. In particular it would be valuable to make systematic comparisons of training programs within industry with those carried on by outside agencies. In addition, we need studies of individual differences relating to differential success in learning and in the carry-over of training to subsequent development of the student.

The programs reported so far have been of short duration—from 16 to 20 weeks—and the average progress has been only 1.5 to 2 grade levels. In this time, only a few trainees reach a point where they are considered functionally literate, i.e., at the sixth or eighth grade level. If these levels are considered necessary for practical effects upon employability or other uses of reading, it is obvious that the programs must be extended in length and that the trainees must be motivated to continue. The most promising way of providing this continued motivation would be the further development of literacy training within industry, linking successive stages of basic education to opportunities for job advancement and specialized occupational training. The present programs by community agencies in providing the first stage of training and in feeding the students into industry cannot be considered as complete solutions to the problem, but as leading to further stages of training through opportunities and incentives offered by industry to its employees.

REFERENCES

Adair, J. B. *Study of illiteracy in Texas as related to vocational education.* Austin, Texas: Texas Education Agency, 1964.

Adult Education Association of the U.S.A. *Federal support for adult education: Directory of programs and services.* New York: The Macmillan Company, 1969.

Assistant Secretary of Defense (Manpower and Reserve Affairs). *Project one hundred thousand: Characteristics and performance of "new standards" men.* Washington: Office of Secretary of Defense, 1968.

Battelle Memorial Institute. *Process paper on the determination of the basic education requirements of a job and/or a training program for that job.* Columbus, Ohio: Battelle Memorial Institute, 1971.

Beck, F. Reading instruction in business and industry. In Vol. 12, Part 1, *Proceedings of the 12th Annual Convention, International Reading Association,* 1967–68, pp. 414–417.

Board for Fundamental Education. *The Dallas Retail Merchants Project, "Manpower Development Through Education."* Indianapolis: BFE, 1967.

Clearinghouse for Offender Literacy Programs. *Reading—where it's at—in prison.* Washington: Clearinghouse for Offender Literacy Programs, undated. [Circa 1973]

DeCrowe, R., Cogan, T., & Furlong, W. (Eds.) *Partners in the Right to Read.* Washington: National Reading Center, 1973.

Department of the Army. *Marginal man and military service: A review.* Washington: Department of the Army, 1965.

Drotning, J. E., Lipsky, D. B., & Fottler, M. D. *Jobs, education and training: Research on a project combining literacy and on-the-job training for the disadvantaged.* Interim Report submitted to the Office of Manpower Research, U.S. Department of Labor, 1969.

Ferman, L. A. *The Negro and equal employment opportunities.* New York: Praeger, 1968.

Ferman, L. A., Kornbluh, J. L., & Miller, J. A. *Negroes and jobs.* Ann Arbor: University of Michigan Press, 1968.

Gassler, L. S. How companies are helping the undereducated worker. *Personnel,* 1967, **44**(4, July-August), 47–55.

Greenleigh Associates. *Field test and evaluation of selected adult basic education systems.* New York: Greenleigh Associates, 1966.

Greenleigh Associates. *Summary: Field test and evaluation of four adult basic education systems.* Washington: Office of Economic Opportunity, 1967.

Greenleigh Associates. *Opening the doors: Job training programs.* A report to the Committee on Administration of Training Programs of the Department of Health, Education and Welfare, 1968.

Hastings, W. H. Improved reading of industrial workers, developmental reading for United Automobile Workers. *Journal of Reading,* 1966, **9,** 253–254.

Kline, B. E. MIND, Inc. system approach to training hard-core unemployables. *Training and Developmental Journal,* 1969, **23**(9), 18–20.

Main, E. D. *A nationwide evaluation of MDTA institutional job training programs.* National Opinion Research Center Report No. 118. Washington: Office of Manpower Research, U.S. Department of Labor, 1966.

Manpower Administration, Office of Manpower, Automation and Training. Formal occupational training of adult workers. *Manpower/Automation Research Monograph,* No. 2, 1964, 1–48.

Marshall, F. R., & Briggs, V. M., Jr. *The Negro and apprenticeship.* Baltimore: Johns Hopkins University Press, 1967a.

Marshall, F. R., & Briggs, V. M., Jr. Remedies for discrimination in apprenticeship programs. *Industrial Relations,* 1967b, **6,** 303–320.

Patten, T. H., Jr., & Clark, G. E., Jr. Literacy training and job placement of hard-core unemployed Negroes in Detroit. *Journal of Human Resources,* 1968, **3,** 25–46.

Portman, L. A reading course for labor unions. *Journal of Reading,* 1966, **10,** 29–32.

Riessman, F. New careers: A workable approach to hard-core unemployment. *Personnel,* 1968, **45**(5), 36–41.

Sticht, T. G. Literature review and general research: Suggestions for the experimental study of foundation education and career education. Monterey, Calif.: Author, 1973.

Sticht, T. G., Caylor, J. S., Kern, R. P., & Fox, L. C. Project REALISTIC: Determination of adult functional literacy skill levels. *Reading Research Quarterly,* 1972, **7,** 424–465.

Sticht, T. G., et al. HumRRO's literacy research for the U.S. Army: Progress and prospects. Alexandria, Va.: HumRRO Professional Paper 2-73, January 1973.

Van Brunt, R. E. Unexpected results when training the disadvantaged. *Training and Development Journal,* 1969, **23**(10), 22–24.

Vineburg, R., Sticht, T. G., Taylor, E., & Caylor, J. Effects of aptitude (AFQT), job experience, and literacy on job performance: Summary of HumRRO work units UTILITY and REALISTIC. Alexandria, Va.: HumRRO Technical Report 71-1, February 1971.

Zaccaria, M. Effectiveness of the basic military training reading proficiency training program. Unpublished Air Force report, circa 1971.

Zeller, F. A., & Miller, R. W. *Manpower development in Appalachia.* New York: Praeger, 1968.

CHAPTER 5

BILINGUAL LITERACY

Vivian M. Horner

We have room for but one language here, and that is the English
language, for we intend to see that the crucible turns our people out
as Americans and not as dwellers in a polyglot boarding house.

THEODORE ROOSEVELT, 1919

It has been more than a half a century since Theodore Roosevelt defined
Americanism in monolingual terms, a half-century during which our schools
have expended enormous energies trying to stamp out in young children
entering the system all traces of any language other than English and
educate them to enter the mainstream. Simultaneously, at the upper end
of the educational continuum, billions of dollars have been spent trying to
teach foreign languages to stolidly monolingual American adolescents and
adults. We have failed at both ends. We have failed to produce literacy
in bilingual children; we have failed to produce bilingualism in literate
adults. We have failed at both ends. We have failed to produce literacy
suggests may offer hope for easing the consequences of both failures.

The title of this paper is somewhat misleading. It is less about bilingual literacy than about bilingual illiteracy. Most of our educational efforts
to date on behalf of non-English-speaking children are producing poor
school learners who are illiterate in two languages.

When we speak of the educational failure of non-English-speaking
children, we must keep in mind that we are not speaking of all children
who do not speak English when first entering school. We are not speaking
of the children of U.N. diplomats, nor of the sons and daughters of wealthy
foreign businessmen conducting their affairs in the United States, nor even
of those immigrants' children who find themselves few in number in their

190

new communities. We are talking in the main about large groups of children who are poor and who are geographically and/or socially isolated, whose mother tongue is not English, and who are attending public schools in which instruction is carried out solely in English. In short we are talking about the children of the poor, stigmatized in the schools by their alien languages and their alien cultures.

The appalling effect of our failure to educate these non-English-speaking children was dramatized a few years ago by the results of a California survey that showed that Spanish-speaking children, who made up only 15 percent of the general school population, constituted 28 percent of the population of classes for the mentally retarded, on the basis of intelligence tests conducted in English. The California survey marked one of the first steps in the raising of public school consciousness, for it was instituted at the insistence of militant Mexican-American parents, and together with a lawsuit, *Diana et al. v. State Board of Education*, resulted in a decision potentially affecting some 22,000 Mexican-American children in mentally retarded classes in California. The Board of Education ruling decreed that all children then in such classes were to be retested in their native language, and that future testing of non-English-speaking children would be done in the language of their homes.

The federal government's involvement in the education of "bilinguals" ostensibly began in 1968 with the passage of Title VII, the bilingual American education section of the Elementary and Secondary Education Act (ESEA). Title VII made available funds for the development of programs utilizing two languages—the non-English mother tongue as well as English —as media of instruction. Title VII was well motivated, but because of its poverty criterion, it made bilingual education a kind of medicine for the poor. Worse, it was, and is, funded at a grossly inadequate level. Worse still, in its conceptualization it was "additive"; that is, it encouraged the development of bilingual programs dependent on federal funding, programs tacked onto existing education structures. Since it required no new commitment of funds on the part of the school systems developing such programs, it tended to encourage schools to count exclusively on increasingly large allocations from the federal government to sustain the programs. This was hardly a set of circumstances designed to bring forth either quality programs or large-scale solutions to large-scale problems.

In 1970 the Department of Health, Education and Welfare (HEW) notified 1,000 school districts throughout the country with a concentration of 5 percent or more non-English-speakers that they would have to take affirmative action to remove the language barriers that handicap children who are not speakers of English, or face a cutoff of federal funds under the Civil Rights Act of 1964. The mandate did not specify bilingual education, of course, but the option to *reallocate* funds for this purpose was a crucial ingredient if Title VII was to make a serious impact. HEW's action might have been a wedge to break into the cumbersome bureau-cracy that had for so long neglected the needs of non-English-speaking children, if federal funds had truly been withheld across the board for programs that did not demonstrate affirmative action to meet the special-ized needs of such children. Instead, what we have witnessed is some minimal reshuffling of existing funds to meet federal requirements and a good deal of demagoguery about bilingual education. Meanwhile, we have not witnessed any marked improvement in the education of our non-English-speaking youngsters. Bilingual education still suffers from "three serious lacks: a lack of funds . . . a lack of personnel . . . and a lack of evaluated programs . . . [Fishman & Lovas, 1970]." Indeed there is still a great deal of confusion among educators about what constitutes bilingual education. In spite of all their good intentions, many still believe that bilingual education means special language classes, such as TESOL (Teaching English to Speakers of Other Languages), for children who can-not speak English well.

I would like to suggest that solving the problem of bilingual illiteracy —at both ends of the educational spectrum—will require a considerably broader understanding of bilingual education than is now prevalent. What will be necessary is the development of educational programs conducted in two languages, with literacy in one, or, preferably, both languages as a goal. Before we talk about literacy, however, we need to clarify a few notions about bilingualism and language learning.

In educational circles the term "bilingual" has commonly been applied to all children with foreign language backgrounds. Obviously this is a misnomer; such children may or may not speak English and may or may not be bilingual. The children about whom we are concerned are those whose "problem" is that they speak only a "foreign" language, those who have little or no mastery of English. Bilingualism itself is not the problem. There are millions of people throughout the world for whom speaking, reading, and writing two or even more languages is natural. There is a problem "only when a population, through emigration or conquest, be-comes part of a community where another language is spoken and this language is imposed on them through the school system or by other authorities" [Andersson & Boyer, 1970, vol. 1, p. 9], and excludes the use of their own language for purposes of schooling.

The notion of imposition makes clear a second aspect of linguistic relationships, that is, that there are status dimensions in any two-language setting that can be ignored only at great hazard both to the child and to the success of the educational undertaking. We know from sociolinguistic research that in some two-language settings one language tends to become associated with formality and the "high" culture, while the other is a part of informal and intimate settings. In the United States it is clear that English is the language associated with formality and the dominant culture, whether high or low, and that its position, as well as that of other languages, is presently fixed by the socioeconomic facts of life. At a minimum, then, the task for education is to make all children functional in domains requiring the dominant language to the level of usage required in them. The school must help non-English-speaking children to develop complex linguistic skills so that they may move as competently in a monolingual society as does a monolingual. This task is formidable enough, but we must do more. Non-English-speaking children must not, in the course of their education, be alienated from their mother tongues and the social and cultural domains in which they already function. We must not only strive to make them competent and literate in English, but we must strengthen their skills in their own language as well.

Which brings us to the nub of the problem. How can we best take children who come to school not speaking English and make them literate? The commonest approach to this task in our public schools is monolithic. It has been best characterized, perhaps, by Gaarder's phrase "cut all ties and Anglicize." In practice this approach has at least three variants. The first is to make the children bilingual, then literate in English. The second, and worse, is to stamp out their languages, replace them with English, and then teach them to read. The third, worst of all, is to try to do both these things at once.

These, of course, are program goals, and even if they were reached, they would not solve the children's problem. As long as literacy is narrowly defined as the ability to read and write English, and as long as we continue to insist that aural-oral skills inevitably precede reading and writing skills, we have little other recourse open to us. We can do nothing other than to try to develop the children's ability to speak and understand English and then to try to teach them to read and write it. One of our most difficult tasks in making non-English-speaking children literate is altering the attitudes that underlie this monolithic approach.

The first thing we must do is to reduce the hostility of the school system toward children's native languages. As a first approximation, there are two models calling themselves bilingual education which share with the approach we have just described the goal of Anglicizing children but which have managed to eliminate the goal of cutting all ties to the native tongue. One such type of program, which according to one typology (Fishman & Lovas, 1970, p. 215) is designated as "transitional bilingualism," utilizes the mother tongue "in the early grades to the extent necessary to allow pupils to 'adjust to school' and/or to 'master subject matter' until their skill in English is developed to the point that it alone can be used as the medium of instruction." A somewhat more extended use of the mother tongue is integral to programs that strive for what Fishman & Lovas (1970) have called "monoliterate bilingualism." In such programs aural-oral skills are developed in both languages, but literacy is developed only in English. Fluency in the native language is encouraged as a way of providing a better link between the home and the school.

If such programs could make non-English-speaking children competent in English *fast enough* without alienating them from their home environments, the educational problem might be reduced to that of teaching them to read. In this task we might at least anticipate the same degree of success we have had in teaching other poor English-speaking children to read. But probably not, for poor native English-speaking children may still have an edge.

> English-speaking children in the United States naturally begin their formal schooling in their mother tongue, while children of Navajo, Chinese, Japanese, Eskimo, German, or any of half-a-hundred other language backgrounds are not encouraged to begin their formal learning in *their* mother tongue. English-speaking children profit from carefully prepared reading readiness and reading programs, whereas children with other language backgrounds have no such provisions for reading in their language. Not only do such practices leave them illiterate in their mother tongue, they also indirectly foster illiteracy in English by forcing the children to read in English before they are ready. Developmental psychology is applied to the education of English-speaking children, but not to non-English-speaking children whose needs are greater. The mediocre results that have been so well publicized of late should hardly surprise us [Andersson & Boyer, 1970, vol. 1, p. 3].

What these authors suggest is that children should learn to read in the language most familiar to them, a point of view that is supported by a small body of research (MacNamara, 1966, 1967; Modiano, 1968) and endorsed increasingly by educators who have tried it. What perhaps needs emphasis where non-English-speaking children are concerned is that there is a distinction between learning to read and learning language. What happens most often in the schools is that the teaching of language and the teaching of literacy skills are attempted simultaneously without any clear understanding of the differences between the two. The result is that neither is taught satisfactorily.

No one would argue that there comes a time when being able to read contributes to the extension and the refinement of language skills for the individual, but learning to read is not language learning; nor is language learning the same as learning to read. They are more than different expressions of an identical underlying structure; they are different tasks. Learning to speak and understand and learning to read are separate sets of complex skills, which at most share certain common prerequisites and certain similar controlling stimuli.

Although we do not fully understand the interrelationships between language and literacy skills, it would seem possible to assert that language skills are essential to learning to read. As I would conceptualize it, the basic task in teaching children to read is to bring a part of their verbal repertoire under the direct stimulus control of black marks on paper. Thus the verbal repertoire must, of necessity, be already in existence. This initial phase of learning to read is a laborious task for the children, and it is reasonable to assume that the existence of *well-established* verbal patterns would make the work easier. Similarly, the initial task in teaching the child to write is that of getting a part of the children's verbal (or vocal) repertoire to come to control their hand movements in such a way as to string letter blocks or make black marks on paper that can in turn control part of their own (or others') verbal repertoire. Again this phase of the learning presupposes *well-established* verbal patterns.

Following this logic, one could assume that if the children are native speakers of, for example, Ojibwa, when they are first introduced to reading, the task of learning to decipher and to construct black marks on paper would be considerably easier if it proceeded in Ojibwa. This assumption presumes, of course, that we are able to make reliable predictions about the structure and the vocabulary of Ojibwa children of this age, just as we make similar predictions about the level of structural and vocabulary mastery for English-speaking children of school age.

It may be that the mastery of the initial level of reading and writing skill proceeds comfortably under these circumstances simply because, as Modiano (1968) has suggested, the task of learning to read has been separated from the task of language learning. It may also be that reading is learned more easily in the native language because the redundancy of overlearned language patterns increases the probability of instant recognition on the part of the children when they "decode," however haltingly, a set of written symbols. Both factors would argue for the advisability of initiating reading (and writing) instruction in the mother tongue of the children.

On the other hand, if the redundancy-recognition factor is not critical in learning to read, an argument can be made for introducing and carefully practicing on an aural-oral level that which is ultimately to be read. I would merely emphasize the point that it is *mastery* which seems to be important in this process rather than the particular approach. If a limited amount of the second language is introduced to the children and the children are given sufficient experience with it to make it functional for them, then they may quickly learn to read it and perhaps to write it.

There is some evidence that such a technique can be effective. The Fleming School in New York City is a French-English bilingual school for children who are native speakers of English; that is, the children are all monolingual English speakers when they enter school. They engage in learning activities throughout kindergarten (and preschool, if they happen to have entered then) in both English and French, being exposed not to bilingual teachers but to various teachers, some of whom are French speakers and some of whom are English speakers. By the time they begin reading instruction, the children know some French—they understand it fairly well within the context of school activities, and some speak it fairly well. None of the children could properly be called bilingual at this point, however. Reading instruction proceeds *in French*, but the techniques of teaching are closely geared to what the children actually demonstrate in the way of mastery of French, and no attempt is made to *teach French* via this early process. Ostensibly, the children are taught to read what they already know in French because the writing system of French is more consistently and regularly related to the spoken forms than is the case with English.

This latter point raises another important issue in the arguments put forth to justify bilingual education, especially for Spanish-speaking children. One of the crucial factors determining whether learning to read is easy or difficult is the phoneme-to-grapheme correspondence. For all dialects of Spanish there is a nearly one-to-one correspondence between the phonemes of the spoken language and the graphemes of the written. For Spanish, moreover, the consistency is far greater than it is for English.

Following this logic, one would predict that Spanish-speaking children would learn to read more and faster at the beginning; that is, they would learn code breaking more easily in Spanish than would an English-speaking child in English. From programs I have observed and from reports from teachers in bilingual programs in the early grades, this would indeed appear to be the case. For example, I visited several first-grade classrooms in a bilingual school in Corpus Christi, Texas, a short time ago and found myself surprised at the level of reading skill demonstrated by the group of Chicano youngsters comprising the classes. The visit was just prior to Christmas, not quite 4 months after school had started. The children were working from experience charts, blackboard exercises, and rexographed phonics work sheets at their desks. The teacher was relaxed and easygoing; she told me to select some children so that she could show me what they could do. I did so, and she put them through their paces, reading, word identification, word attack—one child at a time. It was in fact a very impressive performance, and it was repeated in each of the bilingual classrooms I visited.

To add to the impact, as I was leaving one of the first-grade classes, the principal of the school introduced me to an Anglo teacher who stepped into the hall from a first-grade classroom next to the one we had just left. She apologized to me on behalf of her class, explaining that they had not had the advantage of bilingual instruction and hence were slower than the youngsters I had seen, but that she was doing everything she could to remedy the situation, including taking Spanish classes in night school. She said that during the coming summer she intended to study Spanish intensively, for she had already found that her teaching task had been made easier and her success with the Mexican-American children enhanced by the little Spanish she had already picked up. In addition, she had become convinced by observing the success of the bilingual classes in her school.

Research has not yet provided any clear-cut answers about bilingual education. But on the basis of what we now know, it would appear that programs that attempt to develop literacy in the mother tongue make a great deal of sense, at least in the early years. Although the exact sequencing of instruction in the mother tongue and the other tongue is presently impossible to prescribe, it seems clear that each step in the acquisition of literacy skills should first be mastered in the mother tongue before the same task is introduced at the same level in English.

The question of how far to go in developing literacy in the mother tongue will most likely be dictated by factors other than pedagogical ones. Obviously, there are different problems associated with developing bilingual literacy programs for different language groups. They are determined in part by the relationship of the mother tongue to English and in part by the status of the mother tongue. For children who enter school speaking a language with a strong tradition of literacy and a well-developed body of written material, there is an obvious advantage to a sustained literacy program in their own language. A high level of literacy opens the door to the whole range of experience embodied in the literature of the child's native language.

For example, the greatest number of non-English-speaking children in our schools today are speakers of Spanish. This language, as one of the five most widely used in the world, has a wealth of available teaching materials at all levels. The task of implementing a cogent literacy program in Spanish involves collecting and evaluating available materials, selecting appropriate ones for use in specific Spanish dialect areas, then sequencing and adapting them for use in the schools. It may prove desirable to prepare new materials, particularly for use at the earliest levels of reading ability, but the ready availability of books in Spanish does not make this a *necessity*.

For children who come to school speaking a language without a literary tradition, however, as is the case with some of our Indian and Eskimo children, or for children who speak languages with limited or relatively inaccessible literatures, the implementation of a sustained literacy program in the schools may simply not be feasible. In such a situation the most modest goal, say of preparing only initial reading materials in the child's native tongue, will require intensive activity on the part of linguists to analyze the language, if this task is not yet done, and to design a writing system in which the preparation of literacy materials can proceed. Only then might we begin to think about how to expand.

Gaarder (1968) has offered several useful recommendations as to how the latter task might proceed for American Indian languages. For one thing, he has proposed that for every language with 1,000 or more speakers, the task of recording, writing, and publishing begin at once and include the history, religion, biography, lore, folktales, points of view on current problems, and the essential subject matter of the school curriculum appropriate to the group in question. Although these are worthy and pedagogically necessary steps to take, in the last analysis, the degree to which a literature will be developed in these languages will be for the speakers of the languages, not the school system, to decide.

Fishman & Lovas's (1970) typology of bilingual programs includes two models appropriate to the situations just delineated. The first of these, "full bilingualism," would develop all skills in both languages. Both English and the other language would serve as "media of instruction for all subjects (except in teaching the languages themselves)." Such an approach is only possible within the framework of a language in common use and with a well-developed literature. It is an attractive model to work toward, as it is the most promising possibility we have for developing bilingual literacy and other bilingual skills in many children, regardless of the language in which they begin their studies. Our failure to teach foreign languages well to our stolidly monolingual adults may thus be relieved in the process of meeting another critical educational need.

The second model, "partial bilingualism," has as its goal fluency and literacy in both languages, but "literacy in the mother tongue is restricted to certain subject matter, most generally that related to the ethnic group and its cultural heritage." This approach to bilingual literacy could apply to both types of language situations described earlier. For languages without a literary tradition, it is for the time being the only feasible approach. In view of the attitudinal changes that must occur among educators before the possibility of full bilingualism can be entertained, it may also be for the moment the most practical approach to developing bilingual literacy in children who are native speakers of languages of wider communication.

The extension of the bilingual rationale to the problems of developing literacy skills in speakers of regional and social dialects of English, particularly Black English, is also worth mentioning. The argument is that the task of learning to read would be easier with materials that correspond closely to the children's own speech and that which they regularly hear. It remains to be demonstrated that initial reading materials prepared in the "mother tongue" of black children will facilitate their learning to read. But whether or not success can be demonstrated, the willingness of educators to try new approaches suggests a dawning respect for the child's language.

When that respect has grown firm, perhaps we can abandon the myth of the melting pot and recognize our nation as a mosaic, the strength and beauty of which depend on the richness and variety of the fragments that comprise it. Perhaps then we can abandon our obsession with standard English as the key to all learning and get on with the task of educating our children.

REFERENCES

Andersson, T., & Boyer, M. *Bilingual schooling in the United States*. Washington: U.S. Government Printing Office, 1970. 2 vols.

Fishman, J. A., & Lovas, J. Bilingual education in sociolinguistic perspective. *TESOL Quarterly*, 1970, **4**, 215–222.

Gaarder, A. B. Education of American Indian children. In J. E. Alatis (Ed.), *Report of the Nineteenth Annual Round Table Meeting on Linguistics and Language Studies*. Washington: Georgetown University Press, 1968. Pp. 83–96. (Monograph Series on Languages and Linguistics, No. 21.)

MacNamara, J. *Bilingualism and primary education*. Edinburgh: Edinburgh University Press, 1966.

MacNamara, J. The effects of instruction in a weaker language. *Journal of Social Issues*, 1967, **23**, 121–135.

Modiano, N. National or mother language in beginning reading: A comparative study. *Research in the Teaching of English*, 1968, **2**, 32–43.

CHAPTER 6

THE ROLE OF TELEVISION IN LITERACY PROGRAMS

Nancy Hamilton Markle, David G. Markle, and Nathan Maccoby

INTRODUCTION

A majority of present and past political and social leaders in the United States have held universal literacy to be a desirable national goal. For over 200 years we have not been successful in attaining that goal. Citizens of a democratic, technical society need to be able to communicate and obtain instruction and recreation via printed media. Furthermore, citizens who are literate can achieve the knowledge and sophistication of thinking essential to effective and rational participation in modern, democratic self-government. The less-developed countries of the world are now attempting to leapfrog over past failures and successes of this and other highly developed countries. Is television the way?

The purpose of this paper is to explore some problems and possibilities involved in using mass media for literacy training programs. The purpose of this paper is not primarily to review literature on the psychology of cognition, theories on the teaching of reading, or theories and experimentation on how the skill of reading is acquired. Literature, theories, and research will, however, be considered where they provide illustrations of the advantages or disadvantages of one or another method or medium of instruction. Television will be the medium primarily considered.

GENERAL PROBLEMS IN LITERACY TRAINING

Instruction

Both scientific knowledge and empirical processes must be used in designing an instructional system. The medium of transmission is part of the instructional system and as such deserves consideration during the development process. For example, if the eventual intention is transmission by television, development of a course of instruction entirely apart from television would be a mistake. Nevertheless, many phases of the developmental process can be undertaken without constant recourse to the specific medium of transmission. On the one hand, one wants to avoid having the media dictate what is done. On the other hand, one wants to take advantage of medium-related creative design.

There is a great danger in using ad hoc television presentations. They may be effective, or they may not. Ideas for televised literacy programs must be pretested and modified on the basis of such testing as they are being developed.

Media for Transmission of Training and Information

A good instructional system for teaching reading is more important than the medium by which the instruction is delivered. The means of transmission is important, however, because the correct choices of media will reach the largest audience that will receive the greatest benefit from the instructional system at the most economical cost. Without a sound instructional system there is no possibility of an effective television presentation; with it there is an opportunity for one.

The principal uniqueness of television lies in its transmission capability rather than its instructional capacity. For example, it makes sense to use TV to transmit film or print or audio stimuli, but the relationships are not transitive.

Considerations for an instructional system should include not only the medium of transmission but also the control of other, potentially competing stimuli during transmission time, particularly for nonschool students. For example, are other self-selected activities such as eating, sleeping, and recreation more likely to compete at one transmission time than another? Should all channels or airways be preempted during the time of instruction? How can members of the intended audience be reached who do not have access to the reception system? What will the transmission and reception system cost? What amount of time will be necessary to prepare materials for one transmission system versus another? To what extent should the plan involve a major promotion effort to attract the appropriate audience to televised literacy programs? Would it be feasible to have utilization agents who make home visits to assign lessons and facilitate integration of televised learning with other materials? Would it be equally feasible to have centers to which students could come for certain kinds of group activities that are coordinated with home viewing? The British Open University has successfully used this sort of combined system.

Motivation

Available knowledge and experience should be employed to gain and to keep the attention of the audience. No instructional system can succeed if the students do not interact with that system.

It is wrong to assume that in school the student's attention is controlled and that out of school the student's attention is not controlled. Controlling attention of nonreaders within school is a key problem, and attracting and holding the attention of home viewers is a key problem for teaching them at home via television. Gibbon, Palmer, and Fowles, Chapter 7, below, report success with a system of testing children's television programs, in general, and *Sesame Street* prereading materials, in particular, for motivational and attention-holding value.

Treatments can be readily filmed or videotaped in rough form and pretested. What is being suggested here is not formal testing with large numbers of cases, but rather a more qualitative form of pretesting, in which it can often be discovered with very few cases—sometimes only one or two—that a given treatment needs changing. Filmmakers and program producers should take advantage of the experience of researchers who are willing to forego elaborate designs involving large N's during the process of development in the interest of improving and helping to build good programs, rather than concentrating only on elaborate evaluations of completed programs.

THE INSTRUCTIONAL SYSTEM

A number of general characteristics of a good instructional system can be discussed in the context of television as a transmission and presentation medium.

It must be valid. Here validity refers first not only to the final tests that measure attainment of the objectives but also to the match between the final tests and in-process instructional tasks given the students. In other words, the task being tested for must involve the same skills being performed under conditions similar to those in which the task is to be performed in "real life." Instruction that produces good performance on valid measuring instruments can, itself, be accepted as valid. The medium of transmission is of secondary importance in the establishment of validity.

It must be reproducible. In this instance the medium of transmission is important. The potentiality of television to control real time can contribute to the reproducibility of the instruction. This control potential is greater than that which is afforded by presentation media that do not control time. Little control is afforded by media, such as lectures, which take place in real time but which are not reproducible in a scientific sense. Print media, for example, permit reproducibility of static visual stimuli, but timing of presentation will vary among students, and sequence will vary among some. Critical dimensions of "live" presentations are usually not possible to reproduce reliably.

It should have an integral assessment and measurement system. This cannot be provided if television is used alone as a medium. Thus we conclude that whether or not television is used as a principal medium, it cannot be used exclusively. On-line response capability, such as is presently part of some cable TV experiments, could largely alleviate the assessment and measurement problem.

It should be based on research and generalization of principles, whenever possible. Television has the broadest presentation capability of any common mass medium. It employs both sight and sound and can be transmitted over great distances. It has the advantages of film, in being able to shift dramatically and instantly from one location to another, from one time to another, and from long shot to tight close-up (although not as effectively as film, owing to screen size and definition). It can shift from the speaker to what he is describing and back again. It can show the printed word and emphasize in closeup the relevant part of the word, phrase, etc. Therefore a broad range of principles can be employed via television presentation.

It can be tried out and revised as often as necessary before release. This is possible with television, although it is more expensive than with some other media if studio costs are involved. Although television tapes can easily be re-recorded, detailed editing and revision cannot easily be accomplished without recourse to other technological resources.

It can be called back for revision after release. In view of the ease of control of the distribution system for television presentations, this is one of the great advantages of the medium. Accomplishment of the actual revision may, as previously stated, be somewhat expensive.

It is carefully sequenced. This is a characteristic of the instructional system that should not be affected by the transmission medium. However, owing to costs of production, a higher degree of care in sequencing is needed for television than for some other means of communication.

It should arouse initial interest and maintain motivation. Television has excellent potential for this. It is well established as a source of recreation, relaxation, and entertainment for much of the population. Whether this initially positive valence can be maintained is the responsibility of the instructional system. Certainly many "educational" presentations have failed. On the other hand, *Sesame Street*, of the Children's Television

Workshop, has been successful in holding the interest of its intended audience. The early work investigating motivational characteristics of the material apparently "paid off." Again, the capability is intrinsic to the instructional system, not to the medium of transmission alone.

It should actively engage the learner's participation. This has been hard to engineer with television and for that reason has been largely omitted from most television programs. Again, *Sesame Street* has been successful in this dimension. Its producers have not yet tried many higher orders of participation, such as would be required for much adult learning. Careful instructional engineering can overcome the problems that television poses for active participation in at least two ways. First, empirical work with spot check overt responses in developmental stages can be used to engineer covert responses with fair certainty. Second, the efficiency of overt responding can be accommodated via deliberate response requests, timing of the presentation, and manipulation of external contingencies. In this latter regard, other media, such as printed answer sheets and workbooks, will be needed, along with procedures, rewards, etc., for encouraging their completion. Such overt response provisions can be interspersed during the television presentation, and they can also be independent of it from a timing standpoint. Presumably as skill increases, more independent reading would be encouraged.

It should provide for feedback to the designer. Any current mass medium is inherently a one-way transmission channel. Feedback to the designer should be liberally used in development to minimize problems in transmission. It will be necessary, however, to use other means of communication to obtain feedback for the designer and evaluator during the actual presentation of the course via television, for example. Paper media, as suggested above, would have to be relied on for some types of evaluation and feedback. Personal contacts (interviews) could be used for others. In some situations cable TV installations have provisions for digital push-button responses, which would be a good way of collecting feedback from the student.

It should inform the student of his progress. Mass communication media usually fix the pace of presentation. Thus some students may receive feedback too early, others too late, for "real time" overt responding coordinated with a presentation. This can be accommodated to some extent with techniques that reduce response time variance. Empirical means can then be used to plan timing of feedback that is least undesirable. Timing of feedback is less troublesome for supplemental materials that are solely in print media.

It should be optimally economical. Ideally, the first economic considerations would be of the students' time and money. In reality, the reverse order is usually the case, and if careful attention is paid to all elements, the student's time and money can be preserved reasonably well.

Television is probably economical with regard to the student's money, and if proper considerations in scheduling, programming, etc., are made, television can be economical with regard to the student's time as well. Design costs for any materials that are developed rigorously using empirical methods will be high, as compared with nonempirical text "authorship." These costs are small, however, as compared with professional media-specific design costs when theatrical and broadcasting rates apply. Production time and costs are relatively high for television, but a minimal use of "professional" time and facilities should reduce costs considerably. Although professional production know-how should not be overlooked, most evidence indicates that many production techniques that are used in commercial films and television either do not facilitate learning or are inconsistent with design requirements that have been identified empirically (Hovland, Lumsdaine, & Sheffield, 1949; Markle, 1967). Finally, almost no matter how high the production costs may be, the cost per student, if audiences are at all numerous, can be quite moderate.

Many features of instruction that are generally accepted as desirable in their own right are means to the ends that have been enumerated above. Such features include optimal step size, suitable pacing, appropriate media, simulation of real conditions during instruction, and use of reward rather than punishment.

Making Programs to Teach the Illiterate

Different subsets of the population pose different questions for literacy training. Adults who have been exposed to the school system but cannot read, adults who have had little or no schooling and consequently cannot read, children who do poorly in school, and ordinary school children, for example, pose different instructional, motivational, and transmission problems.

Programs intended to teach those who have not learned or who potentially will not learn to read will require rigorous empirical development. Motivation, transmission, and evaluation must be made part of the design setting. A satisfactory combination may be very difficult to attain and may require many trials and revisions.

In the contemporary professional community, sufficient information, expertise, and experience now exist to produce programs that would very likely be successful in teaching normal adults to read.

ADVANTAGES AND DISADVANTAGES OF TELEVISION

Television is widely available as a medium of reception. For those who cannot read and write, television is more widely available even than paper media—or perhaps we should say *functionally* more available than paper media, for obvious reasons.

Television has great popular appeal. This is one of the strongest points in its favor. Radio also has great popular appeal, as do other entertainment media. Nevertheless, given the present standing of the various media, nonreaders and poor readers are more likely to be reached by a widely publicized presentation on television than by any other available medium.

Many people now allot large portions of their nonworking time to viewing television. Habituation is well established. Further, there are no age limitations or social sanctions associated with television. Television is not confined to a single method of presentation. Almost all other presentation media can be used *via* television. Thus all or nearly all of a production can be coordinated through television.

Television can use important persons with high status to present content. It can also be used to depersonalize instruction if that is desirable. This is a major advantage over nearly all other media. For example, radio can use prestigious figures (with some loss in personal impact) but would not be nearly as successful in depersonalizing content.

Television can employ both motion and sound, with control over synchronization, an advantage shared only by live and filmed presentations.

Size of step and pacing of presentation are controlled in televised presentations. This can be a disadvantage, but in literacy instruction, in which the audience has little or no experience in choosing a suitable step size or pace, the fixed presentation *could be* turned into an advantage. This pacing could be especially effective on television if it were based on careful pretesting of the material to be taught and were carried out with selected individual learners from the target audiences (Sheffield and Maccoby, 1961).

Television is locally controllable in videotape form, but it *can* be centrally controlled via broadcasting if that is desirable.

General Disadvantages of Television

The most needy portion of the intended audience for literacy instruction may not possess or have access to television. This is especially true of the rural black population in the southern United States. More persons have radio, and that medium should be considered.

Television is expensive as an original medium. Costs of design and production are increased by the necessity to employ non-subject-matter professionals. Television is especially expensive as compared with paper media and to a lesser extent as compared with slides and filmstrips. Nevertheless, the practical unavailability of slides, filmstrips, and sound motion pictures to all but those with special projection equipment, argue that television and radio are "first-choice" media.

Television, like film, is a medium that is likely to seduce the developer into concentrating on "artistic" considerations that may be irrelevant to instruction. Proper development should control and constrain this, but this caveat is more difficult to obey than it may seem.

More generally, television is stimulus oriented rather than response oriented. It is as though one put the reward in the hand of the experimenter rather than in the mouth of the rat. Stimulus-oriented systems, consequently, can fail to produce the desired behavior.

The expense and trouble of manipulating videotape may deter tryout and revision of instruction. Planning early developmental tryouts in which a TV presentation is simulated with other presentation means can partly obviate this cost. Paper media are clearly superior in this regard. If paper media were easily distributable and had the intrinsic motivational aspects and auditory advantages of television, they would be superior to other media.

Television does not completely provide active practice, feedback to the student, and feedback to the designer. It may be necessary to present material simultaneously or in coordination by more than one medium, probably including print media. This will cause students difficulties with manipulation and coordination of more than one medium—difficulties that are especially serious with poor readers and nonreaders. Of course, media coordination will be a problem with any system in which the student must do some of the coordination.

Some research shows that certain personality types learn more from live presentations (Snow, Tiffin, & Siebert, 1965), but the study is of doubtful generalization to the illiterate populations. In any event, there is no reason to suppose that human teachers will not be a functioning part of the system, no matter what other media prove useful.

WHAT THE RESEARCH SHOWS

There are a number of models of the cognitive processes employed in reading and in learning to read (as represented by Singer & Ruddell, 1970).

Reading research and methods of teaching reading are much more in the province of the other contributors to this volume. Research findings have been specific and numerous but have thus far not provided a complete gestalt that can guide the preparation of effective courses in reading for any given population at a moment's notice.

Research specifically on the use of television as a transmission system for literacy training is scarce. In 1968 the United States Office of Education and the Carnegie and Ford foundations began sponsorship of a project called the Children's Television Workshop. The objectives were to teach classic stories, the alphabet, language, and the art of reasoning to preschool children. The program *Sesame Street* resulted from this project. Additional programs of this nature—not, however, specifically on literacy —are presently under way. Literature in this area has been well covered in reviews by Chu & Schramm (1968) and by Wade (1969). We have been unable to find much research that includes rigorous evaluation of programs using television to teach reading. We would, therefore, like to turn our attention to goals for the future.

WHAT RESEARCH IS NEEDED

Programs that will teach all our citizens to read cannot wait for all the research that would be valuable or interesting. It is for this reason that empirical development, using what research has indicated thus far, is recommended. But it is not for that reason alone that empirical development should be employed. Empirical development will be needed even when scientific knowledge is far better established. For example, let us assume that it has been established that active practice, when combined with demonstration, will enhance the effectiveness of instruction and learning. How does one apply that principle to teaching a youngster to read via television? We submit that considerable creativity, coupled with repeated testing and evaluation at each stage of development, is needed to make maximum application of such principles to teaching children to read via television or, for that matter, any medium.

If literacy training is to be presented via television, research on reading should involve television. Theory-testing research that is not operationally specific to the literacy program to which this committee is addressed should be undertaken independently with other funds, by other agencies.

WHAT SHOULD BE DONE

Motivation

In investigating television's motivational capacity, attention should be devoted to ways of capitalizing on the initial positive valence, which will quickly disappear if the treatment does not maintain interest. Here are some guidelines: Some portion of the program should have real persons with whom the student can identify and/or who are acceptable to the student as models. This is a very important point, since the educationally deprived population does not identify with traditional figures of status and authority, nor with the so-called average man. Motivational techniques known to succeed with the white middle-class population will not in general succeed with the educationally disadvantaged.

The program should take the dignity of the student seriously. Not being able to read is a serious deficit in our society, but it is neither childish nor undignified. Teaching techniques that talk down to the student (as opposed to making the task simple for him to complete) will instantly lose the audience. Empirical development methods often identify trouble spots, but they do not uniquely identify how to revise materials. It requires fine judgment and restraint to simplify materials without making them simpleminded and offensive. It will be difficult for the developers, no matter how highly motivated, to avoid becoming hostile about their students' failures and equally difficult to keep from letting their hostility indirectly affect the nature of the materials. These problems are common with less difficult subject matter areas and students. We cannot ignore them here.

Materials, instructions, and all portions of the lessons should be attractive but clear. Elaborate "window dressing" should be avoided as potentially more confusing than anything else. This guideline applies under the headings of both instruction and motivation. Active practice is good for maintaining interaction with specifically that which is being practiced. Whether the active practice leads to the intended learning depends on what is practiced, how much at one time, for how long a period of time, and with how many repetitions, and so forth. These questions can only be answered by empirical tryouts. The answers are different for different kinds of material and for different presentations of the same kind of material. Regardless of mode of presentation, however, the basic task is to engineer frequent or continuous practice of an interesting nature.

Probably the most powerful overall motivator will be success. Success is defined here in the students' terms, not the all-too-convenient middle-class teacher's terms. Success is the intersection of tasks that are meaningful to the student, correct performance, and perceptions of success. Perceptions of correctness alone will not do. There will be some students who fail. There will be some small failures for each student. Nonetheless, the system should be developed with the goal of eliminating failure.

A contributor not only to maintaining interest but also to success is proper pacing of the presentation. In fixed time presentations, now common to television, proper pacing will be one of the most difficult engineering tasks. Presentations too slowly paced will bore the faster students, whereas presentations too rapidly paced will lose the slower students. Perhaps this difficulty can be avoided by making a multitrack presentation, in which the student is asked to do a "core" task first, with increasingly enriched but not basically crucial tasks being available to those who finish each core step.

Ideally, the materials will have a variable, controllable pace. This implies, however, that national mass presentation via commercial or educational television is not feasible. In the long run, the pacing problem should probably be dealt with on the assumption that mass presentation will be the only way to reach many adult nonreaders. Materials for use in the schools, on the other hand, could be packaged for videotape viewing, controllable by the individual teacher or student using them. Funds to purchase such viewing facilities should be provided to schools that cannot equip themselves.

If organization of the material to be presented is appropriately conceptualized, it may be possible to maintain a given rate of presentation successfully to a relatively large audience containing individuals who differ widely in their usual rates of learning. The concept developed by Sheffield & Maccoby (1961) of the demonstration-assimilation (D-A) span—the largest amount of material that could be demonstrated and result in immediate successful practice—could perhaps be applied to reading. General percentage criteria for course success can be set before instruction is developed or as a product of development, or both. Sheffield and Maccoby settled for a D-A span that was successful with 75 percent of their audiences. As students learn, larger units—hopefully what they labeled natural units—could be employed for demonstration and practice, and finally still larger units could thus be employed. These principles could undoubtedly be engineered for reading instruction over television.

Although the use of color may make presentations more attractive, we cannot assume that color reception is universally available. Therefore the lessons should be developed, tried out, and revised in black and white. The decision of whether to make the final filming or taping in color then becomes purely economic. There is nothing in the psychological literature to indicate that color pictures instruct better than black and white pictures, *unless* the instruction is color relevant (Kanner, 1968). With limited availability of color-receiving TV sets, it would seem unwise to make treatments for mass projection that use color-dependent teaching techniques. Color may serve as an "irrelevant" motivator, however, and so broadcasting in color may be worthwhile, as long as viewers with black and white reception are not penalized.

Attractive sound can play a role in maintaining interest, but irrelevant musical backgrounds and extraneous or simply distracting noises should be avoided. The professional broadcaster's notion that every moment of "air" time must be filled with some noise or other can be dysfunctional to portions of a good instructional system.

Research on extending motivation to engage in a desirable activity (in this case, reading) outside of the instructional setting was reported by May & Lumsdaine (1958). Essentially the findings indicated that more school children who had seen movies of a specific story or book checked that book out of the school library than did those who had seen no movie.

This indicates that a familiarization program could be used as a motivator preceding introduction of desirable reading material in printed form. This notion should, however, be investigated further with educationally disadvantaged students before the same means of enhancing motivation can be certain to apply to them.

We must distinguish between two types of situations: the first is the one in which the student is motivated simply to watch, listen, and be entertained, and the second is the one in which the student is motivated not only to watch and keep watching but also to participate actively in specific ways. Clearly, the second will be much more difficult to achieve.

Current techniques used on television tend to be aimed toward the first type of motivation. Whether or not those same techniques can be applied toward the second type of motivation is an open question. They include, for example: canned laughter; stories that are predictable, nonthreatening, easy to follow and highly redundant (you miss nothing if you miss one or a piece of one); sex; violence; background music and/or popular music; action, in the sense of "something always happening"; appeals to the need to escape; etc. Although many of these techniques may not be useful in instruction, we should not expect that traditional classroom motivational techniques would be useful either, nor can we expect to get motivation out of a paper bag.

Transmission

Television as a transmission and reception medium exists. The question of whether it is the logical choice for a universal literacy program can only be settled when it is determined that television reception can be made available widely enough to the relevant population. Radio should be considered an alternative to television, even though the instructional problems are much greater, because it is more widely available and lower in cost.

If we assume that television is chosen as the major medium, there are several considerations about the type of transmission.

For the adult nonliterate population, mass presentation with all other air time preempted would be a powerful attention-securing device. Whether or not other air time is preempted, mass broadcasting either on a national or on a local scale is the simplest answer for the adult population.

Scheduling the mass presentations could be done many ways. If all air time is preempted for literacy during prime time for approximately one half-hour daily, other TV channels can have visual programs showing only the texts of various books or printed word media (newspapers, magazines, etc.). These texts on other channels would be of varying difficulty levels—none would be of intrinsic interest (visual, audio, etc.) beyond that conveyed by the verbal text. The sound track for these other texts could be dead or have occasional sound effects—none of any intrinsic interest. Alternatively, or concomitantly, many different difficulty levels could be accommodated. Television stations not presenting one level or the other of the literacy program, and radio stations as well, could present public-service programs: how to register to vote; economics for the housewife; ecological preservation; population planning; etc. For all competing programs, time could be sold (as well as for the literacy program if control could remain with the designers rather than with the admen), but these other programs would be supervised by the literacy team, who would have veto power as well as advisory power. (Remember, this would not be for a long period of time nor for very long in any one day. It must, however, be during prime time, say between 7 and 8 P.M.)

For the person still in school who is not learning to read at a satisfactory level or rate, materials different from those for the nonliterate adult would be needed. Lessons that can be teacher or student paced and controlled would be best for in-school situations.

For prereading training of the child, or better still for reading training of the child, beginning at the prereading level, still another set of materials is needed. Self-pacing or teacher-scheduled pacing is most desirable. Perhaps all three kinds of material (adult, in-school reading disability, and entire reading instruction program from preschool on) could be generated from the same set of basic objectives, but the interim goal points and the lessons themselves would differ from one another.

Two basic kinds of transmission must, then, be planned—mass transmission for mass consumption and individual packaging for individual (or small group) control and consumption. We should consider also a multiple-channel approach beyond the radio-TV parallelism suggested above. If, for example, the print media ran the same lessons for "readers," there would be added reward for nonreaders to keep up with the audio lessons so that they could interact with the readers about the "same" material.

Assessment and Evaluation

An instructional system should include provisions for collecting data both during development and during use. Data are needed on within-course performance, immediate-terminal performance, and delayed performance. Within-course and immediate post-course assessment and feedback are more difficult to design, to distribute, and to obtain returns for some media of transmission than for others.

Television, or any other mass medium, poses severe problems in obtaining ongoing assessment and evaluation. Sampling schemes are necessary, and the proper sampling plan will provide the necessary information for revision and evaluation of the course as a whole. The problem of providing rewards and feedback to the student is a separate one, and we would like to suggest some elements of a reward scheme. The system could be administered from offices much the same as the motor vehicle licensing program is. Graded printed reading material with contributing illustrations could be provided, on loan, contingent on passing a prereading test in the office and registering for the literacy series. If the learner finished the course satisfactorily (i.e., came in and passed intermediate tests, turned in workbooks, and passed the final test in the office), he would be given all the books. During the time of the broadcast, all pencils, free paper, and free workbooks, as well as free "reading" books would be provided for coming in and passing tests and turning in work at the office. Payment of welfare money might be made contingent on *trying* the reading course, but it would be destructive to make welfare payments contingent on *passing* the reading course.

A further consideration is that for some persons who cannot read, association in any way with "welfare people" could stop them from participating in the program.

If competing programs presented on radio and TV are all to be literacy related, they could be stratified by first language, age, or geographic region as well as being presented in tracks, as discussed earlier in this paper.

Instruction

Since this paper is not addressed particularly to the topic of instruction, our comments will be limited to some general ideas about how to approach the teaching of reading and to a methodological discussion of recommended empirical development techniques and procedures.

Use of rote memorization is probably valuable in teaching spelling and letter names and in increasing vocabulary. Repetition in various contexts—visual, auditory, tactile, etc.—would aid learning and retention, and various attractive settings would help insure motivation. Overlearning of many basic tools, such as the alphabet, is critical for the proper utilization of these building blocks easily and accurately in subsequent learning. The optimal degree of overlearning usually involves a considerable amount of practice of the behavior to be learned.

Camera and sound devices can be used to focus attention on critical elements of the presentation. All the aforementioned devices have been employed successfully on *Sesame Street* as well as in many nontelevision productions. We wish merely to point out their potential generality.

In the process of collecting more information specifically about the disadvantaged nonreader and the disabled reader, two sources are suggested. First, a large amount of often ignored information can be obtained by talking with some of the "patients" who actually have the "disease," especially with older students who have gone through the educational system without really learning to read. Testing, discussing, etc., with willing members of the specific populations would be invaluable. Second, interviews and observations of teachers known to be especially good instructors of reading or known to be more than usually successful with students who have reading problems should be useful.

It is clear that television has limitations as a medium for literacy training. Television cannot readily be adapted to individual differences in readiness to learn to read and in the rate and depth of learning to read. There also exist important limitations on the provision of knowledge to the learner of the results of such practice. In spite of these and other limitations of the medium, we have seen that television can play an important role in a major effort to increase and improve literacy. It will, however, take a considerable investment in people, equipment, and funds for any such effort to be even moderately successful.

REFERENCES

Chu, G. C., and Schramm, W. *Learning from television: What the research says.* An occasional paper from ERIC, August 1968.

Hovland, C. I., Lumsdaine, A. A., Sheffield, F. D. *Experiments on mass communication.* Princeton, N.J.: Princeton University Press, 1949.

Kanner, J. H. *The instructional effectiveness of color in television: A review of the evidence.* An occasional paper from ERIC, January 1968.

Lumsdaine, A. A. (Ed.) *Student response in programmed instruction.* National Academy of Sciences—National Research Council Publication 943, 1961.

Lumsdaine, A. A. Instruments and media of instruction. In N. L. Gage (Ed.), *Handbook of research on teaching.* Chicago: Rand McNally & Company, 1963. Pp. 583–682.

Lumsdaine, A. A., and May, M. A. Mass communication and educational media. *Annual Review of Psychology*, 1965, **16**, 175–534.

Maccoby, N., and Sheffield, F. D. Theory and experimental research on the teaching of complex sequential procedures by alternate demonstration and practice. In *Air Force human engineering, personnel, and training research.* National Academy of Sciences—National Research Council Publication 516, 1958.

Markle, D. G. Final Report. The development of the Bell System first aid and personal safety course. Contract AIR-E81-4/67-FR. Palo Alto, Calif.: American Institutes for Research, 1967.

May, M. A., and Lumsdaine, A. A. *Learning from films.* New Haven, Conn.: Yale University Press, 1958.

Snow, R. E., Tiffin, J., and Seibert, W. Individual differences and instructional film effects. *Journal of Educational Psychology*, 1965, **6**, 315–326.

Singer, H., and Ruddell, R. (Eds.) *Theoretical models and processes of reading.* Newark, Del.: International Reading Association, 1970.

Wade, S. E. *Media and the disadvantaged.* A review of literature paper from ERIC, March 1969.

CHAPTER 7

SESAME STREET, THE ELECTRIC COMPANY, AND READING

Samuel Y. Gibbon, Jr., Edward L. Palmer, and Barbara R. Fowles

INTRODUCTION

Sesame Street and *The Electric Company*, two of the most pervasive educational experiments in recent memory, uniquely exploit the special values of the television medium for teaching prereading and reading skills.[1]

Sesame Street,[2] however, was not conceived in response to the nation's reading problem per se but grew out of the prevalent concern during the early and mid 1960s for early cognitive stimulation. It was thought of as a preschool rather than a prereading program, and this perspective was reflected in the series' initial statement of educational objectives, which included a limited set of prereading goals as a part of a far broader preschool curriculum. The first season of *Sesame Street* proved television's efficacy for teaching selected prereading skills. As a result, the second

---

[1] The development and execution of these programs represents the effort of a large number of intelligent, talented, and committed individuals. Many of the ideas discussed here are theirs. The present authors take credit only for organizing and systematizing ideas generated and realized by everyone on the research and production staffs of the Children's Television Workshop.

[2] The present discussions of *Sesame Street* are drawn mainly from an earlier article by Gibbon & Palmer (1970). Many of the same discussions are quoted within a somewhat different interpretive context by Lesser (1974).

season curriculum contained an explicit and considerably expanded emphasis on reading.

Also as a result of the evident success of *Sesame Street*, and in response to the growing concern with the nation's literacy problem, work on *The Electric Company* was begun. Its intended purpose was to provide supplementary instruction in basic reading skills for seven- to ten-year-old children with reading problems. Evaluation of the educational effects of two seasons of *The Electric Company* has demonstrated that television has an important role to play in reading instruction.

The Children's Television Workshop (CTW) was organized from the beginning as a cooperative enterprise involving educational researchers and academic advisers as well as television producers. Formative research, undertaken primarily by the CTW research staff, provides prebroadcast and continuous feedback information about the efficacy of particular production techniques and program segments (Palmer, 1974). Summative research, usually carried out independently of CTW, evaluates the impact of an entire year's series of programs and provides a basis for curriculum revision. Advisers to the Workshop, who are drawn mainly from the fields of child psychology, education, reading, and research design, provide recommendations at critical points in the production/research process.

Sesame Street and *The Electric Company* have been evaluated extensively (Ball & Bogatz, 1970, 1972; Bogatz & Ball, 1971; Herriott & Liebert, 1972). Both series have been shown to achieve their intended objectives successfully, reaching unprecedented numbers of viewers for instructional television programs and producing clear gains in most of the instructional goal areas treated. Since these results are readily available in published reports, discussion of the educational effects of the programs will not be repeated here. Rather, what is presented here is an explication of the reading and prereading goals of the two series and a description of some of the approaches taken in using the television medium to implement them.

Although on the face of it televised reading instruction might seem to be an unlikely hybridization of media, there are in fact several reasons why television can be useful in teaching prereading and reading skills. First, television, no matter what it might teach, is virtually "flunk proof." For many disadvantaged children, school is an exotic subculture whose rituals and demands are baffling. The child who watches *Sesame Street* or *The Electric Company* is being educated by a medium whose visual, auditory, and temporal conventions are familiar. For preschoolers this can mean that their first acquaintances with letters and numbers are pleasant and positive; for older children whose school failures have made print a threat, television can make reading palatable and even enjoyable.

Second, both very young children and slow learners require generous repetition of simple concepts. Television makes it possible, through the use of live action film, puppets, animation, music, and all manner of audio-visual magic, to present the most fundamental material over and over while keeping it fresh and attractive.

Third, broadcast television's ability to bring instruction to literally millions of children, at home and in classrooms, means that the cost per program per child is remarkably small.

Finally, and of special importance for reading instruction, television offers a unique repertory of film and electronic techniques for drawing the child's attention to print, focusing it on critical elements of the printed code, modeling processes of blending and scanning, and relating printed language to its meaning.

This chapter describes the thinking behind the televised prereading and reading instruction offered on *Sesame Street* and *The Electric Company*. Our intention is to delineate the key issues involved in designing such programs and to relate them to actual program design decisions. Most of all, we hope to convey to the reader what we have come to appreciate of the scope, the power, and the sophistication of television as a teaching tool.

SESAME STREET

Sesame Street began as, and continues to be, a true experiment in the use of popular television techniques to teach. Although educational television has been in existence for quite some time, it had previously served mainly to bring conventional classroom instruction to a wider audience. *Sesame Street*, in contrast, represents a deliberate effort to marry the production techniques of popular commercial television programs with educational content. Its curriculum is designed to meet the educational needs of the preschooler, particularly the urban disadvantaged child.

Since learning to read is the major task that the primary school child faces, skills related to reading have an important place in the *Sesame Street* curriculum. For the three- to five-year-old, these skills encompass a broad spectrum of perceptual and cognitive competencies. The curriculum for the first season of *Sesame Street* reflected that spectrum, but it was cautiously limited to such simple prerequisites to reading as letter discrimination, letter names, left-to-right orientation, spoken vocabulary, and the practical and social utility of literacy. After the impressive success of its first season (Ball & Bogatz, 1970), *Sesame Street's* reading goals were expanded to include some actual beginning reading instruction, including sight vocabulary, word families, and blending. There has since been a small retreat from this sophisticated second-year curriculum out of the concern that the program was exceeding the readiness of the disadvantaged viewer.

Some criteria other than explicitly educational ones contributed to curriculum selection decisions. A major one was that whatever was to be taught had to be suitable for television presentation. Parental expectations for an educational program and the contribution of mastery of the curriculum to the self-image of the child were also considered. Obviously a program whose goals are those which most parents agree to be important for their children (like letter names and counting) is readily accepted. This means that children are likely to be reinforced by their parents for viewing.

Success in learning and motivation to learn feed one another. Intellectual accomplishments that would enhance the child's self-image and that the child and his parents would recognize as badges of success were therefore considered important. Furthermore, these achievements could foster the interest in school that would in turn facilitate success in that setting.

The current (1974–75) prereading goals for *Sesame Street*, excerpted from the series' larger set of goals, are presented in Appendix A at the end of the chapter. Some of those goals merit detailed discussion. For example, extensive deliberation preceded the decision to include recitation of the alphabet as a curriculum objective. We were well aware that although studies have shown that ability to name the letters of the alphabet is one of the best predictors of reading success (Chall, 1967), the high correlation between these skills is generally agreed to be explained by some shared antecedent ability. Nevertheless, there were several things to be said for teaching young children to recite the alphabet. First, presentation of the alphabet exposes the viewer to the entire set of letters to be learned; knowing the extent of the learning task may facilitate its accomplishment. Second, recitation of the alphabet can offer a clear invitation for the audience to participate in the television program. Since active involvement is a powerful learning mode for young children, such an opportunity is important. And the inclination to participate may then be generalized to other segments in which the invitation is less explicit. Finally, the motivational value of learning to recite the alphabet can be great, since it is seen by adults and other children as an impressive achievement.

A second *Sesame Street* curriculum area that deserves discussion is the list of Spanish and English sight vocabulary (words to be recognized as wholes). Mastery of a limited English sight vocabulary serves a motivational end similar to learning to recite the alphabet, since the ability to recognize words is a widely acknowledged intellectual achievement for young children. The words taught on *Sesame Street* were selected for their motivational value, their high frequency of occurrence in the environment, and their high functional utility. Finally, some words were selected because they belonged to the same "word family." By becoming thoroughly familiar with several words that have common phonic structures, the viewer may begin to make simple inferences about the sound system, and the spelling system, of English.

Presentation of Spanish sight vocabulary serves the function of assisting the large number of Spanish-speaking children in *Sesame Street's* audience. Inclusion of Spanish vocabulary and bilingual characters tells Hispanic children that the program is for them too and that reading is an activity as appropriate to Spanish as to English. Simultaneously, the message is communicated to non-Hispanic children that other cultures and languages are interesting and that other languages can be written down.

The final area of the prereading curriculum to be discussed is auditory word analysis. This includes identification of individual letter sounds, word families, rhyming, alliteration, and syllable blending. Awareness that spoken words can be analyzed into their component sounds is a critical prerequisite to reading (Mattingly, 1972). Auditory analysis is therefore presented at several levels of precision. The grossest skill taught is analysis of words into syllables ("can-dle"), since syllabic units are much easier to hear than phonemic ones (Gleitman & Rozin, 1973). Therefore, modeling the blending process by using syllabic units, even though the English alphabetic system functions at the phonemic level, makes it easier for the child to grasp the principle of synthesizing smaller units into words. Once this principle is understood, applying it at the phonemic level, and eventually relating it to print, becomes a more manageable task.

Rhyming word families and alliteration are used on *Sesame Street* to introduce the viewer to a finer level of sound structure. Each of these techniques employs a constant plus variation ("jet, met, set"); or ("jet, jam, jar") to focus the child's attention on the regularities of the mapping system.

Finally, individual letter sounds are taught. The difficult process of synthesizing these individual letter sounds into intelligible words is not taught on *Sesame Street*. However, exposure to the blending principle by using syllables, together with mastery of letter sounds, can maximize the likelihood that the viewer will meet with success when confronted with auditory analysis tasks.

The problem of instructional sequence concerned the designers of *Sesame Street* from the very outset. Traditional instructional practice requires that the teaching of any complex skill be carefully sequenced from the elementary to the elaborate. For *Sesame Street* this principle posed serious problems because factors associated with the open broadcast circumstances made conventional sequencing patterns inappropriate. No matter how effective the information campaign might have been prior to going on the air, the audience was bound to start relatively small and grow during the course of the series. Furthermore, it was certain that no matter how entertaining the show proved to be, a sizable percentage of the audience would view irregularly. Then too, members of this heterogeneous young audience would differ widely in age, background, prior experience, and learning style.

Finally, it was desirable to schedule the instruction in such a way that a child tuning in the series late in the season, and perhaps viewing irregularly thereafter, would still be guaranteed at least some exposure to the entire curriculum. The decision was finally made that no single program could require that the viewer have seen any other and every program segment had to be designed with a wide range of individual learning needs in mind. Each program would therefore include instruction in each major goal area. The schedule would include as much review as possible for the sake of the irregular viewer.

Scheduling the letter instruction presented problems of its own. It was impossible to present the letter-related skills in strict accordance with any conventional assumptions about hierarchical acquisition. For example, there was no point in teaching the "short" vowel sounds before the "long" if a sizable portion of the ultimate audience might not yet be watching.

Once these exigencies were recognized, the first season's scheduling of the letters of the alphabet followed logically. The alphabet was regarded as a set of thirty-six letters: twenty-one consonants, five vowels, and the same five vowels repeated twice more. Thus vowels received triple the exposure given to consonants. Three letters were introduced each week in random order, so the entire set could be presented in a period of 12 weeks.

Within each week the scheduling was intricate: On each of 3 days, one of that week's three letters was given major attention; the other two received minor attention for purposes of review and reinforcement. Thus, over the 3 days, each letter was given primary emphasis once and secondary emphasis twice. On the fourth day all three letters were given equal emphasis; and on the fifth day two of the previous week's letters were reviewed, and one letter from the following week was previewed, all three letters receiving equal time. These varying patterns were assigned to different days from week to week so that any child missing the show consistently on a particular day could still encounter all the variations within the schedule.

The entire 12-week schedule was repeated once during the first 26-week season of *Sesame Street*. The pattern of letter instruction in the remaining 2 weeks of the season was initially left undetermined, allowing for experimentation with a different schedule of instruction or different ways of presenting the letters. This complex schedule grew almost entirely out of the need to make the most appropriate use of the open broadcast circumstances and to get as much information as possible to as many children as possible.

These same factors have influenced both the form of the entire show and the construction of its segments. Each program is conceived as a potpourri of short, diverse elements frequently related to one another but often not, all held together by the realistic street setting that functions as "home base" for the program. Each segment was designed to teach on as many levels as possible and to do so in an entertaining fashion.

It was assumed in designing the program that any given child would perceive the show in accordance with his current capacity to understand and that repeated exposure to the program would expand that capacity and raise his level of learning. For this reason individual program elements were designed to embody within them a number of levels of complexity. The viewer could then perceive the material on the level of complexity appropriate to his understanding. Given sufficient repetition of the same or similar segments, the child might sequence himself through the material presented, from simple to complex.

As an illustration, a child starting with only the barest understanding of the nature of the written code might, over several repetitions, get all the following notions from a hypothetical *Sesame Street* segment designed to teach the shape of the letter *W*, its name, and the sound it represents:

1. That squiggle is not a random squiggle.
2. That squiggle has a particular identifiable shape.
3. It must have that shape, or it is a squiggle with another name.
4. This squiggle I see is called "double-*U*."
5. "Double-*U*" is one of a class of squiggles called "letters."
6. The letter *W* represents a particular speech sound.
7. The letter *W* often appears with other letters in groups called "words."
8. Words are things we say when we talk.
9. Written words correspond to spoken words.
10. Many spoken words begin with the speech sound /*w*/.
11. Many written words begin with the letter "double-*U*."
12. The letter *W* represents the speech sound /*w*/.
13. In printed words, "begins with" means "at the left-hand end of."
14. When a printed word begins with *W*, /*w*/ is the first sound spoken.
15. The printed word "Witch" is such a word.
16. "Witch" can occur and be read in other contexts.

This list of concepts is of course hypothetical, incomplete, and not necessarily hierarchical. It is meant only as an illustration of the range of learning opportunities that can be offered to the learner within a single segment.

Acquisition of the concepts almost certainly does not follow the sequence given. A child may sit through many repetitions of a film, apparently merely enjoying it for its humor or other engaging qualities, and then come to understand several concepts simultaneously. Another child may steadily accrue information until some new fact about W conflicts with what he or she has learned earlier. The conflict may lead him to regress temporarily and then to integrate the new understanding with the old in a new, higher-level organization.

Previous learning may alter the order and rate of acquisition, and not always favorably. For example, introduction of the letter *b* immediately after *d* may cause the child to mislabel *b*. The location of points of confusion may vary depending on how many letters the child has already learned and how well he has learned them.

Some of this discussion has been necessarily speculative, because there is much yet to be learned about what transpires between the young child and the program. Our purpose in this discussion has been to illustrate the reasoning behind the design of *Sesame Street's* curriculum and to suggest that the learning processes invoked by instructional television warrant considerable sophisticated research, which has barely begun.

The following section will pursue this theme in discussing the implementation of this curriculum and the matching of instructional goals to the educational means provided by television, focusing on the unique capabilities television has for meeting these instructional objectives. We will look at this process in two ways.

The first type of instructional strategy to be discussed in detail is that which involves the use of a variety of program segments to present a particular goal area. As an illustration, the goal of identifying distinctive letter shapes will be the focus of this discussion. Later, the discussion will turn to examples of segments wherein a particular instructional approach is applied across several learning goals.

The rationale for presenting the same goal area in several different ways is a simple one. Repetition of the same subject matter can remain interesting when it appears in several guises. At the same time, an audience with a wide variety of learning styles can be most effectively accommodated. With animation, letters can form as if by magic, and several films produced for *Sesame Street* take advantage of this visually compelling technique. In one, a ball tossed by a little girl bounces between ruled lines drawn across the screen, leaving a visible wake in the form of the letter *M*. This particular sequence is interesting because it presented a dilemma: on the recommendation of its advisors, the Workshop tries to imitate as closely as possible in all its letter presentations a manuscript alphabet widely used in first grade. The specified order in which the elements of uppercase *M* are to be drawn was not followed in the animated sequence in question. The ball had to form the *M* continuously in order not to violate the premise that it was bouncing up and down between the lines, whereas manuscript order calls for the two vertical members to be drawn first in separate strokes, and then for the middle members to be drawn, also in separate strokes.

Ensuing discussions with the advisors had to weigh the demands of educative consistency against those of dramatic integrity. It was concluded that the main purpose of calling attention to the structure of the letter had been served even if the process of forming it had not been copied faithfully, and that the animated sequence had sufficient value as entertainment to warrant departing from the prescribed sequence of letter formation. Equally often, critical educational considerations have prevailed and have led to the revision or exclusion of contemplated program segments.

In a later part of the same M animation, other effects made possible by animation are used to call the viewers' attention to the structural details of the letter M. Teeth grow in the V-shaped space between the two middle lines that make up the letter and proceed to eat up everything in sight. Then the letter walks along, the two outside lines serving as legs. The correspondence between the printed letter M and its sound is established repeatedly throughout the segment by an alliterative voice track in which the initial (M) sound is sustained to call attention to it. Further, when the M has finished its eating, it emits a satisfied "Mmmm." This familiar sound can serve as an effective mnemonic.

In addition to this primary goal, this segment seeks also to establish that words are individual entities, that words have "first" letters and "last" letters in left-to-right order, that each word begins with a particular sound, and that many different words begin with the same sound. No single segment by itself is expected to teach all these points, but different segments that highlight different points, when taken in combination, can do so. With all its pedagogical freight, a piece such as this "M-Martha" segment rarely runs for more than 1½ to 2 minutes.

In another segment dealing with letter shapes, Big Bird, a gigantic but gentle feathered creature, is left to guard a three-dimensional lower-case i. The dot on the i is in fact a disk manipulated by a puppeteer. As soon as Big Bird is left alone with his charge, the dot jumps down from its position. Big Bird, alarmed that he will be accused of failing his responsibility if the dot escapes, gives chase. The dot eludes him and disappears over the fence. Eventually, however, it returns and Big Bird is redeemed. By endowing the dot on the i with a magical life of its own, the episode makes that distinctive feature highly memorable.

The use of the voice-over technique has special educative advantages when the objective is to elicit the active participation and involvement of the viewing children. In one series of films on letter drawing, the letters are produced by a skywriter. They are integrated into the television program in such a way as to make it appear that the characters on the *Sesame Street* set are actually seeing a given letter being written over their heads. As we see the shape of the letter evolve, the voices of the children on the set are heard trying to guess what letter it will be. They thus both encourage participation and model appropriate responses to the segment. Observations have revealed that the effect, when this technique is used properly, is to engage the viewing children quite actively in the guessing process. For instance, the children delight in trying to think of different letters that could develop starting with a single, vertical straight line. Or, they become thoroughly caught up with suspense and excitement as a letter that starts off as the letter *C* nears the critical point in its construction where it must either remain a *C* or become the letter *O*, or perhaps *Q*. The exercise of gradually reducing the number of possible letters that is modeled by the voices of the child actors contributes to the viewers' capacity to attend to critically differentiating features. The child actors can also serve as competition for the older children who already have acquired a good grasp of the letters.

Early in the program's development, formative research established that a technique called "pixillation" has unusually high viewer appeal. The technique consists of filming live actors a single frame at a time and then (in a process similar to that of animated cartoons) printing the frames together in a sequence so as to make the actors appear to be moving in unusual or normally impossible ways, e.g., floating without ever touching the ground. The result is an incongruous combination of the magical properties of animated films and the antics of actual human characters in natural settings. It has been used with great success in drawing attention to the process of letter formation. In one such use, two characters appear, each carrying part of a huge three-dimensional styrofoam letter. Through grotesquely inaccurate trial and error, accompanied by silent movie chase music, they discover the correct fit. Each time an incorrect assemblage of the letter parts is completed, the two characters stand back to survey it and then indicate, usually by a shake of the head, that it is wrong. When the parts finally are assembled correctly, they indicate that it is correct by vigorous affirmative head nodding, jumping up and down, and finally by shaking hands. As with the skywriting, active participation is encouraged. In this case, it is to recognize when the assembled parts do and do not correspond to a previously familiar letter, and perhaps to supply the name once a correct letter form is constructed. For the very young viewer, the lesson to be learned is that certain configurations are somehow important and somehow right, and others are not. For the somewhat older viewer, who already knows letter shapes and letter names, the segments remain an engaging guessing game.

In many program segments, attempts have been made to point out the similarity between letter forms and the shapes of real objects, thus using the more familiar as a bridge to the less familiar. In an animated film, two boys are invited by an unseen narrator to watch a story about the letter *J*. A large uppercase *J* descends between them. One of the boys remarks that the *J* looks like a fishhook. The voice of the narrator intones, "It's not a fishhook, it's a *J*." The first boy replies, "It still looks like a fishhook to me." The purpose of the shape analogy is to make the new knowledge more accessible and therefore more memorable. Similar shape analogies have been drawn for other letters.

In a related approach, letter forms are revealed to be embedded in the real environment. In one *Sesame Street* segment, a puppet finds the letter E repeated in the structure of a door, and in another, T is discovered embedded in the railing around the basement windows of an apartment house. When such a letter is found, a cutout letter is superimposed on the embedded letter to confirm and emphasize the presence of the embedded form for the child who may not have seen it. The search for embedded letters is, of course, an exercise of wider significance, since it provides training in perceptual decentration by implicating an object first in the framework of a physical structure and then in the category of letters. It also provides practice in distinguishing relevant characteristics from irrelevant ones. Both these activities implicitly invite replication by the child after the program ends, and any home environment offers many opportunities to do so. The child is thus provided with a method of extending and reinforcing learning on his own.

Finally, in many program segments an attempt is made to use cross-modal reinforcement of letter shapes. In these segments the primarily visual experience of letter formation is supported by music or sound effects appropriate to the action as, for example, in the M segment described above, where the bouncing ball is accompanied by "boing" sounds that attempt to focus attention on the bounce points, and correspondingly on these points as distinctive vertices of the letter M. Another type of synesthetic reinforcement is used in a muppet segment in which Kermit the frog describes a letter N as having "three lines. Zap! Zap! Zap!" Even without accompanying gestures (Kermit's manual capabilities are limited), the words are remarkably appropriate to the shape they describe.

The preceding examples help to illustrate how a wide variety of production techniques can be brought to bear on any particular curriculum area. Next we will discuss instructional approaches that can be applied to a variety of goal areas.

Repetition of segments, of course, maximizes consistency of presentation. Repetition as an instructional strategy takes two forms: exact repetition of intact program segments and repetition of program segments with variation. Our focus will be first on the use of a constant format to present invariant or somewhat varied content, since this is the case where television is probably most distinctive in its capabilities.

Varying the content while keeping the format constant promotes familiarity with format conventions that are potentially useful for instructional purposes. The format of any program segment functions as a kind of "frame" for the instructional content, a complex of auditory and visual conventions that the child can master through repeated exposure. For example, the viewer can learn to expect that a particular format will usually deal with a particular category of stimulus (letter, word number, concept) and with a particular intellectual activity (memorizing, sorting or classifying, guessing, combining). A particular sequence of events or types of events will reliably occur; a particular type of feedback to the viewer's implicit or explicit responses will be delivered. Moreover, a viewer's familiarity with a given format can help him determine at what point in the presentation the important information will come, how much of it there will be, perhaps even whether it is likely to be too easy, too difficult, or about right for him. Among the main instructional advantages afforded by these various forms of cueing is that they will entice the viewing child to attend to what is new in each succeeding application of the format, since it will "stand out" against the familiar background more than if the entire presentation were novel. As a result, learning and concept formation are enhanced. In addition, the viewers appear often to derive special pleasure from their familiarity with a repeatedly used format, from their sense of mastery of its special conventions, from the gamelike challenge of making guesses from format cues and then confirming their accuracy, and from a program's frequent use of comic twists, especially when these are parodies of familiar format.

Some of the benefits of repeated application of a particular format are illustrated in the set of pixillated letter construction segments described previously. The child who is familiar with this format knows that the product will always be a member of the class "letters" and that the actors will eventually come to the correct solution by rotation and rearrangement of the pieces. There is, therefore, a strong implicit invitation to anticipate the outcome through mental manipulations analogous to the physical manipulations on the screen. The child who forms a hypothesis about the identity of the letter knows that the hypothesis will be confirmed or disconfirmed by the eventual successful assembly of the letter.

The set of skywriting segments, also described earlier, provide yet another example of the advantages of holding the format constant while varying the content. After the viewing children have seen this format applied repeatedly with different letters of the alphabet, they understand immediately upon seeing the distinctive beginning of such a segment that a single figure is to be formed, that it will be a letter of the alphabet, and that there will be an opportunity to guess its identity prior to its being completely formed.

A set of 10- to 15-second animated films, called "balloon bits," were made for several letters of the alphabet. In these films, a character, different for each letter, appears against a plain white background. The character pronounces the name of the letter, a word beginning with that letter, and the name of the letter again. As the letter name is spoken, a balloon emerges rapidly from the character's mouth, and the letter in its lowercase form appears within it. As the word is spoken, its remaining letters also appear in the balloon. The balloon now assumes life independent of the character who produced it, who is now helpless to control the action that takes place within it. Within the balloon, the word forms into the object it names, or it dissolves into a scene illustrating the use of the word. A quick visual gag ensues, generally involving the original character, and the scene within the balloon then dissolves back to the letter as the character pronounces it the second time.

The word used to illustrate the use of the letter *a*, for example, is "ape." The printed word dissolves into an animated ape, who strums a ukulele and sings in a high falsetto the first phrase of "Tiptoe through the Tulips." The ape disappears, *a* reappears, and the original character, who has been observing the spectacle, turns to camera with a quizzical expression and says, "*a?*"

Repeated use of the balloon convention has motivational and conceptual advantages. First, recognition of a convention whose previous use has been amusing creates a pleasurable anticipation for its subsequent use. Second, if a previous use of the convention has contributed to mastery of the content, similar success with the new material will be anticipated. Third, the speech balloon is such a strong symbol of the correspondence of print to speech that that concept may be communicated without direct didactic reference. Fourth, although twenty-five different letters and the same number of different words are presented through the use of this convention, only these types of units are used in this format. Thus the convention serves to group into a class the symbolic material it presents.

One frequently used format, which turned out quite serendipitously to be useful in teaching prereading and reading skills, was designed originally to teach children to sort and classify objects on the basis of size, form, class, number, and function. A card divided into quadrants shows three identical symbols or drawings and a fourth drawing that is different. In the typical presentation, a performer stands next to the card and sings a song that gives the rules of the game: "One of these things is not like the others/One of these things just doesn't belong. . . ."[3] At the end of the chorus, the screen fills with a shot of the entire card. Instrumental music continues while the child at home selects the picture that does not belong with the other three. The correct choice is then indicated both visually and in a second chorus. At the end of the song, the difference is carefully pointed out in terms of critical features, and where appropriate, a generalization (class name) is offered. Repeating the same song and the same visual context each time the game is played but varying the content of the quadrants on the card has the functions of increasing the understanding of the discrimination task, focusing attention on the critical features of the example presented, and teaching the extension of the classes involved.

---

[3] Music by Joe Raposo, lyrics by Jon Stone. © 1970 Jonico Music, Inc.

When this format is used to present words and letters, it presumably has the same motivational advantages as those enjoyed by the convention of the speech balloon. The concept of classification and the importance of fine discrimination to its successful exercise are the instructional freight carried as conventions within this particular format. To show how this format is applied, in one case the letter *E* appears in each of three quadrants, and the letter *F* in the fourth. In another, the word "who" appears in each of three quadrants, and "why" in the other. The child familiar with the format, from having seen it used previously in connection with the sorting of objects, knows already that one of the entities is different from the others in some visually perceivable respect and that the difference is important enough so that the different entities have different names and perhaps different functions. In short, the repeated use of this particular format teaches generalized skill ·in discrimination and classification, both of which are essential to reading. In the particular case of the "who" and "why" discrimination, there is an opportunity to help overcome the tendency of many beginning readers to notice only the first letters of a word and try to guess its identity from that information alone.

Exact repetition of segments carries the cueing function of the repeated format to the maximum. *Sesame Street* borrowed the notion of short, well-constructed repeatable messages from advertisers, after observing that commercials were frequently more attractive to children than the programs they interrupted. In addition to its attention-getting powers, the effective advertisement has much to recommend it as an educative device. It is short, uses speech sparingly and television technology maximally, makes use of musical jingles, rhymes and slogans, and has as its raison d'être making the message intrinsically interesting and motivating to the viewers.

Exact repetition of animated films and certain videotaped segments has been a highly visible feature of *Sesame Street* instruction in all goal areas. It is assumed that a commercial "selling" a letter is enhanced by repetition in much the same way as a product commercial. Given sufficient repetition, the child will begin to recall elements of visual imagery or soundtrack that may in turn cue rehearsal of the message and reinforce the learning that occurred while viewing. Finally, exact repetition of a well-designed segment can elicit a desirable learning sequence that can be summarized as observation-participation-anticipation. The operation of this sequence will be described as it has been observed to occur in response to a particular *Sesame Street* segment.

The segment is an unadorned film of the actor James Earl Jones reciting the alphabet. Mr. Jones's recitation takes a full minute and a half. He stares compellingly at the camera throughout, his shaven head gleaming. His immense hollow voice booms the letter names ominously. His lip movements are so exaggerated that they can easily be read without the sound. It is a performance that should be seen by every actor who ever complained about his lines. As Mr. Jones recites the letters, they appear to the viewer on alternate sides of his head. Each letter appears visually for a moment before it is named. Once named, the letter disappears, and another brief pause ensues before the next letter appears and is in turn named.

This film produces a well-defined three-stage learning sequence in many viewers. The first time children see the Jones performance, they begin almost at once to respond to the implicit invitation to say the alphabet along with the performer, although the response may take the form of strict attention rather than verbal response at first. On somewhat later repetitions they begin to name the letter readily with Mr. Jones and then as soon as it appears, before the actor has named it. Mr. Jones's naming of the letter then confirms or corrects the child's identification of it. With still further repetition, the child begins to anticipate the printed symbol as well. As soon as the preceding letter disappears, the viewer names the next and sees and hears his or her response confirmed or disconfirmed.

The effect is significant because it demonstrates the feasibility of creating with the one-way medium of television, the feedback situation instrumental to learning. The Jones segment first produced this learning sequence serendipitously, but subsequently, deliberate attempts have been made to evoke similar responses in viewers. For example, in another alphabet sequence, the actor Pat Paulsen dramatizes the invitation to participate even more explicitly than the Jones performance, by apparently faltering in his recitation of the alphabet sequence. The timing is the same as Mr. Jones's: letter appears; pause; letter is named; letter disappears; pause; next letter appears; etc., until Mr. Paulsen falters. At this point, the letter matted next to his head flashes several times to remind him; Mr. Paulsen sneaks a quick look, names the letter in happy relief, and goes on. Clearly repetition, which can often become dull, is useful and attractive when combined with the magic of television.

Humor, particularly humor deriving from incongruity, pervades *Sesame Street*'s approach to teaching. Incongruity arises with the introduction of an unexpected or inappropriate element in an otherwise conventional situation. Aside from the virtue of entertaining the child, incongruity has a more specific role to play in instruction. It appears that the introduction of an unexpected element into the stimulus field both focuses attention on that element and initiates mental processes to resolve the incongruity.

Visual or audiovisual incongruity brings the viewer's attention to the point of conflict or incongruity and motivates the mental activity necessary to resolve it. If the instructional message of the segment can also be the source of the incongruity, it is likely to be the focus of attention, and a powerful teaching sequence is the result—one that allows a medium said to be limited to a passive learning mode to evoke covert cognitive responses in the child.

An example is a muppet vignette involving Bert and Ernie: Bert, in an effort to establish his exclusive right to the cookie cabinet, has painted a capital *B* for Bert on its front doors. Ernie notices that the letter spans the division between the doors and, in apparently innocent elaboration, establishes that the initial on the door designates the name of the person who is allowed to enter the cabinet for cookies. Bert impatiently confirms the rule. Ernie then matter-of-factly opens wide the right-hand cabinet door, removing from sight the bumps on the *B* and leaving a skinny but discriminable *E* (for Ernie), and helps himself to a snack while Bert smolders. Here the letter clearly becomes the center of the dramatic action, and the transformation of the *B* into an *E* presumably will lead the child to reflect on the similarities and critical differences between the letter shapes that permitted this humorous turn of events to occur.

A more elaborate example of the function of incongruity can be seen in an alphabet segment in which a little girl (live) is reciting the alphabet to the frog muppet named Kermit. The little girl recites, and as each letter is spoken, it appears in print in the upper-right quadrant of the screen. During the taping of the segment, the child spontaneously inserted the name "Cookie Monster" (another muppet) at unpredictable points in the alphabet sequence. To capitalize on her ad-lib humor, Kermit acted duly astonished, and the child, delighting in the frog's reaction, proceeded happily with her game until the alphabet was completed. When the letters were superimposed on the videotape afterward, the Cookie Monster's face was made to appear in the sequence wherever his name occurs. Thus the sequence goes "*A* . . . *B* . . . *C* . . . Cookie Monster . . ." and so on, with appropriate visual cues.

This violation of the sequence, which is outrageous enough to be abundantly clear even to the child who is barely acquainted with the alphabet, leads the viewer to an awareness that there is in fact a sequence and that the sequence has been violated at a particular point. Finally, it focuses attention on the letter whose position in the sequence has been usurped. Each violation of the sequence serves to heighten this effect and at the same time increase the humor (although adults may tire of the joke, young children almost never do). The segment has the additional, more general value of modeling the violation of a convention for the viewer and thereby acknowledging that convention. The viewer thus is made aware of a particular kind of "game" that seeks out conventional, ordered bodies of information and violates them in play. Games that focus attention on the structure of language, numbers, or other conventional systems are important in fostering an awareness of structure that can greatly enhance learning and conceptual growth.

This discussion covers only a portion of the goals and instructional strategies that make up *Sesame Street*. Some of these strategies are also used on *The Electric Company*, and many teaching techniques developed for *The Electric Company* have proven to be amenable to the *Sesame Street* curriculum as well.

THE ELECTRIC COMPANY

With the success of *Sesame Street* it became apparent that television could indeed function as a successful and engaging teaching tool. Children's Television Workshop therefore decided to investigate the feasibility of using television to help children with reading problems. The rationale was that television could provide failing readers with a nonthreatening, entertaining treatment of basic skills that could give them the boost needed to escape the downward spiral to failure. Given this intention, corollary decisions about the nature of the program followed:

1. The target audience for the program was designated as seven- to ten-year-olds encountering reading difficulties. The primary intended audience was to be the second grader in the lower half of his or her reading class. The reason for aiming the program at the younger child was that it could then function at least in part as prevention rather than cure. First graders were not included for several reasons. It was felt that careful sequencing is in fact required in the introductory stages of learning. By the second grade, although reading is still taught as a separate subject, the child has presumably had sequential exposure to all the rudiments of reading, which *The Electric Company* can then serve to reinforce and review. First graders might be confused by the variety of instructional approaches offered in the program, whereas an older child might find this variety refreshing. (Nevertheless, large numbers of first graders do watch the program.)

2. The program was not to be a comprehensive reading program but one focusing on a limited number of skills which are most often the source of problems for children and which also tend to be the most difficult ones for teachers to make continually palatable given the amount of repetition and practice these skills require.

3. Emphasis, then, was to be placed on "decoding" skills, that is, the mastery of spelling-to-sound correspondences. According to Chall (1967), these skills are the most common source of problems for children who have difficulty in the beginning stages of learning, and when they are not adequately mastered, the acquisition of higher-order skills is disrupted.

The decision to focus on phonics has a second basis, one that in turn reinforced the decision to aim the program's remedial effort at children in the rather early stages of learning. That is, it was necessary to consider what television could and could not do successfully with regard to reading instruction. Since television, because of small screen size, poor resolution, and the demands of program pacing, could not effectively provide opportunities for extended reading practice, advanced reading skills were not considered to be an appropriate target. On the other hand, the devices television has for creating compelling syntheses of audio and visual cues suggested that the medium would have a special value in teaching symbol-to-sound correspondences. Since this expectation has been confirmed, the decision to emphasize phonics is further affirmed. On the other hand, as techniques for presenting print on the screen have become more sophisticated, it has become possible to provide somewhat greater emphasis on the skills of reading for meaning.

4. *The Electric Company* was intended for viewing primarily at home, a relatively nonthreatening environment. However, it was made available to schools, and public broadcasting stations were asked to distribute information to teachers. Therefore no sequencing of skills from simple to complex over the course of the season was planned. As with *Sesame Street,* such a sequence was thought to penalize irregular viewers and those who discovered the program in the middle of the broadcast season.

However, unlike *Sesame Street,* each half hour of *The Electric Company* has a carefully organized internal structure. This structure is designed to provide high redundancy in order that the child who has experienced failure in learning will be likely to meet with success in his or her attempts to read what is presented on the screen. For example, a typical program begins by introducing the sound of *y* in "cry" and continues with several animated and live segments containing the words "sly," "fry," "dry," and "fly." After two successive segments focusing on "fly," this word appears on the screen without audio support, and the children are asked to read it themselves before it "self-destructs." The focus then shifts to *fl-* (from "fly") and a series of segments containing this blend. The final part of the program is devoted to more general reading practice and a review.

In accordance with these basic design decisions, 130 half-hour programs were prepared for broadcast during the school year 1971–72. The series, now in its fourth season of broadcasting, with a fifth series of 130 programs in production, has generally adhered to the initial decisions described above. *The Electric Company*'s current curriculum appears in Appendix B, this chapter.

This curriculum reflects some shift in emphasis from the first season toward providing opportunities for reading units larger than single words. This shift reflects adviser recommendations that the program could be less cautious after a successful first season and research results confirming the program's usefulness (Ball & Bogatz, 1972).

Phonics has remained a primary component of *The Electric Company*'s curriculum, but an item that has changed from the first season is the treatment of context clues. Initially, an attempt was made to model the utilization of context according to an analytic system that identified three cases: (1) the child has the word in his or her spoken vocabulary but has difficulty decoding it (e.g., "cough"); (2) the decoding process is not difficult, but the meaning of the word is unfamiliar (e.g., "metaphor"); (3) both the decoding and the meaning are sources of difficulty (e.g., "slough"). An attempt was made to show the child strategies for dealing with each of these cases as a discrete condition. This proved to be too rigid and artificial an approach —nearly impossible for the writers to develop material for and perhaps misleading the child into a narrow, rigid conception of how context can be used. Using context clues is a complex process operating at several levels at once and involving flexible use of a variety of sources of information. It has therefore proven necessary to abandon this taxonomy and model the use of context as a process of shifting from level to level, utilizing the information a particular situation offers as efficiently as possible. This more flexible treatment of context clues has proven more workable for the writers; although it loses some of the exactness of the original treatment, it represents a much more realistic situation to the viewer.

Finally, the decision to include spelling patterns that have two or more possible sound correspondences, e.g., *ea*, *ow*, even though these units represent difficult decoding tasks, may seem inappropriate at first, but it was made because children with reading problems are often discouraged by the irrationalities of the code. Acknowledging and confronting some of the inconsistencies directly can be useful when done in such a way as to show the child that the difficulties lie with the code, not with the reader, and when an opportunity to model strategies for coping with this kind of confusion is offered.

In designing the program that was to implement the reading curriculum discussed above, two concerns were paramount. First, there could be no concealing the program's instructional intent. The curriculum for *Sesame Street* is varied. The viewer gets frequent relief from overt instruction about print and numbers in the form of less apparently didactic material about the natural and man-made environments, about feelings, and so on. *The Electric Company* curriculum deals only with reading, and thus the continued presence of a possibly aversive print stimulus on the screen is unavoidable.

Second, although the fast-paced magazine format of *Sesame Street* and many of the production devices employed within it had demonstrable appeal for *The Electric Company* audience as well and were obviously applicable to a reading curriculum, the new program had to look distinctly different from *Sesame Street*, lest it be dismissed as "kid's stuff" by children already self-conscious about being "behind."

The answer to the first problem is easy to formulate, but difficult to implement: print must be presented on the screen in attractive and compelling forms in order to attract and hold the print-aversive viewer. The attractiveness of the print must be reinforced by building an appealing program around it. The primary problem of execution and one that has continually been the focus of formative research for *The Electric Company* has been the design of program segments that will both maintain interest in the program and encourage the viewer to attend to and process print. The primary advantage is in approaching the child with a nonpunitive, "flunk-proof" television program whose reading instruction contrasts sharply in style with his previous experiences in the classroom.

The constant presence of print in itself gives *The Electric Company* an identity distinct from *Sesame Street*. Other design decisions helped still further. Instead of a realistic "home base" like the street setting on *Sesame Street*, *The Electric Company* exists in a fluid fantasy setting. Freedom from the contraints of reality permits the arbitrary introduction of print into a scene through a variety of film and electronic devices without a disturbing clash of representational levels. Instead of a consistent cast of unchanging characters (necessary, it was felt, for the preschool viewer of *Sesame Street*), *The Electric Company* employs a repertory company of actors free to take on a large variety of roles. The range of roles portrayed by each actor permits the delivery of such implicit messages as, for example, the value of reading to many different ethnic and socioeconomic groups, or the value of being bilingual or multidialectal, or that it is not unfeminine, unmasculine, or unhip to be a skilled reader.

The nonrealistic format allows the *surface* of the screen to become the focus of attention, rather than a window on a three-dimensional world. The television screen thus assumes some of the properties of the printed page. Using television this way allows for the uncluttered presentation of print that can compel attention by moving, undulating, blushing, or twitching with the accompaniment of sound effects.

The following sections describe in more detail ways of putting print on the screen to meet particular curriculum objectives and maintain appeal. We will begin with four instructional goals of *The Electric Company* and the diverse ways in which they are implemented. Then production strategies that can cut across several such goal areas will be described.

Since the skill of blending individual sounds together is central to the approach to reading taken on *The Electric Company*, considerable effort has gone into the development of effective ways of modeling the blending process. The most fundamental and yet most difficult level at which blending takes place is in synthesizing phonemes into intelligible words. Through letter movement, carefully synchronized with voice, *The Electric Company* can dynamically depict the information-processing strategy that the child must carry out when faced with the task of phonically analyzing and re-forming a word.

One particularly useful format for modeling this process has come to be called the "silhouette blend." In this series of segments (each member of the series focuses on a different sound unit), the profiles of two actors are face to face, a small distance apart on the screen. Only dark silhouettes are visible so that no facial features are available as distractions. The character on the left pronounces, with slightly exaggerated lip movements, the first element of a word, e.g., "ch." As it is pronounced, the corresponding print unit, *ch*, appears to emerge from the character's mouth and moves to the lower middle sector of the screen. (Formative research on these segments, utilizing eye movement recordings, has shown that the lip movement succeeds in drawing the child's eyes to the point where the print will emerge; the moving print then entices the eye to track it to its resting point.) The routine is then repeated with the last half of the word, e.g., *-ip*, emerging from the mouth of the character on the right. Finally the two print elements slide together to form a single unit ("chip") as that unit is pronounced by the two actors in unison. Several words in succession, tied together by a key phonic element ("chip," "chin," "chop"), are presented in this way, the entire series then being repeated once. The whole sequence is accompanied by engaging syncopated music, which serves as a strong audio cue to the appearance of each print element.

As an experiment, a silhouette blend piece using full profiles of the actors rather than silhouettes was produced. This was not as successful as the original form. Apparently a conflict was set up between the three-dimensional faces and the two-dimensional print. Eye movement records showed viewers spending less time on the print and more time studying facial features with this version.

With these segments, one aspect of the decoding process which the child is expected to carry out "in his head" and which is difficult to describe or to illustrate with static materials is given a compelling visual analog. An additional strength of this format is that it can be used as well to illustrate the combination of units at almost any level (e.g., "can-dle" → "candle"; "cow-boy" → "cowboy"). In doing so, a rather abstract point can be effectively made: The same processes of synthesis are applicable across many levels of the written code.

Manipulation of giant letters by magically diminutive "live" actors is also a visually compelling way of modeling the blending process, as well as offering a visual metaphor for the difficulty of decoding print. Perhaps the relative hugeness of the letters on the screen objectifies some of the feelings that poor readers may have of being overpowered by print. The telestrator, a device that allows obviously handwritten letters to appear by magic (as they are formed by a remote hand writing with a light pen) on the screen, has a similar effect, focusing attention on letter formation and encouraging anticipation of the outcome.

A key aspect of teaching blending skills is drawing attention to the appropriate phonic element at each point in the blending sequence in order to insure that the appropriate auditory-visual match will be made by the viewer. Many powerful means exist for doing this with television. Color contrast is an obvious one. If *ch* in the word "chip" is brighter when the voice-over pronounces /*ch*/, the likelihood that the child will match the sound to this and only this written unit is increased. Blinking, expanding, wiggling, and jumping letters and many other techniques have been used to render key phonic elements salient. The salience cue can shift, smoothly or abruptly, from one unit to another as the decoding process proceeds. This ability to direct attention to appropriate elements is crucial to an educational tool that cannot monitor the reader's response.

The more fundamental problem of integrating print into the "plot" of a segment while at the same time insuring that the viewer will attend to it has been met by transforming all sorts of objects into letter-bearers. Written phonic units have appeared on garbage cans, sides of elephants, balloons, tickertape, soles of feet; in alphabet soup and crystal balls; and written in shaving cream, whipped cream, and pastry dough.

As the current curriculum description for *The Electric Company* indicates, particular items are taught within a framework that will impart to the child some of the fundamental properties of the written code. According to Downing (1973) and others, lack of understanding of these properties is common among poor readers, often because of a lack of preschool experience with books and reading, and can seriously impede the process of learning to read. One such basic principle dealt with on *The Electric Company* is that there is a systematic relationship between print and speech. A corollary to this is that print proceeds from left to right in accordance with the temporal sequence of speech. Although these may seem like trivial notions to the skilled reader, the relationship between print and speech may come as a powerful insight to the struggling learner. *The Electric Company* has employed, in addition to frequent implicit treatments of this principle, several program segments that render this principle of print-speech correspondence explicit, without ever presenting a "rule" per se.

One appealing and effective example is a song sung by a group of rock singers, only slightly older than the average viewer. One member of the group, Kathy, begins a singing game, and as she sings, certain phrases appear above her head (italicized words appear in print):

> *My name is Kathy, Kathy is my name.*
> *My name is Kathy, Kathy is my name.*
> Those words up there are saying just the same.
> *I like to sing and make fine music too,*
> *I like to sing and make fine music too.*
> Those words up there just tell it like I do.[4]

---

[4] Music by Joe Raposo, lyrics by Elaine Laron. © 1972 Instructional Children's Music, Inc., and Sesame Street, Inc.

The others in the group sing essentially similar stanzas. Thus, although the apparent purpose of the segment is to present a pleasant rhyming game that viewers and their teachers can adopt, the song in fact makes the sophisticated metalinguistic statement that what is said can be written down and (from the very first line) that the *order* of words is important, and it touches upon the even higher-level metalinguistic notion that language can be used to talk about language.

Another singing game carries the message of print-speech correspondence with somewhat different connotations. In this instance, the same young singers take turns making up phonically regular words, assigning silly meanings to them, and spelling them magically in the air with the telestrator device described previously. The chorus of this song is as follows:

> You can make up a word.
> Just think it up out of your head.
> You can decide what you want it to mean,
> And how it's said.
> You can make up a word,
> Your own private personal word.
> And then all you do is just say it out loud,
> And your word will be heard.[5]

The correspondence between print and speech is demonstrated forcefully by the fact that the words made up in the course of the song, i.e., "sploosh," and "flibble," and "glunk," are spelled with no difficulty. But the viewer can also come to any or all of the following related insights in the course of viewing this segment, or more likely after viewing it several times. No necessary order of acquisition is implied in this list:

Language is created by those who use it.

The names assigned to things and events are arbitrary.

Meanings are not inherent in words; they must be assigned and communicated to others.

Language is not sacrosanct; it can be altered.

Whatever can be said can be spelled; the mapping rules are reversible.

The sequence of written units corresponds to the sequence of speech sounds.

Whatever can be "said" in a given language corresponds to the phonological rules of that language.

The last is a profound insight about the basis for our productive use of language, and the possibility that a child will come to understand it is remote. Still, the idea is available in the segment, and children who actu-

---

[5] Music by Joe Raposo, lyrics by Elaine Laron. © 1971 Instructional Children's Music, Inc., and Sesame Street, Inc.

ally try to play the game on their own, adding to the set of silly words, probably have a reasonable chance of discovering a simple version of this idea, namely that words they make up and are able to spell will usually resemble other words they know. If the words do not, it is because the children introduce nonspeech sounds like whistles and snorts. Playful violation of this system also serves to heighten awareness of it and to reinforce it.

Animation, of course, offers another effective way of illustrating the relationship between print and speech. Through the use of speech balloons, borrowed from the comic books that are so popular with children, animated characters can speak and have their words actually emerge from their moving mouths and assemble in balloons near their heads in perfect synchrony with the spoken counterparts.

This technique is well illustrated by an animation in which a cheery plumber arrives at the door of a house with his box of tools. He knocks, and a parrot inside squawks, "Who is it?," his words appearing in a speech balloon as he squawks them. The plumber, assuming the parrot's raucous voice to be that of the lady of the house, answers, "It's the plumber. I've come to fix the sink," and his words also appear in a speech balloon. In the absence of further response from within, the plumber knocks once more. The parrot again shrills, "Who is it?" The plumber, irritated, shouts, "It's the plumber! I've come to fix the sink!" Silence is maintained inside, and the door, of course, remains closed. In a rage, the plumber hammers on the door with his fist. Its inflection unchanged, the parrot asks, tirelessly, "Who is it?" The plumber chokes out an apoplectic, "It's the plumber! I've come to fix the sink!" and collapses to the sidewalk. Immediately, the mistress of the house returns, and seeing the plumber prostrate in front of her house, asks, "Who is it?" The parrot answers, "It's the plumber. He's come to fix the sink."

Note that the humor of this segment derives from repetition with a twist. This gives the segment added value because it is likely that repeated exposure allows for the learning of some sight vocabulary.

Another series of animated segments feature a little character who reads posted messages by tracking the words visually with his nose as he painfully decodes them. The poor fellow never quite gets through his message, which always warns of some impending disaster, in time to escape. Thus these segments deal with the functional aspect of print, as well as the structure of the code. The written message clearly conveys information that should lead directly to action. The warning in the message always has very literal consequences so that this point is abundantly clear, and the message of reading rapidly enough and carefully enough to ward off disaster is unmistakable.

The communication function of written language is illustrated very clearly in two simple animations, which appear completely different on the surface but are identical in their pedagogical strategies. The first shows the popular cartoon character Roadrunner being chased by his eternal enemy the coyote. This time, however, as Roadrunner roars away from his pursuer he posts several signs in his path as he goes. The coyote, in hot pursuit, nevertheless reads each sign and religiously follows its instructions to "crawl," "hop," "skip," and so forth. The final sign, however, says "Run," and the chase is on again. The sight of this familiar villain skipping to the accompaniment of saccharine music delights the viewer, but at the same time the segment certainly renders memorable the point that printed messages can influence behavior.

The second is a film in which an unadorned colored dot moves around the screen in accordance with signs posted in its path. An important feature of this segment is that the child is strongly encouraged to read the sign and anticipate the dot's response, because there is a short interval between the appearance of each sign on the screen and the dot's response to it. There is no voice on the film. However, the set of alternatives is so limited, and the response of the dot to the sign so clear and unambiguous, that the child who may be unable to read the signs can tell what they say by observing the dot's response. For example, at one point the dot encounters a sign reading, "Whistle 'Yankee Doodle." The dot whistles the first four lines, bouncing very slightly with the effort. Another sign then appears saying, "All of it." The dot obediently whistles the chorus.

It was first feared that this segment might be too slow to hold viewers' attention, but the combination of good timing, simplicity, and visual humor proved to be very engaging. And the children who are endeavoring to read the words have their hypotheses confirmed or denied by the dot's behavior.

Another series of segments, focused on following written directions, has as its central character a blithely incompetent television cook dubbed Julia Grownup. Julia reads written recipes and follows them to the letter—often at the expense of the spirit. For example, directions to "beat well" result in a flogging of the bread dough with a riding crop. Julia is thus able to make two apparently contradictory points at the same time. That is, the meaningful aspect of print, its relation to behavior, is the ostensible focus of the segment, but since Julia's amusing errors (like the double entendre on "beat" above) are typically hinged on word play, the written words come to be objects of interest in their own right. The use of incongruity as a teaching device, discussed above with regard to *Sesame Street*, is very much in evidence on *The Electric Company* as well. Words become objects of attention as the viewer seeks to make sense of Julia's unexpected actions.

The final goal area we will discuss is *The Electric Company*'s treatment of punctuation. Mastery of punctuation conventions is perhaps of secondary importance for the child who is still struggling with the most basic elements of the written code, but punctuation is an important meaning clue and helps the reader to group words into appropriate "chunks." The lyrics of one popular song about punctuation impart this idea to the viewer in the following words:

> Punctuation!
> Punc, punc, punc, punctuation
> They are the little marks that use their influence
> To help a sentence make more sense.[6]

Television offers a rich store of techniques for illustrating the relationship among punctuation, intonation, and meaning. Research results (Ball & Bogatz, 1972) have shown substantial gains in punctuation objectives for many of the viewing groups tested, even among children with considerable reading problems.

Television has several strategic advantages over conventional materials that have been utilized to teach punctuation. First, freedom, from temporal and physical constraints allows sentence intonation, and the corresponding referent situation, to change simultaneously. An example of this is an animated cartoon in which a single sentence, "I am going over there," with changing punctuation, narrates an entire plot wherein the narrator is matter-of-factly walking over a somewhat surrealistic landscape ("I am going over there.") and spots a giant delectable ice-cream cone in the distance ("I am going over there!"). As he runs eagerly toward it, the huge head of a monster rises from the earth between our protagonist and his goal ("I am going over there?"). He beats a hasty retreat ("I am going over there!") and disappears from the screen. The entire piece takes only a few seconds.

Second, *The Electric Company* can isolate intonation as a variable, related to punctuation, something children have difficulty doing for themselves. This is done in a regularly repeated feature called the "tease." This format presents a "frozen" frame drawn from some segment the viewer is to see later in the program with a caption of sentence length printed below it. The viewer is encouraged by an off-screen voice to decode the sentence in order to watch for it later. The sentence is not read to the viewer, but the sentence contours (phrasing and intonation) are accurately portrayed by a slide whistle. This serves both to support the child in his or her attempts at reading the sentence and to highlight the intonation patterns. Punctuation is not emphasized in these segments. However, in illustrating the role of intonation as a meaning cue, they can nevertheless encourage the viewer to utilize punctuation, which is the key to intonation in print, as an aid in interpreting sentences.

---

[6] Music by Joe Raposo, lyrics by Elaine Laron. © 1971 Instructional Children's Music, Inc., and Sesame Street, Inc.

Finally, animation permits the punctuation marks themselves to come alive, respond to intonational and situational cues and take on the rudiments of personality that can serve as an effective reminder of their function. In one series of films the pianist-comedian Victor Borge was invited to display his classic "phonetic punctuation" routine. Seated in an armchair reading aloud, Borge "reads" the punctuation marks as well as the words, consistently associating a humorous but very apt grunt, spit, or whistle with each type of punctuation mark as it occurs in the sequence he is reading. As he reads, the corresponding words and punctuation marks appear beside him. The punctuation marks are made visually as well as auditorily salient by appearing very large at first and then "sinking" into their appropriate place in the sentence. Children find Borge's sound effects amusing and use them themselves. The sounds thus serve to focus attention on punctuation and help viewers discriminate one punctuation mark from another.

The role of punctuation is elaborated in the calypso song about punctuation, quoted briefly above. The verses of the song explicitly point out the function of each punctuation mark, as the particular mark dances around near the singer's head. Between verses the punctuation marks are used in sentences, and electronic sound effects take the place of Borge's voice effects. Here again animation calls attention to punctuation marks and their placement in the sentence.

We turn next to a discussion of the strategies that have been employed with success across several of *The Electric Company* curriculum objectives. The first such strategy might be termed visual word play, a rubric for techniques that capitalize on television's unique ability to overcome the restrictions of ordinary print media and thereby make available a kind of visual word play that can be comprehensible and enjoyable to poor readers.

One of the simplest of these techniques is to present the word in a visual context in which it is often found in the "real world" and therefore is likely to be recognized. The best examples of this approach are a series of "Sign Songs." The lyrics of these songs are strings of words found on signs.

> Gas, Car Wash, Subway, Don't Walk.
> No Parking, Tow Away Zone
> Uptown, Downtown, First Avenue
> Home Sweet Home.[7]

Each song is set to a lively "hummable" melody, and as each sign appears on the screen, an off-screen chorus of children responds to its appearance by singing exactly what the sign says. The music is repeated

[7] Music and lyrics by Clark Gesner. © 1972 Sesame Street, Inc.

a second time with only the accompaniment of a muted trumpet suggesting the speech contours. The film is repeated exactly, and the viewer is told, "this time we'll be quiet and *you* sing." The visual cues and the trumpet support the viewer's efforts to sing the second chorus on his own.

In the original version of the "Sign Song," all the signs were filmed in typical visual contexts in streets, on buildings, etc., so that the environment might provide further cues. A later version played upon this format by taking signs and pieces of signs out of context and combining individual words from them into quasi-meaningful verse, e.g.,

> I like fish food,
> You do too.
> Don't look now,
> Your hair is blue.[8]

Animation further extends the power of television to provide powerful visual cues for decoding. Animation can create situations where a change in print is instantaneously reflected in a change in some object or situation, thus drawing attention to both the changing features of the word and the meaning of the word as reflected in the situation. A highly popular *The Electric Company* format using this approach is "The Adventures of Letterman," a cartoon feature whose progenitor is obvious as soon as the narrator describes him as "Faster than a rolling *O*, stronger than silent *e*; able to leap capital *T* in a single bound." Letterman's sole purpose in life is to undo the harm done by an infamous little character called Spellbinder, who causes great difficulties by changing letters in words and causing a corresponding change in objects. For example, in one episode, Spellbinder changes "flower" into "shower," ruining a family picnic. Letterman then appears, pulls the appropriate letter, in this case a *t*, off the varsity sweater he wears, and changes "shower" to "tower," providing the grateful family with a lofty perch above the clouds.

Another animation with the same theme features a song about the function of the "silent *e*." In this song the letter itself, silent *e*, becomes the protagonist and demonstrates its power to change a word's structure and meaning. The song begins:

> Who can turn a can into a cane?
> Who can turn a pan into a pane?
> It's not too hard to see,
> It's silent "e."

Silent *e* is personified as something of a wizard, with hands, feet, and

---

[8] Music and lyrics by Clark Gesner. © 1972 Sesame Street, Inc.

a magic wand. As he waves the wand, changes in objects on the screen occur to reflect the lyrics—first a can, then a cane, and so forth.

However, the song continues:

> He turned a dam (Alacazam) into a dame
> But my friend Sam stayed just the same.[9]

The inclusion of the "Sam" → "same" transformation (accompanied by an unchanging portrait of Uncle Sam) serves, in effect, to bring the child back to reality by violating the magical connection between word structure and meaning that is set up in the song, thereby emphasizing the true arbitrariness of the code.

Meaning is sometimes reflected in the way the word itself is printed. The word "caterpillar" can, with the help of computer animation, undulate across the screen; "cold" can appear as a block of ice, "hot" can sizzle, "jam" can ooze onto a piece of bread. Rendering print iconic in this way is a powerful mnemonic device, which can also provide a welcome and perhaps illuminating switch from the strong print-as-code emphasis of the program. This is another case of visual play used to emphasize a convention by violating it. (In this case, it is the convention that meaning is available only by going through the sound system, not by examining the shapes of words.)

The final aspect of *The Electric Company* production to be discussed has to do with the program's continuing effort to achieve desanctification of print. This is of crucial importance since poor readers tend to react to print as an aversive stimulus, and research has indicated that this aversion can be reflected in actual visual avoidance of print that appears on the screen. Therefore *The Electric Company* must do as much as possible to reduce the threatening quality of print. This is not a teaching strategy in the same sense as others we have dealt with here, but it has implications for virtually all the teaching that takes place on the program. Desanctifying print means making it less formidable and mysterious and more approachable for children who have, through failure, come to look upon it with fear and anxiety. *The Electric Company* seeks to communicate a sympathetic understanding of the difficulties that the viewer might have in struggling with the inconsistencies of the written code. It also presents written language as flexible and as a tool for people. The song "You Can Make Up a Word," described earlier, demonstrates this point.

Two of *The Electric Company*'s regular characters work to desanctify print in different ways. J. Arthur Crank, an irritable but lovable fellow, addresses the difficulties of our written code, such as letters that have two sounds, by complaining about them in a straightforward manner. Crank

---

[9] Music and lyrics by Tom Lehrer. © 1971 Maelstrom Music.

can thus give voice to the frustrations felt by the child who is struggling with these inconsistencies. In addition, because of this strong identification with the viewer, Crank can then get away from simply explaining some of these problems to the audience directly without sounding too much like a lecturer.

Easy Reader is a hip, black street character who is wild about reading and is usually found in the street reading signs, gum wrappers, anything at all with print on it. For example, in one segment he borrows a dollar from another character, not to buy something but to read it. By his behavior, Easy Reader communicates the message that reading can be a real joy, that you can be "street wise" and still be a good reader, and that reading is an activity for many more situations than the classroom.

A song that Easy sings shows the nature of the character nicely:

> Easy Reader, that's my name.
> Uh Uh Uh
> Reading, reading, that's my game.
> Uh Uh Uh
> Top to bottom, left to right
> That reading stuff is out of sight.
> Easy Reader, that's my name.
> Uh Uh Uh[10]

Other characters are used to give children who may have bad feelings about themselves because they cannot read well, a chance to feel superior. A series of segments involving actors who cannot read their cue cards correctly offers such an opportunity. In one such segment, Bill Cosby, dressed as Superguy, an incompetent superhero, is to leap through a window and say imperiously "What do you mean by that crack?" in response to a gangsterlike character who remarks, "Superguy's a meatball!" (The cue card has the word "crack" on it.)

Through several trials, as the director becomes increasingly agitated and gesticulates wildly at the cue card, Superguy stumbles through the window and delivers hopelessly muffed versions of his line, e.g., "Who are you calling a meatball?" The director finally announces that she is about to "crack" and rushes off sobbing. By this time, even a nonreading child is sure of the word on the card and can feel superior to the chagrined actor. As the actor makes mistake after mistake, viewers can take great enjoyment both in the amusing errors and in the fact that they know the answer while the actor does not. This can be a rare pleasure for children who may often find themselves fumbling desperately for a correct word just as the

[10] Music by Joe Raposo, lyrics by Elaine Laron. © 1972 Instructional Children's Music, Inc., and Sesame Street, Inc.

person on the screen is now doing. Having these triumphant feelings may help children with reading problems feel more comfortable with print and make them feel like insiders rather than outsiders.

A final program format aimed at desanctification of print is the "Very Short Book." *The Electric Company* has continually been criticized for its lack of opportunities for real reading and for its potential misrepresentation of reading as merely decoding bits of print. Although the program can accommodate to this criticism only partially, since television is simply not suited to present text for extended reading, there is a continuing effort to develop formats that will give the viewer the experience of reading more extended material. At the same time, it has been noted that children who are experiencing difficulty in learning to read are often threatened by books and are easily overwhelmed by any lengthy passage of uninterrupted print. The great value of *The Electric Company* for this group, and its probable source of appeal for them as well, is that it is largely lacking in great expanses of print and is irreverent about the difficult and serious business of reading. "The Very Short Book" then, was devised to accommodate both these needs by providing an experience of real reading brief enough for slow readers to handle comfortably. In addition, "The Very Short Book" parodies classic children's books and treats them with healthy irreverence. One such parody runs as follows:

	Little Miss Muffet
	Sat on a tuffet
(On screen	Eating her curds and whey
and spoken)	Along came a spider
	And sat down beside her
	And said, "What the heck is curds and whey?"
(Spoken only)	"Beats me, tastes kinda yucchy.
	By the way, what's a tuffet?"

THE END[11]

Each line appears on a page that fills the entire screen, with the print across the top and an "illustration" beneath, which is a tableau of actors who occasionally move. As the story is read, the viewer sees the pages turned and has the experience of reading a real, albeit abridged, book.

The desanctification of print is explicitly illustrated by the program segments described, but the whole program by its very nature no doubt serves to make print appear less threatening. Because it meshes reading instruction with material that is very much like what children watch on commercial television, *The Electric Company* brings print into the child's own bailiwick. Although the classroom may be an uncomfortable place for

[11] © 1972 Children's Television Workshop.

many children, particularly those who have not come from middle-class homes, television is part of the child's own turf. Therefore the very fact that print is coming through this familiar medium goes a long way toward making it acceptable and unthreatening.

The intention of this rather lengthy discussion has been to describe in as much detail as possible the process of utilizing the powers of entertainment television, often thought to be a medium antithetical to education, to implement a solid prereading and reading curriculum for young children.

A detailed description of the process of designing this sort of program, of meshing educational ends with material entertaining enough to compete with commercial programming for the target viewers attention, has heretofore been unavailable. This gap needed to be filled since the great success of both *Sesame Street* and *The Electric Company* indicates likely directions for much of instructional television programming in the future.

Further, although the conventional educational outcomes associated with the two programs have, as noted in our introduction, been thoroughly evaluated, we are only beginning to formulate the right questions to ask about the effects of the hybridization of television and print on the cognitive processes associated with reading. If the preceding discussion can provoke more researchers to tackle this intriguing area of investigation, it will have served its most urgent purpose.

REFERENCES

Ball, S., & Bogatz, G. A. *The first year of "Sesame Street": An evaluation.* Princeton, N.J.: Educational Testing Service, 1970.

Ball, S., & Bogatz, G. A. *Reading with television: An evaluation of "The Electric Company."* Princeton, N.J.: Educational Testing Service, 1972.

Bogatz, G. A., & Ball, S. *The second year of "Sesame Street": A continuing evaluation.* Princeton, N.J.: Educational Testing Service, 1971.

Chall, J. *Learning to read: The great debate.* New York: McGraw-Hill Book Company, 1967.

Downing, J. A summary of evidence related to the cognitive clarity theory of reading. In P. L. Nacke (Ed.), *Diversity in mature reading: Theory and research.* Boone, N. C.: National Reading Conference, 1973.

Gibbon, S. Y., Jr., & Palmer, E. L. *Pre-reading on Sesame Street*; Final report, Vol. 5. Children's Television Workshop, December 1970. 89 pp. (ERIC Document Reproduction Service, Document ED 047 825.)

Gleitman, L., & Rozin, P. Teaching reading by use of a syllabary. *Reading Research Quarterly*, 1973, **8**, 447–483.

Herriott, R. E., & Liebert, R. J. *"The Electric Company": In-school utilization study.* Tallahassee: Center for the Study of Education, Institute for Social Research, Florida State University, in conjunction with the Research Triangle Institute, 1972.

Lesser, G. S. *Children and television: Lessons from Sesame Street.* New York: Random House, 1974.

Mattingly, I. G. Reading, the linguistic process, and linguistic awareness. In J. F. Kavanagh & I. G. Mattingly (Eds.), *Language by ear and by eye; The relationships between speech and reading.* Cambridge, Mass.: The M.I.T. Press, 1972.

Palmer, E. L. Formative research in the production of television for children. In D. R. Olson (Ed.), Media and symbols: The forms of expression, communication, and education. *Yearbooks of the National Society for the Study of Education,* 1974, **73** (Part I), 303–329.

APPENDIX A. Excerpts from the "Sesame Street" Curriculum (1974–75)

I. Symbolic Representation
   A. Prereading Goals
   The following is a list of reading principles that illustrate the relationship between the spoken and written language. Although these abstract principles will not be taught directly, each has guided the selection of one or more of the prereading skills that will be taught directly.
      1. Words can be identified as distinct units in writing just as they can be identified as distinct units in speech.
      2. Written words are symbols for spoken words.
      3. Spoken words are made up of distinct speech sounds.
      4. Written words are made up of letters which are symbols for those speech sounds.
      5. Letters combine to make written words just as speech sounds combine to make spoken words.
      6. The order in which letters appear in a written word corresponds to the order in which sounds are produced in saying that word.
      7. Words and sentences are read from left to right.
   B. Letters
      1. *Matching.* Given a printed letter (upper or lower case), the child can select the identical letter from a set of printed letters.
      2. *Recognition.* Given the verbal label for a letter, the child can select the appropriate letter (upper or lower case) from a set of printed letters.
      3. *Labelling.* Given a printed letter (upper or lower case), the child can provide the verbal label.
   C. Letter Sounds
      1. Given a set of words presented orally all beginning with the same letter sound (not necessarily a sustaining consonant), the child can select a picture of an object that begins with the same letter sound from a set of pictures.
      2. Given a sustaining consonant sound, the child can select the corresponding printed letter from a set of printed letters.
      3. For sustaining consonants (f-l-m-n-r-s-v-z), given the printed letter, the child can produce that letter's corresponding sound.
   D. Rhyming
      1. Given a set of rhyming words presented orally and the initial (sustaining) consonant sound of a new word, the child can produce a rhyming word beginning with that sound.

248

2. Given a set of rhyming words presented orally, the child can select a rhyming word from a set of pictures.
3. Given two or more words that rhyme, the child can select or supply a third rhyming word.

E. Verbal Blending
1. Given a two-syllable word presented orally with a separation between the two syllables, the child can blend the two syllables and repeat the word without the separation. Example: Say "ta-ble" to child and ask "What word did I say?" or "Say it fast."
2. Given a three- or four-letter word presented orally with a separation between the initial consonant sound and the rest of the word, the child can blend the word parts together and repeat the word without the separation. Example: Say "c-at" to child and ask "What word did I say?" or "Say it fast."

F. Words
1. *Matching.* Given a printed word, the child can select the identical word from a set of printed words.
2. *Recognition.* Given a verbal label for any of the words appearing in the *Sesame Street* III word list (in English and Spanish), the child can select the appropriate word from a set of printed words presented in a variety of contexts.

Sesame Street Word List

1. bus	8. open
2. danger	9. school
3. exit	10. stop
4. help	11. street
5. love	12. telephone
6. me	13. walk
7. no	14. yes

Spanish Sight Words

1. *cerrado* ("closed")	5. *peligro* ("danger")
2. *abierto* ("open")	6. *casa* ("house"; "home")
3. *salida* ("exit")	7. *beso* ("kiss")
4. *entrada* ("entrance")	8. *agua* ("water")

G. Recitation of the Alphabet. The child can recite the alphabet.

II. Cognitive Organization
A. Perceptual Discrimination and Orientation
1. Visual Discrimination
a. *Matching.* The child can match a given object or picture to one of a varied set of objects or pictures that is similar in form, size or position.
b. *Recognition of embedded figures.* Given a form, the child can find its counterpart embedded in a picture or drawing.
c. *Part/whole relationships.* The child can structure parts into a meaningful whole:
(1) Given a model and an assortment of its parts, the child can arrange these parts to match the model.
(2) Given a model and a selection of parts, the child can select

those parts which are essential to the construction of the model, discarding those parts which do not belong.

(3) Given a model and an assortment of its parts, the child can determine which parts are missing.

2. Auditory Discrimination

a. *Sound identification.* The child can associate given sounds with familiar objects or animals.

b. *Rhyming words.* Given two or more words that rhyme, the child can select or supply a third rhyming word.

III. Bilingual/Bicultural Objectives

A. Finding ways of making the curriculum goals of *Sesame Street* more comprehensible and thus more accessible to the Spanish-speaking child, so as to provide the same learning advantages that the program brings to its English-speaking audience.

1. Reinforcing cultural identity and self-pride in viewers from Spanish-speaking backgrounds. Strategies include presenting the following as an integral part of the program:

a. The Spanish language

b. Spanish customs

c. Spanish art forms: songs and music, theater, dance

d. Spanish-speaking performers: live-action, animated, puppet

2. Presenting educational material in Spanish so that the child will learn the concept first and later be able to transfer the learning to other languages (English), while retaining the Spanish language.

3. Teaching as "sight words" certain Spanish words that are encountered often in the Spanish-speaking child's environment.

4. Emphasizing certain English letter combinations that are difficult for Spanish-speaking children to learn.

APPENDIX B. Curriculum for "The Electric Company" (1974–75)

Reading is presented as a unified process of getting information from print, incorporating units at several levels (letters, letter combinations, syllables, words, phrases, sentences). A problem-solving approach to reading is stressed, so that the children are made aware of all the kinds of clues that are available to assist them. The notion that we read for *meaning* underlies all teaching strategies. Some general guidelines for implementing this are as follows:

1. Decoding segments are followed as often as possible by a larger meaningful unit (phrase or sentence) that presents the sound that has been taught in a clear context.

2. Anything that is sounded out is read through again, preferably twice, in a very natural manner.

3. Words should be meaningful to the target audience child. Unfamiliar words tend to become stumbling blocks, unless they are amusing for their sound alone.

4. Each segment is explicit about what it is teaching and what is expected of the viewer. Devices that isolate the key point—at least briefly—are useful Some such devices are: (*a*) freezing all action while flashing a superimposed word, (*b*) using "old-time movie" style inserts, and (*c*) the usual salience devices such as color contrast, flashing, and especially movement. In using these salience devices, however, it is important to at some point *fade* the salient letters into a word and read the word as a whole.

5. Comments encouraging the viewer and rewarding him for partial success are important.

6. Print does not change rapidly within a single segment. An opportunity for the children to tackle the print before it is read to them is provided.

7. General characteristics of the written code are noted when possible. These are (*a*) reading from left-to-right, (*b*) print follows the temporal sequence of speech, (*c*) longer words usually take longer to say, and (*d*) the code is basically logical.

8. Levels of analysis are not always rigidly separated. It is useful to read a sentence in the normal manner, come upon a hard word, and analyze that word syllable by syllable, or even to analyze a syllable into separate sounds. This gives the child the idea that the same basic process applies at all levels. A segment of this kind generally concludes with a reading of the entire phrase or sentence correctly and with natural intonation.

9. Using context is an important strategy. Wherever possible, decoding strategies are related to the use of context cues. This is especially appropriate in decoding ambiguous sounds (*c, g, ow, ie*), but it is generally useful to balance decoding by reading the decoded word in context.

Following is a list of the basic pieces of the written code that are used in modelling the reading process, and some suggested teaching strategies.

Letters and Simple Letter Combinations

The following units are presented primarily in a blending context. Simple blending (*m-a-n* → man), word families (*m-an* → man; *f-an* → fan) and additive blending (*m-a* → ma; *ma-n* → man) may be used. The consonant following the short vowel should be on the screen when a sound is assigned to the vowel, since that consonant determines the sound the vowel will have.

A. Consonants

b	(as in "bag")
c	(as in "cat" and as in "city")
d	(as in "dog")
f	(as in "fig")
g	(as in "got" and as in "gem")
h	(as in "hot")
j	(as in "jet")
k	(as in "kiss")
l	(as in "lot")
m	(as in "map")
n	(as in "nap")
p	(as in "pot")
qu	(as in "quit")
r	(as in "rat")
s	(as in "sit")
t	(as in "top")
v	(as in "vat")
w	(as in "won")
x	(as in "box")
y	(as in "yell")
z	(as in "zoo")

1. Medial and final consonants are stressed. Since these are less distinct, the best strategy is to present the consonant first in *initial* position and then move it to other positions: b*i*n, so*b*er, ro*b*.

2. Both *c* and *g* have two sounds, but they cannot be treated in the same way. Although both more frequently have a "hard" sound, *c* has a "soft" sound when followed by specific letters (*i*, *e*, and *y*) but *g* varies unpredictably when followed by *e* ("get" versus "gem") or *i* ("gin" versus "gill"). For *g*, the appropriate approach is to model the use of context to determine which sound is correct. Context is the major approach in teaching the two sounds of *c*. Visual arrangements of words, pointing up vowels, can also be useful for *c*.

3. Controlled vowels are taught only when *r* is taught. Our approach will be to show that an *r* is an important cue for pronouncing the vowel, and that "vowel/*r*" is a unit, giving the vowel a different sound than it has alone.

B. Consonant Blends

1. The emphasis in teaching consonant blends is on the blending process. They should not be taught as chunks. The distinction between the approaches to a digraph, and a blend, should be clear.

2. Consonant blends are generally assigned along with a related simple consonant. For example, *bl* and *br* will be assigned with *b*. A two-stage model like the following (which might be used in silhouette blending), is appropriate:

$$b + l = bl$$
$$bl + oom = bloom$$

or a three-stage model:

$$b + oom = boom$$
$$b + l = bl$$
$$bl + oom = bloom$$

3. A single blend is seldom used in a given show. At least two related blends are included in order to avoid making blends seem like unique combinations (digraphs).

4. Final blends are stressed because they are difficult. This is most true for dialect speakers, particularly with the following blends: *-ld, -nd, -sp, -st,* in which the final sound tends to be dropped. Because of their construction, *-lt, -mp,* and *-lp* are not as troublesome. Therefore an ideal strategy is to begin a blending lesson with one of the latter examples, in order to make the procedure clear, and then move on to the more difficult blends.

5. The following *final* blends will be stressed:
-ft, -ld, -lp, -lt, -mp, -nd, -nd, -nt, -nk, -sk, -sp, and *-st*

6. Other consonant blends that may be covered are:
bl-, br-, cl-, dr-, fl-, fr-, gl-, gr-, pl-, pr-,
sk-, sl-, sm-, sn-, sp-, st-, sw-, and *tr-*

C. Consonant Digraphs

Consonant digraphs are presented as single units with a single new sound. Tying the two letters together visually is helpful, for example, moving the digraph *unit* around the screen and dropping it into different words.

ch	(as in "chop")
ph	(as in "phone")
sh	(as in "ship")
th*	(as in "think" and as in "this")
wh	(as in "what")

* No explicit distinction is made between the two sounds. It is likely that the sounds are similar enough for the child to generalize from one to the other.

D. Vowels

1. Vowels always have a context; because their sound is so malleable it makes no sense to present them in isolation. It is particularly important to have the letter or letters following the vowel available while decoding it.

a	(as in "rat")
e	(as in "met")
i	(as in "bit")
o	(as in "hot")
u	(as in "cut")
y	(as in "dry" and as in "happy")

2. Medial vowels are more difficult than consonants. They each have several sounds, and the sounds are more difficult to discriminate from one another. Meaning cues are always required. Vowels most likely to be misperceived are:

> *i* as in "pin"   and *e* as in "pen"
> *a* as in "thank" and *i* as in "think"
> *a* as in "hat"   and *o* as in "hot"
> *u* as in "put"   and *oo* as in "pool"

The first two pairs are much easier to discriminate when they are not followed by nasal consonants (*-n, -m, -ng*). "Pet" and "pit" are used to teach these sounds rather than "pen" and "pin."

E. Vowel Combinations

> *ai*   (as in "bait")
> *ay*   (as in "day")
> *ea*   (as in "neat")
> *ee*   (as in "see")
> *ie*   (as in "die" and as in "thief")
> *oa*   (as in "boat")
> *oi*   (as in "boil")
> *oo**   (as in "food" and as in "good")
> *ou*   (as in "found")
> *ow*   (as in "know" and as in "cow")
> *oy*   (as in "toy")
> *ue*   (as in "blue")

* No explicit distinction is made between the two sounds. It is likely that the sounds are similar enough for the child to generalize from one to the other.

1. Vowel combinations are treated as new sounds, similar to digraphs. They will be "stuck together" visually, as described for digraphs.
2. Vowel combinations with two sounds are taught by using context clues to resolve the ambiguity.
3. With *ie*, casual reference is made to the rule that *ie* followed by nothing is "eye," while *ie* followed by a consonant is "ee." This rule is shown as well as verbalized. The children are not made to feel that they are expected to learn the rule, but its usefulness is noted.

Larger Patterns (Chunks) in Words

These are presented as larger (and therefore more efficient) decoding units. They are amenable to the same process used in simple blending.

A. Larger Spelling Patterns

Segments teaching larger spelling patterns focus on modelling their *use* in the decoding process. Locating larger spelling patterns in the context of words (phrases and sentences) and using them as a "boost" toward reading the larger unit are two strategies that are taught.

> *-alk*   (as in "talk")
> *-all*   (as in "tall")
> *-igh(t)*   (as in "high" and as in "night")
> *-ing*   (as in "sing")
> *-tion*   (as in "motion")

B. Morphemes
   1. Morphemes are presented as chunks, like digraphs or larger spelling patterns, with the additional idea that morphemes carry meaning.

-ed	(past tense)
-er, est	(comparative and superlative adjectives)
-ing	(present progressive)
-ly	(adverbial)
-n't	(negative contraction)
-s	(plural)
-'s	(contraction)
-'s	(possessive)
un-	(negative prefix)

   2. Meanings are illustrated rather than explained.
   3. Explanation of what a contraction is and how an apostrophe functions are not necessary and are probably too abstract for our target audience. However, *reading* units with apostrophes in them is modeled, so that it is clear that one blends the letter sounds as if the apostrophe were not there.

C. Syllables
   1. Syllables are a good vehicle for modeling blending because they are easier to say without distortion, and easier to hear.
   2. Syllables should be recombined in different ways.
      Common syllables with unvarying pronunciation to be combined in larger units:

bat	go	some
can	let	star
car	out	ten
day	sea	

   3. The following words from the sight word list (section D) may also be used as syllables:

to	(to-day)
for	(for-get)
or	(or-der)

D. Sight Words
   (Taught As Whole Words)
   1. Sight words are taught as chunks.

and	stop
danger	the
for	to
if	was
is	who
of	you
or	

   2. It may occasionally be useful to include a familiar sight word in a decoding segment. The child may be more easily able to "hook into" the sound via a word he already knows.
   3. Meaning cues are provided for sight words, and they are integrated into larger contexts like other units.

Scanning Cues in Words

These are included to model the process of using noncontinuous patterns in decoding.

A. Final -*e* Signalling a "Long" Vowel: *

mate	(versus "mat")
Pete	(versus "pet")
bite	(versus "bit")
note	(versus "not")
cute	(versus "cut")

Final *e* is not always presented in contrasting pairs. The attempt is rather to get the child to recognize that "an *e* on the end" acts on the preceding vowel and must be taken into account in decoding that vowel.

B. Double Consonant Signalling a "Short" Vowel: *

1. Double consonants are not taught as chunks, rather the effect of a double versus a single consonant on the preceding vowel is to be stressed. This effect should be presented in both directions, adding and removing the second consonant.

2. Words with double consonants are good vehicles for decoding by syllables, because the syllable boundary (between the two consonants) is very noticeable. Also, with words of this form, the syllables have the same sound when split apart.

* These terms will not be used in the program.

Where pairs of familiar words exist (super"/"duper"), this principle is taught through contrasts. Otherwise the double consonant is taught by itself, again stressing that something that follows (here the double consonant) must be taken into account in decoding the vowel.

Phrases and Sentences

The approach to combining words into phrases and in turn into larger units is presented in accordance with the notion that the same strategies of analysis and synthesis obtain at all levels.

Phrases are sometimes treated as chunks within sentences. Phrases that have been presented earlier in the show can be spotted in the context of a sentence and used as a basis for figuring out the sentence.

A. Combining words into phrases.

B. Combining words or phrases into sentences.

C. Using syntactic and semantic context clues to figure out an unfamiliar word. Strategies for using structural and meaning clues, and shifting back and forth between the two are modeled.

D. Punctuation as a guide to meaning interpretation:

1. A sentence can end with a period, a question mark, or an exclamation point.

2. A capital letter signals a new sentence unless it begins a name.

3. Quotation marks indicate that the writer (speaker) is exactly reporting what someone said. (In dealing with an isolated sentence, the convention is followed that the person being quoted is identified; e.g., "he said," "she said," etc.)

CHAPTER 8

MOTIVATIONAL ASPECTS OF THE LITERACY PROBLEM

Lauren B. Resnick and Betty H. Robinson

It is widely assumed that the "disadvantaged," by virtue of their early and continuing family experiences, are not adequately "motivated" for academic achievement (e.g., Katz, 1967) and that this failure of motivation on the part of children and their families accounts in large part for the existence of the literacy problem in this country. That there is a problem surrounding literacy is abundantly evident. Large segments of our population—usually the poor and racial minorities—are failing to learn to read and write at a level adequate to the demands of our society. Black and

NOTE: The authors of this chapter have been engaged in collaborative development and research work in an urban public school over a period of several years. Our backgrounds and roles in this work are complementary in several senses. We are a black (Robinson) and a white (Resnick), who have worked jointly on a project concerned with the problems of educating young children from varied but predominantly poor and black families. Resnick has served as research and development director of this project, working with a number of faculty members and research staff whose contributions made an individualized instructional program possible. Robinson was the coordinator of activities in the school, working with teachers, parents, and children on the day-to-day problems of developmental instruction and motivation. Our concerns, and sometimes our opinions, have reflected our different backgrounds and orientations. We have not always agreed—except on the commitment to find ways of educating all children. Out of this commitment, over time, a set of practices and related theory has grown. The ideas presented in this paper derive from the special interaction of practice, theory, and empirical research we have been privileged to be part of.

The research and development work that underlies our thinking on the question of literacy was conducted under the auspices of the Learning Research and Development Center, University of Pittsburgh, and the Pittsburgh Public Schools. The former is supported in part by grants from the Office of Research, United States Office of Education, and more recently from the National Institute of Education. Special grants from the Ford Foundation for work on the Primary Education Project also supported this work.

other minority children fall farther behind in basic academic performance with succeeding years in school. Many adults, including some who hold high school diplomas, are unable to meet the minimal literacy demands of any but the least-skilled jobs. In every major city there are schools that routinely fall below both local and national norms on any test of academic performance they choose to administer. In what sense, however, does all this evidence argue for the existence of motivational problems on the part of certain social groups?

CONCEPTIONS OF MOTIVATION

Motivation in a Selective Model of Education

We would like to suggest that the evidence for a failure of academic motivation in the disadvantaged is essentially the same evidence that in times of different social persuasion has been used to argue that the disadvantaged were less "intelligent" than other segments of the population and that concepts of motivational deficit derive from the same educational and social assumptions that underlie concepts of intellectual deficit. The "hard" evidence (on both kinds of deficit) is that within the educational system as now constituted, certain groups of children fail to learn. Traditionally, our response has been to accept the educational system as given and then to seek "explanatory factors" to account for the discrepancies in learning outcomes. Since the educational treatment was assumed to be more or less invariant, it was inevitable that the relevant explanatory factors would be sought outside the educational system, i.e., in differences between children.

This statement requires some explanation. There are, of course, differences from school to school and from classroom to classroom in the resources brought to bear on education and in the specific objectives of instruction. There are also honest attempts on the part of many schools and teachers to make adjustments to individual differences among students. Nevertheless, in all but a few instances, our educational system has worked on the assumption that there is some fixed body of material to be "covered" in a given period of time and that some students would learn it and some would not. "Equality of educational opportunity," as Coleman (1968) has pointed out, has been judged according to whether students had *access* to the same educational experiences, not according to the equivalence of *results*.

Under these assumptions, the educational system has operated in a very real sense as a mechanism of social selection—accepting everyone at the outset, but according the intellectual and social benefits of educational success only to some. The selective aspects of the system are relatively masked in America, as compared, say, with certain European educational systems, but they are real enough even here. They continue to be maintained, even in the face of subtly changing social and legal definitions of equality (Coleman, 1968), by normative achievement testing programs, which rank students in relation to one another, thus implicitly selecting some students as being "better educated" than others.

Tests of "intelligence" were originally designed to predict success or failure within a selective educational system (Hunt, 1961; Glaser, 1969). This means that the test designers deliberately sought items for inclusion in the tests that would maximize differences between successful and unsuccessful students. IQ tests, validated within a selective educational model, have so dominated our thinking about intelligence that in all the discussion generated over Jensen's (1969) thesis concerning the heritability of intelligence, hardly anyone has challenged his assumption that intelligence is adequately defined by what is measured in IQ tests.

A brief scanning of research on academic motivation suggests that a similar concern with maximizing differences between successful and unsuccessful students has dominated our view of the issue. Katz (1967), reviewing research on the socialization of academic motivation in minority group children, mentions the possibility that racial differences in scholastic achievement may be due to failure of the schools to teach rather than of children to be motivated to learn. However, he then directs his attention almost entirely to research (his own and others') that seeks racial differences in achievement motivation, self-evaluation, response to tangible and symbolic rewards, and other characteristics that are presumably socialized early in a child's development and remain relatively stable throughout his lifetime. The attempt, in other words, is to find dimensions that will discriminate as sharply as possible between racial groups—since it is already known that these groups perform differentially in school.

Underlying research of this kind is a conception of motivation as a personality trait, i.e., a behavioral tendency that is stable across situations. This conception, in turn, leads to attributing the causes or failure to characteristics of the individual rather than of the environment (Jones & Nisbett, 1971). In education, in particular, this kind of attribution often is used as an excuse for failure of the institution or its practices (Clark, 1965), rather than as a stimulant to reform. For this reason, most traditional research on motivation offers little guidance for the development of educational intervention programs.

Motivation in an Adaptive Model of Education

What happens when we change from a selective model of education to an "adaptive" one—a model in which it is considered the job of the educator or educational agency to adapt its practices to the requirements of the students, rather than to select those students who can easily adapt themselves to the system? In an adaptive model of the kind we have in mind, learning goals would be set for, by, or with the students, and a contract made—implicitly or explicitly—to meet those goals. Since, presumably, students would differ widely upon entering the system, the school would be required to provide a number of alternative instructional courses in order to fulfill the contract with every student. A minimally adaptive system would be one in which all students are working toward the same goals and in which the same sequence of specific learning objectives is followed by all students, but in which each student is permitted to enter the sequence at a point suited to his own level of development and to proceed through the sequence at a rate determined by his mastery of successive levels in the sequence. There is no fixed time within which a task must be learned; rather, each student has as much (or as little) time as he needs. More extensive adaptation can be provided by offering alternative sequences or instructional strategies toward a given set of goals; or, further, by tailoring the goals themselves to the interests, capacities, and aspirations of the learner.

Carroll (1963) has suggested five variables in terms of which it should be possible to account for the rate at which individuals learn in an adaptive system. These are (1) aptitude (the amount of time *needed* to learn), (2) ability (to understand instruction), (3) quality of instruction, (4) time *allowed* for learning, and (5) perseverance (amount of time the learner is *willing* to spend in learning). The last of these variables, perseverance at learning, constitutes a reasonable operational definition of motivation; such a definition is consonant with findings that high achievement motivation is generally associated with persistence at achievement-related tasks (Weiner, Frieze, Kukla, Reed, Rest, & Rosenbaum, 1971). When this definition is applied, if as much time as is needed is allowed and if one assumes an individual's aptitude and ability for any given task at a given point in time to be relatively fixed, then the two key variables determining learning are quality of instruction and the learner's perseverance, or "motivation."

It will be readily agreed that educators are responsible for the quality of instruction. That schools and other educational agencies can take responsibility for the degree of perseverance at learning exhibited by their students is perhaps less obvious. We shall argue, nevertheless, that perseverance at learning is not a function simply of inheritance, early socialization, or current cultural conditions, but rather of an interaction of these factors with key aspects of the educational environment. Since we are here concerned with the improvement of educational practice, we shall focus our attention on conditions over which educators have, or can gain, control.

MOTIVATION FOR READING

There are four factors in terms of which we believe it is possible to account for perseverance in learning. These are (1) aspiration, (2) expectation, (3) external rewards, and (4) intrinsic reinforcement.[1] In the following sections we shall describe each of these and consider how they may function in the design of an educational program for children and for functionally illiterate older people. For purposes of this analysis, we wish to consider as "children" only youngsters who are being taught reading for the *first* time, at an age (up to approximately 7) considered standard in our society. Older children who are in remedial programs or who for some reason have not been taught at the normal age will probably have motivational characteristics more similar to adults than to children a few years younger. The reason for this distinction will, we think, become clear in the course of our discussion. In the final section of the paper we shall apply the four motivational factors to an analysis of the problem of motivating teachers to adopt new educational practices.

Aspiration: The Desire to Read

Reading is a normative behavior in American life. Everyone is expected to be able to read. The aversive consequences of not reading are great. Illiteracy is a serious handicap, not only in the job market but in numerous aspects of personal life. We assume, therefore, that there are few if any persons who would not prefer literacy to relative illiteracy. Although it is more anecdotal than quantitative, it is worth mentioning some of the kinds of evidence that support our assumption.

Young children, even from the most "disadvantaged" urban homes, usually come to first grade expecting and wanting to be taught to read. They ask explicitly for instruction in reading and respond especially quickly to activities that "look like" reading, such as learning the alphabet. The children want to "know how to read," although they may have little specific experience of what knowing how to read actually entails. These children of 5 or 6 years have learned from their parents and siblings, and indeed from their entire cultural experience, that reading is valuable. They have learned this even though many of their parents and older siblings and neighbors have never learned to read adequately. This fact alone suggests the degree of aspiration for literacy in communities with high rates of functional illiteracy.

---

[1] It should be noted that we use the term "aspiration" in a somewhat different sense from what has been traditional in social psychology. Our distinction between "aspiration" and "expectation" is roughly equivalent to the distinction made by Lewin, Dembo, Festinger, & Sears (1944) between "ideal goals" and "action goals." It is probably best, however, to avoid attempting to draw too close a comparison. Our own terms are defined in the course of our discussion.

The extent to which reading is valued even in the poorest cultures is further suggested by the extent to which functionally illiterate adults will go to hide their difficulties. Early in the development of the Job Corps basic literacy program, designers of the program discovered the elaborate (and highly intelligent) procedures that many young men used to "cheat" on the literacy placement tests, in order not to reveal their inadequacies. At Warrendale, a Youth Development Center in Pennsylvania that has developed a highly adaptive educational program in which boys "contract" for the academic work they will do, instructors report that the biggest step in dealing with the literacy problem is to get the boy to admit that he cannot read and make the first contract. Once beyond this point, progress is usually relatively quick.

What do facts like these imply for the design of educational programs for literacy? For young children, they offer us enormous encouragement. They suggest that the school's main job is to meet the child's desire to be taught to read—by teaching him and making his learning visible to himself and to his family.

Since, despite their desire to learn to read, many children come to first grade without having acquired the necessary prerequisite behaviors for learning, the commitment to teaching will usually imply the use of strong preparatory programs, with a heavy academic component. A motivationally adaptive educational program cannot afford to wait for "readiness" to develop. It must teach whatever readiness skills are truly prerequisite and then go ahead and teach reading, using whatever materials and methods seem to do the job best.

The requirement of visibility means that the materials and methods used in teaching must be clearly interpretable as "real reading" by the children and the community. Long periods of preparatory linguistic, visual or auditory training, for example, however well-founded from a pedagogic point of view, may flounder because they fail to make contact with the child's and the community's aspirations. Instead, readiness activities should involve work with letters as early as possible, and children should read early in "books," even if the books have only one word per page! The books and other materials with which they work should be available to take home as each successive level is mastered. The terminal behavior of reading, in other words, needs to be approximated as early as possible, and the developing skills of children need to be shown in concrete form to their families.

For adults, or for children who have already experienced failure in the first try at learning to read, the motivational problem surrounding aspiration is more complicated. The key step is to get the individual to admit that he has something to learn. There are several conditions that seem likely to contribute to a social-learning environment that will make this admission least uncomfortable and most likely to occur.

First, anonymity, or at least privacy during the instructional sessions, may help. It is not uncommon to find adults traveling across a city to a literacy class, bypassing one in their own neighborhood where attendance would be an admission to friends and neighbors that they could not read. And having admitted the need for help by entering a program, adults often withdraw from class situations in which they must expose all the specifics of their failure to public view. While anonymity may be outside most educational agencies' powers to arrange, privacy is not. Provision for privacy with respect to what one works on and where should do much to maintain participation in adult literacy programs. This makes an individualized program, with provision for tutorial instruction where necessary, close to a requirement in an adult literacy undertaking, for motivational as well as cognitive reasons.

A second need in adult programs is for some parity of relationship between instructor and student, with this need becoming greater the older the student. The traditional school authority relationship has failed for the functional illiterate. Thus the traditional "teacher in front of the class" is unlikely to work in adult or adolescent programs. Instead, some sense of "colleagueship" between instructor and student probably needs to be developed. In the two adult and adolescent programs we know best (Warrendale and the Bidwell Cultural and Training Center, in Pittsburgh), the physical arrangement is informal and not reminiscent of the schoolroom. Furthermore, there is considerable real power given to the students—not only to select their own learning activities and manage their own time but also to affect certain basic organizational features of the institution. Ideally, the teacher's authority should derive from the students' recognition of his competence as a teacher of something the student wants to learn, rather than from formal authority relationships. Just how to manage this and how to balance the student's need for autonomy with the teacher's need to instruct and set tasks are questions that need considerably more investigation.

A third factor that may increase the likelihood of enrolling and remaining in an adult literacy program is the visibility of "models"—other individuals who have admitted the need for literacy education and who are engaging in it. The existence of such models may function both to lower the perceived likelihood of unpleasant consequences for admitting the need of education and to demonstrate that literacy goals are realizable. As the models advance through the program and publicly demonstrate increasing competence, they may provide a form of vicarious positive reinforcement, which can function to increase the likelihood of the observer's engaging in the modeled behavior (Bandura, 1971). The effectiveness of such models of success has been demonstrated at the Bidwell Center, where enrollment increased sharply after the first 12 trainees passed the General Educational Development (GED) exam and were treated to an expensive dinner by key members of the center's board.

Finally, responsibility for another's education may serve to promote the desire to pursue one's own. Probably everyone who has worked with disadvantaged youngsters has encountered cases in which a parent returned to night school as his child developed increasing reading skill, in order to "keep up" or "be able to help." We have already noted that the culture of the poor—at least of the urban black—values literacy, and that this valuation is commonly expressed in great aspirations for its children. Educational programs that systematically capitalize on this sense of responsibility to the young child have only begun to be explored (e.g., Melaragno & Newmark, 1969; Ellson et al., 1965). By making an older child or adult responsible for tutoring a younger one, it may be possible not only to give the younger one valuable individual attention but also to provide the older person with an excuse for engaging in special study activities himself in order to "prepare for his job." These considerations suggest that cross-age tutoring programs should examine the effects on tutors as well as on tutees.

Expectation: Goal Setting

We have noted our belief that children from all kinds of homes enter school with high aspirations concerning reading and that these aspirations derive from their families and communities. Yet it has been widely hypothesized that disadvantaged children have weaker "self-concepts," lower "need for achievement," and generally more depressed expectations of success than their more advantaged peers. In other words, within a short time of entrance into school, children from poor and minority homes no longer expect to do well in school. Nor do their parents and teachers, whatever their aspirations concerning reading, have any great expectations for the children's success.

It is our own observation, shared by colleagues working in similar educational environments, that many parents who desperately want their children to do well nevertheless do not expect them to. This appears to be part of a general attitude on the part of people from relatively powerless groups in society that they cannot significantly control their environments or succeed through their own efforts (Lefcourt, 1966). This failure of expectancy is most often demonstrated in withdrawal and apparent apathy with respect to school and school achievement. Occasionally, however, most often when an intensive intervention program has dramatically raised a parent's hope for his children and thus his functional expectations for them, it is expressed directly.

Goldman (1970), for example, trained a small group of mothers in the use of positive reinforcement (praise) while teaching and playing with their own children. In interviews at the conclusion of the 3-month training program all the mothers expressed the expectation that they could now work effectively with their children and that the children would therefore probably do much better in school than they themselves had or better than

older siblings had. Parents of children in our developmental program sometimes tell us that their older children's experiences in school had led them
to give up hope for their children's learning, but that the progress of a
younger child in the program has raised their expectations.

Teachers' expectations of learning in the disadvantaged are also
characteristically low even as the child enters school (Rosenthal & Jacobson, 1968). These expectations probably derive from a combination of
"folklore," subtle forms of class and race bias, and teachers' own cumu-
lating experiences in which, under the existing educational system and
given the training and materials available to them, they have been unsuccessful in teaching such children. Rosenthal and Jacobson, in the studies
described in *Pygmalion in the Classroom,* have attempted to show that
teachers' initial expectations for their students can significantly affect
actual achievement. Although the Pygmalion studies have been severely
criticized on methodological grounds (Thorndike, 1968; Elashoff & Snow,
1971), the hypothesis of self-fulfilling prophecies in the area of academic
achievement seems sufficiently compelling to warrant further investigation
and analysis (Finn, 1972; Rosenthal & Rubin, 1971).

Assuming for the moment that the effects of teacher expectation on
learning are real, it is appropriate to ask how expectations might function
to produce differences in performance. It seems likely that teacher expectation affects ultimate performance both at the point of setting tasks and at
the point of evaluating performance. With respect to task setting, differential expectations, particularly where some measure of individualization of
learning tasks is possible, probably lead to differential assignment of tasks.
A child who is not expected to learn easily or well may be assigned fewer
tasks, or repetitive tasks at the same level of difficulty. If he has trouble
with a task, the teacher may move him back to an easier task without
carefully determining the source of difficulty or trying to help him solve
the problem. He will not, in other words, be regularly required to "extend"
himself. Where the child's and the parents' expectations are similarly low,
the teacher's failure to demand high performance will be compounded by
the child's withdrawal from serious efforts.

The child for whom there are high expectations, by contrast, will be
asked to do more and harder work and will not be permitted to "give up."
At the point of evaluation, as tasks or subtasks are completed, it seems
likely that children for whom there are high expectations will be more
warmly praised and more publicly recognized than children for whom
there are low expectations. Sheer amount of attention for appropriate
behavior may also be greater.

It is essential to note that, however important the effects of initial
expectation, the ultimate effect on the child will result from a cumulative
cycle in which the actual performance confirms and therefore strengthens
both the teacher's and the child's initial perception. The child for whom

expectations are low often actually does perform badly, in smaller and larger ways. This is why small differences in expectation can potentially have so great an effect. It is also one of the reasons why well-controlled research on the question is so difficult and why it is likely to be a long time before the effects of task setting, evaluation, attention, and other more subtle variables can be isolated.

With respect to the design and the staffing of educational programs, the potential effects of expectations on achievement point to the need for selecting and educating teachers in ways that will lead to changed initial expectations. This may be less a matter of college courses or other formalized training than of designing institutions and social support systems within the schools that will mitigate against the development and maintenance of negative expectations. With respect to parents' expectations for their children and to children's own self expectations, the job seems to us to be primarily one of visible demonstration of learning and of convincing learners that their own efforts can result in real achievement. Parent involvement in the educational process is vital if changes in expectation are to be effected. Yet the parents whose expectations are lowest are, as we have noted, the ones most likely to have withdrawn from active contact with the school. Thus special efforts at initiating and sustaining parental contact will be needed.

External Reinforcers for Learning to Read

Our initial section discussed the motivation deriving from the desire to *be able* to read, that is, to be an already accomplished reader. But *learning* to read is a long process, and many of the specific tasks involved may appear far indeed from reading itself, particularly if the individual's entering repertoire is weak and a period of preparatory instruction is required. Thus, even assuming that the basic desire to read exists, and even if expectations of success are maintained, other kinds of rewards, coming from the teacher and the school rather than from the student himself, may be required to initiate and to maintain the actual process of learning.

We mean by "external rewards" any rewards for learning or performance that are offered to the learner by some outside agent (teacher, peer, parent) rather than deriving either from the student's striving for some distant goal (such as literacy) or from intrinsic pleasure in performing the task at hand. Examples of external rewards range from tangible reinforcers (perhaps mediated by a token or point system) to praise from parent or teacher or recognition by peers. Defined in this broad way, it is clear that external reinforcers function in virtually every social situation. Thus the question for educational design is not *whether* to use external reinforcers but *which ones* to use and *how* to use them. Let us consider, therefore, some alternative external reinforcement systems, their characteristics, and their effects on learning and other characteristics of the school environment.

Token economies or point systems. Systems in which learners earn points or "tokens" for the work they do in an academic setting have been used with groups ranging from normal preschoolers through institutionalized delinquents (O'Leary & Drabman, 1971; Kazdin & Bootzin, 1972; Staats, 1973). Although details of the systems used have varied, token economy experiments have generally shared certain key features. First, there is usually a sequentially arranged curriculum (often no more than an ordering of the lessons in standard school textbooks). Second, there are standards of achievement for passage from one level to the next (these standards being intrinsic to the curriculum itself rather than to externally normed achievement tests). Third, there is the opportunity to earn points or tokens for attending to one's work, for completing work, or for passing tests that measure performance on the established objectives. Finally, points or tokens accumulated can be traded for privileges, consumable items, or other "goods" in the equivalent of a "store." In most cases, there is a mix of relatively immediate exchanges (each evening or the end of the work hour, for example) and relatively delayed exchanges (a monthly trip or an expensive catalogue item, for example).

A variant of the token economy is the reinforcement "menu" or contingency contract (Homme, Csanyi, Gonzales, & Rechs, 1969). Here, immediate access to desirable activities is made contingent on completing a unit of work. Such systems have worked rather well in maintaining work behavior in elementary school classrooms. They are appealing but are not always easy to organize. In addition, since access to reinforcement is tied to task completion and there are no systematic mediators, such as tokens, the teacher is provided few tools with which to shape and maintain perseverance in children who have difficulty in simply maintaining attention to a learning task through the time needed to complete it.

Projects using token or contract reinforcement in conjunction with individualized instruction have frequently been able to produce marked gains in reading performance after only a few months of participation in the program. These instances indicate the potential power of systematic programs of tangible reinforcement when skillfully and adaptively applied. However, it should be noted that the use of even very powerful tangible reinforcers does not free educational designers from concern with establishing conditions in which aspirations to literacy can be expressed (particularly in the case of adults) and in which expectations of learning are carefully nurtured. Rather, it seems appropriate to view the use of such reinforcement systems as a means of initially involving the student. As the student's expectations of success develop and as his increasing competence brings him into contact with intrinsic intellectual pleasures involved in reading and with social and perhaps (for adults) monetary reinforcers, the need for token economies and other incentive systems can be expected to diminish.

Token economies are relatively expensive to establish and operate. The expense lies only partially in the cost of the tangible rewards themselves. Other costs are social: the need to convince teachers that rewarding learning is not "bribery" and to train them in the use of the tokens to "shape" new behaviors rather than simply to reinforce already adequate behaviors. Still more important, we think, are the dangers inherent in a situation in which one group (teachers) seeks to establish control over another group (students), using resources available only to the former group. Social reinforcement systems avoid some of these problems.

Systematic social reinforcement. The effect of systematic social reinforcement (praise and contingent attention) in the classroom has been demonstrated in a number of studies (Glaser & Resnick, 1972). Most studies of this kind have concentrated on diminishing disruptive behavior and/or increasing overt "study behavior." While quiet classrooms and much "on task" behavior are undoubtedly reinforcing to teachers, it remains to be demonstrated that these characteristics of classrooms are directly associated with increases in learning.

Social reinforcement has a number of advantages over token or other forms of tangible reinforcement. First, it is cheap. It uses exactly the same resources as the teacher has used all along but distributes them more "rationally" and intentionally. Second, it is a step closer to the "natural" environment, that is, to an enviornment in which reinforcers are not systematically programmed. This is an advantage both to teachers who are troubled by the notion of "paying for" a child's learning, and to children, who move somewhat closer to being able to operate in the natural environment. Finally, social reinforcement is a mutual process, children and teachers dispensing it with more nearly equal power than is the case with tangible reinforcers.

Social reinforcement, like tangible reinforcement, can be distributed on a variety of schedules. It is our observation that many children, particularly from disadvantaged homes, enter school with relatively few "work skills," that is, abilities to follow directions, to follow through on a task, to ask for help when needed in appropriate ways, etc. In addition, with little experience of success in academic matters, such children may need especially frequent reinforcement. It is essential that such children be met where they are. Their attentional and work behaviors must be shaped by direct reinforcement, either tangible or social. As the ability to complete longer and more complex tasks develops, the contingencies can be shifted to *task completion*. This shift represents a move closer to natural reinforcement conditions, for traditional teacher practices place heavy emphasis on accurate and timely completion of work.

We know of no studies of systematic social reinforcement with adult functional illiterates. It seems unlikely that social reinforcement from an instructor will function in the same way as it does with children, since the effect of social reinforcement depends on perceived status and other relationships of the individuals involved (Blau, 1964). Nevertheless, for designers of adult literacy programs it is worth considering the social reinforcement resources of peers and families and seeking ways of making prestige and recognition in the community become dependent on progress in learning.

Although it is important to consider the means by which systematic external reinforcers can be gradually eliminated, it is also important to recognize that both social and tangible reinforcers constitute a part of the "natural" environment for children and adults. Thus there is no need to seek conditions in which parent and teacher praise is completely eliminated, in which no prestige accrues for literacy performance, or in which all tangible reinforcers (such as money) are removed. One of the characteristics of families and schools that are academically successful is that parents and teachers continue to demonstrate pleasure at children's learning and that individuals look forward to the dignity and the earning power of respected work. We must seek to make this the case for poor families and for impoverished schools as well.

Intrinsic Reinforcers for Learning to Read
The systematic use of external reinforcers for learning activities need not imply a disregard for the forms of reinforcement that are commonly termed "intrinsic"—either self-administered or built into the learning tasks themselves. In fact, it is useful to think of external reinforcement systems as establishing the conditions under which certain kinds of intrinsic reinforcement can become effective, particularly for individuals who have had little experience of academic success and who have reinforcement histories tending to produce devaluation of their own efforts. We shall consider two main categories of intrinsic reinforcers, with particular reference to the features of an educational program most likely to enhance their functioning among the disadvantaged.

Self-evaluation and self-reinforcement. Bandura (1971) and others have recently stressed the role of self-administered reinforcement and punishment in controlling an individual's behavior in the absence of, or in the intervals between, external reinforcements. Presumably, self-reinforcement in the form of positive self-evaluation mediates access to the external reinforcers available in the individual's environment much as tokens mediate access to tangible reinforcers in a token incentive system. Katz (1967) suggests that lower-class children, particularly blacks, tend to evaluate their performances more negatively than do middle-class children. This would imply that lower-class children's mediating reinforcement schedule is much "thinner" than that of middle-class children. Further, individuals from relatively powerless groups in society typically tend to perceive less opportunity to control the environment and therefore to achieve goals through personal effort (Lefcourt, 1966). For both these reasons it would not be unexpected to find a lower level of perseverance among lower-class children and adults, given equivalent difficulty of task and delay of external reinforcement.

It seems likely that one's evaluation of one's own learning will be closely tied to one's expectations for achievement and for control over learning. In the section on expectations for learning we spoke of the way in which repeated visible success might function to raise expectations of learning in students and in their parents. We would like to suggest now that, in addition to raising expectations, success can itself come to function as a self-mediated reinforcer of learning. This hypothesis is based on the assumption that people are reinforced by their "competence" (White, 1959). Behaviorally, it implies that people will keep doing things (1) that they are able to do well, (2) in which they can make clear judgments of their own competence, and (3) in which they attribute their success to their own abilities and efforts rather than to external factors such as luck (de Charms, 1968; Rotter, 1966; Weiner et al., 1971).

This definition of success as a reinforcer of learning suggests three conditions that should be met by educational programs. First, programs must be designed so that most individuals are successful at most tasks that they undertake. Second, there must be clear standards of success against which individuals can measure their own performance. Third, individuals must feel that they have met these standards through their own efforts and that their successes are real; warm praise for indifferent efforts and mediocre performance will quickly lose value.

Frequency of success can be best assured by offering an appropriately sequenced series of tasks, each developing the competence needed to succeed at learning the next. The steps must be small enough that a discernibly separate task is mastered frequently; and at the same time, they must be large enough to be perceived as significant markers of effort and achievement. At the outset, social or other external reinforcement should probably be offered for each task mastered, both to maintain learning behavior before success itself becomes functional as a reinforcer and to provide "models" of appropriate self-reinforcement behavior. Forms of record keeping, such as individual graphs and progress charts, which offer visual evidence of progress through a sequence of tasks, can do much to enhance the effect of frequent mastery. To function as reinforcers, these records should be available to the student; where possible, they should be maintained by the student, who must then discriminate more sharply the occasions when he is judged successful from those when he is not.

At first, as we have indicated, judgments of success or failure at a learning task will probably need to be largely external, provided by the teacher or perhaps another student. As experience builds, however, it should become possible for the student to take on much of the evaluative function himself. It is at this point that control over reinforcement is transferred to the student, and it becomes appropriate to speak of "self" or "intrinsic" reinforcement and, concomitantly, of internalized control.

Where the student is to be judge of his own performance, it is important that standards of success be as unambiguous as possible, at least at the outset. Two kinds of standards of success are possible. One, the most widely used in our current educational system, is one's standing in relation to others. This represents a "norm-referenced" standard of behavior and is embodied in our standardized aptitude and achievement tests. Motivationally, the difficulty with norm-referenced standards, whether the normative group is a single classroom, a school, community, or the entire nation (as in standardized achievement tests), is that for someone to be ahead, someone else must always be behind. For this reason, we would advocate the use of "criterion-referenced" standards, that is, standards in which a particular performance goal is described in detail and the student compares his performance with the described optimal performance (Glaser, 1963). In such a system, everyone can be successful, although there will be differences in the rates at which individuals meet successive performance standards. In addition, criterion-referenced tests provide a clearer description of the kinds of competence to be developed than do normed tests.

Pleasure in reading. In an experimental after-school program for black, intermediate-grade students who were significantly below grade level in reading (Wolf, Giles, & Hall, 1968), token reinforcement for completing math and reading assignments was temporarily dropped as part of a test of the tokens' effectiveness. Work rates dropped, but for at least some children they dropped markedly less in reading than in math. Here we have experimental evidence for the intrinsic pleasures of reading, even in a "remedial" population. For those with adequate reading skill, the pleasures of following a story or obtaining new information will often maintain reading activity for extended periods of time with no outside reinforcement at all. To what extent can pleasure in reading be used to maintain perseverance at *acquiring* reading skill?

In considering this question, it is necessary to distinguish between initial and later stages in learning to read. The initial stages of learning are necessarily concerned primarily with learning to recognize or decode words—to make the appropriate oral responses to written symbols. Whatever methods of reading instruction is used, reading vocabulary at the outset is extremely limited. As a result, it is difficult to write stories with much intrinsic interest that beginning students can read by themselves. Thus it seems most profitable at the early stages of reading to rely on other forms of motivation (including the intrinsic pleasures of success in decoding) and to use the most efficient teaching methods available in order to establish as extensive a reading vocabulary as possible, as quickly as possible.

At the same time, generous access to *orally* presented stories and other materials of high interest and quality can be used to maintain a general interest in reading and to provide some introduction to comprehension skills. In this regard, the use of audio recordings, keyed to printed stories that students can follow along with, is worth considerable attention. In addition to making the readings available on a more individualized and frequent schedule than "live" readings permit, "reading along" can probably be effectively used to develop certain visual attention skills. Comprehension skills can be developed on the basis of these oral presentations, thus establishing the groundwork on which skills in comprehension of written texts can later be built. Finally, for adult students, recordings of texts may be the most practical means of maintaining privacy while still offering a wide variety of listening/reading material. The possibilities for the kinds of texts that might be available in an adults' "listening library" are, at least theoretically, as wide as the printed material available in our society. Even the daily newspaper might be recorded each morning by students at a more advanced level in the program to be listened to by beginners.

As word attack skills and reading vocabulary expand and the student can read more and more on his own, the possibilities for readable texts of high interest built into the instructional program itself increase. It was in recognition of this possibility that various "reading laboratory" programs have been developed and also that reading series with "urban content," expressly intended for minority group and other disadvantaged city children, have been published. We are unaware, however, of a varied set of selected readings with an adequate range of content specifically suited to poor and minority group children. Perhaps this need can best be filled by making use of the wide variety of full-length children's "trade books" already on the market. A reading program built on such books could offer far more variety of format and content than any set of prepared selections and would also probably do more to engage children in extended reading efforts. Comprehension and related skills might be built on the basis of these texts, as might middle- and advanced-level word analysis skills. In this respect, approaches initially developed for adults, as in the Job Corps reading program, might well be imitated in programs for younger children.

MOTIVATING TEACHERS TO ADAPT TO STUDENTS

We have proposed a number of ways in which schools might adapt their practices in order to meet a commitment to teach all children to read regardless of their entering level of skill or motivation. Some of the changes proposed involve deep and extensive modifications in teachers' attitudes and day-to-day conduct with children. At least in the public schools, it is not always possible to select teachers with the most favorable attitudes and teaching skills for working with disadvantaged children. It is important, therefore, to consider what kinds of staff development practices within the schools themselves might bring about and maintain the kinds of behavior toward children that is needed. Since the changes required on the part of teachers will require much expenditure of energy on their part and since the ultimate payoff for these changes (i.e., schools full of literate children) may be some time in coming, administrators seeking to develop new teaching practices in their schools will need to develop and support considerable perseverance on the part of teachers at this difficult task. Administrators will, in other words, have to deal with the problem of motivating teachers to teach.

Standard supervisory practices in public schools offer little support to teachers working with lower class and minority group children. The principal is rarely seen, except when the class is disruptive, and for an annual or biannual rating of the teacher. A supervisor who travels from school to school may visit a few times a year to observe and, again, rate the teacher's performance. In general, a teacher receives external reinforcement (good ratings and promotions) largely on the basis of the external (i.e., nondisruptive) behavior of the children rather than their learning. The children's achievement levels are expected to be low anyway. The unusual teacher who does not accept these low expectations finds little encouragement. Most such teachers either leave the system or succumb to its low expectations. It is easier to blame the child for being unable to learn than to continue to blame oneself for being unable to teach.

Although the picture is bleak, we do not believe that it is hopeless. We think it may be possible to apply some of the same principles of motivation developed earlier in this paper to shaping and maintaining teachers' perseverance at the difficult but rewarding task of teaching disadvantaged children in an adaptive educational system. In this final section of the paper, therefore, we shall briefly discuss the implications of our analysis of motivation for the training and support of teachers in urban schools.

Aspiration. We begin with a proposition concerning aspiration—aspiration to teach. We think it is reasonable to assume that teachers want to succeed in the classroom and that the definition of success adopted by teachers will, in the long run, be determined by the professional/social environment in which they find themselves. Thus a school that is seeking to make major impact on the problem of functional illiteracy must begin by establishing a "culture" in which it is made clear to teachers at the outset that their success in the classroom will be measured by their ability to invoke learning in children, particularly in children who are not normally expected to learn. Through group meetings, individual conferences, and public commitments, the school must seek to establish in each teacher a frame of mind in which his or her aspirations as a teacher will only be satisfied if there is success in teaching all the children, including the "unteachable."

Expectation. If aspiration to teach is high, the problem becomes one of expectation—expectation of the children's ability to learn and of one's own ability to teach. Teachers' expectations, like those of children and parents, can probably best be changed by the experience and recognition of success. This means that teachers must be provided with models of successful teaching—a supervisor or other teacher who succeeds in teaching a child considered "unteachable." It means, further, that teachers must be provided with the technical skills and the instructional materials needed to facilitate children's learning. They must be educated in methods of diagnosing specific learning needs and in providing the varied approaches to learning that result in frequent success for both child and teacher. Further, they must have means of making their successes visible to themselves and their supervisors as well as to the children and the parents. Thus many of the techniques suggested earlier for enhancing children's motivation for learning can be viewed also as a means of enhancing teachers' motivation for teaching.

External and internal reinforcement. During initial periods of a teacher's work, generous use of external social reinforcers can help to sustain motivation. Probably most important in this regard is the recognition and responsiveness of supervisors and other teachers to small successes in teaching and learning. Other forms of social reinforcement might include the opportunity to talk with visitors to the school or to represent the school on visits to other schools. Staff meetings, formal or informal, can also become occasions for mutual social support. All these things can help to establish an environment in which intrinsic reinforcement from success in teaching can continue to build. Just as children are reinforced by visible evidence of their increasing mastery, so teachers can be reinforced by evidence that children are progressing. Thus, in addition to serving as the basis for planning a child's program, individual records on children can serve to make visible to teachers their own success in teaching. Regular supervisory conferences that focus on children's learning rather than on the external aspects of teacher behavior can do much to change the supervisory relationship from an evaluative to a collegial one, in which supervisor and teacher are mutually reinforced by successful teaching and learning.

What we are advocating, to state the case as generally as possible, is the use of the teaching experience itself as a means of changing teacher attitudes, rather than the more conventional approach that treats changed attitudes as a *prerequisite* to effective teaching in difficult settings. We have outlined, very briefly, a set of principles for staff development that has guided our initial work in developing an adaptive educational program in the context of an urban public school. The principles have been stressed, rather than the specific practices used in our school, because we are not prepared to offer a detailed prescription for school organization or super-visory practice on the basis of this experience alone. There is much yet to be learned both about how to train teachers in the technical skills that are needed to succeed in their work and about how to establish and support the attitudes toward children and toward their families that will make teaching effective and humane. What we would like to stress, however, is the necessity of paying at least as much attention to methods of motivating and training a teaching staff as to methods of teaching children. This concern for staff development is particularly crucial where students' level of motivation for learning is initially low, since it is only through appropriate social design of the school that perseverance at learning can be developed. Instructional methods and materials may be improved immensely. However, we see no substitute for the teacher as a person who establishes the expectation and provides the reward for initial learn-ing—and by so doing sets conditions under which learning can eventually be motivated largely by the expectation of continuing success.

REFERENCES

Bandura, A. Vicarious and self-reinforcement processes. In R. Glaser (Ed.), *The nature of reinforcement.* New York: Academic Press, Inc., 1971. Pp. 228–278.

Blau, P. *Exchange and power in social life.* New York: John Wiley & Sons, Inc., 1964.

Carroll, J. B. A model of school learning. *Teachers College Record,* 1963, **64,** 723–33.

Clark, K. B. *Dark ghetto.* New York: Harper & Row, Publishers, Incorporated, 1965.

Coleman, J. S. The concept of equality of educational opportunity. *Harvard Educa-tional Review,* 1968, **38,** 7–22.

deCharms, R. *Personal causation.* New York: Academic Press, Inc., 1968.

Elashoff, J. D., & Snow, R. E. *Pygmalion reconsidered.* Worthington, Ohio: Charles A. Jones, 1971.

Ellson, D. G., Barber, L., Engle, T. L., & Kampwerth, L. Programmed tutoring—a teaching aid and a research tool. *Reading Research Quarterly,* 1965, **1**(1), 77–127.

Finn, J. D. Expectations and the educational environment. *Review of Educational Re-search,* 1972, **42**(3), 387–410.

Glaser, R. Instructional technology and the measurement of outcomes: Some questions. *American Psychologist*, 1963, **18**(8), 519–521.

Glaser, R. Adapting the elementary school curriculum to individual performance. In B. S. Bloom (Ed.), *Proceedings of the 1967 Invitational Conference on Testing Problems*, Princeton, N.J.: Educational Testing Service, 1967. Pp. 3–36.

Glaser, R. Individual differences in learning—recent research. Paper presented at a conference on Individualized Curriculum and Instruction, University of Alberta, Edmonton, Canada, October 29–November 1, 1969.

Glaser, R., & Resnick, L. B. Instructional psychology. *Annual Review of Psychology*, 1972, **23**, 207–275.

Goldman, R. M. Development of a training program to increase the use of reinforcers in informal teaching by mothers of educationally disadvantaged children. Unpublished doctoral dissertation, University of Pittsburgh, 1970.

Homme, L., Csanyi, A. P., Gonzales, M. A., & Rechs, J. R. *How to use contingency contracting in the classroom*. Champaign, Ill.: Research Press, 1969.

Hunt, J. M. *Intelligence and experience*. New York: The Ronald Press Company, 1961.

Jensen, A. R. How much can we boost IQ and scholastic achievement? *Harvard Educational Review*, 1969, **39**, 1–123.

Jones, E. E., & Nisbett, R. E. *The actor and the observer: Divergent perceptions of the causes of behavior*. New York: General Learning Press, 1971.

Katz, I. The socialization of academic motivation in minority group children. In M. D. Levine (Ed.), *Nebraska Symposium on Motivation*. Lincoln: University of Nebraska Press, 1967. Pp. 133–197.

Kazdin, A., & Bootzin, R. The token economy: An evaluative review. *Journal of Applied Behavior Analysis*, 1972, **5**, 343–372.

Lefcourt, H. M. Belief in personal control: Research and implications. *Journal of Individual Psychology*, 1966, **22**, 185–195.

Lewin, K., Dembo, T., Festinger, L., & Sears, P. S. Level of aspiration. In J. McV. Hunt (Ed.), *Personality and the behavior disorders*. New York: The Ronald Press Company, 1944. Pp. 333–378.

Melaragno, R. J., & Newmark, G. A study to develop a tutorial community in the elementary school. Technical Memorandum. System Development Corporation, Santa Monica, California, 1969.

O'Leary, K. D. & Drabman, R. Token reinforcement programs in the classroom: A review. *Psychological Bulletin*, 1971, **75**, 379–98.

Rosenthal, R. & Jacobson, L. *Pygmalion in the classroom*. New York: Holt, Rinehart and Winston, Inc., 1968.

Rosenthal, R., and Rubin, D. B. *Pygmalion* reaffirmed. In Elashoff and Snow (1971), pp. 139–155.

Rotter, J. B. Generalized expectancies for internal versus external control of reinforcement. *Psychological Monographs*, 1966, **89**(1, Whole No. 609).

Staats, A. Behavior analysis and token reinforcement in educational behavior modification and curriculum research. In C. E. Thoreson (Ed.), *72nd yearbook of the NSSE, behavior modification in education*. Chicago: University of Chicago Press, 1973.

Thorndike, R. L. Review of *Pygmalion in the classroom. American Educational Research Journal*, 1968, **5**, 708–71.

Weiner, B., Frieze, I., Kukla, A., Reed, L., Rest, S., & Rosenbaum, R. M. *Perceiving the causes of success and failure.* New York: General Learning Press, 1971.

White, R. W. Motivation reconsidered: The concept of competence. *Psychological Review*, 1959, **66**, 297–333.

Wolf, M. M., Giles, D. K., & Hall, R. V. Experiments with token reinforcement in a remedial classroom. *Behavioral Research and Therapy*, 1968, **6**, 51–64.

CHAPTER 9

NATIONAL IMPLEMENTATION OF A REWARD SYSTEM

Norris G. Haring

If reading involves associating a written word with a spoken sound until the written words evoke the concepts for which they stand, then the stimulus-response-reinforcement paradigm devised by B. F. Skinner (1953) to explain behavior is admirably suited to reading instruction. The behavioral techniques in education that have been based on Skinner's concepts have proved to be powerful tools in teaching children. According to the paradigm, a stimulus evokes a response and that response is strengthened by the presentation of a rewarding consequence. The principle of reinforcement states that a response that is followed by a pleasant stimulus will tend to recur. If a stimulus is presented, a response is evoked, and the response is reinforced, the response will be likely to occur again in the presence of the stimulus, and the original stimulus will exert control over the response because the stimulus is discriminated by the learner. If the stimulus is a written word and the response is the spoken word, and if the spoken word is followed by an M & M,[1] then the written word will tend to become a controlling (or discriminative) stimulus that always evokes the spoken word (assuming, of course, that getting an M & M is a pleasant consequence). If the stimulus is a spoken word, the response is the writing of the word, and reinforcement follows, the spoken word is the controlling (discriminative) stimulus, in the presence of which the child will always make the same response. This, in a very simplified form, is the behavioral

[1] M & M is the brand name of a candy that comes in small pieces.

approach to the teaching of reading. A child's response to the spoken (or written) stimulus is conditioned by reinforcement. The behaviorist is concerned with the active, i.e., observable, responses emitted by the learner, and it is in the making of the response that learning takes place (Buchanan, 1969).

The measurement of a student's responses to stimuli can be an indicator of learning. A high and error-free rate of oral responses to written stimuli would indicate that the learner was reading the material presented and that he or she had learned to discriminate the words as stimuli that evoked the responses. A high and error-free rate of written responses to comprehension questions would test mastery of material that had been read silently.

If learning takes place in the active responses of the learner, then a record of those responses yields vital information about the appropriateness of the arrangement of the instructional environment—whether the stimuli in the environment are evoking the proper responses and whether subsequent events are strengthening those responses. Before any measurement can take place, the responses to be measured must be observable and carefully defined.

The most important aspect of measurement is in its use to determine the relationship between the responses and the reinforcement. A response is strengthened (its frequency is increased) if it is followed by reinforcement. But if a response rate is not increased when responses are followed by some event, then that event is not reinforcing. If a child does not like M & M's, then his or her response frequency will not increase even though he or she is offered an M & M after each response.

If the change in frequency were slow, it would be difficult to determine that the frequency was changing at all unless some form of continuous measurement were devised. An accurate reflection of behavior is the response rate. To determine a rate, one simply measures the number of responses over a period of time and then divides the total number of responses by the total number of minutes (or hours or seconds) to find the response rate. By noting the changes in the rate, the observer can see how the frequency changes in the presence of subsequent events. A rise in the frequency of the occurrence of a response would indicate that the subsequent events were rewarding (reinforcing) for the learner.

The use of reinforcement is a powerful technique in a teaching situation, and the arrangement of reinforcing events is known as contingency management, because the reinforcement is contingent on the emission of the response. Most teachers use reinforcement in some way to modify the behavior of students. "When you have finished your arithmetic assignment, you may go out for recess." "If you all have your work done on time, we may take 30 minutes for a party this afternoon." Some teachers give praise, which can be a very rewarding thing for many children, and some give gold stars as a tangible reward accompanying the praise. However, most teachers do this sort of thing on a very irregular basis or only as a special incentive. The systematic use of reinforcement techniques in a classroom, however, can have a great effect on the performance of children in that classroom, and a teacher who has a record of the rate of responding in the presence of subsequent conditions can determine which of those conditions are reinforcing and thus can be used to increase the frequency of desirable behaviors.

Poor readers in schools are subjected to very unpleasant consequences as a result of their reading behavior. Children who stumble over oral reading assignments are often laughed at. The teacher may speak sharply to them or criticize them. The material may be too difficult for them, but they may still be expected to keep up with the rest of the class and be humiliated by their failure to do so. For poor readers, the act of reading is an unpleasant one to be avoided.

If children are successful in the process of learning to read and if reading is an activity that always leads to satisfying and pleasant consequences—such as praise—then the children will enjoy reading, and they will read often, thus increasing their skills. In the home and the classroom, the beginning reader must find that reading is a pleasant and satisfying experience, rather than a frustrating and painful one. A reading program must incorporate principles of positive reinforcement where rewarding consequences follow responses. When a poor reader learns to read well, the act of reading will become a pleasant one.

Reinforcement techniques where consequences are rewarding rather than unpleasant can work in any teaching situation. Employees may take special training courses in their jobs, the reinforcement being the promise of a raise in pay. College students are generally working on degrees with the hope that they will get good-paying jobs when they graduate. These examples show reinforcement in terms of long-range goals, but reinforcement techniques are used in situations where the reward is more immediate. A program has been initiated at Fort Ord, California, that allows men in the basic training program to earn merits by performing assigned duties. Better-than-average performance earns a proportionately higher number of merits than does average performance. The merits can be cashed in for privileges such as passes, movies, and promotions, on the basis of the number of merits earned—high earners are promoted more rapidly ·than average earners. Although the program is still in a trial period, ". . . it does appear that the reinforcements proffered do serve as powerful motivational forces, that the trainees are enthusiastic abut the system, that attitude toward training is improved, that absenteeism is reduced, and that good performance is maintained throughout the cycle."[2]

[2] Personal communication from Robert L. Steward, Information Officer, Fort Ord, May 13, 1970.

The effectiveness of token reinforcement techniques in classrooms has been demonstrated (Nolen, Kunzelmann, & Haring, 1967; Haring & Kunzelmann, 1966; Haring & Hauck, 1969). Tokens may be stars, marbles, or plastic poker chips. Tokens may be points awarded by the teacher, which can then be cashed in for some reward such as food, a toy, or free time.

The use of free time as a reinforcement is based on the Premack (1959) principle. According to Premack, any activity will reinforce any other activity if the first occurs at a higher rate (is more probable) than the second. If kicking a wastebasket is an activity that is likely to occur at a higher rate than doing arithmetic problems, then the rate of doing arithmetic problems will increase if the child gets free time to kick the wastebasket when he or she has completed a certain number of problems. Homme (1966, 1968) has developed classroom situations where high-probability behaviors are used to reinforce low-probability ones.

High-strength areas are a part of the classrooms at the Experimental Education Unit of the University of Washington's Child Development and Mental Retardation Center (Nolen et al., 1967; Haring & Kunzelmann, 1966). The combination of a token system with a high-strength system is perhaps the most flexible arrangement for a classroom. If tokens are given in the form of points and the points can then be used for free time to engage in one of a variety of high-strength activities, the child will not become satiated on one reinforcer, and the high-strength activities will retain their strength as reinforcers. The element of choice prevents satiation.

When reading is defined in behavioral terms as stimulus-response (sound-symbol) association, the value of a reinforcement program is evident. Some forms of reading may be rewarding in themselves. For example, hard-core pornography appeals to many people. But there is little intrinsic reward in reading a newspaper (in fact, even for the skilled reader, much of the news may be unpleasant), and one certainly finds little inherent pleasure in reading an instruction manual or a textbook. For those with a reading disability, the act of reading is probably unpleasant and frustrating. Token reinforcement where tokens can be cashed in for things or events that are rewarding is an effective way to increase the responses of the learner, and it is in the responding that learning takes place (Buchanan, 1969). Lovitt, Eaton, Kirkwood, & Pelander (1971) demonstrated that oral reading performance of learning-disabled children is responsive to various reinforcement contingencies.

To this point the discussion has centered on the technique of reinforcing responses, but nothing has been said about the stimuli that elicit the responses that will be reinforced. Programmed instruction can fulfill the role of stimulus material. The format of programmed instruction is based on the stimulus-response-reinforcement paradigm (Buchanan, 1969).

The stimulus is the question or statement that demands an active response from the learner, and reinforcement usually comes in the form of the satisfaction of making the correct response. The learners receive immediate feedback because they are able to compare their answers with the correct answer provided in the text (Scriven, 1969). A good programmed text proceeds by small increments so that the learners are almost assured of getting the correct answer every time. They are able to work at their own pace and are not pressured to complete an assignment in a certain amount of time. The nature of programmed instruction is such that it demands active responses, and these responses can be measured.

As has been stated, measurement is necessary to determine whether events that follow a response are actually strengthening the response. An increase in rate indicates that they are. Responses have to be precisely defined so that they can be counted, and they must be of comparable complexity or duration. For example, if on one day the learners must respond to each of a series of single sentences and the next must respond to entire paragraphs, then changes in their response rates would not accurately reflect their learning because they could not respond to a series of paragraphs at the same rate that they could respond to sentences. Most programmed texts require responses over approximately equal amounts of material, thus assuring a constant rate. The variations in rate that appear would thus be due to the management of reinforcement contingencies rather than to changes in the material format.

The debates over teaching methods have produced no agreement among authorities as to what method is best. The wide variety of methods and reading materials in use have produced a wide variety of reading skills in the population. But if a comprehensive program of reading instruction were developed and if the process of reading was broken down into a carefully defined sequence of behaviors, each of which was taught by the program, then there would seem to be no need for the multiplicity of material available now. Individualized instruction does not have to mean a different textbook for each student. If the basic skills to be acquired are the same for every learner, then the program could be the same. The individualization would come in the self-pacing nature of a programmed text, where the learner works at his own rate of progress, and in the arrangement of reinforcing consequences. Measurement of responses allows a teacher to assess the effectiveness of reinforcing events and to arrange those which analysis of data has shown to be most effective for each individual. A comprehensive national reading program could serve the needs of all readers with a well-programmed sequence of material and a system of individualizing instruction through response measurement and arrangement of reinforcing events.

For a national program to deal with reading disability in children and adults, an integrated program of reading, writing, and phonics could be developed. It is generally agreed that many people who are labeled dyslexic have poor handwriting (Hermann, 1959). It may also be accepted as a premise that a phonetically oriented linguistic method of teaching produces better results than a look-say method (Chall, 1967). The concept of an auditory-visual-kinesthetic approach (Fernald, 1943) in which the learner looks at, says aloud, and traces the letter he or she is learning involves the senses of sight, hearing, and touch in the learning process. (One could, perhaps, use M & M's with different letters of the alphabet printed on them as rewards for accurate responses and thus involve the sense of taste as well.) An integrated program of reading, writing, and phonics is simply an example of the auditory-visual-kinesthetic approach.

Such a program would have to specify precisely the terminal objectives that the learner should achieve in each step of the program. It should also specify the behaviors that are required to enter the program. To determine whether a learner has the behaviors required to enter the program, a series of probes or tests taken from the material covered in the program could be constructed. If the entering behaviors were recognition of the letters *A*, *N*, and *P*, the tests would show whether the learner could indeed identify those letters. If not, a readiness program would be available to teach those letters, and when they had become part of the learner's repertoire, he or she could then begin the program.

Probes could also be used to determine the level at which a student should be placed in the program. The specific deficits of each child would be revealed through testing and the teacher would know that certain material should be stressed to overcome a particular deficit. Probe tests taken directly from the material covered by the program are the most effective means of determining entering behaviors and response deficits so that a student can be placed at the proper level in the program.

The probes developed for assessment would also be useful for taking daily data on the child's performance in the target skill. Often traditional classroom materials, even programmed texts, vary in response format from day to day. While working in his or her workbook on Monday a child may be required to insert long vowel sounds in words, whereas on Tuesday the format might include a review of the six consonant sounds learned earlier that week. Understandably, the rate data from Monday and Tuesday should not be compared to ascertain progress. To solve the problem of varying format within traditional materials, many teachers will use probes for a daily data collection tool. These probes consist of pages of the same class of problems from day to day (i.e., a probe on long vowels, a probe on short vowels).

In order to use the probes effectively, the teacher pinpoints through the assessment procedures outlined above the skills each child has not mastered. The teacher then works on these skills, one by one, using whatever instructional materials he or she chooses. In order to evaluate the effects of his or her instruction, the teacher takes data daily on probes that measure that skill. When the child has demonstrated mastery, the teacher moves on to the next skill while administering periodic review probes to assure that mastery is attained.

Once the learner has begun this type of program, he or she will progress through a series of small steps that approximate the terminal behaviors, each step requiring an active response and each step so designed that the response elicited is the correct one. For elementary school children, reinforcement in the form of tokens or praise would be given after a certain number of correct responses. For adolescents and adults, the reinforcement could perhaps be a certificate indicating mastery of the material at that step, and the certificate might entitle the individual to some reward such as a job promotion. Such a program must also be made teacher-proof by specifying the teacher's behavior as well as the responses of the learner. With the directions for administering the probes built into the program itself, any teacher could function successfully even with no specific training in the principles of programmed instruction.

Some of the newer beginning reading programs that have been marketed in the last 5 years are attempting to meet these needs. One in particular, the Distar program, utilizes the concept of reinforcement, progression by small increments, and similar format from day to day. Also, the teachers' behaviors are well specified so that the program can be successfully conducted by volunteers and classroom aides. This program, however, because it is usually group administered, still does not allow students to move at their own pace and does not allow them to skip portions of the material that they may already know.

The terminal objectives of a program designed to eliminate illiteracy in the general population should be based on a functional reading level—the ability to read and understand a newspaper article, to read and understand the issues on a ballot, instructions on a voting machine, instructions on how to run a household appliance, ability to read a driver's manual to pass a driving test, to read printed instructions on how to perform one's work. If a person can read on the purely functional level to acquire information, he or she has the skills that can be developed for reading for pleasure.

Once a program is devised, the question becomes how to make it reach all those people in the population who have difficulty in reading. The most important aspect of implementing the program is that it must be free and readily available to those in need of it. Obviously, the first place to implement such a program will be at the elementary school level. The best way to contend with the problems of reading disability is to prevent them altogether. Every school reading program should include a parent education program, for parents may not realize that a great deal of their children's success in reading depends on their own attitudes. If they read to their children, provide a wide range of reading material in the home, and encourage their children to read and praise their efforts, they are doing much to make reading a pleasant activity. Although the teaching of reading should be left to trained specialists, parents must realize the effect of the home environment or a child's reading behavior, and they should be informed of the ways in which they can provide a pleasant home environment where reading is encouraged and is a pleasant activity.

For the adult who cannot read, there are other places where reading programs could be set up. Reading centers could be established in public schools to serve adults in evening classes, and the tokens could be certificates issued at the completion of various levels of the program. Such certificates could be required by employers as prerequisites for pay raises or promotions (the tangible reward for which the token certificate could be exchanged). For adolescents in high school, the form of token reinforcement could be combined with the use of rewarding high-strength activities. Points earned in reading classes could be exchanged for tickets to athletic events, school dances, or special activities. The privilege of participating in such activities as band, choral club, or drama and art classes could be made contingent on the accumulation of a certain number of points. After-school jobs might be dependent on a number of points or a certificate of reading competency.

Reinforcement can take the form of money payments. A project has been conducted by Clark, Lachowicz, & Wolf (1968) with high-school dropouts involved in a Neighborhood Youth Corps group. As members of the youth corps, they went to school half a day and worked the other half. One part of the group worked at jobs for which they were paid a regular salary. Another part of the group received pay for academic responses in school. Results showed that the group who were paid for their academic responses showed higher gains in educational levels than those whose salaries were paid contingent only on their jobs. Employers in business and industry can institute on-the-job programs of reading instruction, the level of material based on the functional requirements of the job (such as reading technical material or instruction manuals). Higher levels of skill could be rewarded by promotions or financial bonuses. The federal Job Corps program has instituted reading instruction as a major part of its job training program (*Reading Disorders in the United States*, 1969), and a program of reading instruction such as has been described earlier using reinforcement techniques could be implemented in Job Corps Centers.

In penal institutions the overall educational level of inmates is only 7.2 grade years, and studies indicate that seventy-five percent of all juvenile delinquents are significantly retarded in reading (*Reading Disorders in the United States,* 1969). For the captive audience in such institutions, the points earned in reading instruction might be used to lessen the length of the sentence. Training programs in the armed services should be instituted. Certificates of reading competency or points earned in a reading program could be used for special privileges. A program of merits for performance previously described is already in effect at Fort Ord, California. Instruction in reading could simply be considered a part of basic training for the military services.

In order to achieve a functional level of literacy in the population as a whole, it is necessary that the instruction be individualized as far as possible to allow each learner to proceed at his own rate and with the form of reinforcement that is most motivating for him. The programmed instruction described earlier would meet these criteria. A programmed text allows the reader to proceed at his own rate and evokes measurable responses in small increments. A record of these responses will allow the teacher to determine which consequences will reinforce the reader's responses. If the use of tokens exchangeable for tickets to high-school dances does not increase the response rate of an adolescent, then perhaps a direct monetary payment will be more reinforcing and will cause a rise in the rate. A standardized program would assure that all learners would at least achieve a minimum level of functional reading ability. An individualized application of the program would assure that each person could proceed at the maximum rate of which he or she was capable without experiencing undue pressure.

To implement a nationwide program of reading instruction, teachers would have to be trained. It would appear that a major deficit in the American educational system today is not that children do not learn to read but that teachers are not trained to teach them to read. Teacher training should involve a basic understanding of the skills and behaviors involved in the process of reading, and procedures of defining and measuring behaviors, charting data, and interpreting the data to determine whether events subsequent to a response (giving points, tokens, or praise) were actually reinforcing the response.

The success of a program to deal with problems of reading disability demands a coordinated effort among colleges and universities where research on reading instruction is being done and teachers are being trained, government agencies (both state and federal) that administer programs such as the Job Corps, and public schools where children are taught to read. With a full-scale, frontal attack on the problems of reading disability in all elements of the population, those problems could be overcome, and many individuals who are now handicapped by a reading ability inadequate for their needs could be helped to become more productive members of society.

REFERENCES

Buchanan, C. D. Programmed learning in spelling. In A. D. Calvin (Ed.), *Programmed instruction: Bold new venture.* Bloomington: Indiana University Press, 1969.

Chall, J. S. *Learning to read: The great debate.* New York: McGraw-Hill Book Company, 1967.

Clark, M., Lachowicz, J., & Wolf, M. A pilot basic education program for school dropouts incorporating a token reinforcement system. *Behavior Research and Therapy,* 1968, **6,** 183–188.

Fernald, G. M. *Remedial techniques in basic school subjects.* New York: McGraw-Hill Book Company, 1943.

Haring, N. G., & Hauck, M. A. Improved learning conditions in the establishment of reading skills with disabled readers. *Exceptional Children,* 1969, **35,** 341–352.

Haring, N. G., & Kunzelmann, H. P. The finer focus of therapeutic behavioral management. In J. Hellmuth (Ed.), *Educational Therapy.* Seattle: Special Child Publications, 1966.

Hermann, K. *Reading disability: A medical study of word-blindness and related handicaps.* Springfield, Ill.: Charles C Thomas, 1959.

Homme, L. E. Human motivation and environment. In N. G. Haring & R. J. Whelan (Coordinators), The learning environment: Relationship to behavior modification and implications for special education. Symposium sponsored by the School of Education, University of Kansas, 1965. *Kansas Studies in Education,* 1966, **16**(2), 30–47.

Homme, L. E. What behavioral engineering is. In N. G. Haring & A. H. Hayden (Eds.), *The improvement of instruction.* Seattle, Wash.: Special Child Publications, 1972. Pp. 154–169.

Lovitt, T. L., Eaton, M. D., Kirkwood, M. E., & Pelander, J. Effects of various reinforcement contingencies on oral reading rate. In E. A. Ramp & B. L. Hopkins (Eds.), *A new direction for education: Behavior analysis.* Lawrence: University of Kansas Press, 1971.

Nolen, P. A., Kunzelmann, H. P., & Haring, N. G. Behavioral modification in a junior high learning disabilities classroom. *Exceptional Children,* 1967, **34,** 163–167.

Premack, D. Toward empirical behavior laws: Positive reinforcement. *Psychological Review,* 1959, **66,** 219–233.

Reading Disorders in the United States: Report of the Secretary's (Health, Education, and Welfare) National Advisory Committee on Dyslexia and Related Reading Disorders. Report issued by United States Department of Health, Education, and Welfare, Public Health Service, National Institute of Health, August 1969. Available from Developmental Learning Materials, 3505 North Ashland Ave., Chicago, Ill. 60657.

Scriven, M. The case for and use of programmed text. In A. D. Calvin (Ed.), *Programmed instruction: Bold new venture.* Bloomington: Indiana University Press, 1969.

Skinner, B. F. *Science and human behavior.* New York: The Free Press; London: Collier-Macmillan, Limited, 1953.

CHAPTER 10

THEORY-BASED RESEARCH ON READING AND ITS IMPLICATIONS FOR INSTRUCTION

Eleanor J. Gibson

Despite a long history of research on reading, it is only within the last decade that some of this research can be characterized as theory based. I mean by theory here a psychological analysis of cognitive development in general and of the processes involved in learning to read in particular. The theory must also make an analysis of the task confronting the child at all stages of his progress, and it must relate the task to the information to be dealt with. What kind of information has to be picked up? For example, is it encoded in an alphabetic system or, on the other hand, in a syllabary such as the Katakana system in Japan? The information to be picked up, and the nature of the pickup processes that must be developed are two aspects that a good theory tries to match to one another.

Educational research on reading has been notoriously unhelpful (Chall, 1967). A book published by Huey (1908) more than 60 years ago, and recently republished, summarizes practically all the psychological research on reading that was of interest until the new theory-based effort began about 10 years ago, an effort that was greatly advanced by Project Literacy.[1] Now there is a fair collection of research findings generated by

[1] Project Literacy was organized at Cornell University in February 1964, with Harry Levin as its director. It was supported by a developmental projects award from the Cooperative Research Branch of the United States Office of Education. For 4 years it attempted to bring together psychologists and educators from a variety of disciplines

relevant psychological theory. Can these findings be integrated into a general picture of how reading skill develops? And do they lead, then, to any principles useful for guiding instruction?

Issues for reading research have derived from several theories: from Piaget's theory of cognitive development; from stimulus-response (S-R) theories like the Russians' motor-copy theory, and operant conditioning theory; and even from mysterious recapitulation theories that advocate exercises beginning with crawling. Because of the limited space available, only the author's own analysis of the processes involved in acquiring reading skill will be emphasized, although leeway in the direction of eclecticism will be introduced when promising work is available.

AN ANALYSIS OF READING DEVELOPMENT

The material to be presented must be organized in some useful fashion. The following outline based on the author's analysis is proposed. It emphasizes the cognitive aspect of the learning process, not the motivational, but the two aspects coincide in places, and the tie will be followed up. The analysis is developmental, and so the major divisions are called "phases." The word "stage" implies less docility, less flexibility due to educational intervention, and less overlap than. is intended, and so "phase" seems to be the better word. The fundamental skills in phase I may continue to develop in parallel with phases II and III.

Phase I. Development of Skills Fundamental to Learning to Read
  A. Speech (hearing-speaking)
    1. Phonological aspects
    2. Semantic aspects (conceptual system and words)
    3. Syntactic aspects
  B. The "graphic" act and its perceptual feedback
    1. Perceptual differentiation of "writing"; of distinctive features of graphemes; letter identification
    2. Development of active perceptual strategies (comparison, "decentration," ordering, systematic scanning, analytic strategies)
Phase II. Decoding (mapping written text to speech sounds)
  A. Factors facilitating learning to decode
  B. Factors facilitating transfer in decoding
Phase III. Learning rules of unit formation (progressive economy of in-

---

to plan research aimed at understanding the acquisition of reading skill. Microfilm or photostatic copies of Project Literacy Reports and of the Final Reports referred to elsewhere in this paper can be obtained by writing to ERIC Document Reproduction Service, Leasco Information Products, Inc., P.O. Drawer O, Bethesda, Maryland 20014. [See also Levin & Williams, 1970.—Ed.]

formation processing by use of structural principles inherent in the informational system itself)

A. The nature of the informational system
B. Spelling-sound correspondences
C. Orthographic rule structure
D. Morphological and syntactic rule systems

The plan is to raise critical issues under each of these headings, to describe briefly the relevant research, if any exists, and to propose implications for instruction, if these follow from the research.

PHASE I. DEVELOPMENT OF SKILLS FUNDAMENTAL TO LEARNING TO READ

Speech (Hearing-Speaking)

There are many skills that are fundamental to learning to read, even though they may not seem to be part of the reading process as such. Producing and comprehending speech is one of these skills. Reading is a symbol system that normally decodes to speech. It follows that the child must have a reasonable competence in hearing and speaking before he or she can make smooth progress in learning to read. Deaf children are notoriously hard put to learn reading as a first-order symbol system. They may know manual sign language, but it is ideographic, except for finger spelling, and appears to afford less transfer to reading. There is the possibility of much transfer from the child's knowledge of his or her spoken language, for many parallels exist between the two symbol systems, hearing-speaking and reading-writing.

What should the child know about spoken language before serious reading instruction will be profitable? (Spontaneous attempts to read on the child's part should never be discouraged, any more than we would discourage spontaneous attempts to speak; we are talking of *instruction*.) We can divide the useful propositions into three parts, representing three aspects of language, the phonological system, the semantic system, and the syntactic system. Information about all three aspects exists in the world of stimulation engulfing children, and it is their task as well as their nature to extract this information as experience reveals it to them.

Phonological aspects. For children to decode writing to speech, or to write what they hear, they must have differentiated the distinctive features of phonemes. They must *hear* the difference between "bet" and "get," "bat" and "bed," "cat" and "tat," "ham" and "hem," "little" and "riddle," and so on. Probably nearly all children have mastered these distinctions before entering school, but there are exceptions. Some children still do not produce all phonemes distinctly. Although this fact does not necessarily reflect tardy perceptual development, it might. Such children should be given discrimination tests with pairs of words containing confusable phonemes. If discrimination is imperfect, the child should be given training in *listening* for the distinction. Material used for such training should *never* be in units smaller than a syllable. It has been demonstrated by scientists at the Haskins Laboratory (Liberman, Cooper, Shankweiler, & Studdert-Kennedy, 1967) that phonemic invariance cannot be extracted from a smaller speech sample. Asking children to do so is not only artificial (and absurd to them), it is impossible.

What units of speech does a child hear? Speech consists of an infinite number of combinations of a small number of components. Fragmentation and recombination of sounds would appear to be essential for mastery of the speech system and for decoding it to written symbols. It is this fragmentation and recombination in innovative utterances that seems to be beyond the ability of any animal but man. Children must have developed the ability to hear *segmentation* in what is spoken to them before we can reasonably expect them to learn to map the written code to speech. Children do not necessarily hear speech segmented into words. (Remember the story of "Gladly My Cross-Eyed Bear"?) Children can be examined for this ability by asking them to indicate (by handing the teacher a block, for instance) each word they hear in a sentence. Giving them the concept of a word may help. (I know of no research on children's concept of a "word" and how it influences either speech segmentation or reading.)

What about the phonological rule system? The child's native language is characteristically structured so that certain phonemic sequences are highly probable in certain orders and are not permissible in others. Certain consonant clusters typically begin a word but never end one, and vice versa (Zettersten, 1969). These very lawful orders are reflected in the spelling patterns that the child must learn. There might be transfer value from a highly developed sensitivity to the typical phonological patterns. Children ordinarily would pick up a knowledge of these patterns from the speech they hear in the world around them. But children need to hear good speech and may be at a disadvantage if they hear a dialect that does not map neatly to the orthographic rule system. Because this was a serious problem in England, where upper-class and lower-class speech have (or had) little in common, a standard "BBC" dialect was developed and literally taught to radio announcers and speakers. Perhaps we should pay more attention to the kind of speech children hear on the public media.

The role of dialect differences in learning to read is receiving study (Goodman, 1965; Cohen, 1966; Labov and Cohen, 1967). Eliminating all dialectical differences would seem a drastic and probably needless cultural impoverishment. Comprehension of standard phonological rules is undoubtedly important for discovering correspondences with the orthographic rule system, but Labov and Cohen report that speakers of nonstandard dialects may be quite capable of mastering the comprehension of both standard and nonstandard speech.

Semantic aspects. The semantic aspect of spoken language reflects meaning; a conceptual system that has to do with relations, objects, places, persons, and events in the world and a set of symbols to which these are mapped—a lexicon. The point of reading, we are always told, is to get meaning from the printed page. But we do not expect children to learn all the semantic aspects of language as they learn to read. Deaf children are deprived with respect to concepts of relations that are usually expressed verbally, "opposition," for instance (Furth, 1961), and typically have trouble making this up. Hearing children are not ordinarily so deprived, but they can be helped, so that meanings may hopefully transfer from spoken to written language.

Concepts such as "same" and "different" can be taught to children (Caldwell and Hall, 1969), and their discriminative performance is greatly refined as a result of it. Concepts, especially relational ones like equivalence, should be taught in kindergarten. That this can be done in interesting ways has been shown by the television program *Sesame Street.*

One of the concepts that may usefully be taught prereading children is the idea of a code. They are going to learn to use written characters as symbols for words with meanings, and it may be useful to teach them in gamelike ways what a code is. This was tried in an experimental classroom by Levin and Mitchell (1969) and appeared to be successful.

The most important preparation for reading as regards the semantic aspect of language is teaching children that there *is* meaning to be found from the printed page and that it generally contains information that they want very much to know. The obvious way to do this is to read to children before they can read themselves and to let them observe closely, by following along, what the adult reader is doing. The best motivation for reading is certainly the information one gets from doing it, and children should learn very early that great reward is in store for them if they attain this skill. Autonomous reinforcement for learning is the ideal kind, and discovery of meaningful information is reinforcing. Cognitive learning is the result of reduction of uncertainty (Gibson, 1969), and finding meaning reduces uncertainty.

Syntactic aspects. The child's knowledge of syntax and morphology is basic to reading and is made use of in the reading process, as we shall see. The rules simply carry over from the speech system, and so we expect transfer from a sure mastery of them. Children normally induce these rules for themselves. They can productively demonstrate considerable morphological knowledge when they are 4 years old (Berko, 1959), but there are limits to this knowledge. Even children beyond 8 years of age show increasing abilities to take advantage of both semantic and syntactic properties of word pairs (Gallagher, 1969).

These facts suggest that the child's comprehension of syntactic properties of language (as well as semantic ones) continues to develop through the early school grades and should be considered as playing a role in reading instruction.

The "Graphic" Act and its Perceptual Feedback

Visual differentiation of written symbols. While children are learning to hear and speak their native languages, they are also, in nearly every culture, allowed marking tools to play with. These tools can vary from sticks for drawing in mud to pencils and painting sets. In watching young children scribbling—the normal child of 18 months scribbles spontaneously when given pencil and paper according to Cattell (1960)—it is striking to note that they are fascinated by the tracings that they are producing. They are not scribbling for the sake of exercising their arms and hands but because they are interested in looking at the marks they are making (Gibson and Yonas, 1968). This tendency to explore visually the results of tracing seems as species-specific as language itself. Furthermore, children learn something from this activity. They learn to suit the size of their marks to the paper, and they learn what kind of features marks on paper may *differ* by. They perceive continuity, intersection, overlapping, straightness, curvature, connectedness, and termination, and learn that they can produce these variants.

Obviously, children should be supplied at an early age with pencil and paper and be given an opportunity to explore the possibilities quite spontaneously. They may imitate an older sibling or their parents (as they might the parents' speech), but they should not be pressed to do so too early. Scribbling seems to be its own reward, and furthermore it furnishes an unparalleled opportunity for learning the relations between the finger movements that guide the tool and the resulting visual feedback.

That children do learn a great deal spontaneously from scribbling, imitating marks of others, and observing writing has been demonstrated by L. Lavine (1972). She found that children differentiate simplified line drawings of objects from writing of all kinds by age 4 or earlier and that scribbling is usually differentiated from cursive writing by age 5 or 6, even when the child cannot write or even name a single letter. This learning occurs as spontaneously as speech perception, and it is self-motivating and painless. It should be encouraged by supplying every environmental opportunity, as one would expose a child to speech.

Once children have differentiated "writing" as a category from "drawing," they must learn to differentiate the set of forms that comprise the alphabet for their language. They can perceive artificial graphemes and other kinds of script (Hebrew, for instance) as writing, we have found,[2] but the time comes when they must learn the set of distinctive features that distinguish the particular set of symbols they are going to decode. That there is development in the ability to differentiate letterlike forms has been shown by Gibson, Gibson, Pick, & Osser (1962).

Can children be given assistance, in kindergarten and early in the first grade, in learning to differentiate graphic symbols? They surely can. An experiment by Pick (1965) demonstrated that training in matching letterlike forms improved discrimination and resulted in transfer, the amount and type of transfer depending on the kind of material given the child during training. Practice in discriminating transformations of a standard form appeared to be particularly effective, especially when new sets of forms were presented that varied by the same transformations. Comparison of a prototype form with that same form rotated, or changed by substituting a curve for a straight line, will teach the child to notice these differences, which we might refer to as the distinguishing features of letters.

What are the distinguishing features of letters? And are letters really differentiated on the basis of a set of distinctive features? There is good reason to think that they are, and some progress has been made in defining the set for the upper case Roman capitals (Gibson, Schapiro, & Yonas, 1968). Latencies and confusion errors for making same-different judgments of pairs of letters were collected for seven-year-old children and for adults and were analyzed by a hierarchical cluster analysis. Very similar tree structures (i.e., stages of differentiation) resulted from this analysis for the children and adults, and identical ones resulted from errors and latencies. The feature responsible for a split at any point in the tree is evidently being used, and some features have priority in the discrimination process. The curve-straight distinction, for instance, always (in many replications and with different samples of letters and artificial graphemes) comes out in the first branching.

Supposing we knew what the important feature contrasts were, how should we make use of this knowledge to promote faultless discrimination of the letters? By giving some kind of practice that would enhance the critical features, presumably. We know little about methods of enhancing a feature contrast so that it will be abstracted as an invariant feature (over

---

[2] It is interesting to compare the young child's ability to classify examples of various scripts as "writing" with the archaeologist's ability to classify undecoded symbol systems, such as "Linear B," as writing and perhaps even as a subcategory, such as ideographic, alphabetic, or a syllabary. There are conventions and regularities in writing, whatever they are, that permit it to be classified as such before its decoding system has been penetrated. Is it possible that "linguistic universals" include some writing universals?

irrelevant and "noisy" variations). Presenting the same contrast over differing base forms (as Pick did) is one fairly obvious way. This is often done with pairs of letters that differ mainly by their orientation on the page (*b-d, p-q, N-Z*, etc.). But letters differ by many features. Even without knowing exactly what these features are, we can give practice in discriminating highly confusable pairs (*E-F, P-R, M-W*).

How should the pairs be displayed? Under conditions of noise, such as different handwriting on different trials, to "force out" the invariant? Should a redundant, very noticeable feature be added, even though it is not critical? An example would be using color to enhance a difference, like coloring the diagonal stroke on the *R*. There is little good research on this problem, but caution is indicated, since the child may rely on the redundant feature instead of the critical one (Samuels, 1968). (This has proved to be the case in teaching children notes of the musical scale.)

Should the letters be presented as part of a word (e.g., "PAM" and "RAM") or separately? Probably both. It is not necessary to make a decision here. Is there any point in demonstrating or giving practice with a single letter, not presented in contrast with another? Having the child copy it, for instance? The answer appears to be that there is not. Tracing or copying single letters is far less effective for later recognition of letters than giving practice in discriminating (without reproduction) "hard" pairs that vary only slightly (Williams, 1969).

Letters must be identified as well as discriminated. We teach children the alphabet (the names of the letters), and there is some reason to think that this is a useful preliminary to reading (Chall, 1967, Chapter 5). I hope that it really is, if we are going to teach it, because we have found the task a very hard one for five-year-old children in a Head Start group, and one grows concerned that the boredom and distraction encountered in accomplishing this feat of memorization will put the child off when real reading begins. Is it possible that we "lose" some children at this early stage? One does not get much information from calling a *B* a *B*, and reinforcement with candy, stars, etc., proved (we found) thoroughly artificial and ineffective.

Can one find any structure in the alphabet that could reduce the information processing and thus give the child an opportunity for intrinsic reinforcement by reducing uncertainty? It occurred to me that we might take advantage of the fact that names of letters fall, in a number of cases, into rhyming groups (e.g., *A, K, J*). They could be confused, for that reason, but any kind of classification reduces information and is potentially useful at some point in the learning process. An experiment (Gibson and Shepela, 1968) was run, making color of print redundant with rhyming groups. Three groups of children (redundant color, nonredundant color, and all-black print) learned nine letters. Correlated color and rhyme increased errors within the the set but did not impair actual speed of learning over trials. The experiment could not be carried to a conclusion beause of available time and difficulty of the task. But the children (age 5) remembered the colors better than the names of the letters, so as a method it was a failure, as we ran it. Yet, some such principle would be useful if it cut down the memory load.

It has often been suggested (Fernald, 1943) that making a "motor copy" will somehow mediate between a visually presented stimulus and a verbal, naming response that has to be learned. The rationale is that giving added response-produced stimulation increases the cue value of the stimulus (Arnoult, 1957) or develops a "schema" of the stimulus, since this is constructed via sensorimotor activity (Elkind, 1967). The fact that coincidence tracing or copying is not particularly effective as practice for recognition does not exclude the possibility that motor pretraining might help in forming an arbitrary association, such as a letter and its name. Levin, Watson, & Feldman (1963) investigated this possibility, using artificial graphemes arranged in a string, each grapheme paired with a sound. Pretraining conditions included tracing the graphemes, copying them, just observing them, etc. A small amount of motor pretraining before learning the verbal response was totally ineffective. Repeated tracing of an initial grapheme only, gave slight facilitation for later association of the grapheme string and the verbal response. Tracing a medial or a terminal grapheme was actually worse than no tracing at all. There is no clear evidence that motor practice such as tracing or copying will facilitate learning a verbal naming response to the visually presented graphic stimulus.

Active perceptual strategies. Besides "content" learning, such as distinctive features and shapes of the letters, perceptual development includes active strategies. Perception is an activity (Gibson, 1966); it searches, explores, compares. The fact that coincidence tracing is not an effective kind of practice is not so surprising. It is not really an active perceptual strategy. Different theories of the active nature of perception have been formulated by such varied theorists as J. J. Gibson (1966), Held (1965), Piaget (1961), and the Soviet psychologists. It is agreed by all of them that skill develops in perceiving strategically. The perceptual activities required for reading are to some extent obvious. Feature analysis demands active comparison, and this develops with age, as Vurpillot (1968) has shown by studying children's eye movements during visual comparison. Asking the child to find contrasts can be an interesting game and may provide effective practice for a child who is slow in discriminating fine differences. I know of no relevant research.

Systematic scanning is another perceptual strategy that must be developed for effective reading. Preschool instruction usually gives practice for this purpose. Just how formally programmed this practice should be is a question. Is it a good thing to use moving devices to force the reader's eye movements to go in a given direction at a given pace? Conclusions from experiments with older readers trying to expedite their scanning are generally negative (Glock, 1949). Forcing a path or a pace does not develop an *active* perceptual strategy. The child must be led to develop this himself. Research on games or self-directed exercises that would be effective is indicated.

We know that perception during reading takes place during the fixation pauses. The information taken in during a fixation increases as reading skill increases. Is there any way we can help a child to learn to "take in more at a glance"? This question has generated a lot of argument. Practice with tachistoscopic devices (Goins, 1958) has not proved to be effective in promoting reading skill. Proponents of "speed reading" make claims for increasing the amount of material picked up at a glance, by some mysterious process of relaxing fixation. They may have something, but I know of no research on it, and the thing sounds suspiciously like a fad, as the tachistoscopic training programs were. There is a rhythm to reading, but it must fit the task (e.g., What do I want to get out of this page? Maybe only a telephone number.), and the material being read. We simply do not know how to develop active perceptual reading strategies that can change with the task. Perhaps spontaneous practice is enough, but any preschool play or exercise that encourages active exploration and "looking" is potentially good (Elkind & Weiss, 1967).

Piaget, in particular, has insisted on the development of perceptual activities. His research in this area has been almost exclusively with illusions, but Elkind (1967) has applied his ideas to reading. Perceptual activities, according to Piaget, include exploration, schematization, reorganization, and transport. "Decentration," the evidence of perceptual activity, is the ability to free perception from field effects produced by insistent features of the stimulus display.[3] Elkind feels that this ability is particularly essential in reading English, because letters and sounds do not have a consistent one-to-one correspondence. The child must develop skill in perceptual reorganization, and he thinks that children can profit from training in reorganization. An experiment (Elkind and Deblinger, 1969) gave second-grade inner-city black children perceptual exercises, such as solving anagrams and matching scrambled words, that presumably promoted development of appropriate perceptual activities. Measurements of reading achievement after a number of such training sessions indicated that certain aspects of these children's reading had benefited somewhat as compared to a control group. Elkind's exercises were aimed particularly at getting the children to discover the "arbitrariness of visual symbols" (per-

---

[3] Thurstone called one of his perceptual factors "freedom from Gestalt-binding." It was not clear from his research that it is related to reading, however (Thurstone, 1944).

sonal communication). This issue leads us directly into the next phase of learning to read, the decoding problem.

One point should be emphasized, however, before proceeding to the learning process involved in decoding, namely, the nature of the child's motivation to learn. Even Pavlov, the spiritual father of the stimulus-response (S-R) psychologists, pointed out again and again the child's natural interest in getting information about his environment, as witness the following paragraph:

> It is scarcely rated highly enough—this reflex that one might call the investigatory reflex, or, as I call it, the "What-is-it?" reflex; this is . . . one of the fundamental reflexes. Both we and the animals, at the slightest environmental variation, dispose the appropriate receptor apparatus in the direction of the agent of the variation. The biological significance of this reflex is enormous. If an animal lacked this reflex, then its life would every moment hang by a thread. And for us this reflex goes a very long way indeed, appearing finally in the form of that curiosity which creates science and gives and promises us supreme, unlimited orientation in the surrounding world.

It seems as though we often manage in the school to kill this active urge to seek information. Everything should be done to build on it rather than extinguish it with boredom, confusion, or failure to provide the appropriate kind of reinforcement.

PHASE II. DECODING

Factors Facilitating Learning to Decode

The heart of learning to read would seem to be the process of mapping written words and letters to the spoken language; a process of translating or matching one symbol system to another. It is often said that this is merely a matter of paired-associate learning. A visual display is presented to the child, and he or she memorizes a spoken response. It may be right here that we get in trouble. For one thing, memorizing an arbitrary association is an unnatural act and brings with it little cognitive reinforcement. For another, what are these S-R units going to be?

Units. Since letters are the elements of the code that are combined in infinite variety, it is natural that methods of instruction have often (perhaps mainly) emphasized decoding letters as units. But, as spelling reformers are fond of pointing out, the letter-sound correspondence in

English is irregular. Several expedients have been tried to get around this difficulty. One is the position advocated by the linguist Bloomfield: begin by teaching the child only regular correspondences and save the difficult ones till later (but then one cannot use the word "the" in the child's earliest stories). Another is Pitman's Initial Teaching Alphabet, which presents forty-eight written symbols, each ostensibly decoding to a unique sound. I will not go into research on the results of instruction with this method, except to say that the latest data suggest that any early advantage washes out (at best) by later grades. A third is the suggestion that colors be taught the child for different sounds and that letters or clusters of letters be presented in color so that a color image will eventually mediate the letter-sound relation (Gattegno and Hinman, 1966).

All these suggestions are based on misunderstandings of the psychological process of reading. For one thing, people do not read letter by letter (either good readers or bad readers, but especially good readers). Cattell showed long ago that with tachistoscopic exposure of words or letters, a five-letter word could be read with as short or shorter an exposure as a single letter. Later research (Kolers and Katzman, 1966; Newman, 1966) has shown that words presented to an observer letter by letter so as to project on the same retinal area are extremely hard, if not impossible to read. There is information in the adjacent context that the reader needs and uses. A single letter is in fact itself detected more easily when it is presented in a word than when it is presented without context. Lott, Cronnell & Smith (1968) and Smith (1969b) found this to be true, not for kindergarteners to be sure, but for third and fifth graders. The result has been replicated in several experiments with adults.

Moreover, a single phoneme cannot be perceived as invariant over a unit smaller than a syllable. It has been demonstrated by scientists at the Haskins laboratory (Liberman et al., 1967) that acoustic information from the context is essential for hearing the intended phoneme. So one-letter-to-one-sound cannot work even in a language with more consistent mapping relations than English. Having a child "blend" sounds together is a very unnatural business. If one wishes to teach a sound for an *a*, for instance, it should be presented in a word or a syllable, with a number of examples ("man," "cat," "ham," "bad," etc.) so that an invariant or common feature can be learned as a concept (which it is).

There have been many studies of cross-modal matching (visual-to-auditory and auditory-to-visual patterns) on the assumption that more knowledge about the matching process would help to understand what goes on in the case just mentioned. Although these experiments are interesting in themselves (see Pick, 1970, for a summary), they do not throw much light on the process. The experimental task of matching a sequence of clicks to a pattern of dots or a sequence of flashes is not really analogous to the task of discovering a cross-modal invariant relation, because that is a conceptual task and not mere matching. There is no amodal *similarity* in the visual and auditory information in reading; the code mapping is arbitrary.

If one accepts this fact, he may try, as Silberman (1964a) did, to teach the invariances by making children discover them in a learning setup arranged so that they might induce them for themselves. With very young, disadvantaged children this procedure, straightforward as it seems, was not very successful. It was too difficult and did not hold the child's attention.

Words are far more natural units, and they have the advantage of carrying meaning. One can use them at once to construct a message and get across the whole purpose of reading. The "whole word" method has long had its advocates, and with good reason. But the matter does not end with agreeing that words are units that carry meaning. Children do not automatically perceive words as units on the printed page. They have to learn that they are displayed with spaces between them, and they still must be differentiated, even as wholes.

Graphic features of words. Suppose we agree that we should start with words (and indeed sentences that convey a message), what features of the written word are we going to teach so that it will be differentiated from other words and recognized on a later occasion? If it is a visual display that is to elicit a verbal response, what features of this complex stimulus display are going to function as effective cues? Overall word shape has often been proposed (especially by "whole word" enthusiasts) as the critical feature. A kind of contour or outline of vertical and horizontal extremities of the word presumably give it a global form without concern about internal graphic detail. Research (Edelman, 1963; Smith, 1969a) has tended to refute this precept. Overall word shape is not a sufficiently good differentiator, and children do not use it. Analysis of features, using an optimal set as regards distinctiveness and economy is indicated. Not only is differentiation poor without internal analysis, but transfer to new words cannot occur. It also has been shown (Bowden, 1911) that this analysis does not necessarily take place automatically.

How fine an analysis of graphic features is necessary for identifying words? Computer programs for pattern recognition may eventually help us here, but the psychologist's intuition and a few experimental facts are the best we can provide now. The most informative parts of a word are its beginning and its end, and children who learn to read soon find this out. They process the information giving priority to the beginning first and the end next (Edelman, 1963; Marchbanks and Levin, 1965). This is borne out also by research with adult subjects by Bruner and O'Dowd (1958) and by Horowitz, White, & Atwood (1968). Subjects were asked to recall words on the basis of word fragments. Fragments presented as "cues" were initial, medial, or final clusters. Initial clusters were most informative, and final clusters were next in order.

Consider the following list of words:

> quick
> script
> cling
> drink
> swift

They all begin with a consonant cluster that can only begin a word and not end it. They all end with consonant clusters that can only end a word but not begin it. The medial vowel is the same in all and provides little information. But noticing the beginnings and the ends maximally reduces the number of alternatives and the uncertainty. A word such as "script" is unique; there is nothing else that it can almost be. As Garner (1970) has shown, this makes it a "good" pattern, and it should be easily learned. Children who have learned to pay attention to word beginnings and endings have found (consciously or not) its economy for information processing. Slow children can be helped to do this (but probably not by mere verbal admonition).

In pointing out the informativeness of initial and final portions of words, I do not mean that the matter ends here. There is a rule structure to orthography that goes beyond attention to ends, as we shall consider in the next section. But attention to the ends of words will lead to discovery of a lot of it. Even noting final *e*'s will do this. So many English words end in *e* that one might, on superficial consideration, think it noninformative. But that is not the case, because the marker *e* tells the reader about a higher-order pattern, cutting across literally thousands of words, that reduces uncertainty about spelling-to-sound correspondences. Compare the two lists below; they are examples of a very general rule.

hat	hate
dot	dote
cut	cute
met	mete
kit	kite

Emphasis and redundancy. Suppose we want to call a child's attention to informative features of the visually presented word, are there optimal ways of doing this? Just making a verbal statement to him may help, of course, but it is very apt to be misunderstood. Emphasis of the feature by the use of redundancy or eliminating noise or by providing contrasts are the other obvious ways (Gibson, 1969). There is little research specifically on this problem in reading instruction.

How could one introduce redundancy in normal reading and would it be useful?[4] Visual-aural redundancy, where clusters give good spelling-sound correspondence, seems obvious. Presentation of correlated visual-aural displays may help the child to extract the invariant mapping relation. Like a concept, this is a relation that holds over varying context. Trying to transmit some kinds of information over two sensory channels at the same time may, however, interfere rather than facilitate (Van Mondfrans and Travers, 1964, 1965). The closeness of spelling-sound correspondence and the relative obscurity of the feature to be isolated would presumably make a difference. Visual-aural redundant presentation is most effective for recall when spelling and pronunciation are maximally congruent (Nelson, 1969).

Methods like presenting the critical feature in a common color, or presenting skeleton words to enhance contrast (e.g., ... T versus . . . . TE) are possibilities, but there are problems such as how to fade out the redundant property and what happens when the context is put back. We could use some well-controlled research on this subject.

Role of articulation. What is the role of "pronouncing a word to oneself" in learning to decode written material? Is implicit speech useful, because it adds further redundancy and potential distinctiveness, or is it bad because articulating might slow down the process? Is it possible that hearing onself say the word is what pulls out the meaning? Consider what Huey (1908) said about this question 60 years ago:

> There can be little doubt that the main meaning comes to consciousness only with the beginning of the sentence-utterance, and the reader does not feel he has the complete sense until he has spoken it. He is almost sure to deliberately say the passage over to himself if it is difficult, and persons who do not read very much must usually use an actual whisper, even in easy reading, if the meaning is to be obtained [p. 147].

It is possible to reduce articulation during reading by giving the reader feedback about the muscular activity (Hardyck, Petrinovich, & Ellsworth, 1967). But this does not automatically increase the skill of the reading, in terms of getting the message. For a child who is learning, subvocal speech may be essential for getting the message. If we rely on

---

[4] An example of redundancy in instruction is the presentation of material to deaf students at a college for the deaf. The teacher lectures, aloud. He accompanies his speech with a translation of the same message into sign language. A student with some residual hearing has three potential redundant inputs; acoustic, visual input from lip-reading, and visual input from manual signs. A deaf student has two, lipreading and the manual signs. I do not know of research investigating how useful this redundant input actually is.

direct transfer of meaning to reading from speech, articulation should not be discouraged in early stages, at least.

Not everyone would agree with this point. Bever and Bower (1966) argued that "visual" readers are faster than "nonvisual" readers and that they can be trained. How children beginning to read would be trained to skip an auditory stage and still get any meaning was not indicated, however.

Meaning. Does meaning simply carry over from speech to reading? Has the child "got" the meaning when he or she can pronounce the word? Again, our earlier concern with preparing the child for reading leads to a question. When we have prepared children by providing them with an environment rich in opportunities to learn meanings and concepts, will the meaning roll out automatically when they hear themselves produce a familiar word? I simply do not know (especially for the Appalachian child, or the ghetto child who may hear an unfamiliar idiom in school), and I think some research should be planned on this issue at once. Teachers have intuitive opinions about it, but that is not good enough. Children make meaningful errors by guessing from context when they begin to learn to read (Biemiller, 1970), but it is not the printed word itself that is eliciting meaning. For an older reader, the meaning of the word is so insistent that it can interfere with a simple response of naming the color it is printed in, as the Stroop test shows, but how the meaning becomes literally embedded in the printed word is a mystery. That it does is proved by the experiments on semantic satiation. Staring at a word long enough extinguishes its meaning temporarily. But the fact that it can be extinguished proves that it was there. How can we help it get there?

Role of pictures. Children's readers nearly always contain pictures. What is the function of the pictures with regard to the child's learning to code writing to speech? The child has looked at pictures and understood them for years before he or she began to read. They interest the child and make the book attractive. But if they give the same information as the text, will they not actually remove the incentive to discover the printed message? Will the child not be distracted by the picture from paying attention to the text itself?

But perhaps a picture presented with a word by itself might serve as a kind of mediating image to elicit the spoken word and facilitate forming of an association between the printed and the spoken one. Myrna Shure (unpublished manuscript) conducted a preliminary experiment on this issue. Children in the second term of kindergarten were given practice with three-letter common words ("cat," "bed," "dog," etc.) on flash cards. In one group, the word on the card was accompanied by the appropriate picture. In another, it appeared alone. Training trials, in which the experimenter pronounced the word as it was displayed to the child, alternated with test trials when the child was shown the word alone and asked to say what it was. The picture group made significantly more errors and took longer to reach criterion than the group without pictures. The pictorial redundancy appeared to be distracting rather than useful. Similar results were obtained by Samuels (1967).

Does this mean that pictures are generally valueless or interfering? I do not think so, but I believe that we should discover what their function is and consider how they can serve it best. Children love comic strips and comic books, and at least one child I know taught himself to read with them. Why would he do this when the story was told by the pictures? I think the answer may be that all of the story was not found in the pictures; it is (in a good comic strip) interwoven with the comments of the characters. A comic strip with no printed messages at all seldom survives. The text is important, as Hochberg (1968) pointed out. He also said that "picture-text amalgams are essentially teaching machines in that they convey information in a self-paced and self-reinforcing process." But this is only potentially true. Most are not. What makes the successful ones work? Except for Hochberg's (1964, 1968), preliminary work, I know of no research on this really important problem. In a successful illustrated text, do the pictures contribute sequential or substantive information, or only a connotative setting for the story carried by the text? The question has not been answered, and so of course we cannot answer the question of whether, for learning, pictures *should* convey information in addition to the text, or whether they should only serve an incentive function for initiating interest in the text. They could, for instance, pose a question that only reading the text will answer.

Reinforcement. The role of pictures in a text brings us again to the question of reinforcement. I agree with Hochberg that reinforcement in procedures for teaching can only be internal. Reading should be a consummatory activity that functions as its own incentive and reward because of the appeal of the information to be procured. The consummatory value does not have to lie in a "sexy" text. Reduction of uncertainty is a potent internal reinforcer. Finding an answer to a practical question can do this and can be introduced immediately if the child's first two words are just "yes" and "no." I shall not go into the function of external reinforcement (praise, monetary rewards, etc.). They have been used with (reportedly) a certain amount of success with retarded, disadvantaged readers. Their function appears to be simply keeping the child at the task and has no relevance to learning as such. In an ideal instructional setting, we would never to have to resort to such artificial devices.

Factors Facilitating Transfer in Decoding

Analysis of component correspondence. The big objection to the "whole word" method of teaching beginning reading has been, on the one hand, that it fails to take advantage of an alphabetic writing system (we might as well use ideographs) and that poor readers result from its use because they have not learned anything that they can transfer to decoding new words. Certainly we want as little rote learning in our instructional procedures as possible, and that means that we should maximize transfer. Is it true that some analysis of the internal structure of the word—the location of component correspondences—is necessary for transfer to decoding new words?

Bishop (1964) worked on this problem, using college sophomores as subjects in a simulated learning-to-read situation. Different groups of subjects were given training by a whole word method or by a component letter method, with Arabic words, letters, and appropriate word and phoneme pronunciation. After training, new words made by recombining the already presented components were presented for the subjects to learn to read. In comparison with a control condition, the component training group showed very significant transfer. The whole word group also showed some. The subjects were examined, at the end, for knowledge of component grapheme-phoneme correspondences. It turned out that *all* the transfer in the whole word group was accounted for by a fraction of the subjects who had induced the component correspondences for themselves, without teaching. A similar experiment was conducted by Jeffrey and Samuels (1967) with six-year-old children and English words, again with the result that transfer only occurred when training with component correspondences or analysis had taken place.

For transfer, then, there must be some analysis. How it should be done is not an easy question, for reasons presented earlier. (Letter-by-letter mapping is inconsistent in the English language and anyway is unnatural to the reader-speaker.) Letters need to be presented in context, and the only natural way to learn component relations is to induce them as a conceptual invariant from a variable context. Some children will do this quite automatically by themselves, but some appear not to. Let us return briefly to Silberman's experiments.

Silberman (1964b) prepared an iterative reading program designed to teach children to read aloud combinations of four initial consonants (*f, r, s,* and *n*) and four vowel-consonant word endings ("an," "it," "at," and "in"). It was expected that children would automatically induce the internal correspondences if given enough contrastive practice with a sample of the possible combinations (e.g., "fan"-"fin," "sat"-"fat," "ran"-"fan," etc.). He should be able to transfer the induced mapping invariant to a novel combination that had not been taught (e.g., "rat"). The children in the experiment were in the lowest quartile in reading readiness in the low first grade in a "culturally deprived" neighborhood. They did not show automatic transfer until they had specific practice in decoding novel words *within* the training program. Teaching sounds independently and then "blending" was not successful. They needed practice in *generalizing the decoding skill*. This procedure proved effective for reading novel words.

Because practice in generalizing proved effective, we have tested a learning-set procedure designed specifically to promote interproblem transfer where the problem is to learn a concept—a letter-sound invariant embedded in variable contexts. This work will be described in Phase III, since the concept taught was a more constrained pattern than the single-letter components used by Silberman, and is properly considered as part of a rule system. We know that the most powerful kind of transfer is not transfer of identical elements but transfer by rule. It is the rule system we should look to, then.

Set for diversity. The suggestion has been made that because English does not incorporate tidy one-to-one mappings of single letters to sounds, or vice versa, children should not be encouraged to think that it does, but on the contrary should be given some kind of instruction or exercise that emphasizes diversity of these relations. This applies, of course, to transfer. If each word were memorized separately, it would not matter if component correspondences were inconsistent.

Levin and his co-workers (Levin and Watson, 1963a, 1963b; Levin, Baum, & Bostwick, 1963) investigated this issue in a number of experiments. The method was to present a list of paired associates for learning in which correspondences within the pairs were constant or variable as regarded repeated elements. Artificial graphemes were displayed visually, paired with familiar words. A trigram of three artificial graphemes might be paired, for instance, with the word "his." Other trigrams contained the same medial grapheme. In the "constant" lists, this medial grapheme was always paired with a sound comparable to the media vowel in "his" (words like "hit," "sit," etc.). In the variable lists, there were two or three vowel sounds, but they were all represented by a single written symbol.

Transfer lists of new pairs followed learning of the first list. For some groups, the transfer list was a "variable" list, and for some a "constant" list. For original learning, there was little difference in difficulty of learning the variable list versus the constant list. But when the transfer findings were compared, the group whose variable list was preceded by an original variable list was at an advantage. The authors concluded that a set for variability was engendered by the first list and transferred as a general set to learning the second list.

This experiment was repeated (Levin and Watson, 1963b) with variable-versus-constant correspondences in the initial position of the word with similar results. Most efficient learning of the second list occurred when a variable list was preceded by a different variable one. These results suggest that teaching children at first to *expect* one-to-one constant mappings of letters to sounds is the least effective way to promote transfer in decoding at later stages of learning to read. The nature of the correspondence system should be revealed in the earliest stages of training if transfer is to be optimized.

PHASE III. LEARNING RULES OF UNIT FORMATION

The skilled reader takes advantage of every conceivable principle for organizing the information in larger units. Perceptual pickup develops in the direction of greater and greater economy of information processing by using structural principles that are inherent in the informational system itself (Gibson, 1969). We want children to learn to read in larger units, and we know, if they progress, that they will. How can we help them? Finding rules and structure of any sort that serve to combine subordinate units into superordinate ones must be the way. Hochberg and Brooks (1970) believe that accomplished readers sample the redundant sequence of print, anticipate what is to come, and form and test hypotheses. If that is the case, they must have learned about the redundancies.

The Nature of the Informational System
What structural principles are inherent in the informational system? If there are correspondences between the phonological system and the graphological system, there must be mapping rules from one to the other. Since the mapping is not simply a one-to-one letter-sound relation, this is a critical area for research. Venezky and Weir (1966) have investigated these correspondence rules and have made it clear that correspondences are not chaotic, when clusters of letters and sounds in context and morphemic information are considered. Their findings provide a basis for preparation of instructional materials (Weir and Venezky, 1965).

Besides the spelling-sound correspondence system, which may provide a rule structure, there are rules of orthography whether or not sound is considered. We seldom verbalize them, but in doing crossword puzzles or playing scrabble we recognize possible initial clusters, final clusters, and contextual constraints like the necessity of a *u* following a *q*.

Besides the constraints within a word, the system has grammatical rules connecting words. Rules of morphology and syntax are part of the language system, and they serve to organize units. They do this for spoken language, and they could do so for reading as well. We shall inquire below to what extent they do.

Meaning also groups words. Sentences have underlying "thoughts," and so do paragraphs. So do whole books. Outlines and summaries that we find helpful for reading a text economically would seem to prove the force of meaning as an organizing principle. It provides context and expectancies, hypotheses about what will follow. A word in context is more easily and quickly recognized than the same word without context (Morton, 1964). I doubt that we can do better at present than consult our common sense as regards the use of meaning in reading; it just "comes natural." We have the habit, when we hear a sentence, of looking for its semantic interpretation, and this carries over to reading. But the other types of structure have inspired some research within the reading situation that may have applications for instruction.

Spelling-Sound Correspondences

Are there spelling-sound correspondences, rules that relate spelling to sound? According to Venezky (1967), there is a complex and reasonably regular relationship, wherein phoneme and morpheme share leading roles. Venezky tabulated spelling-to-sound correspondences in a corpus of the 20,000 most common English words, after devising a computer program for the purpose. Positions of the letters in the word were taken into account. Word lists for all correspondences were provided. Suffixes and word endings were studied for their function in determining correspondences. Consider the words "relate" and "relation." The spelling-to-sound correspondence for the *t* depends on whether it is followed by a marker *e* or the suffix *ion*, but this is a perfectly rulelike pattern. Functional spelling units must be defined for specifying the rules, and these units are not necessarily single letters. They may be units composed of several letters that have a correspondence that cannot be predicted from the individual letters (like the *dg* in "edge," "hedge," "badge," etc.).

Venezky points out that spelling units are not related directly to sound but to an intermediate morphophonemic level first and then to sound. I note this because it turns out, I think, to be important for reading instruction. Morpheme boundaries predict many spelling-to-sound correspondences (e.g., *ph* at the beginning of a word or of a base word, as in "morpheme," versus *ph* across morpheme boundaries, as in "shepherd"). I think that this can be an easy thing for a child to learn, because it operates rather like a syllabary system and that, it seems, is very easy for a child to master (Makita [1968] reports that there are less than 1 percent reading disabilities in Japan, where the children first learn a syllabary, the Katakana script). It also has underlying ties to meanings (the "shep" and the "herd") that define units and classes of words.

Suppose there are predictable functional relationships between spelling patterns and sound correspondents; are these used by the reader in such a way as to facilitate reading new, unfamiliar words? This was the issue investigated in an experiment by Gibson, Osser, Pick, & Hammond (1962). Pseudowords were invented with two versions matched in pairs so that one member incorporated a letter string arranged to be pronounce-able; the other had the same letters rearranged with initial and final consonant clusters reversed, making them unpronounceable (e.g., "glurck" and "ckurgl"). The words were displayed tachistoscopically to college students, with several different response measures, with the result that the "pronounceable" words were perceived far more accurately than the "unpronounceable" ones. The pronounceable words were rated more pronounceable on a rating scale, and when they were read aloud, they were given more consistent pronunciations and read with lower latency than the unpronounceable ones. Biemiller and Levin (1968) displayed the same pseudowords to third- and fourth-grade students. The children took longer to read aloud the less-pronounceable words.

How early do children begin to differentiate rulelike word forms from illegal ones? Again, pseudowords that followed simple spelling-sound correspondence patterns were compared with ones that did not (Gibson, Osser, & Pick, 1963). Subjects were children who had just completed the first and third grades. Some 3-letter strings (real familiar words, pronounceable pseudowords, and unpronounceable pseudowords) were presented tachistoscopically, as well as some of the 4- and 5-letter strings used in the previous experiment. An example of the 3-letter combinations might be *ran*, *nar*, and *rna*. The first-grade readers read (and spelled out) most accurately the familiar 3-letter words but read the pronounceable trigrams significantly better than the unpronounceable ones. The longer pseudowords were seldom read accurately and were not differentiated by pronounceability. The third-grade girls read all 3-letter combinations with high and about equal accuracy but differentiated the longer pseudowords; i.e., the pronounceable 4- and 5-letter pseudowords were more often perceived and spelled out correctly than their unpronounceable counterparts. Rosinski and Wheeler (1972) obtained similar results when they asked first- and third-grade children to judge which of a pair of pseudowords was "more like a word." The words varied in length from 4 to 8 letters and were matched as in the preceding experiments. The first graders made chance judgments, but the third graders made the judgment with about 90 percent accuracy. In this case, when there was no time limit for making a response, length was not a factor in the judgment.

These results suggest that a child in the first stages of reading skill has begun (with 3-letter strings) to generalize certain simple regularities of spelling-to-sound correspondence. As skill increases, longer items that involve far more complex conditional rules are brought under control, so that the children can perceive longer strings as units and can generalize their knowledge of regular correspondences to new items. The children must do a lot of the rule induction for themselves, since the complex correspondences are seldom explicitly taught. The opportunities for discovering the correspondences might well be enhanced in programming reading materials, since it is likely that the task is a hard one for many children. The children in the Rosinski and Wheeler experiment came from a good school, and nearly all had parents who were professional academics. Children from a less reading-full environment may be slow in getting enough exposure to the redundancies of the code to internalize them.

Other evidence that pronounceability (spelling-sound correspondence) structures units for perception, and for memory as well, comes from an experiment by Gibson, Bishop, Schiff, & Smith (1964). Meaning, as well as pronounceability, was contrasted with control items (unpronounceable and meaningless) in this experiment. Both properties facilitated perceiving and remembering an item; pronounceability was more effective for tachistoscopic perception, and meaning was more effective for retention. Clare (1969) found that pronounceability of a target word greatly favored its discovery in a visual search task, with other factors, such as meaning and familiarity, controlled.

We want children, therefore, to learn to take advantage of "pronounceability" in reading. What exactly do we mean by this? Pronounceability may be considered the regularity of correspondence of either simple or complex spelling patterns to sounds, conditional upon context, location in the letter string, and morpheme boundaries. If so, how does the reader use this correspondence? Must he articulate an unfamiliar visually presented word and match it to some stored acoustic or articulatory pattern before he detects it as a potential lexical item? This hypothesis was suggested by Biemiller and Levin (1968). If it is true, we would expect congenitally deaf readers to show less benefit from pronounceability of unfamiliar pseudowords than hearing subjects show.

This prediction was tested by Gibson, Shurcliff, & Yonas (1970). If pronounceability, in the above sense, is what facilitates reading the so-called pronounceable items, we should find an interaction with the ability to speak and hear them. With the cooperation of the students and faculty at Gallaudet College, this hypothesis was tested. There was no interaction. The deaf subjects profited just as much in reading the pronounceable combinations as hearing subjects did. I believe we can only account for this finding by recognizing that the two types of pseudowords are differentiated not only by ease of pronunciation but by rules of orthography, that is, spelling patterns alone. There is a kind of grammar for letter sequences that generates permissible combinations. It can tell us, without pronouncing it and even if it were unfamiliar, that "string" can be an English word but "ngistr" cannot.

Conrad (1970) divided profoundly deaf schoolboys into two groups, those relying on "articulatory coding" and those relying on visual information alone. The two groups differed on several tests. The nonarticulatory group made more recall errors when they had been required to read aloud. The articulatory group made more errors when lists consisting of pairs of homophones were presented. The latter had no effect on the nonarticulatory readers.

Orthographic Rule Structure

It would seem, at this state of our knowledge, that there are spelling-sound relationships that may affect facility of reading, and also solely graphic spelling patterns that may affect reading facility. Both have been demonstrated to facilitate perception and retention. Let us call the graphic spelling patterns the orthographic rule structure. Although congruence of two rule systems (phonological and orthographic) should give the most powerful set of generalizations, regularity in the orthographic information can be quite effective alone. Nelson (1969) has shown that recall of pseudowords is most facilitated by congruence of spelling and pronunciation but that similarity to English spelling is a highly significant variable by itself. That being the case, how do we promote the learning of what I shall call spelling patterns?

Two hypotheses that seem reasonable are (1) that there must be abstraction of an invariant pattern over many variable contexts and (2) that a learning set gradually develops for finding regular patterns in orthography. Should one teach verbal rules, such as "When two vowels go walking, the first one is talking," or is there a better way? Surely we can expect more transfer if the learner succeeds in making his own inference, for reduction of uncertainty is reinforcing.

Gibson, Farber, & Shepela (1967) attempted to develop a training procedure aimed at providing opportunities for abstraction of a regular pattern and for developing a learning set. They constructed a large number of problems that required the subject to sort positive from negative instances, like a simple concept-learning experiment. All the problems had four positive instances, each of which contained a cluster of two letters in an invariant position—initial, medial, or final (e.g., *qu*, *ea*, *ng*). The other letters always varied. The children were given one problem at a time for sorting, with one negative and one positive instance indicated when the problem was presented. They were corrected when they were wrong. They sorted for one problem four times and then went on to another, whether they had succeeded in a perfect sort or not, following a procedure much like a discrimination learning set experiment.

This training procedure was first tried on kindergarten children and first graders, running them on six problems a day for five consecutive days. The task was extremely hard for the kindergarten children. Only one out of twelve developed an indubitable learning set. This child could sort *all* the problems correctly on the first sort by the fifth day. The task was somewhat easier for first-grade children; about half of a first-grade sample showed evidence of developing a learning set to abstract common patterns of orthography.

It was not clear whether these subjects had really attained a set to search for invariant structure over a series of items or whether more specific habits had already been learned in first grade that helped on this task. We therefore tried an experiment comparing success on the spelling pattern problems with success on analogous problems in which the elements were color chips instead of letters. Subjects for this experiment were first- and third-grade children, some run first with colors, and some run first with letters. For the first-grade children, color and letter patterns were equally (and very) difficult; success on the color problems, however, transferred to the spelling patterns. For the third-grade children, the letter patterns were much more easily picked up than the color patterns; and color problems were far more likely to be solved if they followed solution of letter problems than if they were given first.

It appears that a set to look for structure can be developed and can transfer to new problems; and that the ability to detect structure in letter patterns improves with age and schooling. It seems that this is more than specific learning, since it transferred to color patterns. The third graders easily succeeded in searching actively for invariant spelling patterns. Following a task in which a child found them, he or she could pursue an analogous search for color patterns. *Finding structure* is rewarding, and when these children had found it, they repeated their successful strategy.

How could the first graders be assisted toward success in finding the structure, so as to facilitate transfer to new cases? Lowenstein (1969) compared three procedures in a new experiment with first graders. One group was given *no* special hints or help, as in the preceding experiments. One group was given *specific* help. When a problem was first presented, the experimenter said, "You will be able to find your own mail, because all the cards will have *these two* letters on them." The pair of common letters was pointed out. This was repeated for each problem. A third group was told, "You will be able to find your own mail because your cards will have the same two letters on them." But they were never told which letters. After two days of practice, all the subjects had a posttest set of problems without any further instructions.

The group given specific help made very few errors during training, even on the first day. The group given no help made many, although some improvement occurred. The group given the general hint made many more errors to begin with than the children given specific help (a mean of 6 errors) but they improved steadily, and on the posttest had a median of zero errors; whereas errors ro*e on the posttest to a median of 5.5 for the group that had received specific help. This was more than 5 times as many as they had made on day 1. Although 70 percent of the subjects in the "specific" group made no errors on day 2, only 20 percent made no errors on day 3, the posttest. But in the group given the general instruction to look for an invariant letter pattern, 40 percent made no errors on day 2, and 60 percent made none on day 3. Response latencies confirmed these results. The "specific" group showed *no* change from day 1 to day 3, whereas the group given the general hint showed a steady and significant decrease in latency over the three days.

It may be concluded then that first-grade children can easily sort words on the basis of presence or absence of two specific letters that have been pointed out to them. But it is not this ability as such that leads to detecting common spelling patterns across items. There must be a search for an invariant pattern and discovery of such structure for transfer of this kind of abstraction to new problems. Subjects given no special instructions or hints may eventually accomplish this on their own—20 percent of the subjects in the control group made no errors on day 3 (the same percentage as the "specific" help group on day 3). But it is clearly better to have attention directed to search for invariant features in the stimulus array, and finding them is reinforcing; it leads to repetition of the successful strategy and thus to consistently accelerated performance.

This is the point that I wish to emphasize again. Motivation and reinforcement for cognitive learning, such as speech and reading, are internal. Reinforcement is not reduction of a drive, but reduction of uncertainty, specifically the discovery of structure that reduces the information processing and increases cognitive economy. This is perceptual learning, not just remembering something. Learning to read involves active participation by the scholar, not memorizing a verbal rule followed by a pat on the back.

Morphological and Syntactic Rule Systems

Language in its morphological and syntactic systems offers a higher-order rule structure beyond the level of the word that the speaker-hearer takes advantage of in comprehending and producing messages. It seems obvious that the same process must occur with written language for the skilled reader-writer, since the motivation is identical. Is there proof that it does? How early can a young reader do this? Will it occur naturally, as a kind of incidental learning, as it apparently does with spoken language? Are there underlying structures of grammar (and meaningful content) at some deep cognitive level that make themselves available to the reader, as well as to the speaker, at some stage (when?) in his or her learning? Chomsky (1970) seems to assert something like this.

Weber (1967, 1970) studied the errors of children reading aloud to each other at the end of first grade. Most of these errors did not comprise grammatical mistakes. When a mistake occurred, it was followed by an ungrammatical conclusion only 29 percent of the time. The good readers, in particular, tended not to violate grammaticality, or they corrected the error if they did. These findings show that grammatical rules are in general available to children at this age. But the important question is whether the child *uses* this knowledge to carve out units for reading. Use of this redundancy to form "chunks" should be a great aid to economical processing.

This question has been the subject of a number of experiments by H. Levin and his students (Levin and Kaplan, 1970). At what age does a child stop reading word by word and begin making use of textual redundancies, such as syntactical contraints in sentences? The technique employed was the so-called Eye-Voice Span. It is the distance, measured in words, that the eye is ahead of the voice. It has long been known that the eye-voice span increases with age, and that it is affected by the difficulty of the reading material. The more difficult the material, the shorter the span. It seems likely, also, that the more structured the material, the longer the span. It is longer for a sentence, for instance, than for a random string of words of equal length.

Is the eye-voice span directly influenced by units of grammatical structure, in the sense that these create boundaries for the eye? If this is true, we have evidence that the reader is making real use of the syntactical rules to form units. He is actively searching for and picking up units composed of multiple words. In one experiment, Levin and Turner (1968) studied eye-voice span for simple active sentences with subjects at six grade levels. There were active sentences made up of 2-word phrases, active sentences of 3-word phrases, and active sentences of 4-word phrases. Unstructured word lists were also included. The mean length of the span was significantly longer for the sentences than for the unstructured word lists, and there was a tendency for the span to be longest on the sentences of 3-word phrases. Older subjects had longer spans than younger ones, and faster readers had longer spans than slower readers. The eye-voice span tended to extend to a phrase boundary, except in the youngest (second-grade) sample.

Other experiments have elucidated still further the role of syntactic constraints in creating units for reading. It has been shown that the latter half of passive sentences is more highly constrained than the corresponding part of active sentences. It was predicted, therefore, that the eye-voice span should become longer toward the middle of the passive form but not for the active form. Levin and Kaplan (1968) demonstrated that with college students this is indeed the case; the eye-voice span was longer for passive sentences at that point where the active and passive forms began to be differentially constrained.

Another type of constraint, the difference between left-embedded and right-embedded sentences, was explored by Levin, Grossman, Kaplan, & Yang (1972). By using a modified cloze procedure, it was ascertained that right-branching sentences are more highly constrained than left-branching ones. Eye-voice spans were then determined for these sentences, with college students as subjects. As predicted, the eye-voice spans were longer for the more highly constrained right-embedded sentences, once again suggesting that skilled readers actively search for and use regularities in language structure. Their knowledge of the rules tells them where and how far to look and thus assists them to chunk the material in higher-order units.

How early is this admirable cognitive economy available to young readers? The Levin and Turner study suggested that even by the end of second grade there is a difference in eye-voice span between random strings of words and sentences, although there was progress after that in using intrasentence constraints such as phrase boundaries. Perhaps it is the meaning in the sentences, rather than grammatical structure, that is responsible for the difference observed in the second graders. The question may not have a simple answer, for syntactic markers are important clues to meaning (Fodor and Garrett, 1967). But we still need to explore much farther the developmental progress in pickup of constraints and redundancies of both kinds. We do not know how this learning occurs. Are habits of doing this already internalized for spoken language and simply transferred to reading? I do not think the answer is this easy; I think there are clues to syntax on the printed page that are perhaps comparable but not identical with those in heard speech.

An analysis of the progressive use of finer clues to syntactical units was undertaken by Gibson and Guinet (1971). They studied pickup of morphological transformations (verb inflections) in third- and fifth-grade children and college sophomores. Words were flashed one at a time on a screen with a brief exposure for the subject to read and record. There were three types of stem words (real words, pronounceable pseudowords, and unpronounceable pseudowords). The words varied in length from four to seven letters. There were four versions of each one; the stem word, the third-person singular (*s* added), the past tense (*ed* added), and the progressive (*ing* added). The questions were whether the verb ending functioned as a unit, resisting errors and permitting a longer word to be read, and whether such a tendency, if present, was learned by third grade or only later.

As in earlier experiments, the real words were read with fewest errors, and the pronounceable pseudowords with the next fewest. A stem word lengthened by an inflectional suffix was *not* read more correctly than a word of equivalent length that did not contain a suffix. But the inflectional endings themselves were read with fewer errors than noninflectional endings on words of equivalent length. Furthermore, if an error was made on the inflected ending, there was a tendency to substitute one of the other inflections (for example, *ing* for *ed*). Both these latter tendencies increased from the third to the fifth grade. Thus inflectional endings do tend to be processed as unitary word features, and this is done increasingly as reading skill develops. They can therefore serve as clues to the structure of a phrase or a sentence.

Is there redundant information beyond the sentence that can improve the economy of reading? Intuitively, we certainly suppose so. The paragraph, for instance, is a form of organization that groups information. An experiment by Koen, Becker & Young (1969) investigated whether subjects agree in identifying paragraph boundaries in unindented prose passages. They were interested in whether there existed formal cues to paragraph structure, as well as semantic cues. Content words (nouns, verbs, adjectives, and adverbs) were replaced in some of the passages by nonsense paralogs. The subjects marked paragaph boundaries in both types of passages. For adults, the reliability (agreement) in identifying paragraph boundaries of the original English passages was very high (0.86). But the reliability for the nonsense versions of the same passages was also quite high (0.71), and so there are evidently formal indications of paragraph structure as well as thematic indications.

This experiment was repeated with children of three age groups (ages 7–8, 10–12, and 14–16). There was an increase in interjudge consistency with increasing age and experience. Surprisingly, the correlations between adults and children in the two younger groups were greater for the nonsense passage than for the original English version. The authors concluded tentatively that the development of the syntactic system is more rapid than that of the semantic. At least, before the age of 14 or so, children do not behave like adults in using thematic structure to organize units of paragraph length.

Much more research is needed on the problem of how we learn to read in units beyond the word. Skilled adult readers do use morphological, grammatical, and semantic structure. But we know very little about how this skill develops. We do not even know how early semantic structure influences sentence processing in reading. How the structural information is incorporated in our reading habits is as much a mystery as the same question is for speech. It is not something that is explicitly taught, for the good reason that perceptual learning is involved, so reinforcement must be internal and self-regulated. It is possible that exercises in placing phrase boundaries, sentence boundaries, and paragraph boundaries can help, but hard data are not available,

CONCLUSION

I do not believe that there is one ideal reading program that should be mechanically spread through the land by computerized instruction or even simpler programming of a rigid sort. Children are different. Some learn to read overnight, as if by magic, and some struggle, undoubtedly for different reasons. It is the teacher who must cope with these children. What we must do, first and foremost, is see that the teacher is well-educated in the basic psychology of reading, so that he or she will have some wisdom to apply to the individual case. A child's lacks or problems may be centered on any of the aspects of the reading process that I have been describing. The teacher must understand what these aspects are and be ready to diagnose a child's needs in terms of them. There is no magic, comprehensive program or all-sufficing model (see Gibson and Levin, 1975), but there is a psychology of reading with some general principles that afford a basis for understanding the individual case.

REFERENCES

Arnoult, M. D. Stimulus predifferentiation: Some generalizations and hypotheses. *Psychological Bulletin,* 1957, **54,** 339–350.

Berko, J. The child's learning of English morphology. *Word,* 1958, **14,** 150–177.

Bever, T., & Bower, T. How to read without listening. *Project Literacy Reports,* 1966, No. 6, 13–25. (ERIC Document ED 010 312.)

Biemiller, A. J. The development of the use of graphic and contextual information as children learn to read. *Reading Research Quarterly,* 1970, **6,** 75–96.

Biemiller, A. J., & Levin, H. Studies of oral reading. II. Pronounceability. In *The analysis of reading skill: A program of basic and applied research.* Final Report, Project No. 5-1213, 1968, Cornell University and the U.S. Office of Education. Pp. 116–125. (ERIC Document ED 034 663.)

Bishop, C. H. Transfer effects of word and letter training in reading. *Journal of Verbal Learning and Verbal Behavior,* 1964, **3,** 215–221.

Bowden, J. H. Learning to read. *Elementary School Teacher,* 1911, **12,** 21–33.

Bruner, J. S., & O'Dowd, D. A note on the informativeness of parts of words. *Language and Speech,* 1958, **1,** 98–101.

Caldwell, E., & Hall, V. The influence of concept training on letter discrimination. *Child Development,* 1969, **40,** 63–71.

Cattell, P. *The measurement of intelligence of infants and young children.* (Rev. ed.) New York: Psychological Corporation, 1960.

Chall, J. S. *Learning to read: The great debate.* New York: McGraw-Hill Book Company, 1967.

Chomsky, N. Phonology and reading. In H. Levin & J. P. Williams (Eds.), *Basic studies on reading.* New York: Basic Books, Inc., Publishers, 1970.

Clare, D. A study of principles of integration in the perception of written verbal items. Unpublished doctoral dissertation, Cornell University, 1969.

Cohen, P. S. Outline of research results on the English of Negro and Puerto Rican speakers in New York City. *Project Literacy Reports,* 1966, No. 7, 13–18. (ERIC Document ED 010 313.)

Conrad, R. Short-term memory processes in the deaf. *British Journal of Psychology,* 1970, **61**, 179–195.

Edelman, G. The use of cues in word recognition. In *A Basic Research Program on Reading.* Final Report, Project No. 639, 1963, Cornell University and the U.S. Office of Education. (ERIC Document ED 002 967.)

Elkind, D. Piaget's theory of perceptual development: Its application to reading and special education. *Journal of Special Education,* 1967, **1**, 357–361.

Elkind, D., & Deblinger, J. A. Perceptual training and reading achievement in disadvantaged children. *Child Development,* 1969, **40**, 11–19.

Elkind, D., & Weiss, J. Studies in perceptual development. III. Perceptual organization. *Child Development,* 1967, **38**, 553–561.

Fernald, G. *Remedial techniques in basic school subjects.* New York: McGraw-Hill Book Company, 1943.

Fodor, J. A., & Garrett, M. Some syntactic determinants of sentential complexity. *Perception and Psychophysics,* 1967, **7**, 289–296.

Furth, H. G. The influence of language on the development of concept formation in deaf children. *Journal of Abnormal and Social Psychology,* 1961, **63**, 386–389.

Garner, W. R. Good patterns have few alternatives. *American Scientist,* 1970, **58**, 34–42.

Gattegno, C., & Hinman, D. Words in color. In J. Money (Ed.), *The disabled reader.* Baltimore: Johns Hopkins Press, 1966, Chap. 11.

Gallagher, J. W. Semantic relationship and the learning of syntactic word pairs in children. *Journal of Experimental Child Psychology,* 1969, **8**, 411–417.

Gibson, E. J. *Principles of perceptual learning and development.* New York: Appleton-Century-Crofts, Inc., 1969.

Gibson, E. J., Bishop, C., Schiff, W., & Smith, J. Comparison of meaningfulness and pronunciability as grouping principles in the perception and retention of verbal material. *Journal of Experimental Psychology,* 1964, **67**, 173–182.

Gibson, E. J., Farber, J., & Shepela, S. Test of a learning set procedure for the abstraction of spelling patterns. *Project Literacy Reports,* 1967, No. 8.

Gibson, E. J., Gibson, J. J., Pick, A. D., & Osser, H. A developmental study of the discrimination of letter-like forms. *Journal of Comparative and Physiological Psychology,* 1962, **55**, 897–906.

Gibson, E. J., & Guinet, L. Perception of inflections in brief visual presentations of words. *Journal of Verbal Learning and Verbal Behavior,* 1971, **10**, 182–189.

Gibson, E. J., & Levin, H. *The psychology of reading.* Cambridge Mass.: MIT Press, 1975.

Gibson, E. J., Osser, H., & Pick, A. A study in the development of grapheme-phoneme correspondences. *Journal of Verbal Learning and Verbal Behavior,* 1963, **2**, 142–146.

Gibson, E. J., Pick, A., Osser, H., & Hammond, M. The role of grapheme-phoneme correspondence in the perception of words. *American Journal of Psychology,* 1962, **75**, 554–570.

Gibson, E. J., Schapiro, F., & Yonas, A. Confusion matrices for graphic patterns obtained with a latency measure. In *The analysis of reading skill: A program of basic and applied research.* Final Report, Project No. 5-1213, 1968, Cornell University and the U.S. Office of Education. Pp. 76–96. (ERIC Document ED 034 663.)

Gibson, E. J., & Shepela, S. Some effects of redundant stimulus information on learning to identify letters. In *The analysis of reading skill: A program of basic and applied research*. Final Report, Project No. 5–1213, 1968, Cornell University and the U.S. Office of Education. Pp. 63–75. (ERIC Document ED 034 663.)

Gibson, E. J., Shurcliff, A., & Yonas, A. Utilization of spelling patterns by deaf and hearing subjects. In H. Levin & J. P. Williams (Eds.), *Basic studies on reading*. New York: Basic Books, Inc., Publishers, 1970.

Gibson, J. J. *The senses considered as perceptual systems*. Boston: Houghton Mifflin Company, 1966.

Gibson, J. J., & Yonas, P. A new theory of scribbling and drawing in children. In *The analysis of reading skill*. Final Report, Project No. 5-1213, December 1968, Cornell University and the U.S. Office of Education. Pp. 355–370. (ERIC Document ED 034 663.)

Glock, M. D. The effect upon eye-movements and reading rate at the college level of three methods of training. *Journal of Educational Psychology*, 1949, **40**, 93–106.

Goins, J. T. Visual perceptual abilities and early reading progress. *Supplemental Education Monograph*, 1958, No. 87.

Goodman, K. S. Dialect barriers to reading comprehension. *Elementary English*, 1965, **42**, 853–860.

Hardyck, C. D., Petrinovich, L. F., & Ellsworth, D. W. Feedback of speech muscle activity during silent reading: Rapid extinction. *Science*, 1967, **154**, 1467–1468.

Held, R. Plasticity in sensory-motor systems. *Scientific American*, 1965, **213**, 84–94.

Hochberg, J. Stimulus factors in literacy: Graphic communication, verbal and non-verbal. *Project Literacy Reports*, 1964, No. 1, 17–18. (ERIC Document ED 010 307.)

Hochberg, J. Studies in reading. *Project Literacy Reports*, 1968, No. 9, 25–37.

Hochberg, J., & Brooks, V. Reading as intentional behavior. In H. Singer and R. B. Ruddell (Eds.), *Theoretical models and processes of reading*. Newark, Delaware: International Reading Association, 1970. Pp. 304–314.

Horowitz, L. M., White, M. A., & Atwood, D. W. Word fragments as aids to recall: The organization of a word. *Journal of Experimental Psychology*, 1968, **76**, 219–226.

Huey, E. B. *The psychology and pedagogy of reading*. New York: The Macmillan Company, 1908. (Republished, Cambridge, Mass., The M.I.T. Press, 1968.)

Jeffrey, W. E., & Samuels, S. J. Effect of method of reading training on initial learning and transfer. *Journal of Verbal Learning and Verbal Behavior*, 1967, **6**, 354–358.

Koen, F., Becker, A., & Young, R. The psychological reality of the paragraph. *Journal of Verbal Learning and Verbal Behavior*, 1969, **8**, 49–53.

Kolers, P. A., & Katzman, M. A. Naming sequentially presented letters and words. *Language and Speech*, 1966, **9**, 84–95.

Labov, W., & Cohen, P. Systematic relations of standard and non-standard rules in the grammar of negro speakers. *Project Literacy Reports*, 1967, No. 8, 66–84.

Lavine, L. O. The development of perception or writing in prereading children: A cross-cultural study. Unpublished doctoral dissertation, Cornell University, 1972.

Levin, H., Baum, E., & Bostwick, S. The learning of variable grapheme-phoneme correspondences: Comparison of English and Spanish speakers. In *A basic research program on reading.* Final Report, Project No. 639, 1963, Cornell University and the U.S. Office of Education. (ERIC Document ED 002 967.)

Levin, H., Grossman, J., Kaplan, E., & Yang, R. Constraints and the eye-voice span in right and left embedded sentences. *Language and Speech*, 1972, **15**, 30–39.

Levin, H., & Kaplan, E. Eye-voice span within active and passive sentences. *Language and Speech*, 1968, **2**, 251–258.

Levin, H., & Kaplan, E. Grammatical structure and reading. In H. Levin and J. P. Williams (Eds.), *Basic studies on reading.* New York: Basic Books, Inc., Publishers, 1970.

Levin, H., & Mitchell, J. R. *Project Literacy: Continuing activities.* Final Report, Project No. 50537, 1969, Cornell University and U.S. Office of Education.

Levin, H., & Turner, A. Sentence structure and the eye-voice span. In *The analysis of reading skill: A program of basic and applied research.* Final Report, Project No. 5-1213, 1968, Cornell University and the U.S. Office of Education. Pp. 196–220. (ERIC Document ED 034 663.)

Levin, H., & Watson, J. The learning of variable grapheme-to-phoneme correspondences. In *A basic research program on reading.* Final Report, Project No. 639, 1963a, Cornell University and U.S. Office of Education. (ERIC Document ED 002 967.)

Levin, H., & Watson, J. The learning of variable grapheme-to-phoneme correspondences: Variations in the initial consonant position. In *A basic research program on reading.* Final Report, Project No. 639, 1963b, Cornell University and U.S. Office of Education. (ERIC Document ED 002 967.)

Levin, H., Watson, J. S., & Feldman, M. Writing as pretraining for association learning. In *A basic research program on reading.* Final Report, Project No. 639, 1963, Cornell University and U.S. Office of Education. (ERIC Document ED 002 967.)

Levin, H., & Williams, J. P. (Eds.) *Basic studies on reading.* New York: Basic Books, Inc., Publishers, 1970.

Liberman, A. M., Cooper, F. S., Shankweiler, D. P., & Studdert-Kennedy, M. Perception of the speech code. *Psychological Review*, 1967, **74**, 431–461.

Lott, D., Cronnell, B., & Smith, F. The use of featural redundancy by beginning readers. Research Memorandum, 1968, Inglewood, Calif.: Southwest Regional Laboratory. (See ERIC Document ED 002 967.)

Lowenstein, A. M. Effects of instructions on the abstraction of spelling patterns. Unpublished master's thesis, Cornell University, 1969.

Makita, Kiyoshi. The rarity of reading disability in Japanese children. *American Journal of Orthopsychiatry*, 1968, **38**, 231–250.

Marchbanks, G., & Levin, H. Cues by which children recognize words. *Journal of Educational Psychology*, 1965, **56**, 57–61.

Morton, J. The effects of context on the visual duration threshold of words. *British Journal of Psychology*, 1964, **55**, 165–180.

Nelson, T. O. Spelling-pronunciation integration: Determinant of bimodal recall. *Journal of Verbal Learning and Verbal Behavior*, 1969, **8**, 118–122.

Newman, E. B. Speed of reading when the span of letters is restricted. *American Journal of Psychology*, 1966, **79**, 272–278.

Piaget, J. *Les mécanismes perceptifs.* Paris: Presses Universitaires de France, 1961.

Pick, A. D. Improvement of visual and tactual form discrimination. *Journal of Experimental Psychology*, 1965, **69**, 331–339.

Pick, A. D. Some basic perceptual processes in reading. *Young Children*, 1970, **25**, 162–181.

Rosinski, R. R., & Wheeler, K. E. Children's use of orthographic structure in word discrimination. *Psychonomic Science*, 1972, **26**, 97–98.

Samuels, S. J. Attentional process in reading: The effect of pictures on the acquisition of reading responses. *Journal of Educational Psychology*, 1967, **58**, 337–342.

Samuels, S. J. Relationship between formal intralist similarity and the von Restorff effect. *Journal of Educational Psychology*, 1968, **59**, 432–437.

Silberman, H. F. Empirical development of a beginning reading skill. *Project Literacy Reports*, 1964a, No. 4, 11–13. (ERIC Document ED 010 310.)

Silberman, H. F. *Exploratory research on a beginning reading program.* Santa Monica, Calif.: System Development Corporation, 1964b.

Smith, F. Familiarity of configuration vs. discriminability of features in the visual identification of words. *Psychonomic Science*, 1969a, **14**, 261–262.

Smith, F. The use of featural dependencies across letters in the visual identification of words. *Journal of Verbal Learning and Verbal Behavior*, 1969b, **8**, 215–218.

Thurstone, L. L. A factorial study of perception. *Psychometric Monographs*, 1944, No. 4.

Van Mondfrans, A. P., & Travers, R. M. Learning of redundant material presented through two sensory modalities. *Perceptual Motor Skills*, 1964, **19**, 743–751.

Van Mondfrans, A. P., & Travers, R. M. Paired-associate learning within and across sense modalities and involving simultaneous and sequential presentations. *American Educational Research Journal*, 1965, **2**, 89–99.

Venezky, R. L. English orthography: Its graphical structure and its relation to sound. *Reading Research Quarterly*, 1967, **2**, 75–106.

Venezky, R., & Weir, R. H. A study of selected spelling-to-sound correspondence patterns. Final Report, Cooperative Research Project No. 3090, Stanford University, 1966. (ERIC Document ED 010 843.)

Vurpillot, E. The development of scanning strategies and their relation to visual differentiation. *Journal of Experimental Child Psychology*, 1968, **6**, 622–650.

Weber, R. M. Grammaticality and the self-correction of reading errors. *Project Literacy Reports*, July 1967, No. 8, 53–59.

Weber, R. M. First graders' use of grammatical context in reading. In H. Levin and J. Williams (Eds.), *Basic studies on reading*. New York: Basic Books, Inc., Publishers, 1970.

Weir, R. H., & Venezky, R. L. Rules to aid in the teaching of reading. Final Report, 1965, Cooperative Research Project No. 2584, Stanford University. (ERIC Document ED 003 357.)

Williams, J. P. Training kindergarten children to discriminate letterlike forms. *American Educational Research Journal*, 1969, **6**, 501–514.

Zettersten, A. *A statistical study of the graphic system of present-day American English.* Lund, Sweden: Studentlitteratur, 1969.

CHAPTER 11

THE POLITICAL IMPLICATIONS OF A NATIONAL READING EFFORT

Natalie Saxe and Richard H. de Lone

It has been five years since the late James E. Allen, then the newly appointed Commissioner of Education of then newly elected President Nixon, began to formulate the idea for a national Right-to-Read program.

Dr. Allen, a liberal, was seeking a viable initiative in a conservative administration that since confirmed suspicions that it was not very much concerned about education. Reading seemed to be an emphasis that could unite different socioeconomic groups and appeal to both liberals and conservatives. Dr. Allen himself used the analogy between a commitment to wipe out illiteracy and the commitment made under President Kennedy to land a man on the moon in a decade.

Five years later, however, it is apparent that no such commitment was forthcoming. The Right-to-Read program exists as a phrase and a niche in the U.S. Office of Education (USOE). The administration has supported the primacy of reading in urging that a major portion of the shrinking funds of the Elementary and Secondary Education Act (ESEA) be devoted to reading improvement. But Dr. Allen certainly had more in mind than a slogan, an office, and a fiscal trade off when he proposed a major national reading effort. No quantum leap toward this goal has been made. The rockets are not even on the launch pad.

In discussing political implications of a national reading effort, this brief background leads us to one order of question that we will consider: what are the political obstacles to developing a constituency and will for such a program? Here one deals with the issues that most of us think of when we speak of politics: how to read the climate, how to build coalitions, how to muster the votes, how to follow up on implementation.

But such tactical questions, critical as they are, require a broader context, which constitutes another aspect of the politics of a national reading effort. The shape of this context depends on how we answer the following related questions:

What are the goals of a national reading effort?

What claim do these goals have on national priorities?

Who is to benefit?

How and by whom will the program be planned and implemented?

In this paper, we will attempt first to analyze these larger, contextual questions. In doing so, and in discussing issues of constituency as well, our attempt will be not so much to answer questions as to frame them.

GOALS AND PRIORITY

The most obvious question is whether a national reading effort is aimed at wiping out illiteracy (however defined) or at a general improvement of reading skills. While this question has pedagogic implications, it has considerable political implications as well. The former goal necessarily involves a smaller, less-articulate, less-powerful constituency than the latter. Its successful implementation, then, depends on developing a powerful advocacy for the needs of the illiterate among the literate, the kind of advocacy that was closer to existing in the days of the "Great Society" than it is currently. This is a political hindrance. On the other hand, a program with broader goals might find a more ready-made constituency of self-interest, but programming would inevitably become less targeted and more diffuse.

However one handles this tradeoff, the more obvious but less frequently asked question remains: what kind of goal—and, particularly, what social change—does one expect to achieve through improving reading skills? This question is more slippery than it immediately appears to be. One might expect, for instance, the answer that reading skill is prerequisite to equalizing status. But if a program has a broad constituency, there is likelihood that the advantaged will benefit more than the disadvantaged: inequality, if anything, will be increased. On the other hand, even the best-intentioned reforms have a habit of simply consolidating the power of those who already have the power to institute the reforms: "helping" turns into a paternalism that either leaves the status quo un-

changed or makes things worse.[1] Put in other terms, if illiteracy constitutes, among other things, a condition of powerlessness, one must examine
closely the distribution of power and the implicit power relations within
a program to combat it.

Neil Postman has argued one line of this reasoning that will suffice
as an example.[2] Postman dismisses most of the standard reasons for the
importance of teaching reading. To the argument that reading skills as
such are necessary to obtain good jobs, he replies that only a few areas
of employment require more than minimal reading competency. To the
argument that reading produces more cultivated, inquiring minds, he
simply points to the kinds of TV fare literate Americans watch in lieu of
reading. (Indeed, it would be interesting to know how many books the
average reading teacher reads in a year.) Rather, he speculates, there
may be other motives operating. "Every medium of communication contains a unique metaphysic," he writes, "which is to say that every medium
makes a special kind of claim on our senses and therefore on our behavior." He observes that Socrates "took a very dim view of the written
word on the grounds that it diminishes man's capability to memorize and
that it forces one to follow an argument rather than participate in it."
Taking his cue from Socrates, Postman suggests that the primary reasons
for emphasizing reading instruction are (1) to give students the skills
they need to be accessible to "political and historical myth (and) standard
brand beliefs," e.g., the notion that it is important to learn to read because
it is important to graduate from high school or college to be a success,
and (2) to give consumers the skills necessary to "develop a keen interest
in all products." (This reason, of course, may be less compelling in the
era of television.)

In short, Postman suggests that reading is taught as a means of
political subjugation. To the extent that this is true, it is hardly surprising
that pupil motivation becomes an obsessive concern. And while it is fairly
easy to scoff at Postman, it is harder to refute him, especially if one recalls
Colonial era stress on teaching indentured servants, apprentices, and
others at the bottom of the ladder to read so that they would understand
the laws governing their status.

It is possible to argue, however, that literacy can be taught for exactly
the opposite purpose (and with a substantially different pedagogy): the
purpose of liberation from social, political, and economic impotence, as

[1] See, for example, discussions of the work of New York City's Public Education
Association as part of the Progressive reform movement of that city in Sol Cohen,
Progressives, and Urban School Reform (New York: Teachers College, 1964), espe-
cially chapters 1–3.

[2] "The Politics of Reading," *Harvard Educational Review,* 40(2), May 1970:
244–252.

Paulo Freire has argued in *The Pedagogy of the Oppressed*.[3] Literacy, defined as the power to collect, analyze, spread, and communicate ideas and to persuade through information, has long been a tool of revolution. In a technocratic society, where armed insurgence is highly unlikely, it may be all the more central to the empowerment of individual and powerless groups.

It is ridiculous, of course, to think of any federal government of the nation's schools embarking on a national reading effort as part of a revolutionary program. Paulo Freire is not going to become the guru of USOE. But it is conceivable that a new administration, come 1976, will address itself seriously to an attempt to redistribute influence and wealth through reformist strategies. A reasonable goal, and one that is likely to increase the efficacy of a national reading effort targeted primarily to those who are not functionally literate, is that it be a part of such a broader reform. Indeed, a growing body of social science evidence suggests that unless it is so linked, the likely impact will be negligible.[4]

This, however, raises clearly the question of priority: increasingly, it makes sense to ask whether social policy should focus on services and categorical programs or on redistributing wealth and income. If funds were unlimited, of course, the arguments for doing both would be strong. But funds are not unlimited, and in the current administration there has already been debate that flirts, at least, with this question. For instance, President Nixon vetoed the Comprehensive Child Development Act of 1971 at least in part, it would seem, because the daycare system it proposed was seen as competing with his now moribund Family Assistance Plan. If funds are limited, and if redistribution of wealth and influence are seen as major goals, it is possible to view a major reading program that requires substantial new increments of funding as a conservative, even reactionary, thrust.

On the other hand, it might be argued that a reading effort should not be the result of added funding but should be a redirection of existing funds. Such a program, however, is almost inevitably going to omit adults from its target population and focus on the schools for its means of implementation. To a certain extent, one could argue, this is already happening in a reemphasis on basic skills instruction in many American classrooms. That it is happening does not eliminate the question of whether it is the top priority for educational change, however. Nor does it eliminate

---

[3] (New York: Herder and Herder, 1970). See also his "The Adult Literacy Process as Cultural Action for Freedom," *Harvard Educational Review*, 40(2), May 1970: 205–225.

[4] For example, the arguments throughout Christopher Jencks et al., *Inequality: A Reassessment of the Effect of Family and Schooling in America* (New York: Basic Books, 1972).

the question of whether or not the schools can do the job to solve a problem that, in some sense, is the result of their failure to do the job.

In schools, as well as in the larger society, the lulling rhetoric of reading improvement, precisely because it does have the broad appeal that Dr. Allen identified, may simply tranquilize concern for more important issues of school reform, such as rethinking the goals of schooling or altering the institutional format of instruction.

WHO IS TO BENEFIT?

The obvious answer to the question of who is to benefit from the program is that this depends on how it defines its target population. Certainly that target population should include both adults and children. But there are also secondary beneficiaries of any funded program: the people who are paid to implement it. It should be remembered that education provides the largest source of publicly funded jobs outside the military, and it can be plausibly argued that the history of American education is the history of the growth of a public employment sector. In thinking about the politics of a national reading effort, the question of secondary benefits may turn out to be primary. It is problematic whether or not the pedagogic know-how and delivery systems exist to eliminate illiteracy. But it is a sure thing that if funds are appropriated there will be beneficiaries.

It is not cynical to suggest that the chief beneficiaries of the Elementary and Secondary Education Act (ESEA) have been the members of school systems—both professional and paraprofessional—for whom new jobs were created. Seven years and as many billion dollars later, the children of the poor have not been "compensated" as clearly as the employees of school systems through this investment. A major reading effort funded through the existing school system would imply a faith that past failures of the system can be remedied through cash. It would further imply that the school establishment and the educational materials industry are the proper recipients of that cash. Both assumptions are clearly subject to debate, if only on the basis of past performance.

There are, of course, those who argue that the reason increased federal and other investments in education have not yielded high returns is the lack of professional accountability. This hypothesis remains to be demonstrated, but if one believes it, it creates another magnitude of political issues. And it suggests that a step prior to mounting a massive reading improvement program through the schools should be developing systems of accountability. In turn, it may well be necessary to establish binding arbitration as a principle in teacher contract negotiations before developing such systems; the political base of teacher organization is generally much stronger than that of school boards, and accountability is an issue closely tied to collective bargaining.

HOW AND BY WHOM WILL THE PROGRAM BE PLANNED AND IMPLEMENTED?

As the above suggests, a first step in answering the question of who will plan and implement the program is deciding whether or not a reading effort should begin by trusting the educational establishment, changing it, or attempting to bypass it. Each method implies very different answers. In the first instance, one simply passes a bill and then passes the money on—presumably, given the current trend, to state departments of education (although cities will then suffer from antiurban bias).

If one attempts to work through the existing structure while modifying or changing it, a new set of questions arises. At what point does one enter the system to change the syndrome? Options include teacher education, curriculum, changing staffing patterns, management structure, and so on. Cases can be made for any and all of these, and a certain amount of experience and literature exist about the pros and cons, and dangers of each. Each, in turn, raises enough political and tactical questions to require another paper to discuss them.

If the decision is to bypass existing educational institutions, then the difficult questions of establishing a new delivery system arise. Does one set up competing, specialized institutions for teaching reading/literacy (e.g., anything from television programs to community corporations to subcontracts with industrial/publishing concerns to a network of reading labs or a volunteer "readings corps")?

Or does one go directly to the consumer-client—the student and/or his parents—establishing a modified voucher system and calling it the Reading Stamps Program?

We believe that an *effective* national reading effort should bypass the existing education macrostructure. At a minimum, it should provide alternatives to that structure. That is, the planning, implementing, and discretionary powers of budgeting should not rest with those most likely to have a vested interest in maintaining the status quo, especially given their unpromising "track record." We further believe that a modified voucher program, with strong consumer safeguards built in (as opposed to a pure free-market voucher system), at least in theory meets several important criteria: it facilitates accountabilty to the client; it thus gives the client a certain amount of power both to set his own goals and to influence the nature of the pedagogy involved; and it can be regulated in a way that fosters development of a wide array of alternatives to existing school systems without necessarily ruling out of eligibility those school systems which demonstrate capability in meeting the need. That is, a program that includes performance standards and audits as a precondition for eligibility to receive voucher payments to some extent makes it possible to "have our cake and eat it too," to bypass the education system without excluding it.

We realize, of course, the difficulty inherent in developing such a system from a purely administrative point of view, but we will not concern ourselves with the question here. Setting aside the likely opposition that such an approach would raise from the education establishment, which constitutes the strongest, best-organized lobby for an education legislation, there are some immediate objections worth discussing:

1. Does not something have to be done to improve existing school systems? After all, they will not go away.

2. Is it not the case that school systems will be best prepared to gear up for such a program, if they are eligible, and as such will drive other approaches from the market? Or, secondly, is it not true that teachers—especially given the latter-day surplus—will end up staffing almost any efforts and will do more or less the same things schools do?

3. Is it not a little starry-eyed to expect even a regulated free market to pay more attention to client needs than, say, doctors or even General Motors?

To the third question, we can only respond, "No more starry-eyed than thinking that the school system will do much more than gratefully absorb added funds, as they absorbed the 153 percent increase in budgets from 1960 to 1970." The truth is that it is a risk. To the second question, we respond "not necessarily," if built into the effort is a serious period of "lead time" to develop alternative program models. And this notion is, to a certain extent, related to the first question. The best way to change school systems is not, in our opinion, to give them more money (just as the best way to improve reading instruction in schools may not be to hire more reading teachers). We are suggesting that the drive toward uniformity and redundancy is so great, given the internal politics of school systems, that external leverage is critical to effecting internal school system change. A voucher system that places schools in competition with other institutions in a carefully regulated market suggests itself as an appropriate model for this strategy.

In turning to the more typical political issues that any public effort faces—the creation and organization of a constituency, the passage of legislation, and follow through of implementation—specific strategies will be conditioned by the way one answers some of the questions posed above, although certain generic political questions (e.g., how to build a coalition, timing, and identification of sponsors) crosscut all approaches. To adopt the idea that a national reading effort should at least partially bypass the educational establishment and use a voucher system, for instance, raises a different set of problems from simply trying to rally the education profession around a bill that, if it accomplished nothing else, would be a pork barrel for educators. In the former instance, it would be necessary to mobilize community organizations, civic groups, labor unions, and the like. Such an approach requires much greater effort than simply rousing the education lobby. Indeed, the puzzling question is just who can or would do this organizing?

This question merely illuminates, in a roundabout way, the more basic problem of constituency. At its simplest, this problem is intimately linked to the status of illiteracy as one of the great nonissues of our time. To be sure, everyone is against it, and millions of parents fret about their children's reading scores, but illiteracy simply does not show up on any of the polls of America's great problems, or even of its minor problems. Nor does America appear to be in a mood at present to discover any "new" problems—as it "discovered" poverty a decade ago. Preoccupations with Watergate, the economy, and the energy crisis, on the one hand, and an apparent swing to the right in city and town alike, on the other, have replaced the crusading zeal of the sixties. From 1968 to 1974, the country approved, at least complied with, a national administration whose domestic initiatives were limited to law enforcement, revenue sharing, a limp effort at welfare reform, and some interest, apparently growing as this paper is written, in national health care legislation. The latter, of course, is a program of universal benefit, as opposed to a literacy program.

None of this suggests a propitious moment for launching a reading effort. If the effort seems worth trying, anyway, it clearly requires a prior effort to elevate the issue into a problem of national concern. Dr. Allen's analogy of a reading program to the space program was no doubt flawed— the goal lacks the drama, the specificity, and the chauvinistic appeal of the moonshot—but the analogy would be closer to appropriate if illiteracy in America was seen as a major problem, a crisis, a point of honor, a national shame, or any similar rallying symbol. Whether issues can be created out of whole cloth, as opposed to arising from broader trends, is problematic. However, a first step toward elevation of such an issue might be, for example, the creation of a commission or a national organization that essentially propagandized the need. As far as we know, however, no such effort has been undertaken in the past five years. If it has, we take our ignorance of it as a comment on its efficiency.

Politics is not only the art of the possible, but it is the art of situation. Therefore, it would be useless for us to attempt a "battle plan" for such a hypothetical body. However, there are a few general considerations that any effort begun at the present moment will have to bear in mind.

First, a promotional and lobbying campaign needs to recognize that the sixties are over. The most important consequence, perhaps, of this fact is that it is now poison, and probably will be for some time, to promote a cause that is identified specifically as an urban or minority group cause. This was the fate of much Great Society legislation, and it could easily become the fate of a literacy campaign: Americans tend to see all social problems as black problems, and the result is frequently as pernicious as the analysis is faulty.

A second, related distinction is that the seventies are to some extent the decade of the suburbs. Not only does suburban growth increasingly account for the continued urbanization of the country, but the political power and influence of suburbia have been reaffirmed through reapportionment. The increased power of the suburbs and the racist stigma attached to "urban" bills both argue for a generous definition of illiteracy, one that would include a much broader spectrum of potential beneficiaries than typical definitions of functional illiteracy, even at risk of diluting program impact by increasing the target group. (A voucher plan that was income conditioned would, however, tend to mitigate this dilution.) The failure of the recently well-publicized problem of hunger in America to stir more than a political yawn may in part be attributable to the well-stocked refrigerators of suburbia.

A second general consideration is that a promotional effort has to start from a premise of involvement, as distinct from an effort to sell. That is to say, grass roots input into the nature of the ultimate effort has become increasingly important to the creation of an authentic constituency that will actually make itself heard. The blue-ribbon committee lacks whatever clout it once had—partially as a fallout from the growing popular mistrust of officialdom and experts that was so well illustrated by the public attitude toward both Watergate and the energy crisis. Broad-based, vocal support will be especially crucial to an effort that partially bypasses the profession.

A third general consideration involves the struggle for power between the executive branch and the legislative branch. Although it is premature to declare that Congress has raised itself from the dead, there are decided indications that members of both houses are looking for legislative initiatives they can take as part of a reassertion of Congressional prerogatives. That is, it is no longer as true that vigorous administration support is a sine qua non for a major program effort. For the duration of the present administration, this is a hopeful sign for those who wish to continue the business of remedying social inequities—including the distribution of literacy skills—in America. The question becomes whether a national reading effort can be cast in a light that makes it sufficiently appealing for a core of key Congressional figures to make it a hobbyhorse.

There is also some cause for optimism in thinking ahead to 1976.

The bicentennial year might create a national tolerance, if not enthusiasm, for fresh social programming. It may very well bring with it a new national administration with just such an interest. A promotional and lobbying campaign should weigh carefully the uses it can make of bicentennial symbolism, a 1976 election, and the party platform process. Reading still just might be the kind of issue that suggests bold new steps without really upsetting any applecarts. As we have suggested above, however, a reading program divorced from realignment of power, influence, and income has dismal prospects for success. The trick, as a result, is the creation of coalitions behind a platform that skillfully interweaves such nonthreatening items as a national reading effort with more controversial ones, such as tax reform and, optimally, a negative income tax.

To enumerate these issues is not to exhaust the question. We have said little about that classic problem of all education legislation—church-state relations. Suffice it to note that a voucher plan raises these issues to a major level and that a program that aims at a suburban as well as an urban constituency may have difficulty maintaining the principle of aid to the child, not the institution, that ESEA utilized. Further, the issues of block grants versus categorical aid, and grants to localities versus grants to the states, raise a host of other questions, if a voucher plan is not adopted. Finally, there is the question of whether a reading effort should rely wholly on federal funding or whether the federal share should be seen as an incentive. (On pragmatic grounds, we prefer the latter.) However, these are not issues peculiar to a national reading effort. Therefore we raise them only to drop them.

This paper has touched briefly a series of complex problems which can each be the basis of lengthy discussion and which can each, in the final analysis, be resolved only in the real situation in which they are raised. We believe that these are soluble problems, but we are not optimistic that they will be solved. First, the tradition that education—which may be the most highly politicized social venture there is and which certainly includes as much "politics" as any other public expenditure—is apolitical remains alive in the behavior of many educationists, who think of politics last and most skimpily, if at all, in going after a goal. Certainly the history to date of a Right-to-Read program suggests that this has been the case.

Second, if any group is most likely to lead the drive for a national reading effort, it is the education profession, spearheaded by the reading establishment within that profession. For reasons we have discussed, we doubt whether such an effort, if it did pay off in additonal funds, would have a commensurate payoff in additional literacy.

And third, despite the few hopeful signs that the drought for social programs may end, the current economic outlook leads to a gloomy prognosis for a national reading effort. Social programming usually occurs on the margins of the American economy, financed by the leftovers of rapid growth. There is little reason to hope this situation will change and much reason to doubt that the margin in the years ahead will be very large. It is doubtful that a national reading effort, even in theory, has a very high claim on our priorities for that small margin. It is even more doubtful that its claim will be translated into effective action.

CHAPTER 12

AN ECONOMIC AND FINANCIAL PERSPECTIVE ON A NATIONAL TEN-YEAR READING EFFORT

Oliver S. Brown and Guilbert C. Hentschke

INTRODUCTION

Purpose and Scope

The purpose of this paper is to examine the possibility of a 10-year national reading effort from an economic and financial management perspective. Not knowing the details of the alternatives proposed makes specific financial forecasting tenuous at best. We have, however, provided some basic financial information and some general alternative approaches that may be useful.

Summary and Conclusions

We think that a 10-year reading project, carefully planned, programmed, budgeted, operated, and evaluated, could have a tremendous impact on the productivity of the whole educational enterprise. Substantial benefits, additional to higher reading performance, could result from this project. Apart from the general concept, however, the magnitude of the positive impact will be largely a function of the design and operation of the delivery system, the discrete components of which are discussed in this paper and summarized here.

Goals and objectives. The goals and objectives of a 10-year reading project ought to be developed with wide participation but should be nationally determined in some detail in order that national resources will be used for the national purposes intended.

Audit procedures and public disclosure. In addition to the normal external financial audits, results and costs should be reviewed (perhaps audited) by a team of local citizens under guidelines developed at the national level, and the performance and financial results actively communicated to the public.

National determination of allocation. The basis upon which resources are allocated to states and districts should be likewise determined at the national level in detail, with only necessary flexibility allowed at the state level with regard to administrative procedures.

Guidelines for the local district. Guidelines for the equitable and effective allocation of resources within districts and schools should be developed at the national level if, and to the extent that, resources are allocated to individuals as in Title I of the Elementary and Secondary Education Act (ESEA).

Phasing the resource allocation. The first year should be devoted to planning, the second to partial implementation, and the third to complete implementation with 20 percent, 75 percent, and 100 percent funding in order to avoid the confusion and the waste that occurred with the hasty introduction and implementation of several titles of ESEA. Funding levels should rise at the rate of 5 percent to 10 percent per year for years thereafter.

Use of socioeconomic factors for allocative purposes. An index of socioeconomic factors that is highly predictive of reading performance ("need") should be used to allocate the resources to the states and districts.

Management development. Provisions should be made to assist local administrators in developing modern managerial skills as part of the planning, implementing, and evaluating processes for this program.

Interface with overlapping operations. Where feasible, the programmatic effort in reading should build upon, borrow from, and "piggyback" complementary systems such as state testing systems, existing in-service training programs for administrators, national professional associations

(ASCD, IRA, AASA, etc.). The Title I, ESEA, delivery system serves as an example of the way such interface might look. Title I of the Elementary and Secondary Act is aimed largely at the same constituency and at many of the same objectives as the Right-to-Read program. U.S. Office of Education officials have estimated that 70 percent of the Title I allocation goes to reading or reading-related activities. It is clear that some or substantially all of Title I administrative machinery and funds could be folded into a 10-year reading project, thereby reducing overhead and start-up costs, and increasing the likelihood of effective program coordination. To the extent that added sources are available, they should be focused on other requirements of the Right-to-Read Program. Examples of other programs that should be examined for possible interface might include statewide assessment programs and curricular programs that include reading components (like Title I). This interface concept applies to many of the other management considerations listed here (e.g., planning, evaluation, and information systems).

Long-range planning. As a part of the phasing of the resource allocation, mentioned above, the 3-year reading project, planning, programming, and budgeting of all resources allocated locally for teaching of reading should be required as a condition of the grant. This relates closely to the prior point of interprogram coordination.

Tax incentives and special subsidies. Tax incentives and special subsidies for firms or institutions developing reading instructional systems should be further explored as a means of stimulating competition that would result in more effective reading programs.

Reading product and system evaluation. A national agency for the evaluation of reading systems should be developed or designated with adequate resources—*specifically to accomplish independent cost-effectiveness studies for the principal purpose of providing local authorities with the means of making more rational choices among available alternatives.*

National reading performance information system. A national agency (as suggested above) for communicating with teachers, principals, parents, board members, superintendents, commercial firms, universities, and others should be established to transmit information about what systems, techniques, and products work and how well they work, how much they cost, and how they may be implemented.

The twelve program ingredients that have been isolated above treat three general themes: defining and implementing public intent, stimulating related activity in both the public and private sector, and determining the feasibility and effectiveness of alternative delivery systems. The next three sections of this chapter treat each of these three themes, while elaborating on the twelve recommendations made earlier.

DEFINING AND IMPLEMENTING PUBLIC INTENT

Establishing Goals, Objectives, and Evaluation Plans

Defining precisely the goals and objectives is an essential first step in a rational allocation process. We know that the general goal—improving reading performance—has its roots deep in public demand. Although most people are aware of this discontent in the inner-city communities, the fact is that professional experience intense concern in all types of communities, including suburbs, whose average performance is well above national forms.

Comparing performance against specific objectives when no common measures exist presents a difficult problem. Each local district has a different set of tests given at different times and under varying conditions, with the exception of states such as New York and California, which have a basic statewide mandated testing program. From a resource allocation point of view, this means that funds cannot be granted to districts as a response to a direct and comparable measure of the problem at this time.[1] This funding could be made within districts, however. Whether it is worth the resources to invest in a uniform, national, mandated testing program for all schools in reading skills is as much a political and educational problem as a financial one. Current problems associated with the National Assessment Program should be instructive here. A single, national measure would definitely facilitate comparative cost benefit analysis after the project is underway. However, the feasibility of pursuing such a program at this time is questionable.

Perhaps the most efficient way to attain results is to define precisely the goals and objectives of the project at the national level in some detail and then to consider, by exception, any request for revisions, additions, or deletions. Barring changes, the state and the district would agree to

---

[1] This is not to say that notable progress is not being made in test comparison strategies. For example, the Anchor Test Study (Peter Loret, "The Anchor Test Study," Educational Testing Service, 1973, mimeographed), recently completed, was an attempt to statistically equate seven of the major standardized tests in reading. The resulting manual will contain complete sets of four types of tables: raw score equivalencies, individual pupil norms, school mean norms, and comparison of individual pupil norms developed from the Anchor Test Study data with those provided by the test publishers. This type of activity has implications for the specific nature of any national reading program.

the national goals and objectives as a condition of receiving the funds. Given that reading is a skill and that the goal of literacy for all is not a controversial one, the acceptance of national goals represents much less of a problem than a comparable program dealing with the content and the attitudes to be taught in, for example, U.S. history.

State, school district, school, class, and individual student reading objectives would then relate (1) to reasonable degrees of progress that might be expected (e.g., "To improve performance in reading comprehension so that ten months of progress is achieved at the sixth-grade level in a year or two"), or (2) to management questions (e.g., "To complete a comprehensive reading development plan for the school system on or before March 15, 197x").

Given these types of objectives, the national, state, and local governing bodies might expect a degree of accountability for results. In any case, at the local level some kind of related formal testing, evaluation, and reporting program is required within each district if the setting of goals and objectives and the allocation of resources are to have meaning. Consideration should be given to making test scores available by school, especially with data on *program achievements*. Again, testing plans that did not deal with actual and emerging testing programs will be something less than efficient.

Defining the Allocation Policy

Local educational autonomy versus national intent. Allocating resources at the national level for a national purpose subverts local autonomy to the extent that money is taken from the community and returned, if at all, with constraints on its use. If, however, there is substantial congruency as to the overall goals of such a project (and we believe this to be the case), the real nub of this problem centers on the proportion of the resources that each state receives and the proportion each district, school, and student receives.

At the state level, we have had a history of resources being diverted from cities. Within cities, there is some evidence that resources have been diverted from those who need them most. There is no question that a national reading program implies a subversion of state and local autonomy to the national interest to the extent that resources are committed from the federal level in a way that state and local legislative bodies would not commit these resources.

Allocating resources among states. The target population of students should be that group that fails to meet some criteria of achievement in reading. Since no direct, comparable measure of the problem exists at this time, a socioeconomic index that closely relates to reading achieve-

ment must be substituted. Requisite data could be generated in cooperation with several agencies (the Bureau of the Census, the Department of
Labor, etc.).

For example, state "A" would receive the highest ("a") rate for half of
its students and the "b" rate for the rest; state "B" would receive the "a"
rate for a few of its students, and so on. Consideration would have to be
given to the issue of cost differentials among states, as well as among
regions within states.

Allocating resources among districts. The same criteria for defining
the population for distribution of funds among the states could be used
within each state. In the example above, "state A" becomes "district A."
The existing machinery for administering and controlling money to districts within a state would be used here.

Intradistrict resource allocation. One of the essential questions that

Figure 1
Determining a State's "Need"* for Project Resources

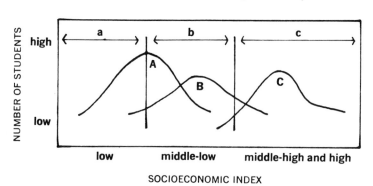

SOCIOECONOMIC INDEX

KEY
Subsidy Rate
    a higher rate
    b lower rate
    c no subsidy
Distribution of Students in Three States
    A state A
    B state B
    C state C

*Need=Number of students who fail to meet a criterion in reading achievement as
measured indirectly by a socioeconomic index based on 1970 Census.

must be answered in the process of defining public interest and the most cost-effective way to achieve results involves (1) whether the project ought to aim at the particular students who have, by some definition, "a reading problem," (2) whether the aim is to improve reading instruction and performance generally in schools and districts that have low performance scores, or (3) whether both aims should be pursued.

The financial implication of this question may not be immediately apparent. If resources are to go to the individual students with reading problems, a much larger investment must be made in control and reporting systems. The individuals must be identified, and plans for each school developed and supported in such a way that they can be audited at the individual student level. Resources allocated for this purpose (control) would presumably be diverted from the primary purpose—learning to read.

If, on the other hand, the resources are allocated to set in motion improvements in reading programs generally in schools and districts where performance is low, the management and control problem is simplified. This strategy suffers from a relatively diminished ability to "target" the effort. The underlying assumption is that large amounts of resources will be drawn to the effort at the local level when board members and professionals have enough solid information to predict that one or more systems carefully implemented will actually work.

To allocate to schools within districts, it must be assumed for the moment that socioeconomic indicators are often not available by school attendance area except through a process of manually prorating data. Assuming that some of the resources are allocated to schools, the following approach, similar to that outlined above could be used:

School "A" would receive the highest subsidy rate for over half its students ("a" rate) and the "b" rate for the rest. School "B" would receive the "a" rate for a few of its students, the "b" rate for about half, and no subsidy for the remainder. School "C" would receive the "b" rate for a few of its students. This system would mean that every state and district, including the suburbs, would receive some funds.

Since most school systems utilize a more direct measure of performance (standardized tests), it is reasonably possible that these scores could be used within a district on the same basis as the socioeconomic indicators. Use of such tests for this purpose would be in accordance with federal guidelines.

This system will work fairly well as long as funds are spent on things like reading teachers, books, and supplies. If, however, the district spends its resources on support systems development so that it can play its part in managing the project, making better informed decisions, and insuring success, then it is much more difficult to determine which individual children actually benefit. In fact, under conditions of high turnover in low socioeconomic areas, the resources might have greater impact on high

Figure 2
Determining a School's "Need" for Project Resources

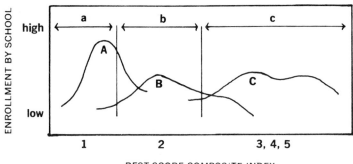

KEY
Subsidy Rate
   a · higher rate
   b lower rate
   c no subsidy
Distribution of Students in Three Schools
   A school A
   B school B
   C school C

socioeconomic regions of a city. It is important to view this project along with Title I, which could be the means of fostering implementation of improvements where the improvements are needed most.

Our conclusion is that no financial and management system within the constraints of reasonable cost can track resources inside most school districts except in a gross way, given the state of school districts accounting systems. The answer lies in large part in (1) accurate public information directly from the government about the project; (2) mandated, local public disclosure of plans, results, and costs;[2] (3) budgets by school which show added direct project expenditures; (4) expansion of the normal external audits to include both the project itself and the equality of allocation as related to stated board policy; and (5) a local results review or audit procedure and disclosure of findings by citizens appointed by the Board, approved by the state, performed under federal-state guidelines, with state advisory assistance.

---

[2] Public disclosure of these kinds of data on a school-by-school basis has recently been required by law in the state of Florida. See *Improving Education in Florida* (Tallahassee, Florida: The Governor's Citizens' Committee on Education, 1973), p. 186.

Improving Educational Management

Positive side effects. One very significant, positive side effect of a 10-year reading project could be a vast improvement in management practices of public education. As a requirement for receiving the funds and with proper assistance from the state, Department of Health, Education, and Welfare (HEW) regional offices, and private contractors, school district administrators (especially curriculum and instruction administrators) could have guided practical experiences in most of the newer planning and management techniques. It would not be long before other problems of the schools would receive far more effective leadership.

A 10-year reading project could be a far more productive investment with far wider impact if this possibility is recognized and taken advantage of. As an example of this effect, many of the most competent school administrators have had federal project experience with Title I and Title III, ESEA projects, etc.

Long-term planning, programming, and budgeting. Rational choices in education are extremely difficult if the time frame is only 1 year. This is especially true if subsidy levels vary considerably from one year to the next, with little assurance that the district can count on any funds at all. From the national as well as the local perspective, resources are wasted.

There is another reason for a long-term commitment to a reading project. At present, general and federal fund budgets of most districts are developed in a separate process, on a separate time schedule, and often by different people. Much of the project planning of a national reading effort must be accomplished at the local level. If the most productive use of all resources is to result, *all the resources to be committed to the project must be considered together.* Even voluntary services and contributions should be planned at the same time if maximum effect on students is to be attained.

We feel that (1) the subsidy should be on a 3-year basis, with annual review[3] and extension 1 year to a total of 10 years; (2) the resources should be phased in at 20 percent the first year, 75 percent the second year, and 100 percent the third year, with an added factor for inflation and salary increases (5 percent to 10 percent) thereafter; (3) a comprehensive (all resource) 3-year plan, program, and budget should be a condition of receipt of funds; and (4) management and program guidance should be made available to the districts from the state or HEW offices (especially where the largest numbers of low-performance students exist —the cities).

---

[3] Annual review should not negatively affect the budget year or budget year plus one funding levels.

Subverting Program Goals and Allocation Policy

Although no regulations can prevent misuse of resources altogether, we believe that well-documented, publicly disclosed plans, approval procedure, and audits are the best means of countering improper diversion of resources. The following examples illustrate the kinds of diversions that take place when districts and states receive categorical aids. Specific delivery plans should address these kinds of problems.

Overhead costs. Pushing overhead costs as high as possible in order to divert categorical aid to general purposes is a common strategy. However, given the need for better management support for a project management approach, this may be difficult to control. For example, is a systems analyst to be used for the reading project or to improve payroll and accounting procedures to better control reading and other expenditures? How will the analyst really be used after he or she has been with the project for 6 months? To the extent possible, though, this issue should not be confused with the "legitimate" efforts by the district to improve program management.

Sinking categorical aid. The effects of increased aid to low socioeconomic areas granted for the purpose of equalizing educational opportunities are often offset from general funds.

What happens looks like this:

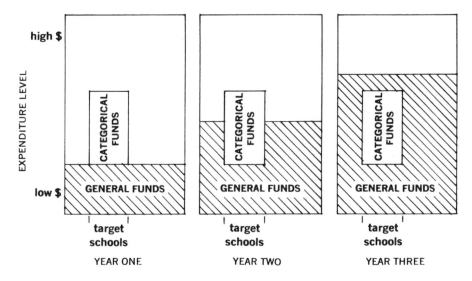

Figure 3
School by School Expenditure Levels over Time

For example, staff development expenditures and music teachers funded with categorical aid for disadvantaged students have been matched wholly or partly by similar expenditures in high socioeconomic areas of a district. This funding may occur a little at a time, so that control is difficult without longitudinal analysis of expenditures or an explicit controlled allocation policy and procedures.

Shifting students. Another tactic is to shift enough students from a low socioeconomic area by open enrollment or otherwise to justify shifting substantial categorical funds for the benefit of all students in the receiving school. (This strategy could be used to encourage integration.)

Rebate. By paying the full list price on equipment the district can use the dollar value of the discount or rebate to acquire other nonreimbursable equipment items.

Enrollment versus attendance. States, by using attendance rather than enrollment as a basis for disbursing aid, can automatically divert general funds from low socioeconomic areas. Generally, because of more family sickness, poorer medical care, poor nutrition, working parents, fear of gangs, the need to earn money, and other reasons, attendance is necessarily lower in economically deprived areas. By basing an aid formula on attendance, the targeting intent is accordingly weakened.

Formula development. Although most aid formulas contain elements that, if properly weighed, could produce greater equality of allocation, the fact of the matter is that a proposed formula is usually analyzed by the legislature first on the end totals it produces for their own constituencies. The elements are reweighed to produce end totals that more accurately reflect the distribution of power. As a result, the cities receive relatively less in relation to need and the cost of operating schools. *Any "play" in the allocation formula as it comes from the federal government will probably be used to divert funds from those constituencies with proportionately less power, which in most states are the cities.*

STIMULATING COOPERATION AMONG VARIOUS SECTORS

Recently, the concept of an operations or education audit has been applied to educational programs and institutions to help schools confirm their results, much as accounting firms normally review the accuracy and propriety of income and expenditure statements. We suspect that external audits of performance will become increasingly common and that many established accounting and general management consulting firms may eventually enter the field, as well as various branches of state and federal education agencies. As indicated in this example, *the success of a national reading program will depend in large part on the ability of the program designers and managers to call up useful competencies in a variety of sectors and organizations.* To that end, those program components which require extensive interorganizational and private sector cooperation are discussed here.

Product and System Evaluation

At present, there are a number of competing firms with competing claims as to the effectiveness of their reading programs. The buyer has little to go on except his instinct and the reputation of a firm. This results in the kind of confusion that preceded federal standards and inspections in many other industries. Such confusion can and should be curtailed in a national reading program. What may be needed is an independent, national agency whose reputation is above reproach to supervise the testing of educational products, especially reading systems (whether or not this would fall within the domain of the National Institute of Education, a professional association, or other type of agency is an open question at this time). Its reports, which would include results, conclusions, and costs, would be rendered in such a way (cost-effectiveness analysis) that (1) others could review their methods and findings and (2) teachers and principals could readily understand and use the information. The purpose would not be to prevent a product from going on the market or to remove a product, but to inform professionals and board members of the apparent effects and costs of implementation of each competing reading system.

We believe that the results of a modest, national investment would be (1) the improvement in the quality of reading systems, (2) the tendency of poorer systems to drop from use, (3) the tendency on the part of the industry to develop whole reading systems, and (4) the improvement of decision making at local district and school levels.

Another function of such an agency might be to review and suggest standards for a variety of types of performance contracts in reading.

National Reading Performance Information System

The key question for the professional and for commercial interests in the field is "What works?" or "What works best under what conditions?" In order for both to respond more quickly and to reduce the time when "best practice" becomes a part of the school program, we believe that the same organization that reviews systems and products could develop a communication strategy to key people in the reading field, commercial, professional, and public, to keep each well informed of developments. We are not thinking of a single newsletter, but a series of communications efforts, each specifically aimed at discrete audiences.

In addition to the communications aspect of such an information system, the more technical aspects of data collection, storage, and retrieval will need to be addressed. In both cases, efforts should be directed toward cooperation with existing agencies that are already performing parts of these functions (e.g., Education Commission of the States, the National Association of School Boards, etc.).

Tax Incentive and Special Subsidies

The federal government has often used tax reductions or subsidies to stimulate private industry, individuals, and institutions to do what is in the national interest. Undoubtedly, the apparent success of *Sesame Street* and *The Electric Company*, which were and are subsidized, has and will bring far greater amounts for educational television. There are other possibilities, a few of which are listed below.

1. Reading systems and product development costs are high if the job is done well and the methods and results are documented and reproducible at reasonable cost. Favorable tax treatment of development costs might stimulate more and better commercially produced reading systems. In the case of a school system, a direct grant in payment for a successful, externally validated system might be more feasible.

2. To protect investment in the specialized training and experience of teachers of reading in low socioeconomic areas and to reduce high turnover, direct grants (salary adjustments) from federal sources could be given. This approach might or might not circumvent local contract provisions.

3. Secondary students could earn further education in the form of vouchers good for postsecondary education on the basis of increased competency in reading (administered like the "GI Bill"). The greater the progress or the higher the absolute level, the larger the size of the voucher.

4. The voucher system has been described as a method of giving parents much wider choice of schools. A supplemental voucher system that could be used for educational summer schools or camps, specifically aimed at higher reading performance, might be developed as a variant on the original ideas to make use of some of the excellent private and public camping facilities (possibly in conjunction with private concerns in the reading field). The results of current evaluation efforts in this area[4] should

---

[4] One example is the current evaluation of the Alum Rock, California, voucher plan by the Rand Corporation. Early analyses of these data indicate the presence of several severe measurement problems, and the probable impacts of the experiment are as yet unclear. For a discussion of this, see R. Gary Bridge, "Some Results of the First Educational Voucher Demonstration," paper presented at the annual meeting of the American Educational Research Association, Chicago, Illinois, April 1974.

be instructive and have implications for the administration of this program.

5. Individual teachers, universities, and private concerns could bid on federally funded supplemental vouchers for teaching children to read, the value of which would be determined by the sustained progress of the student in reading.

6. Colleges and universities could do a far more effective job of teaching teachers to be effective reading instructors if they and/or the teachers were subsidized in this effort.

COSTS OF ILLUSTRATIVE AID SCHEMES

This section of the chapter has been developed in order to give the reader an impression of the general magnitude of factors that could affect the cost of a 10-year reading effort. Knowing the particular form of such a program would, of course, sharpen an estimate of costs. The cost parameters included here, however, are to serve in determining what the particular form of a program might be.

Numbers of Children

The United States had approximately 17.22 million[5] children under 5 years of age in 1970. Approximately 1.4 million children attend public and nonpublic independent nursery schools and kindergartens. This figure is expected to rise sharply to 3.2 million by 1979.[6] (See also Table 1.)

TABLE 1
Public and Nonpublic School Enrollment for the Years 1970 to 1979*
(Values are in millions)

Grades	Public		Nonpublic		Total	
	1970	1979	1970	1979	1970	1979
Elementary	27.3	25.1	4.2	4.0	31.5	29.1
Secondary	18.7	20.4	1.4	1.4	20.1	21.8
Total K to 12	46.0	45.5	5.6	5.4	51.6	50.9

* Based on latest estimates, HEW Office of Research, adjusted for fractions.
SOURCE: National Center for Educational Statistics, *Projections of Educational Statistics*, Washington, D.C.: U.S. Government Printing Office, 1971, p. 21.

[5] *Statistical Abstract of the United States, 1972*, Washington, D.C.: U.S. Department of Commerce, Bureau of the Census, p. 32.

[6] From National Center for Educational Statistics, *Projections of Educational Statistics*, Washington, D.C.: U.S. Government Printing Office, 1971, p. 21.

TABLE 2
Cost of $25 per Pupil General Aid
(Values are in billions)

Grades	Public		Nonpublic		Total	
	1970	1979	1970	1979	1970	1979
Elementary	$0.68	$0.99	$0.11	$0.16	$0.79	$1.38
Secondary	0.47	0.80	0.04	0.05	0.51	0.66
Total K to 12	$1.15	$1.79	$0.15	$0.21	$1.30	$2.04

Cost of General Aid to All: $25 per Pupil

Table 2 shows the annual cost in the periods 1969–1970 and 1979–1980 of $25 per pupil of federal aid to all public and nonpublic school students, assuming a 5 percent escalation per year to $39 per pupil in 1970.

Cost of Aid Alternatives Based on "Need"

1. Table 3 shows the annual cost in the periods 1969–1970 and 1979–1980 of $100, $50, $25, and $0 per pupil to public and parochial school students, K to 12, for the first through the fourth quartiles with a 5 percent inflation factor. It assumes full funding in year 1 (which we do not recommend).

TABLE 3
Estimated Costs $100, $50, $25, and $0 per Pupil Aid for
Public and Parochial Schools
K-12, 1st, 2nd, 3rd, and 4th Quartiles, Respectively,
1969, 1979, 5% Inflation Factor
(Values are in billions)

Grades	Quartile 1		Quartile 2		Quartile 3		Quartile 4		Total	
	1970	1979	1970	1979	1970	1979	1970	1979	1970	1979
Elementary	$0.79	$1.19	$0.40	$0.60	$0.20	$0.30	...	...	$1.39	$2.09
Secondary	0.50	0.85	0.25	0.43	0.13	0.22	...	...	0.88	1.50
Total K to 12	$1.29	$2.04	$0.65	$1.03	$0.33	$0.52	...	...	$2.27	$3.59

2. Table 4 is similar to Table 3 except that $200, $100, $50, and $25 per pupil aid have been substituted for the original figures.

3. Table 5 is similar to Table 3 except that $75, $50, $25, and $0 per pupil aid have been substituted for the original figures.

Early Childhood Program Costs

We show here Selma Mushkin's[7] estimate of the total and net tax cost of a comprehensive preschool child development program.

---

[7] As reprinted in the *NEWS* of the National Committee for the Support of Public Schools, April 1970.

TABLE 4
Estimated Costs $200, $100, $50, and $25 per Pupil Aid for
Public and Parochial Schools
K-12, 1st, 2nd, 3rd, and 4th Quartiles, Respectively,
1969, 1979, 5% Inflation Factor
(Values are in billions)

	Quartile 1		Quartile 2		Quartile 3		Quartile 4		Total	
Grades	1970	1979	1970	1979	1970	1979	1970	1979	1970	1979
K to 8	$1.58	$2.38	$0.79	$1.19	$0.40	$0.60	$0.20	$0.30	$2.97	$4.47
9 to 12	1.00	1.70	0.50	0.85	0.25	0.43	0.13	0.22	1.88	3.20
Total K to 12	$2.50	$4.08	$1.29	$2.04	$0.65	$1.03	$0.33	$0.52	$4.85	$7.67

TABLE 5
Estimated Costs $75, $50, $25, and $0 per Pupil Aid
Public and Parochial Schools
K-12, 1st, 2nd, 3rd, and 4th Quartiles, Respectively,
1969, 1979, 5% Inflation Factor
(Values are in billions)

	Quartile 1		Quartile 2		Quartile 3		Quartile 4		Total	
Grades	1969	1979	1969	1979	1969	1979	1969	1979	1969	1979
K to 8	$0.60	$0.90	$0.40	$0.60	....	....	....	....	$1.00	$1.50
9 to 12	0.38	0.65	0.25	0.43	....	....	....	....	0.63	1.08
Total K to 12	$0.98	$1.55	$0.65	$1.03	....	....	....	....	$1.63	$2.58

How much by way of resources is required to make a full-scale attack on early childhood education? The numbers of children under five by 1975 are estimated at 21 to 27 million, depending upon the fertility rate.

To try to approximate the costs that would be involved in providing child development services with an educational component and to provide preprimary education, account must be taken of the following:

1 The numbers of children in each of the age groups of preprimary children.
2 The number of children from among those in these age groups who would make use of such child care and preprimary education facilities.
3 A reasonable nationwide cost per child that would take account of professional and para-professional salary levels five years or so hence, material and equipment cost, etc.
4 The scope of the services provided [to what extent health service component, dental care, nutrition services are included, as well as educational services].

5 The period of the year, the length of the week, and the hours per day for which services are provided.

The issue of how such costs should be financed is essentially a separate one from the question of availability of the services. Consideration in program development should be given to service for the community as a whole, with appropriate charges imposed in relation to the payability of the families and with safeguards to assure that the care of the child does not depend upon the payments made.

Following are estimated total costs for a nationwide early childhood effort in 1975.

TOTAL PROGRAM: Tax costs	
(combined program 0–5 year olds)	$5,483–7,667 million
PROGRAM FOR 3–4 YEAR OLD GROUP	
a. Total cost, program for 3–4 year olds	$10,000–12,500 million
b. Total costs (assuming an average for one-third the children)	$3,333–4,167 million
c. Total number of preprimary children (3 and 4 year olds)	8–10 million
d. Average cost per preprimary child (average per ¾ day)	$1,250 per child

PROGRAM FOR CHILDREN 0–3 YEARS OF AGE	
a. Total cost (at $2,500 per child)	$6,500–10,250 million
b. Tax costs: Total	$2,125–3,500 million
i. Children paying part costs (on average of one half cost)	$375–500 million
ii. Children receiving services without charge	$1,750–3,000 million
c. Total number of children	13–17 million
d. Total number of children of working mothers (low estimate: low fertitilty, 25% of mothers working) (high estimate: high fertility, 30% of mothers working)	3.3–5.1 million
e. Total number of children using facilities (assumes 80 percent will use)	2.6–4.1 million
i. Full cost covered by charges	1.6–2.5 million
ii. Part cost covered by charges	0.3–0.4 million
iii. No charge (30% of the children)	0.7–1.2 million

Other Financial Information

1. Table 6 represents typical costs of elements that might be a part of a reading project. They are based on the authors' knowledge of Philadelphia and other urban systems. Rural school costs would be less.

TABLE 6
Estimated Typical Costs for Urban Systems

Item	Cost per Year	Cost per Year per pupil	Pupils per Class
Teacher, Reading Specialist	$15,000	$492	25
		$615	20
Teachers, Classroom	$11,000	$300	30
		$360	25
Aide	$ 5,000	$133	30
		$160	25
Helper	$ 4,000	$100	30
		$120	25
Books and Supplies	....	$ 25	
Equipment	....	$ 5	
Staff Development*	....	$ 17	30
		$ 19	25

Reading Program Costs

Company A	....	$ 27	No guaranteed performance
B	....	$ 40	Some guarantee
C	Grade 1	$ 85	
	Grades 2–6	$135	
	Grades 7–9	$180	
D	0–1.5 yr. growth		
	1.6–2.0	$100	
	2.1–2.5	$200	
	Per ½ yr. above	$ 30	
E		$ 40	

* One week's instruction for each teacher, $200 per week for teachers.

2. Table 7 shows the annual and total cost of a $1 million investment over a 10-year period—with 5 percent and 10 percent inflation after the third year.

As was stated earlier, the above tables are intended to serve as representative examples of the kind of data that would go into the generation of specific alternative programs. More definitive, detailed, and complex analysis of program cost factors will aid in determining the most effective 10-year reading program package.

TABLE 7
Escalation of \$1 Million over a 10-Year Period*
(Values are in millions)

Year	5 percent	10 percent
1	0.20	0.20
2	0.75	0.75
3	1.00	1.00
4	1.05	1.10
5	1.10	1.21
6	1.16	1.33
7	1.22	1.46
8	1.28	1.61
9	1.34	1.77
10	1.41	1.95
Total	10.51	12.38

* At 5 percent and 10 percent inflation, assuming 20 percent, 75 percent, and 100 percent funding in the first 3 years, respectively.

Notes on Committee Members and Contributors

JOHN R. BORMUTH, born in 1928, is associate professor of education and of psychology, chairman of the Committee on Language and Instruction, and director of the Reading Research Center at the University of Chicago. He is the author of *On the Theory of Achievement Test Items* and of a number of studies on educational evaluation and readability.

OLIVER S. BROWN, born in 1931 in Boston, is assistant superintendent for business management services of the Cambridge (Mass.) School Department. Previously, he served in the public schools of Philadelphia, Washington, D.C., Weston, Mass., and Fair Haven, Vermont. From 1970 to 1973 he worked with Price Waterhouse and Company performing management consulting assignments in educational and governmental agencies. He is the coauthor of a chapter in *Educational Planning* entitled "Results Oriented Budgeting" (1970) and of "All Kinds of Ways to Reduce Costs" in the *American School Board Journal* (May, 1972).

JOHN B. CARROLL, born in Hartford, Connecticut, in 1916, is Kenan Professor of Psychology and Director of the L. L. Thurstone Psychometric Laboratory at the University of North Carolina. Previously, he was on the faculty of the Graduate School of Education at Harvard University (1949–1967) and Senior Research Psychologist at Educational Testing Service, Princeton (1967–1974). Among his publications are *The Study of Language* (1953), *Language and Thought* (1964), and (with S. M. Sapon) the *Modern Language Aptitude Test* (1959). He has served on the National Advisory Committee on Dyslexia and Related Reading Disorders, and on other committees concerned with problems of language learning.

JEANNE S. CHALL, born in 1921 in Poland, is professor of education at Harvard University. She is a member of the Board of Directors of the National Society for the Study of Education, a past president of the National Conference on Research in English, and a past member of the Board of the International Reading Association. She has served on the National Reading Council and the National Advisory Committee on Dyslexia and Related Reading Disorders. Among her publications are *Readability: An Appraisal of Research and Application* (1958) and *Learning to Read: The Great Debate* (1967).

KENNETH B. CLARK, born in 1914 in Panama, is a professor of psychology with the City College of the City University of New York and president of Metropolitan Applied Research Center, Inc. He is a member of the New York State Board of Regents and also a member of the Boards of Trustees of Howard University and the University of Chicago. He is author of several books and articles, including *Prejudice and Your Child* (1955) and the prizewinning *Dark Ghetto: Dilemmas of Social Power* (1965), coauthor with Jeannette Hopkins of *Relevant War against Poverty* (1968), and coeditor with Talcott Parsons of *The Negro American* (1966).

JAMES S. COLEMAN, born in 1926 in Bedford, Indiana, is professor of sociology at the University of Chicago. He is the author of *The Adolescent Society* and (with others) of *Equality of Educational Opportunity*. His research has been concerned with the effects of school resources on achievement and with the education of adolescents and youth.

RICHARD H. DE LONE, born in Philadelphia in 1940, has taught at the University of Massachusetts and been an educational administrator in Philadelphia and New York. He is currently coordinator for educational policy research at the Carnegie Council on Children in New Haven, Connecticut.

JOHN H. FISCHER, born in 1910, was president of Teachers College, Columbia University, from 1962 to 1974. From 1930 to 1959 he was a teacher and administrator in the Baltimore Public Schools, serving as superintendent from 1953 to 1959, when he was appointed Dean of Teachers College. He has served on numerous governmental commissions and has been Chairman of the Educational Policies Commission and of the Boards of Trustees of Educational Testing Service, Institute for Educational Development, and Center for Urban Education. He is currently chairman of the trustees of the Metropolitan Applied Research Center. His articles on educational policy and administration have appeared in various journals.

BARBARA R. FOWLES, born in Manchester, Connecticut, in 1945, is associate director of research at Children's Television Workshop in New York. She has served as adjunct assistant professor in developmental psychology at the State University of New York at Stony Brook and in educational psychology at Ferkauf Graduate School of Yeshiva University.

WILLIAM FURLONG, born in 1937 in St. Paul, Minnesota, is now president of Resources in Education, Inc., in Crofton, Maryland. As a reading specialist, he has had teaching experience in secondary schools and in adult education programs. He currently teaches graduate reading courses at The Johns Hopkins University. As a former assistant director of the National Reading Center, he has had extensive experience with the National Right-to-Read effort.

SAMUEL Y. GIBBON, JR., born in Philadelphia, is executive producer at Children's Television Workshop in New York and lecturer on education and research associate at Harvard University Graduate School of Education. He worked for six years as associate producer and writer of *Captain Kangaroo* before joining Children's Television Workshop as one of the original producers of *Sesame Street*. He developed *The Electric Company* and served as its producer and executive producer.

ELEANOR J. GIBSON, born in 1910 in Peoria, Illinois, is the Susan Sage Professor of Psychology at Cornell University. She has served as president of the Eastern Psychological Association and is a member of the National Academy of Sciences and the National Academy of Education. She is author of *Principles of Perceptual Learning and Development* (1969) and coauthor with Harry Levin of *The Psychology of Reading* (1975).

JOHN I. GOODLAD, born in 1920 in North Vancouver, British Columbia, is professor and Dean of the Graduate School of Education and director of the University Elementary School, University of California at Los Angeles, as well as director for research for the Charles F. Kettering Foundation's Institute for Development of Educational Activities, Inc. His books include *The Elementary School* (1956), *Educational Leadership and the Elementary School Principal* (1956), *The Nongraded Elementary School* (1959), *School Curriculum Reform in the United States* (1964), *The Changing School Curriculum* (1966), *School, Curriculum, and the Individual* (1966), *Behind the Classroom Door* (1970), *Early Schooling in England and Israel* (1973), and *Early Schooling in the United States* (1973).

NORRIS· G. HARING, born in 1923 in Kearney, Nebraska, is director of the Experimental Education Unit, Child Development and Mental Retardation Unit; professor of education, and adjunct professor of pediatrics at the University of Washington. Previously he was the educational director of the Children's Rehabilitation Unit in the Medical Center of the University of Kansas. He has served as a member of several national and state committees concerned with handicapped children. His recent publications include *Behavior of Exceptional Children; An Introduction to Special Education* (editor); *Analysis and Modification of Classroom Behavior* (1972, with E. Lakin Phillips); and *The Improvement of Instruction* (1972, with Alice H. Hayden), in addition to journal articles and chapters in collected volumes.

GUILBERT C. HENTSCHKE, born in Glendale, California, in 1944, is associate professor of administration in both the College of Education and Graduate School of Management at the University of Rochester, where he directs the Program in Educational Finance and Business Administration. He is editor of *Management of the Educational Enterprise* (1971) and author of *Management Operations in Education* (1975).

VIVIAN HORNER, born in Canton, Ohio, in 1934, is director of research for *The Electric Company* at Children's Television Workshop in New York. She is also associate professor of psycholinguistics and education at The Ferkauf Graduate School of Yeshiva University. Her teaching and research have spanned a variety of language-related areas, including reading, foreign-language teaching and learning, language acquisition, and bilingualism. Her publications include *Early Childhood Bilingual Education* (1971) and "John and Mary: A Pilot Study in Linguistic Ecology," in *Functions of Language in the Classroom* (1972).

HARRY LEVIN, born in 1925 in Baltimore, is the William R. Kenan, Jr., Professor of Psychology and dean of the College of Arts and Sciences at Cornell University. He is the coauthor of *Patterns of Child Rearing* (1956), *Basic Studies in Reading* (1970), and *The Psychology of Reading* (1975).

NATHAN MACCOBY, born in 1912 in London, is professor of communication and director, Institute for Communication Research at Stanford University. He has served as professor and chairman of the Department of Psychology and of the Division of Research of the School of Communication, Boston University. His publications include "Communication and Learning" and he is coeditor of the *Handbook of Communication* (1973) in which it appears. He is coauthor of several chapters in *Student Response in Programmed Instruction* (1961) and his research has focused on learning and persuasion via mass media.

DAVID G. MARKLE, born in 1937 in Easton, Pennsylvania, is codirector of Communication Research Laboratories, Inc., Denver. He has been involved in research and instructional development with several nonprofit organizations, and has taught and consulted extensively on the design of training in industry. Among the multimedia courses he has developed is one for the American National Red Cross entitled *Basic First Aid/Audio-Visual*, designed for adults who cannot read. He is coauthor, with Nathan Maccoby, of a chapter entitled "Communication and Learning," in the *Handbook of Communication* (1973).

NANCY H. MARKLE, born in 1934 in Erie, Colorado, is codirector of Communication Research Laboratories, Inc. She has been involved in research, development, and consulting activities with several private nonprofit organizations. She was a coauthor of the multimedia course, *Basic First Aid/Audio-Visual*. She has been a research associate at Stanford University in connection with evaluation of an educational television satellite demonstration in Denver. Some of her research has concerned differential response to instruction designed to call on spatial and verbal aptitudes.

EDWARD L. PALMER, born in 1933 in Oregon, is vice president for research at Children's Television Workshop in New York. He was research associate with the Oregon State System of Higher Education in 1967, and prior to that, a member of the graduate faculty at Florida State University. His publications are in the areas of children's thinking and learning and educational communications.

HELEN M. POPP, born in 1928 in Marlboro, Massachusetts, is associate professor of education at Harvard University. She worked with young children, first as a librarian and then as a teacher, for ten years before returning to university life. She is the author of the 21-Inch Classroom production of *Word Workers*, produced by WGBH, and of several articles related to beginning reading instruction. She has served as consultant to projects at the Learning Research and Development Center at the University of Pittsburgh, the Bureau of Curriculum Innovation in the Massachusetts State Department of Education, Project Literacy at Cornell University, the Children's Television Workshop, and the Vermont State Department of Education.

LAUREN B. RESNICK, born in 1936 in New York City, is associate professor of psychology and education at the University of Pittsburgh. She also serves as director of research and development at the Learning Research and Development Center there. She has been active in the development of individualized preschool and elementary school programs and in research on processes of learning and instruction. Her publications include "Instructional Psychology" (with Robert Glaser) in *Annual Review of Psychology* (1972), "Hierarchies in Children's Learning: A Symposium" in *Instructional Science* (1973), and several articles on open education in the United States and Great Britain.

BETTY H. ROBINSON, born in 1929 in Indianapolis, is currently an instructional specialist with the Pittsburgh Board of Education. She was previously an elementary school teacher for eight years. In her present position, she has concentrated efforts on development and implementation of individualized elementary school programs in conjunction with the Learning Research and Development Center at the University of Pittsburgh.

THOMAS A. RYAN, born in 1911 in Batavia, New York, is professor of psychology at Cornell University. He was chairman of the department of psychology there from 1953 to 1961. He is the author of *Work and Effort* (1947), *Intentional Behavior* (1970), and coauthor with P. C. Smith of *Principles of Industrial Psychology* (1954). His current interests concern motivational factors in learning.

NATALIE SAXE, born in Philadelphia, is a graduate of the University of Pennsylvania who for the last eight or nine years has been special assistant to the Philadelphia Superintendent of Schools. As legislative consultant for the school district of Philadelphia, she has worked principally with the Pennsylvania Legislature, but also at both local and federal levels. She served for six years on the board of directors of the Pennsylvania School Boards Association. Prior to that, she was an executive assistant to the mayor of Philadelphia. She has been active in local, state, and national political campaigns and affairs for many years.

MARK R. SHEDD, born in 1926 in Quincy, Massachusetts, is visiting professor of education at Harvard University. The former general superintendent of schools in Philadelphia, Mr. Shedd has been a teacher, principal, and superintendent of schools in the public schools of Maine, Connecticut, and New Jersey.

ROSE-MARIE WEBER, born in 1938 in New York City, is professor of linguistics at McGill University. She teaches sociolinguistics and has done research on the implications of linguistics for the study of reading in conjunction with Project Literacy at Cornell University.

INDEX